BASKET DIPLOMACY

BASKET DIPLOMACY

Leadership, Alliance-Building, and Resilience among the Coushatta Tribe of Louisiana, 1884–1984

Denise E. Bates

Epilogue by David Sickey

UNIVERSITY OF NEBRASKA PRESS   LINCOLN

Library of Congress Control Number: 2019015628

Set in Adobe Text by Laura Ebbeka.
Designed by N. Putens.

CONTENTS

ILLUSTRATIONS

ACKNOWLEDGMENTS

Writing this book was a humbling and profound experience. I could never have written it without the support of numerous colleagues, friends, and family. Primary among those supporters is the Coushatta Tribe of Louisiana, which has shown me (and my family) great warmth and hospitality over the years. Being invited to write the tribe's history was a gift that has genuinely enriched me as a historian and as a person. I'm grateful to all of the Coushattas, as well as their friends and allies, who shared their insights and time as I collected hundreds of hours of interviews, piecing together a story that could have never been told through archival evidence alone.

I would particularly like to thank Ernest Sickey for his time and dedication to this project. He was a true collaborator, and I have enjoyed every moment we spent together, whether it was visiting over a meal or traveling in a car trying to navigate the heavy rains of a Louisiana storm. In spite of his retirement from tribal leadership, his deep commitment to the developmental success of southern tribal nations keeps him engaged in any new happenings in Indian country and always ready to assist those who may benefit from his experience and wisdom. It's truly inspiring. Next, I would like to express my gratitude to Chairman David Sickey, whose support and contributions to this book have greatly enriched it. His leadership is a credit to his tribe and to the legacy he inherited. I consider myself fortunate to have witnessed some of the outcomes of his efforts firsthand and look forward to seeing what is on the horizon for the Coushatta people. I also would like to thank Bertney Langley, Linda Langley, and Marianna Luquette of the Coushatta Heritage Department, without whose assistance this book would not have been possible. I owe them a debt for consistently going the extra mile to help me by sharing materials, responding to seemingly endless queries, offering feedback on drafts of this manuscript, and, along with Raynella Thompson Fontenot and Loretta Williams, translating the chapter subtitles into Koasati. For offering their stories and experiences, I'm grateful to Lelia Battise, Leonard Battise, Rod Bertrand, Kevin Billiot, Kenneth Bruchhaus, Jeanette Alcon Campos, Dewith Carrier, Jonathan Cernek, Lora Ann Chaisson, Bonner Miller Cutting, Pratt Doucet, Darlene Langley Dunnehoo, Hiram F. "Pete" Gregory, Leonard Knapp Jr., Barbara Langley, Eleyna Langley, Eli Langley, Robin Langley, Tyler Langley, Stanley Leger, Paula Abbey Manuel, Anna Neal, Gene Paul, Layla Pedigo, Ronnie Petree, Donna Pierite, Jean Luc Pierite, Jeanine Langley Ramirez, Ray Rush, Kelly Rush Savoy, Clark Sickey, Kelly Sickey, Crystal Williams, and Heather Williams. They, along with those previously mentioned, shared enough with me to fill multiple volumes. I would also like to express my gratitude to those who provided additional materials and insights along the way, including Victor Alcorta, Mike Liotta, and Jay Precht.

Researching this book took me on many adventures. Not only did I enjoy the hospitality of those who opened their homes to me, I also found myself at numerous libraries, archival collections, and administrative offices. In some cases I was able to access information remotely through interlibrary loan or digitized archival collections. For her assistance in helping me navigate these resources, I would like to thank Joyce Martin, Arizona State University librarian and curator of the Labriola National American Indian Data Center. The College of Integrative Sciences and Arts at Arizona State University provided the majority of financial support I needed for research travel. This institutional support was accompanied by a Princeton University research grant that allowed me to work with the university's Public Policy Papers, which greatly enriched this book when new, previously unseen materials turned up. During my time at Princeton's Department of Rare Books and Special Collections, I benefited from the generous collegiality of Daniel Linke, Sara Logue, and Rachel Van Unen. Dozens of other librarians and archivists also assisted me through this journey. I would like to specifically express my appreciation to Desiree Wallen of the National Archives at

Atlanta, Gina Rappaport of the Smithsonian National Museum of Natural History, Melanie Counce Montanaro of the Louisiana State Archives, Rose Buchanan of the National Archives and Records Administration, Laura E. Smith of the Archives of Appalachia, and Margaret Schlankey of the Dolph Briscoe Center for American History at the University of Texas at Austin. Finally, I would like to thank the staff of the Inter-Tribal Council of Louisiana, particularly Kevin Billiot, who hosted my visit to Houma, Louisiana, in April 2016. Kevin shared his office space for several days as I looked through old boxes of the Inter-Tribal Council's founding documents that he and John Silver had pulled out of storage for my visit. It was quite a treasure trove, and I was grateful to be given the opportunity.

I'm fortunate to be surrounded by so many supportive and generous colleagues. I would like to thank Kelly Nelson for her friendship and for being my patient and encouraging soundboard all these years. She knew I should embark on this journey even before I did. I'm also grateful to the members of my reading group, K. Tsianina Lomawaima, Katherine Osburn, and Susan Gray, whose feedback proved critical during the early framing of this project. I'm incredibly lucky to have them in my life as mentors, colleagues, and friends. I'm also thankful to others who have provided me with feedback to various iterations of this book or simply offered support and encouragement along the way. In particular, I would like to thank Kevin Ellsworth, Duane Roen, Bryan Brayboy, Jeanne Hanrahan, Mai Trinh, Elizabeth Castillo, Robert Kirsch, Allison Ellsworth, Erica Peters, Stephanie deLusé, Jessica Hirshorn, Mike Rubinoff, Marie Wallace, Stephen Davis, Jennifer Chandler, Matt Rodgers, David Wells, Emily Mertz, David Thomas, Eric Nystrom, Andi Hess, Jay Klagge, Leesa Bowman, Michelle Hale, Brooke Bauer, and Margaret Mortensen Vaughan. I have also benefited from other sources of support that have helped me keep up the momentum in completing this project. In particular, my broad network of Senior Ford Foundation Fellows, although hailing from a variety of fields, has proven to be an invaluable professional resource. Also, attendees at the Native American and Indigenous Studies Association Conference in Vancouver, BC, where I presented this research in 2017, offered feedback that was useful and timely. Finally, I would like to thank Matthew Bokovoy, Heather Stauffer, Elizabeth Gratch, and the anonymous reviewers from the University of Nebraska Press. Their encouragement and suggestions helped pinpoint the "rough" edges and have undoubtedly improved this book.

Last but not least, I would like to acknowledge my incredible family. It was their patience and love that helped me reach the finish line. They have put up with many long nights and even longer research trips. My parents, in-laws, and grandmother have been an amazing source of support not just by encouraging me throughout the research and writing of this book but also by providing the peace of mind that I needed to get it done. They took turns ensuring that my travel schedule never interrupted my children's lives and that there was always family around to pick up any slack, even if that meant traveling across the country to be here for us. For this I would like to thank my parents, Allen Barber and Naomi Clayton; my grandmother, Wanda Tully; my mother-in-law, Alice Bates; and my sister-in-law and niece, Kim and Ruth Ann Bates. My wonderful children, Claire, Aidan, and Lila, have grown so much since I first began this endeavor. They bring me great joy and inspire me with their intelligence, curiosity, and sense of adventure. Finally, with deep love and admiration, I thank Kevin Bates for being an incredible partner, confidant, and father. His love and humor has kept me grounded, and his close reading of this manuscript has generated many thoughtful conversations that have greatly enriched my approach to this work. Words cannot express how grateful I am to be on this journey with him.

INTRODUCTION

In 1972 a thirty-year-old Ernest Sickey was greeted with the fluid rhythm of the Koasati language as he made his way around the Bayou Blue settlement, visiting the homes of Coushatta basket makers to collect their delicate pine needle or swamp cane creations.[1] He carefully tucked the expertly stitched baskets into a briefcase and set off on his next excursion, to Baton Rouge and then onward to Washington DC, to use these tribal treasures to engage in a practice he called "basket diplomacy." Dozens of politicians, lawyers, and government staff received these gifts—imprints of an enduring culture—as Sickey traversed his way into the highest reaches of Louisiana government to lobby on behalf of his impoverished tribe. These efforts were vital to the nearly 280 Coushatta people who lived in the woods of Allen Parish in southwestern Louisiana and who had endured multiple relocations across hundreds of miles and over many generations.[2]

Sickey's pursuits emulated the advocacy and political acumen of previous generations of Coushattas, who, in an effort to protect the community, navigated Louisiana politics and purposefully engaged the American legal system. Their efforts ensured the survival of the Coushattas who first arrived at Bayou Blue in the late nineteenth century with no land base, no existing allies, no political relationship to the state, and no federal acknowledgment of their presence in Louisiana. "[They] worked so hard to maintain what little bit of resources they had," Sickey said, and it was this very determination that allowed them to settle into their new home, acquire homesteads, and find ways to make a living.[3] While many Coushattas found work in agriculture and the timber industry, others looked to applying traditional knowledge to their new environment through basket production and sales. Weavers regularly interacted with the public, serving as economic and cultural brokers, a role that evolved over time as the tribe later nurtured a tourism enterprise and, as demonstrated by Sickey, incorporated basketry into its public relations campaigns.[4] The tribe's increased visibility fueled the curiosity of onlookers, who speculated on where the Coushattas had originated and the circumstances that had brought them to the area. The mystery that surrounded the tribe was evident in local newspapers that, until recently, referred to them as a "lost tribe." Some Coushattas even claimed the tribal name Koasati, derived from the word *Koasat*, or "they are lost," which was a phrase repeated by European explorers who encountered a group of Coushattas during their travels.[5] Other explanations on the etymology of the tribal name tie it to certain environmental descriptors or locations, such as a "white reed brake" or the Coosa River in Alabama, one of the places Coushattas once lived.[6]

No matter what hypothesis the Coushattas' neighbors believed to explain what brought them to southwestern Louisiana, it was likely not nearly as complex as the reality. Like other descendants of the Mississippian chiefdoms of the South, the Coushattas' history was shaped by a lengthy and difficult diasporic migration that led them across treacherous terrain and hostile territories.[7] References to the tribe first appeared in European records in 1540, when Spanish explorer Hernando de Soto encountered the tribe in the Tennessee River basin.[8] By the 1700s they had settled near the convergence of Alabama's Coosa and Tallapoosa Rivers and joined the powerful Creek Confederacy, a political union of the Muscogee family of tribes that extended into Georgia, Alabama, and northern Florida.[9] Coushatta leaders held important political roles within the Confederacy and participated in signing treaties with the United States and several European nations.[10] Soon an increased English presence near their villages prompted some Coushattas to again embark to other locations.[11] Others, however, remained to negotiate land claims and fight in the Creek War of 1813–14. After the conflict, which killed more than three thousand people, most of the remaining Coushattas split into several small bands and followed those who had previously left. According to the tribe's account, they "continued their search for a land offering peace and dignity."[12]

Although gaps in the narrative exist, we now better understand the Coushattas' early cultural and political history and can track the tribe's multiple migrations to present-day settlements in Oklahoma, Texas, and Louisiana.[13] In particular, records from before the Creek War offer insight into their travels. In the late eighteenth century, leaders Stilapihkachatta (Red Shoes) and Pahimikko (Grass Chief) guided nearly one thousand Coushattas to lands held by Spain and established villages along the Red River in northern Louisiana.[14] Because of disputes fueled by political struggles and jockeying for land, these years were significantly unstable for the Coushatta people, who were repeatedly pushed from their settlements within a region that stretched across Louisiana and Texas and which served as a buffer zone between the Spanish, French, Americans, and Mexicans.[15]

The Alabama people, also previously part of the Creek Confederacy, had a migration history similar to that of the Coushattas, and the tribes often crossed paths or traveled together. Because of their westward movement, both the Coushattas and Alabamas were caught in the crosshairs of a volatile frontier disrupted by jurisdictional disputes and war.[16] These upheavals pushed the tribes even further west into the Big Thicket region of Texas, where they carved out settlements and used the rough terrain as a natural barrier against intruders. Unfortunately, their ability to live undisturbed was temporary as they found themselves drawn into conflict, resulting in both tribes assisting the United States to secure the independence of Texas from Mexico in 1835–36. In spite of their help, however, many Texans demanded that the Coushattas and Alabamas be removed from their lands, which forced the intervention of tribal allies, such as land commissioner Jorge Antonio Nixon, who attempted to prevent their dispossession by insisting that his surveyors respect tribal land claims.[17] The famed General Sam Houston also tried to prevent the forced removal of the tribes, even moving to secure more land for them.[18] Not until 1853, however, did Texas purchase 1,110.7 acres in Polk County, about twenty miles from Livingston and seventy-five miles from Beaumont, for the Alabama Indians—known today as the Alabama-Coushatta Reservation. Officials also earmarked money to purchase 640 acres for the Coushatta people, but this purchase never

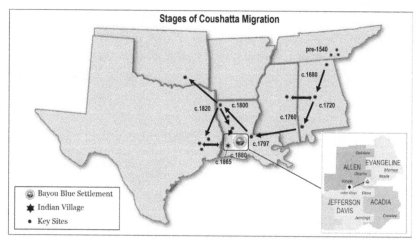

Map 1: Stages of Coushatta migration. The Coushatta Heritage Department is currently identifying and mapping additional village sites, traditional cultural properties, and sacred sites. In creating this map, I consulted David H. Jurney, "Diaspora of the Alabama-Koasati Indians across Southeastern North America" (PhD diss., Southern Methodist University, 2001). The tribal seal was used with permission of the Coushatta Heritage Department. Map by author, with data provided by the Coushatta Tribe of Louisiana.

occurred, and although some Coushatta families remained with the Alabamas at their Texas settlement, most of them decided to resume their journey in search of an undisrupted life. In the face of uncertainty about what might be awaiting them if they continued to push further west, the travelers redirected their movement eastward, returning to Louisiana by the mid-1860s (map 1).[19] Coushattas living in Texas today are connected to the Alabama people as a jointly federally recognized tribal entity, one politically distinct from the Coushatta Tribe of Louisiana.[20]

There is little known about the details of the Coushattas' final return to Louisiana from Texas. Ernest Sickey explained that he believed they were motivated to relocate because "these were the survivors . . . [who] were so determined to [stay together] . . . to be a community that they once were." They sought a home where they could live free from the turmoil of warfare and the resentment of white settlers.[21] While this journey brought them back into Louisiana during the final months of the Civil War, they managed to find a quiet location in the southwestern portion of the state to develop a new settlement called Indian Village, situated along the Calcasieu River and near what came to be known as the town of Kinder. Coushattas lived there for nearly two decades before, once again, being pressured to relocate as white settlers began purchasing the lands around Indian Village.[22] This time, however, the tribe's journey only took them fifteen miles east, where many Coushattas were able to acquire title to land legally as homesteaders around a waterway called Bayou Blue, located just north of what would become the town of Elton.

In this new home Coushattas became part of a culturally rich and racially blended region that was anchored by ancient roots but also stirred by transformation upon an influx of new settlers. Residents had arrived from places nearby, such as eastern Louisiana, and also from farther afield, such as the Midwest, New England, and Europe. The new population included Civil War veterans hoping to become entrepreneurs, midwestern and Cajun farmers eyeing homesteads and large-scale agricultural operations, and timber executives and wage laborers searching for work. The locals knew of the Indians living around Bayou Blue, and many of them even held neighboring homesteads. They saw them in town selling baskets or shopping for supplies, they worked alongside them in the fields and sawmills, and some of their children attended school with Coushatta children in Elton. While it took years for the tribe to appear on the government's radar, by the early twentieth century they had attracted the attention of an assortment of anthropologists, folklorists, and linguists. Researchers were excited about the small, close-knit community, which still spoke its ancestral language, and they wanted to capture remnants of what they considered part of America's dying past. According to sociologist A. L. Bertrand, the Coushattas were a "cultural island" where "the ways of the old-world still live."[23] In the first few decades of the century, anthropologists such as Mark Harrington and John R. Swanton created a trove of detailed notes that later attracted new generations of researchers to the Coushatta community.[24]

While the struggle to find a permanent home had finally come to an end, the Coushattas continued to face the difficult challenge of improving their living conditions, addressing chronic health concerns, and building a future for their children. After years of lobbying the federal government, by the 1930s they finally began receiving federal Indian funding for education and health care. This aid was short-lived, however, when in 1953 the tribe's services were discontinued following passage of legislation aimed at terminating federal trust relationships to tribes. Deviating from the policy's protocol, the federal government never abdicated its trust responsibility to the Coushattas through a congressional action when their services ceased, inciting much confusion and serving to further marginalize the tribe as it slipped deeper into poverty.[25]

This was the story that Ernest Sickey shared when seeking assistance for his tribe from legislators and other public officials in the early 1970s. It was a story of struggle and persistence, and it was relayed during a particularly fortuitous time. Politicians were under tremendous pressure to institute social reforms in the wake of civil rights activities, creating opportunities for southern Indian people to develop their own social and political movement.[26] Coushattas were at the forefront of the charge in Louisiana, and in 1972 they became the first tribe to be formally recognized by the state. In the same year the Louisiana Office of Indian Affairs (LOIA) was created, and the governor appointed Sickey as the first Indian hired by the state to coordinate Indian affairs.[27] This was a monumental moment in Louisiana's history, as the state Indian office represented the potential to define a supportive relationship between Louisiana and its 5,294 documented Indian residents.[28] Following the Coushattas, Louisiana also formally acknowledged the Chitimachas (previously recognized by the federal government in 1916), the Jena Band of Choctaws, the Tunica-Biloxis, the United Houma Nation, the Clifton Choctaws, the Choctaw-Apache Community, and the Louisiana Band of Choctaws. While state recognition didn't carry the broader implications of federal recognition, it did provide tribes with modest resources, technical support, and opportunities to coordinate intertribal efforts around particular issues. Moreover, the Coushattas were able to use it as leverage to generate support in their efforts to be reinstated to a federally acknowledged status. They succeeded, and in 1973, twenty years after being terminated, the Coushattas were administratively reestablished as a federally acknowledged tribe by the U.S. secretary of the interior. This reinstatement was due in large part to the legal assistance of national advocacy groups, such as the Association on American Indian Affairs (AAIA) and the Native American Rights Fund (NARF), which compiled a formal case on behalf of the tribe.[29] The evidence was then used by Louisiana legislators to champion the Coushattas' case, using emotional appeals and aggressive lobbying. The tribe received support from both seasoned and novice politicians who, for the first time in their careers, ventured into the Indian affairs arena. Their experience with the Coushatta tribe later encouraged many of them to continue this work by joining debates or taking policy stances on the federal-Indian relationship as Congress reassessed its obligation to tribes in the years leading to the Indian Self-Determination and Education Assistance Act (1975).[30]

I began this book intending to build upon my previous work on the development of tribal-state relationships in Louisiana, aiming to focus on Coushatta political activities during the 1970s. I wished to better understand the complex circumstances behind their struggle for tribal sovereignty and self-determination. However, as the genesis of the Coushattas' establishment in southwestern Louisiana attests, this is a story with much deeper roots, making it necessary to broaden the scope of this study to begin with the tribe's initial settlement at Bayou Blue in 1884. By then carrying the story to 1984, one hundred years later and over a decade after the tribe's federal status was reinstated, we also are able to examine the early years of modern tribal development as it laid the groundwork for the tribe today. Coushattas worked together, with each generation laying a foundation for the next, and leveraged opportunities so that existing and newly acquired knowledge, timing, and skill worked in tandem. The tribe established stability in their new home by embedding themselves into the region's cultural, economic, and political domains—all while maintaining their distinct identity as Coushatta people. Through the generations Coushattas forged long-lasting alliances with civic and business leaders, charitable organizations, aid groups, legislators, and other tribes. They also engaged the public with stories about the tribe's culture, history, and mutual economic interests, which helped them navigate the social pressures of a region shaped primarily by race and class. This was particularly challenging given their legal marginalization resulting from an elusive and misunderstood history, a diminution caused by inconsistent government reports regarding their citizenship status, past involvement in treaty negotiations, and eligibility for federal Indian services. Expanding the scope of the tribe's history also allows us to better appreciate how the Coushatta people adapted to changing circumstances and protected what was most important to them: their language, culture, and continuity in self-governance.

Basket Diplomacy is about Coushatta activism and self-determination. It examines how, over the course of a century, tribal citizens accepted different roles in order to transform their political and economic status and shifted their focus from survival to nation building.[31] They made decisions collaboratively, often when the heads of families or representatives from the seven clans convened.[32] Over time tribal representatives comprised the advisory board of the Indian Church, and then, as the Coushatta political structure evolved further, members served on the boards of the tribe's nonprofit corporations and later the tribal council. And although external circumstances kept changing, the culture of collective decision making remained.[33] Historian Mikaëla M. Adams identifies a similar continuity among six other southeastern tribes that faced the issue of determining criteria for tribal citizenship in the twentieth century. "Although federal and state policies influenced them," Adams wrote, "tribes did not simply abandon older ways of reckoning belonging in favor of bureaucratized and racialized criteria. Instead, they looked for ways to repackage older concepts into new forms that fit their changing circumstances."[34] While this book highlights the Coushattas who held official positions and interacted with the public, many more worked in less visible but no less important, interlocking leadership roles.[35] Everyone played a part—from bringing in income by working outside the community to maintaining family gardens and repairing homes. Some Coushattas were cross-cultural translators between the tribe and local business owners, farmers, and civic leaders. Others provided spiritual guidance and healing or improved the community's economic well-being and visibility by selling baskets and other handcrafted items. The tribe's survival, however, depended upon the elders. They provided the educational foundation that guided younger generations of Coushattas through increasingly complex terrain, all while continuing to foster shared values and a strong sense of peoplehood. Elders connected the community to its past and helped it envision a better future.[36]

Drawing on a theoretical framework described by public policy scholar Laura E. Evans, this study examines how, despite disadvantages, the Coushatta people developed strategic networks and found opportunities to exploit niches within the local, state, and federal political systems to attain their goals.[37] The tribe acted in what Daniel M. Cobb called "politically purposeful ways"—seeking legal advice, meeting with legislators and civic leaders, writing grants, organizing community meetings and programs, and building intertribal alliances.[38] Throughout the twentieth century Coushattas also strategically redefined their image from a "lost tribe" to a sovereign nation. They ran public awareness campaigns and worked directly with newspapers and other media outlets, demonstrating an ability to communicate across multiple divides, to protect their cultural distinctiveness, and to elevate their economic situation. This was no small task given that English was a second—and sometimes third language—acquired by Coushatta leaders and advocates.

This book offers a unique vantage point from which to better examine race in the New South by illustrating how Indian experiences under Jim Crow were locally dictated. Unlike many other Indians across the region, the Coushattas were incorporated into a segregated system that permitted them to share schools and public spaces with local white residents. Prior to the desegregation of Elton schools in 1965, the tribe also informally interacted with African Americans. Marriage to non-Indians was rare, however, with the tribe carefully maintaining its racially distinct status.[39] Coushattas self-identified as full-blooded Indians and used their baskets to reinforce their Indigenous identities.[40] Yet the access that Coushattas had to the local white power structure secured them early allies, and as the civil rights movement heightened awareness of racial inequality, the tribe was able to leverage these alliances to build an even broader base of support.[41]

While racial politics certainly provided the backdrop for which the Coushattas' story unfolded, class tensions also played a critical role.

Conflict between Louisiana's wealthy and the rural poor fostered a legacy of programs influenced by populist ideologies. Although Indians utilized the by-products of such programs, such as charity hospitals, the majority of early-twentieth-century Louisiana politicians had little knowledge of the state's tribal populations. When the needs of the Coushattas came to the forefront, however, so did the debate over who should take responsibility for providing them services, as their status as "poor" and "Indian" created an elaborate shoving match between the state and federal governments.[42] By strategically drawing on the language of economics, Coushatta leaders acquired alliances in high political offices by midcentury. Tribal representatives emphasized their goal of self-sufficiency coupled with a strong sense of responsibility to assist in boosting the region's economic outlook. This dual mission became the cornerstone of the Coushattas' public identity in the years following federal reinstatement as they executed a highly successful campaign to acquire a tribal land base, build infrastructure, and launch a series of economic ventures. They pushed boundaries and asserted sovereignty in ways that solidified their relationship with the state and federal governments as they moved toward becoming a prominent economic force in Louisiana.

Beyond the local context, this story offers significant contributions to broader lines of inquiry aimed at examining the historical circumstances of Indigenous peoples. As relative newcomers to Louisiana, Coushattas made the Bayou Blue settlement their permanent homeland amid non-Indian homesteaders. Their example, as well as those of other southeastern tribes designated as "refugee-traditional" cultures by anthropologist J. Anthony Paredes, resonates with the scholarship of Paige Raibmon, who argued that Native identity isn't always place bound and that mobility doesn't necessarily equate to shiftlessness or cultural demise. Rather, it was a means of survival and resilience.[43] *Basket Diplomacy* also contributes to the scholarship of Sheri Marie Shuck-Hall on the early history of the Alabamas' and Coushattas' migration and resettlement by extending the narrative to the Coushattas' final settlement in Louisiana.[44] Additionally, the story that unfolds in this book speaks directly to the complexity and subjective nature of federal Indian policy as the Coushatta people were frequently at the center of debates about federal responsibility, seeing highly inconsistent outcomes over the years. While the tribe was unilaterally terminated from federal Indian services without consent or congressional approval, it was later burdened with arbitrary and capricious demands as conditions for reinstatement. Other well-documented cases of termination and reinstatement followed a similar trajectory, but the Coushattas' story remains unique and largely untold. Moreover, this study also enhances the growing scholarship on the challenges and outcomes of federal recognition and the different paths tribes have taken in the twentieth century. Brian Klopotek's book, *Recognition Odysseys: Indigeneity, Race, and Federal Tribal Recognition Policy in Three Louisiana Indian Communities*, in particular, illuminates the roles of race and politics in the federal recognition process among southern tribes. By examining the experiences of three other Louisiana tribes—the Tunica-Biloxi (federally recognized in 1981), the Jena Band of Choctaw (federally recognized in 1995), and the Clifton-Choctaw (recognized by the state in 1979)—he demonstrated how each encountered its own challenges that were partially dictated by how the tribe fit into the local racialized hierarchy. Klopotek also argued that federal recognition is only one milestone in a longer journey—a point that resonates with the Coushattas' experience, for it took the tribal economy years to stabilize following reinstatement.[45] Finally, this book contributes to a growing body of culturally and-contextually specific scholarship, providing insight on "strength-based" leadership in Indigenous communities that emphasizes listening, situational fluidity, community-based initiative building, innovative thinking, and sacrifices.[46]

This story unfolds over six chapters. Chapter 1 focuses on the early years of homesteading and settlement around Bayou Blue. Coushattas adapted to their new home by finding employment, carving footpaths to connect their homesteads, and transforming a Congregational Church into a centralized community hub. Chapter 2 covers the period 1913–51, during which two generations of tribal leaders laid the groundwork for subsequent advocacy by aggressively campaigning for the introduction of federal Indian services to the community. They succeeded, and the tribe began receiving limited resources for education and health care in the 1930s and 1940s. Chapter 3 reveals the fleeting nature of this funding, which was withdrawn in 1953. Spanning the years 1951–62, this chapter covers the aftermath of the termination policy and the election of a new chief. Chapter 4 covers 1962–69 and examines the effects of the War on Poverty within the Coushatta community. In this period the tribe initiated its first revenue-generating enterprise and began reshaping its governing structure. Chapter 5 delves into a shorter period, 1969–73, when Coushattas and their allies leveraged a shifting political landscape within the state and federal governments to secure an opportunity for the Coushattas to become the first tribe to be recognized by Louisiana, with federal reinstatement soon to follow. The book ends, in chapter 6, with the period 1973–84, a time of growth and strategic planning. During these years the Coushattas acquired a reservation, expanded their economic enterprises, developed a series of social programs and services, and launched various public education activities to share their story as members of an emerging tribal nation—one that would continue to set precedents, push boundaries, and become among the top private employers in the state in the decades to follow.[47]

Basket Diplomacy coalesced through a myriad of Coushatta voices as well as Native and non-Native friends, partners, and advocates. They provided hundreds of hours of personal narratives to give this story a level of depth and emotion not yet heard by a wider audience.[48] These narratives complement ethnographic fieldwork and extensive source materials gathered from public and private collections that contribute to an immense documentary record. Although this study provides a deeper understanding of Indian affairs at multiple levels, my primary objective was to foreground the Coushattas' experiences, concerns, and decisions on how best to interact with different institutions and power structures. Although I sought to incorporate representatives from a diverse cross section of the tribe, not all perspectives are presented. When quoting or summarizing, I tried to accurately reflect the speaker's intent, but I know that my interpretation shaped my choices of what to include, and any errors are my own. Consent for this research was provided by the Coushatta Tribal Council, and personal consent was given by those who were interviewed. The Coushatta Heritage Department was instrumental in providing resources, translations, and feedback on this manuscript. In turn I shared interviews and resources collected for this book to include in the tribe's archival collections.[49]

This project was first conceptualized in 2012 following a presentation on southern Indian activism that I was invited to give on the Coushatta reservation. Addressing an auditorium full of Coushattas and their many longtime friends and advocates, I was struck by the scarcity of published information available on the tribe's history, particularly given its broader political and economic impact on the region. Although the historiography of the Native South has grown significantly over the last few decades, it seems that with but a few exceptions the Coushattas have been largely overlooked.[50] This study would not have come to fruition without the encouragement and generosity of Ernest Sickey. As the tribal chairman who shepherded his community to state recognition and federal reinstatement, his perspective and experiences offered critical insights to this work. His ability to recall past events in vivid detail helped convey the urgency that propelled the advocacy work of several generations of Coushatta leaders who paved the way for him. While there were many reoccurring themes to our conversations, one that continually emerged was the importance of the Koasati language to Coushatta identity and survival. And, although the Coushatta tribe continues to have a high percentage of Koasati speakers relative to national averages, fluency has declined over the years. As a result, language retention has thus moved to the forefront of contemporary tribal initiatives.[51] Today the language is seen and heard at every turn around the reservation, appearing on tribal buildings and service vehicles, and it is spoken at the tribal preschool and at departmental and community meetings. It is in this spirit that the Koasati language also is featured throughout the subtitles of this book, both to guide the narrative and to remind the reader what generations of Coushattas have fought so hard to protect.[52] Their sacrifices and struggles fill these pages, sharing a collective story of a resilient people.

BASKET DIPLOMACY

1

"Don't Forget Your Gumbo Bowl"

Building a Life at Bayou Blue

I remember our grandparents taught us a lot about our duty . . .
they set the standards for us to follow.
—Barbara Langley, 2003

Louisiana bustled in 1884. That year the World's Industrial and Cotton Centennial Exhibition was held in New Orleans to celebrate the anniversary of the first documented shipment of cotton sent from the United States to England. The festivities lauded financial prosperity yet also served as a reminder of the slave labor that had built the foundation of the region's economy. In fact, racial tensions were still high amid the celebration, just a decade removed from one of the worst instances of racial violence in Louisiana history: the Colfax massacre.[1] Among many attractions, the New Orleans exhibition showcased an array of what historian Daniel H. Usner Jr. identified as "starkly contrasting Indian scenes," with depictions portraying a nearly vanished Indigenous Louisiana population next to Buffalo Bill Cody's Wild West Show that featured Plains Indian performers engaged in war dances and mock stagecoach attacks. Just as in other locations where the Wild

West show ran, spectators at the New Orleans exhibition were quick to adopt—even appropriate in some instances—popular depictions of Plains Indians as the basis of what constituted "real Indians" of the post-Reconstruction era.[2] This mind-set reinforced the marginalization of local Native peoples, whose presence was commonly dismissed during a time when increasing economic opportunities and the opening of homesteads introduced a new surge of people into the area. Louisiana was like other states in experiencing dramatic demographic changes as fresh railroad tracks traversed the landscape, bringing more people to previously isolated places. Joining this wave of newcomers were several hundred Coushattas, who, like Louisiana's existing Native population, didn't conform to the popularized version of Indians featured in Wild West shows but nonetheless came to contribute to a rich and diverse array of cultures that came to coexist. By the 1880s the Coushatta people had finally found a permanent home in southwestern Louisiana, more than 160 miles from New Orleans, deep within a heavily wooded area dominated by yellow pine, cypress, and diverse wildlife along a waterway called Bayou Blue.

Imishahpafạ Ohtistọ
Settling into Their New Home

Twenty-seven Coushattas and nine Alabamas filed homestead claims on scattered plots of unsettled public lands beginning in the 1880s, acquiring over four thousand acres of "farmland, forest and lush, green swamps" in Allen Parish within the first decade of the twentieth century.[3] The original homesteads were recorded in Calcasieu Parish, but in 1912 Calcasieu was subdivided into the current Allen, Jefferson Davis, and Beauregard Parishes.[4] Many of the Indian homesteaders were assisted through the legal process of acquiring land by James Cole and Richard E. Powell, who were both white landowners in the area and familiar with the opportunities provided by the Homestead Act of 1862.[5] Significantly, at the time Coushatta and Alabama homesteaders obtained their patents, the United States government was on course to deplete Indian-held lands on a national scale. The passing of the 1887 Dawes Severalty Act (also called the General Allotment Act) was part of a larger civilization project aimed at assimilating Indians by transforming them into yeomen farmers and U.S. citizens—a mission that involved breaking up tribally controlled lands into 160-acre allotments, with the "surplus" lands made available to non-Indians. Under this legislation, as well as the previously enacted Indian Homestead Act of 1884, federal protection was extended to Indian-held allotments for twenty-five years, after which the land was privatized and taxed, leading to vulnerabilities that proved devastating—as the loss of 86 million acres of tribal lands between 1887 and 1934 attests.[6] Although historian Angie Debo took a sympathetic position toward the intentions of federal officials, she denounced the policy as an "orgy of plunder and exploitation probably unparalleled in American history."[7]

While land policies of the late nineteenth century served as one part of a larger project to rid the federal government of its treaty obligations to tribes, the Coushattas—like many other southern Indian communities—were not considered "wards" of the federal government. In spite of earlier diplomatic dealings in which Coushatta leaders signed treaties with the United States and several European powers, a later history of migration and isolation left them well outside of the attention of the Office of Indian Affairs (OIA). In deciding to file homestead claims in Louisiana to secure a future in their newfound home, the Coushattas leveraged the very tool intended to undermine tribal cohesion. Historian Jay Precht posited that "homesteads provided Coushattas places to maintain the kin relationships that held the community together . . . and provided a context for building community institutions over time."[8] A legally secured land base not only provided permanence but also presented new opportunities for Coushattas to emerge from the legal shadows and interact with their neighbors as property owners, U.S. citizens, and contributors to the social, political, and economic development of the region.[9]

Of all the Coushatta homesteaders Sissy Robinson Alabama (1873–1914) was the only one whose 160 acres of property wasn't recorded under the authority of the general Homestead Act of 1862.[10] Instead, she recorded her acreage under the Indian Homestead Act of 1884 and placed it into federal trust in 1898.[11] The reason for the inconsistency

in how Alabama acquired her land versus the rest of the tribal homesteaders has been a point of speculation for some time. A 1950 land
claims case made the argument that the majority of Coushattas had to
acquire property under the terms of the general Homestead Act because
in spite of "several notations, referring directly, or by inference, to the
fact that an Indian is involved," the Coushatta patentees must have been
classified as "non-tribal Indians," a category reserved for Indians who
had "abandoned any tribal relations . . . and have adopted the habits of
civilized people."[12] The problem with this argument was that the Coushattas had not abandoned their tribal structure, language, or culture and,
therefore, challenged the distinction these categories were intended to
delineate. Plus, this explanation didn't account for the inconsistency in
how Alabama filed her patent, casting further doubt on whether there
was even a conscious enforcement of policies employed by the local
land office in responding to Indian petitions. The probability that the
Coushattas acquired land patents under terms of their own choosing is
the most reasonable explanation. In exercising control over how their
property was recorded, it is likely that they made the choice to follow
in lockstep with their non-Indian neighbors. Previously landless, Coushattas valued the security of controlling their private domain, and the
notion of inviting federal supervision over their land for the twenty-five
years required by the Indian Homestead Act was a prospect they likely
resisted. Given the general Homestead Act's requirement that filers had
to be at least twenty-one years old, it is also plausible that Sissy Robinson
Alabama would have followed their lead had she not been eighteen years
old when she first initiated the process to acquire a homestead patent.[13]
For whatever reason, Alabama's homestead was the outlier—one that
later proved to have implications that extended beyond her lifetime.
Once taken into trust, hers became the first contemporary case of the
federal government exercising its trust obligation to the Coushattas,
despite not being accompanied by services or an acknowledgment of
tribal sovereignty. Because Alabama's land was under federal jurisdiction, unlike the other Coushatta homesteads, it was not subject to ad
valorem taxes—although Allen Parish did attempt to tax the land in
1916 and was sued by the federal government because of it.[14] The trust

status of her homestead not only allowed Alabama to maintain her estate for her descendants; it also played a vital role in the Coushattas receiving federal Indian services in the 1930s.[15] Anthropologist George Roth identified this as "the most important example of use of the Indian homestead law by a southern tribe."[16]

The Bayou Blue settlement quickly became a home to the Coushatta people, who became an integral part of the rich cultural makeup of Allen and Jefferson Davis Parishes. They joined a unique demographic, composed primarily of African Americans, Cajuns, and German immigrants whose local histories then evolved concurrently with the tribe's.[17] Coushatta families lived interspersed throughout the area, which was characterized by a checkerboard pattern of homesteads, creating opportunities for building cross-cultural alliances over the years. Farmers from midwestern states also began acquiring land in the area as transportation options increased when the Missouri-Pacific Railroad intersected with the Southern Pacific Railroad. These newcomers were eager to try rice farming, a crop introduced into the region by Cajuns, whose ancestors grew rice in small prairie ponds. By the turn of the century new technologies had mechanized rice farming, and it wasn't long before both Coushatta men and women found seasonal agricultural work alongside their new neighbors.[18] Many locals worked for farmers such as Odell Bertrand, who owned property near the Coushatta homesteads and was known for sharing surplus milk, meat, and rice to supplement the Coushattas' wages, which in the first decades of the twentieth century ranged from $1.50 to $3.50 per day.[19] The rich timber resources in southwestern Louisiana—a region advertised in a 1922 publication as offering "the easiest logging of any in the United States or Canada"—provided Coushattas additional opportunities for employment in sawmills, such as one operated by Richard E. Powell.[20] John Albert Bel also had a great deal of influence on the area's development. Bel, who was hailed a "pioneer lumberman and leading capitalist" by the Lake Charles American Press, had vast landholdings that included plots that both divided and adjoined Coushatta properties.[21] His companies, the Bel Lumber Company and later the Bel Oil Corporation, were major employers that drew widely from the local population.

While Coushattas interacted with all of their neighbors to varying degrees, particularly close friendships developed with Cajun families. Dewith Carrier, a Cajun who grew up near Bayou Blue, noted, "The Indians [and] the Cajuns have a lot in common . . . we could relate to the Indians and the Indians could relate to us because we were [all] poor people." Because they spoke French and adhered to their Catholic beliefs in an area predominantly populated by English-speaking Protestants, many Cajuns felt marginalized and discriminated against. Like the Coushattas, Cajuns also obtained homesteads and worked as tenant farmers or in the timber industry. Carrier remembered how Coushattas collected turtles from the bayous to sell to Cajuns, and many even learned to speak French. For the Coushatta families who owned radios, listening to Cajun music was among their favorite pastimes.[22]

As a result of the growing population of homesteaders, several surrounding towns sprouted up to accommodate the influx of new arrivals. The town of Oberlin, which was incorporated in 1900 while still part of Calcasieu Parish, became the seat of Allen Parish in 1912. Named after Oberlin, Ohio, the town was settled initially by migrants from the Midwest who found the location appealing because it served as an intersection point for a train that ran from Lake Charles. Farther south, the town of Kinder (near Indian Village) was founded by the enterprising Jim Kinder, who arrived in 1885 from Mississippi to open a small store.[23]

Although Coushattas often visited Oberlin and Kinder, as well as the other nearby towns of Eunice, Basile, and Jennings, to purchase supplies or sell their wares, the town of Elton emerged as the most prominent location in the establishment of the tribe in the area. Located just a few miles from the Bayou Blue settlement, Elton was founded in part by Isaac M. Henderson of Des Moines, Iowa, a veteran of the Union army who survived a stint in the infamous Confederate Libby Prison. In the decades following the war, Henderson decided to make Louisiana his home and, like Jim Kinder, seized a business opportunity to serve a rapidly growing region by opening a general store. One account claimed that Henderson chose the name Elton after a town in England. His grandson Dr. Harold Sabatier offered another account, saying the town was initially called Hollings after a railroad executive but Henderson later changed it to Elton after his late daughter. By 1896 Henderson had established Elton's first post office and served as the postmaster.[24] After the Southern Pacific Railroad line reached Elton, the population steadily climbed to about one thousand by 1912, the year after the town's incorporation. Initially, Elton fell within the boundaries of Calcasieu Parish but was redistricted to the new Jefferson Davis Parish, and it soon became a thriving prairie town budding up against a combination of thick pine woods and rich agricultural land. The *New Orleans Times-Democrat* named Elton among the "coming great towns of Southern Louisiana" based on its thriving rice industry (shipping out approximately 100,000 bags in 1912) and lumber companies, which shipped out tons of yellow, longleaf, and shortleaf pine.[25] By 1920 the population of Jefferson Davis Parish had reached nearly nineteen thousand and then grew steadily to thirty thousand by 1960.[26] During its heyday in the first half of the twentieth century, Elton had several grocery stores and a meat market, drugstore, bakery, hardware store, clothing store, pool hall, and movie theater. A dirt road ran through the town, and a train depot gave people easy access to New Orleans and Houston.[27]

As the Coushatta people developed enduring friendships with their neighbors, who also lived in what came to be considered "the outskirts of the Cajun Prairie," they became a point of curiosity among the people living in Elton and other nearby towns. Indian families traveled the footpaths that laced through the woods or arrived by wagon as they shopped for necessities, such as seeds for their gardens.[28] As a child, Stanley Leger lived in Kinder, where his mother was born and raised, and he recalled how the residents frequently saw Coushattas come to town. Many of the townspeople were fascinated with them and noticed that they were reluctant to talk with strangers. The Coushattas' reticence fueled speculation about where these "wandering" people had originated and the circumstances that had brought them to southwestern Louisiana.[29] During a 1908 visit to Elton, anthropologist Mark Harrington captured this sentiment, describing Coushattas as wearing "citizen's clothing," almost exclusively speaking Koasati, and posing such a mystery to locals that they didn't even know what tribal name to attribute to them.[30]

Fig. 1: Mother and son, Emily and Bruce Abbey, sell baskets near Elton, 1930s. Courtesy of the State Library of Louisiana, Works Progress Administration Collection.

Coushatta women were particularly visible. Some earned income as domestics in the homes of white families, while others were seen about town or along roadsides selling their swamp cane and pine needle baskets. Baskets were purchased for both their ornamental and practical values, with farmers often using them to carry produce or eggs. Coushatta women filled wagons with baskets and traveled to different towns to sell or barter.[31] Doris Robinson Celestine Battise shared her experiences as a young child going on these trips to trade baskets for food: "The people were very glad to see we brought food home when we got back. That's how we lived and survived back then, we traded our baskets, and got rice, and beans, and potatoes, and live chickens . . . We'd trade baskets for whatever we could, so we could eat" (fig. 1).[32] Other times they would trade for clothing or other supplies. "The baskets were our major source of income," said weaver Loris Abbott Langley. "We could even build our houses with supplies traded for the baskets." If money was exchanged for these baskets, it was "around twenty-five cents for a big basket."[33] As Linda Langley, Claude Oubre, and Jay Precht explained, Coushatta women had "a long tradition of wielding economic and social influence" as major contributors to the production of supplies and items that the Coushattas sold or traded throughout their history.[34]

As Indian-made items became increasingly commodified for primarily white middle- and upper-class consumption, Coushattas saw greater demand for their baskets. During this "basket craze," generated by a growing appreciation for Indian arts as part of the Arts and Crafts movement of the Victorian era, Indian baskets became fashionable as people paired them with other "curios" to decorate their homes.[35] Although fueled by romantic notions of Indians as a people plucked from another time and situated in stark contrast to modernity, the increased exposure provided Indian artisans with opportunities to foster alliances with non-Indian patrons and establish a foothold in tourism.[36] Scholarship on the Indian arts and crafts market among western tribes has provided a deeper understanding of this process. Yet it is the work of Sarah H. Hill on the Cherokees and Daniel H. Usner Jr. on the Chitimachas that demonstrates the role of basket weavers as cultural mediators and significant contributors to the broader social and economic development of the New South.[37]

Basket weaving requires a lot of skill and labor—and the woods around Bayou Blue provide much of the materials that weavers need. "I love the environment we live in," Rosabel Sylestine related, "among the pine timbers which have provided me all the wares I needed to do this work."[38] Over time the gathering trips took weavers farther afield as logging practices depleted their viable resources. Loris Abbott Langley explained: "People think you can just pull any needle off and use them all but that's not how it works . . . Some of the needle[s], like those where bugs have gotten into them, are not long enough. Some needles are just too short." Once collected, needles are sorted and bundled. "We'll wrap them up and find a place like in an attic where the sun's not going to get to them." They are put in rows and carefully turned every two or three months so that they dry evenly. Just before they get too dry and brittle, weavers begin working with them. "It's a complicated process that takes a long time just to get to a point to start making the basket."[39] Once the materials are ready, sewing the basket is another time-consuming endeavor that requires a great deal of patience, dexterity, and arm strength. Depending on the weaver's skills, a basket can take anywhere from days to weeks to complete. Although some Coushatta men also participated in the late nineteenth and early twentieth centuries, it was primarily women who engaged in basket production. In many cases, however, men helped gather materials, and those who worked in the timber industry sometimes gathered swamp cane when out on the job.[40]

While baskets played a critical role in economically sustaining the community, they also contributed to the validation of the Coushattas' identity as Indigenous people in a region preoccupied with race. Usner makes a similar argument for the Chitimachas, describing how basketry became "tightly interwoven with their racial identity," enabling them to mark "bolder boundaries with others" in asserting themselves as Indians, which contributed to the Chitimachas becoming Louisiana's first federally recognized tribe in 1916.[41] Life under the system of Jim Crow was locally dictated, however, and the manner in which it affected—or didn't affect—Indians varied across the region. In Allen and Jefferson Davis Parishes the Coushattas maintained an unquestioned racial identity as Indians, although this designation did not always guarantee access to federal Indian services. Yet despite being categorized as people of color within a system intended to promote white privilege, they were freely admitted into white public spaces, and their children attended white schools. This distinction offered Coushattas access to education all the way through high school, whereas local segregated black schools ended after the seventh grade.[42]

This was an atypical experience—one that deviated from that of many Indians across the South whose racialized identities were carefully scrutinized, barring them from attending white schools and even preventing them from self-identifying as "Indian" on birth certificates or driver's licenses.[43] In describing the experiences of the Tuscaroras and Lumbees in North Carolina, for example, attorney Raymond Gibbs claimed that one "doesn't have to go to Africa to find apartheid; he can come to

Robeson County."[44] Similarly, in characterizing life for the Monacans of Virginia, American Indian Studies scholar Samuel R. Cook wrote: "By the turn of the twentieth century separate schools had long been established for local blacks, and the Monacans were given the choice to attend these schools or do without. Almost without exception, the Indians opted to refrain from indulging in an education system that would deny them equal opportunities with other individuals regardless of race, and more critically would deny their existence as Indians."[45] In much of Louisiana, Brian Klopotek argued, "Indian integration happened haphazardly." For example, Houmas living in Lafourche Parish were integrated into white schools in the 1930s, while those living in Terrebonne Parish weren't fully integrated until the 1960s.[46] The Choctaw-Apaches of Ebarb had similar experiences with a lack of educational access, which prompted them to establish their own school. They weren't even allowed into most sections of the nearby town due to strict segregation practices.[47]

There are a few explanations for why the Coushattas' experiences were different than those of other Louisiana Indian communities. For one, the specific demographic makeup of the area may have contributed to a greater level of tolerance of local Indian residents than in other parts of the state. Ernest Sickey credits the large population of transplants from midwestern states who arrived without the racial baggage that influenced attitudes and permeated other, more established Louisiana communities.[48] Plus, the fact that Coushattas were landowners who were residentially integrated with whites around Bayou Blue also may have contributed to their access to white institutions. Land often was used to enforce the boundaries of white privilege, and as tribes such as the Jena Band of Choctaws farther north were prevented access to land in the early twentieth century, the Coushattas leveraged their position as property owners.[49] Different perspectives on race can also be understood in terms of geography. Precht situated the town of Elton on a "cultural boundary between South Louisiana and North Louisiana" where the influences of the French Catholics—largely associated with the southern part of the state—"moderated the extent of racism, making it less institutionalized than in other parts of the South."[50] Finally, the place on which the Coushattas fell within the local racial hierarchy may

Fig. 2: Above: John Abbey, c. 1905. Courtesy of the Coushatta Tribal Archives.

Fig. 3: Opposite: Sissy Poncho Abbey poses with baskets on her porch, c. 1910. Courtesy of the Coushatta Tribal Archives.

have hinged on a presumption of them being of "pure Indian blood"—a notion that challenged many other southern Indians, who were frequently classified as being "racially mixed." Long-held anxieties about miscegenation embedded in Louisiana law initially prohibited Indians from marrying whites and later extended prohibitions to marriages between Indians and African Americans.[51] So, the decision to admit Coushattas into white schools and public spaces may have been based more on who they were not, rather than who they were.

Even if the Coushattas were on the privileged side of the color line, they still experienced racism and discrimination. One tribal member remembered walking to Elton as a child with his parents to pick up some supplies and having to pay in cash "because most of the merchants would not extend credit to the Indian families."[52] Another recalled how, though she felt the store merchants didn't overtly discriminate, "they didn't like or trust Indians. You could feel it by the way they looked at us and treated us."[53] As the entire region developed, the Coushattas also largely were overlooked for public services, such as electricity, water, and the paving of roads. As one neighbor remembered: "It was all dirt roads . . . Even the police didn't service that area. [The tribe] were the last ones to get sewage, probably were the last ones to get electricity."[54] "We were the lowest of the low," said Ernest Sickey, who remembered how many of the local non-Indians treated the Coushatta people. While developing tribal friendships later mitigated some of these attitudes, in the early days, Sickey claimed, "when we needed help . . . [many] didn't help us. They could care less."[55]

Naasǫhyạlttimawiichitǫ
Everyone in the Community Helped One Another

Homestead patents, census data, and missionary records reveal that two to three hundred Coushatta people were living in Louisiana by the turn of the twentieth century, representing extended families with no less than fifteen surnames. Although the community traveled together, each family had its own unique experiences and hardships shaped by loss and economic struggles. They cared for each other because survival was a cooperative effort. Although Coushatta homesteads were divided—interspersed between those held by non-Indians—they continued their communal practices. Everyone played a part in leading, nurturing, healing, and teaching the next generation.

The guidance and wisdom of tribal leaders such as John Abbey (1832–1910), who served as the Coushattas' chief until his death, was a valuable resource to those looking to lay the foundation for a new settlement (fig. 2). Abbey lived through the community's multiple relocations in the nineteenth century. He shared traditions and stories with his children and imparted what it meant to be a Coushatta. This helped to prepare one of his sons, Jefferson "Jeff" Abbey (1854–1952), to take on the role of chief by the 1930s. The specifics of the education Jeff Abbey received from his father, as well as from others within the community, survived in his own teachings as he went on to provide guidance to many generations of Coushattas over the years. The younger Abbey later acquired the largest homestead on the eastern side of the Bayou Blue community and developed a reputation for his intelligence and keen business acumen. In spite of speaking very little English, he had an innate ability to develop friendships with his non-Indian neighbors and negotiate deals for land, livestock, and other resources that the tribe needed.[56]

Jeff Abbey and his wife, Sissy Poncho Abbey (1856–1936), helped the community remain cohesive, even in the face of tragedy (fig. 3). For instance, when Charley and Mary Sickey moved with the rest of the tribe to the Bayou Blue settlement, they joined in the efforts to create a permanent home for their family.[57] Although they were not among the original homesteaders, census records indicate that they owned their home. By 1905 they had their first child—a son they named Davis. A few years later their daughter, Gladys, was born. In 1910 Mary died, at the age of thirty-eight, from what appeared to be complications from childbirth, and within days the death of her newborn baby was also recorded.[58] Soon afterward Charley Sickey made the decision to leave his two surviving children at the Bayou Blue settlement while he moved to Texas to live with relatives and work in a sawmill. Although he later returned, in 1920 Sickey turned a fifteen-year-old Davis and a thirteen-year-old Gladys over to the care of Jeff and Sissy Abbey.[59] The Abbeys raised the children, even giving them land to establish homes of their own once they came of age. In addition to seeing that the children had what they needed to build a future for themselves, Jeff Abbey also mentored Davis, sharing his vision for the future of the Coushatta people and encouraged Davis to take an active part in helping the tribe establish a strong foothold in the area.

In 1930 Davis Sickey married Daisy Langley and set out to clear and settle the land that had been given to him by the Abbeys. Like Davis, Daisy had also lost a parent at a young age. In her case her father, Alcide Langley (1882–1919), a Coushatta man who, according to military records, was drafted to fight in World War I. He left behind his wife, Arzile Roy Langley, and several children, including a nine-year-old Daisy.[60] Unlike her husband, Arzile wasn't Coushatta but from a Choctaw community residing in the Basile area—less than ten miles from the Bayou Blue community.[61] Arzile's father was a Frenchman named John Roy, but she was raised by her mother, from whom she learned traditional medicine, and later became a well-respected medicine woman among both the Choctaws and Coushattas. The subject of a 1991 essay on lost pan-tribal traditions, Arzile was called "a woman of power, a Choctaw herbalist and seer . . . [whose] skill as a medicine woman earned her a place in the folklore of native communities throughout Louisiana and Texas."[62] She lived for fifty-six more years (until 1975) as a widow and chose to continue residing among the Coushattas, where she practiced traditional medicine while caring for her children by working as a laundress in a nearby town. She eventually came to live with Davis and Daisy Sickey and their children, Ernest and Bernetta. Ernest wanted to practice medicine like his grandmother. "I grew up being the pharmacist," he remembered. People with different illnesses visited her, and she frequently told him to "'go in the woods and dig up this root' or 'go get this bark' or 'go get these leaves from this tree.'" That was his job, and he enjoyed it—it made him feel connected and special. Sitting at his grandmother's knee, Sickey had great respect for the work she did. "It's sacred . . . asking the Creator to help heal, to be a part of the healing process, to heal the body, to heal the voice of mankind through medicine [that] had been given to them for thousands of years." He was eager to learn and carry on her work and people often asked if he was planning to practice medicine himself. "I would pester her until she [got] annoyed," Sickey recalled, "because I wanted to learn. I wanted to know." It wasn't long before she revealed to him that it was not his path, and as a result, she never taught him the prayers or songs behind her medicine. "If you don't have that gift, you just don't have it," she told him. Besides, she said, "you'd be doing other things." At the time, Sickey's disappointment likely made it difficult to accept that those "other things" may not have involved practicing medicine, but, instead, would involve a very different type of work and sacrifice. For the work to come she armed him with some specially prepared medicine and presented it to him with the promise that "this will protect you for the rest of your life." Sickey didn't take this offering lightly, as he explained during a 2015 interview when he carefully retrieved it from his pocket: "It's about sixty-five years old, and I still carry it to this day."[63]

Although Langley practiced Choctaw medicine, she had a lot of interactions with the Coushatta medicine people. Among them was Ency Robinson Abbey Abbott (1897–1956), the youngest sister of Sissy Robinson Alabama and one of the last Coushatta women to practice traditional medicine. Like Langley, Abbott was widely sought after and respected for her knowledge and skills. She was known to be approached "at all hours of the day or night" and would selflessly leave whatever she was doing to assist in alleviating pain and sickness.[64] Traditional healing practices were closely guarded and passed down through specialized training. It was assessed that Abbott's medical knowledge may have derived from her maternal grandfather, August Williams, who was identified as a "doctor" in a 1908 photograph taken by anthropologist Mark Harrington while visiting the community.[65] The knowledge and techniques associated with practicing traditional medicine had deep historical roots that persevered through the Coushattas' many travels. It was a resource that Coushattas who remained in Texas continued to access through frequent visits to southwestern Louisiana, the location of what Crystal Williams, a Coushatta who grew up in Texas, called the "core" community.[66]

In fact, movement between the two settlements was fluid. It was common for Coushatta families living in Texas or Louisiana to walk back and forth to visit their relatives, marry, or settle down for a long stay.[67] Some Coushattas living in Texas resided with the Alabamas in Polk County near the town of Livingston, while others lived in Houston.[68] In total it was about two hundred miles from the Louisiana settlement, taking several days to walk or travel by horseback. Travelers generally found safe places to camp for two nights along their journey. This was how connections between the extended families were maintained as they shared concerns and information about the types of services that other tribes received.[69]

In addition to visiting relatives in Texas, the Bayou Blue community also participated in intertribal gatherings around Louisiana. Anthropologist Hiram F. Gregory discussed the gatherings that used to occur among the Tunica, Coushatta, and Jena Band of Choctaw peoples in the early 1900s. The tribes communicated using a Mobilian trade language that largely derived from Choctaw. Arzile Roy Langley was one of the last Mobilian speakers and worked with linguist Emanuel Drechsel to capture recordings of the unique language before she died.[70] Many tribes living in Louisiana also engaged in cultural sharing, such as basketry techniques and songs. Jean-Luc Pierite, of the Tunica-Biloxi Tribe, described these interactions as an intercultural dialogue: "We used to have cane baskets, and my great-aunt actually adopted the Coushatta style of long-needle pine basketry because of our interaction with the Coushatta Tribe." Pierite also learned from his elders how these intertribal gatherings brought people together for Green Corn ceremonies.[71] In addition to the culture sharing, these meetings promoted coalition building to help advocate for tribal interests. The Tunica were particularly active on this front, promoting advocacy in the early twentieth century and bringing together groups of Choctaws and Biloxis, and even attempting to build coalitions with the Coushattas and Chitimachas.[72]

Despite their multiple relocations, the Coushattas maintained a system of shared governance—a practice that went back centuries.[73] Authority rested with the matrilineal clan system that not only defined the tribe's marriage patterns and kinship relationships but provided a mechanism for ensuring equal representation across the broader community. Leland Thompson explained that "each clan had its own head speaker who in turn

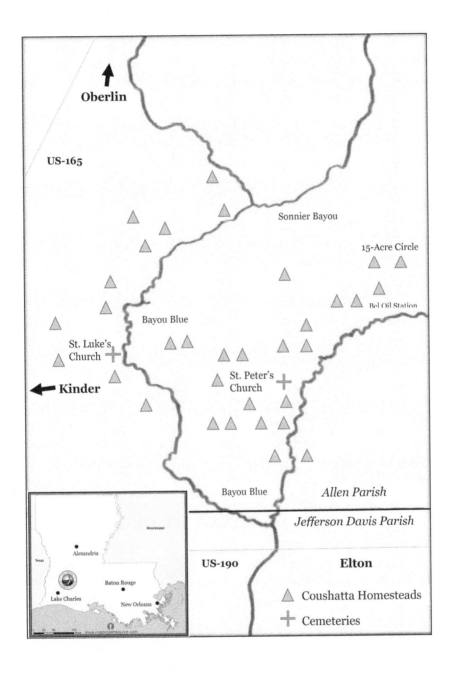

Oberlin

US-165

Sonnier Bayou

15-Acre Circle

Bel Oil Station

Bayou Blue

St. Luke's
Church

Kinder

St. Peter's
Church

Bayou Blue

Allen Parish

Jefferson Davis Parish

US-190

Elton

△ Coushatta Homesteads

✝ Cemeteries

Alexandria

Texas

Mississippi

Baton Rouge

Lake Charles

New Orleans

Map 2: Coushatta homesteads, 1880–1920. Map by Mike Liotta and author.

worked with the chief."[74] "They were the ones that made the decisions," Ernest Sickey added. "They were the ones that created policy, and they were the ones that elected their own leadership. Each family had a say so in the community." When issues impacting the tribe arose, such as a dispute, representatives from each area of the community served as a judicial body, meeting to share perspectives and render a decision on how best to proceed. Although decisions were often discussed collectively, through the mid-twentieth century the Coushattas still had individuals serving under the traditional title of "chief," or *mikkó*.[75] The chief's role was to serve as a communication conduit within the community and facilitate the shared governance as well as to represent the tribe to the outside world—a particularly important role as the tribe established their new home in southwestern Louisiana.[76]

Coushatta landholdings determined the configuration of the settlement, which was geographically divided into three segments—the central, western, and eastern communities—with Bayou Blue serving as the natural boundary that separated the eastern and western sections (map 2). In the early days pathways wound their way through the woods linking Coushatta families who lived within a radius of several miles. Many of them were small paths suitable for foot traffic, but some families carved out wider trails to accommodate wagons. The community relied on these pathways to share food, medicine, and information. Before parts of the woods were cleared and roads were built, the trails were also used to walk to town. Most paths met in the central part of the community, where a small schoolhouse was built in the 1890s but was used only a few months of the year.[77] This is also where people met to socialize and engage in lively stickball games.[78] The paths emanating from the center of the Coushatta community were later described by Bel Abbey as resembling "the spokes of a wheel." It was a settlement pattern consistent with traditional practices common among the Coushattas at the time of European contact that had been modified to suit their shifting needs and geographical placement around Bayou Blue.[79]

The community found every opportunity to come together socially. They had frequent cookouts, and families would show up, each with its own contribution to the feast (fig. 4). As Sickey remembered, "We didn't

Fig. 4: Davis Sickey at a community gathering in 1962 with Lizzie Robinson (right) and Anna John Thompson (back). Courtesy of the Coushatta Tribal Archives.

have much, but . . . enjoyed getting the community together." Birthday parties provided a particularly joyful opportunity for a celebration to which the whole community was invited. "It was a wonderful thing because every weekend . . . there was a party or some kind of birthday gathering . . . Everybody that had a birthday party always used to make chicken gumbo. The joke around the community was, 'Don't forget your gumbo bowl' . . . Gumbo was a big deal, especially in the wintertime." Guests weren't expected to bring gifts, just their own plates, bowls, and utensils packed neatly into paper sacks. Because these were community events, everyone was invited. "You didn't have to be a relative, just show up," Sickey recalled. Funerals also served as an occasion for the entire community to gather. When someone died, people brought food. They built bonfires and stayed up all night visiting and bringing comfort to the family of the deceased. A steady stream of people came through the night to bring more firewood and pay their respects.[80]

Life in the community was defined by a system of reciprocity. "Everyone in the community helped one another," explained Barbara Langley. "If there was any [need], they were all there. If there was food, [they had] a little food fest or something, they would all come together. We didn't have cars so whenever you went out to visit somebody, you spent the night there with them."[81] Rodney Williams also shared with his daughter Crystal "that if someone was moving from house to house, the whole community would come in and help them move. Let's say there was someone cooking, or shot a pig, anything, the whole community was there . . . It was pure family, pure community support for each other. That's what they had, that's all they had. That's what they built their values on."[82]

These values were also the basis of what Coushatta children were taught. It was an educational approach that was intentional and systematically addressed the community's shared pedagogical goals.[83] While everyone contributed, women played a particularly significant role in educating the tribe's children. They not only took care of their own households and, in some cases, worked for wages; they also served as tradition bearers. According to Langley, Oubre, and Precht, "They taught their children traditional stories, songs, and beliefs, transmitting their language as well as their values to each new generation."[84] Passing on the knowledge and techniques of making baskets was also an important part of child-rearing as young weavers perfected their craft under the watchful eyes of their teachers, knowing they ran the risk of having to start again if it wasn't done right.[85]

Children were also taught to hunt, fish, and do chores at an early age. Lelia Battise grew up in the eastern part of the community and explained that each family member had a role to play in order to make a household function: "We had to take care of everything. My mom and my dad had to cut the wood . . . When we got home, we'd get the wheelbarrow . . . and bring it home and stack it up. We had to have everything ready for the fire to cook on the wood stove because there was no electricity at all. No bathrooms or anything. We had to go to the little creek in the back [to get our water] . . . We collected the rainwater . . . Then, later on, they had to dig a well and we had to pump the water."[86] In addition, children helped maintain and harvest the gardens. One common task was corn shucking, pounding, and sifting to help in the preparation of *chawahka* (also known as *sofkee*), a corn soup prepared in a black kettle over an open fire over the course of several hours.[87] The recipe and technique involved in making *chawahka* has been passed down through the generations, as were the tools, pots, and basket sifters used to make it. "It is more precious than gold," explained Jonathan Cernek, who continued the tradition of making *chawahka* for tribal gatherings well into the twenty-first century.[88]

For Coushatta children the woods was their playground. Paula Abbey Manuel recalled what she had heard from the elders: "They'd tell me they'd play in the woods . . . They were always in a group . . . They didn't play on their own. Then the parents didn't have anything to worry about. As far as they were concerned, they'd be back by the time it got dark."[89] Bertney Langley had his own fond memories of playing in the woods, climbing trees, fishing, and swimming in the bayous: "We had to think of ways to entertain ourselves, especially in the worst heat of summer . . . Often we would decide to go swimming or fishing. My mother didn't know how to swim, and she was afraid we would get hurt in the bayous, so she always told us to stay away from them. We knew how to swim before my mother ever knew we had learned. When she told us we couldn't go swimming. . . we would just sneak off and go [anyhow]. We would wait a couple of hours and then come back home after our clothes dried."[90]

While Coushatta children enjoyed a great deal of independence, they also spent countless hours with their elders learning about what was important to them, the challenges they faced, and their hopes for the future. Davis Sickey made certain that his own children benefited, as he had, from the wisdom of people like Jeff Abbey. His son Ernest said: "The best education I ever got was from the old people. All of the history and the tradition and the values that I acquired and learned about was [from] listening to them." Like other Coushatta families, the Sickeys had frequent visitors. "Sometimes you would have five or six old people sitting around and talking and sharing what their ancestors talked about, what they knew . . . Growing up, I was very curious about what these elders were talking about, and sometimes I would sit in on a conversation and not say a word and just listen." They were concerned with how the tribe could survive potential changes. Sickey related how "it seemed like the old people knew what was coming in the next fifty [or a] hundred years. I've always wondered how they knew that we would be facing those kinds of challenges," such as climate change, the discovery of new illnesses, water shortages, and the future direction of federal Indian policy. The specific details of these prophecies continued to resonate with Sickey throughout his life, for he saw many of them come to fruition and thought, "Hey, I heard that when I was a kid." One prediction in particular perplexed him: "A lot of them used to say, 'One day white people are going to shoot the moon.' And as a little boy, I would think, 'Why would they do that? Why would anybody want to shoot the moon?' Later on, they were shooting rockets to the moon."[91] Bertney Langley also talked about the impact of prophetic stories on his childhood. He specifically recalled what his uncles Bel and Gilbert Abbey shared with him. While Bel liked to share funny stories, such as rabbit tales, Gilbert was more serious. "We'd go sit down in his house," Langley recalled, "and he'd tell me about how he grew up with his grandmother. She had prophecies she would tell him, and he told [them] to me. He said, 'This is what's going to happen around this time' . . . [and] I've been able to see most of it come together."[92]

Anticipation of what was to come helped the Coushattas survive through the generations. Many of these insights came as warnings about the loss of language and culture—the basis of Coushatta identity. As a result, strict measures were taken to ensure that, as much as possible, marriages occurred within the tribe, for elders anticipated that "one day there will be intermarriages, and when that happens, we start losing culture," Sickey shared. There was also concern about the loss of traditional medicine: "They used to talk about how if we lose medicine, then what? Because in the white man's world, everything you did was paid for. You had to pay for services, and in the Indian world, at least in our community, the medicine people treated you and took care of you for nothing. It was a gift that they shared among their own people."

As a young child, Sickey felt the urgency of the elders' warnings—a pressure that never relented. "They knew that one day assimilation would pose a threat to their way of life . . . So, I could feel the pressure even as a child," he explained. The same insights created the framework for the Coushatta teachings that shaped generations of children born at the Bayou Blue settlement who were taught to emulate the resilience of their ancestors and navigate through different environments to secure their continuation as a tribal people. Sickey heard this message from his elders, including his father, and he also heard it from Solomon Battise, the Indian preacher.[93]

Ischobak Imittanahhilkoto
The Church Was the Center of the Community

It was a historic moment when Solomon Battise (b. 1911) became an ordained minister at the Indian Church, known as St. Peter's Congregational Church, located in the central part of the community. The son of Ellisor and Burissa Battise, who were among the first wave of Coushattas to be baptized in the first decade of the twentieth century, Solomon and his siblings grew up during a time when the tribe negotiated the role that the church would play in their lives.[94] A World War II veteran who had been awarded a Purple Heart, Battise quickly earned the respect of his people as both a religious and cultural leader who positioned the church as a stabilizing force within the community, one that ensured the continuation of the Koasati language.

Although Sickey was a young boy when Battise returned from the war, he recognized the role he played in helping the community cope with the challenges the elders were concerned about: "Things that I heard many years before, that we have to adapt and adopt certain ways in life . . . it was foreign to us at the time, but yet the transition was made easier because of a man like him [Solomon Battise], who was one of us, who stepped up and took the responsibility of being a representative of both the Christian world and the community." Battise was admired for his communication style and the way he served as a bridge between the tribe and public. "There was never a conflict in the traditional and the Christian world when we had people like him that was able to communicate in our own native language," Sickey said.[95] While Battise didn't serve as the tribal pastor until he returned from the war—work he continued for a half-century, until his death in 2003—he benefited from the mentorship of previous Coushatta leaders within the church who also worked alongside the founder, Rev. Paul Leeds.

Reverend Leeds arrived in southwestern Louisiana in 1893, just a few years after the Coushattas resettled around Bayou Blue, as a representative of the Congregational Home Missionary Society based in Dallas, Texas. Originally from Michigan, Leeds dreamed of beginning his ministry in Central America; however, he changed his mind after arriving for his first assignment in the piney woods of Louisiana, where he found adventure and potential.[96] He set to work preaching among the white homesteaders, first in Jennings and then in the nearby towns of Welsh and Kinder. It wasn't long before he first encountered the Coushatta settlement, at which time numbered up to three hundred people.[97]

There are a few stories that Leeds liked to tell about his first encounters with the Coushattas. In one rendition of the tale, he emphasized their shyness, saying, "They would hide behind the trees to listen to his talks." In another version he told how he first came upon two Coushattas while walking along a trail. "I was badly frightened," Leeds recalled, "for they were rough looking, they were shouting, and they were very drunk." Although it is difficult to ferret out truth from hyperbole, both versions of the story presupposed Leeds's return seven years later to begin his mission work after he was invited by some Coushattas to hold his first meeting at the schoolhouse with approximately forty to forty-five in attendance.[98] According to Leeds's records, within two months of the meeting he was approached by Paul Williams, a Coushatta homesteader and father of a growing family, who expressed the tribe's interest in building a church. Williams donated two and a half acres of his own land, and four months later a little white building was dedicated as St. Peter's Congregationalist Church of Bayou Blue.[99] The first service was held on September 29, 1901. Leeds documented the event, recording the names of the eighteen men and twelve women in attendance, among them John Abbey and Charley Sickey.[100]

Reverend Leeds preached at the Indian Church on a semi-regular basis, even opening another church on the west side of Bayou Blue called St. Luke's Congregational Church, which was active from 1913 to 1921.[101] He also made house calls to attract new members and started a summer tradition of camping in the woods with Coushatta families for ten days while he held "intensive service" and his wife, Marie, played with the children.[102] Over the course of half a century, Leeds baptized, married, and buried hundreds of Coushattas at the Bayou Blue settlement as membership in the Indian Church steadily expanded from about 60 in the mid-1920s to 167 by the early 1950s. For all of his work and dedication, Leeds received attention and praise. Popular narratives cast him as a "savior" to the Indians, while others dubbed him the "Apostle of the Piney Woods."[103] In his later years Leeds received frequent requests to address other missionaries working in tribal communities because he was hailed as a model missionary—one who "worked out forms of worship comprehensible and acceptable to the Koasati, yet he did not violate his own fundamental faith nor the doctrines of the Congregational Church."[104] In 1958 he was named "Rural Minister of the Year in Louisiana" by *Progressive Farmer Magazine* because of his influence in organizing not just the Indian churches but twenty-six other missions and churches in "the Piney Woods area."[105]

The Coushatta people didn't see the Indian Church as a replacement of their culture. Rather, it was a source of continued community cohesion and cultural endurance. The church served a prominent role in preserving the language, as sermons and parables delivered in Koasati were recorded and efforts were made to translate the Bible. It was also built largely by the Coushatta people themselves and reflected many traditional characteristics, such as its centralized location within the community and the doors that open to the south. As a result, it became an important gathering place for the tribe's decision makers or where the community convened for social and political purposes (fig. 5).[106] In enduring the hardships of their migrations over several centuries, Coushattas learned to adapt and survive, and the arrival of Reverend

Fig. 5: Coushattas gather by the Indian Church, c. 1938. Courtesy of the Coushatta Tribal Archives.

Leeds into their newly established settlement helped shape the terms by which they interacted with outsiders and fostered alliances with those who would go on to serve as friends and advocates to the tribe.

Although Leeds disapproved of Coushatta traditional dances and cultural practices, many families who became active in the church continued to celebrate the four seasons of the year, hold stomp dances, and play stickball. Until World War II these activities occurred in secret locations away from the church so as to not come under the reverend's scrutiny. As a child in the 1930s, Edna Langley attended these dances. "We were not permitted to ask questions," she related, "[because] these dances were held at night in secret, way out in the swamps, in order to hide from the preacher."[107] Over time many of the traditions went dormant. Curtis Sylestine discussed the missionary perspective, stating: "They saw our dances and ceremonies as a form of heathen worship and told us that we would have to stop . . . What they did not understand was that our music was very important to us, and that among other things it was a way of worship, just as King David wrote in the Psalms that we should all 'Make a joyful noise unto the Lord.'" Although it seemed "the traditions had been lost for good," Sylestine continued, "overnight it just seemed to happen that our traditions re-emerged full blown . . . the church people told us not to practice our traditions, so we pushed them underground all these years, but they never really went away."[108]

As Leeds began working with Coushatta translators and interpreters to further his work within the community, the church offered a new arena for tribal leadership to emerge.[109] By 1906 Mark Robinson, Boyd Williams, and Alex Johnpierre became deacons. Robinson, a mere twenty-three years old when he first took on a leadership role, served the church for twenty-seven years—first as a deacon and then as the first licensed Coushatta preacher. Leeds called him "a mighty influence" among his people given the significant role he played in helping to establish the community.[110] His sisters, Sissy (whose homestead was placed into federal trust), Lucy, Susie, and Ency (a traditional healer), also held prominent roles in the church administration as officers and deaconesses. Running the Indian Church was a shared responsibility taken on by the broader community. In fact, according to Leeds's records, between 1906 and 1956 nearly seventy Coushatta men and women held positions within the church or Sunday school—as officers or trustees (see appendix). Members of the community also took care of the church and prepared it for services, such as Houston Williams, who was the church sexton throughout the 1940s and 1950s and faithfully prepared it for services every Sunday.[111]

As the years progressed, Leeds found his attention divided among several churches, so he only preached at the Indian Church once or twice a month in the years before his death in 1958. This provided the tribe an opportunity to handle every aspect of church affairs, and Solomon Battise, along with Kent Sylestine, Douglas John, and others, gave sermons in Koasati.[112] And like Robinson before him, Battise accompanied Leeds on home visits, later sharing these fond memories with his grandson while "rocking on the porch." Jonathan Cernek was a teenager when his grandfather died but remembered the many stories of his adventures as a young man taking all-day expeditions with Leeds to visit Coushatta homes and preach.[113]

Every Sunday Coushattas would travel from different areas of the settlement to meet, listen to the bilingual sermons, and socialize. Bertney Langley remembered how he spent his youthful Sundays: "We would all pack lunches. We'd walk to church, because church [was] all day. We'd have services in the mornings. Then we would break for lunch. Everybody would go have a picnic. I remember playing with the other boys in the woods, running, climbing trees . . . Come back again in the afternoon, and have another service. People would just pack up and walk back home."[114] Eventually, a ball field was developed on the west side of the church, where people would congregate and play. The church also factored prominently in Ernest Sickey's childhood, for his grandfather Charley Sickey became a church trustee, song leader, and musical director in the 1940s, after returning from Texas. Ernest's father, Davis, also was a trustee, and his mother, Daisy, dreamed of the day that her son would follow in the footsteps of Solomon Battise by standing behind the pulpit and leading the tribe as a pastor. Like his predecessors, Battise positioned the Indian Church as a force within the community, using his oratory skills to unite people and to carefully craft the Coushattas' image to outsiders. "I looked up to him," Sickey shared, "because he spoke well. He represented the community well."[115]

The Indian Church helped the tribe remain cohesive through the generations as it anchored them in their new home. Although historian Bobby H. Johnson argued that the tribe's culture "suffered" at the hands of the church, he neglected to consider the strategic role the Coushatta people themselves saw for the church in their lives.[116] They survived, despite difficult odds, because they curated their environment to be a safe space that would fit their specific needs.[117] And they did this on their own terms. From relocating and acquiring homesteads to transforming a church into a vehicle to maintain community cohesion and language preservation, the Coushattas exhibited an incredible strength of will, one that carried them through each era brimming with fresh challenges.

2 Refusing to Be Overlooked

*Tribal Leadership and the Introduction
of Federal Indian Services, 1913–1951*

We need better schools, better medical care, and the younger
generation are badly in need of land for homes . . . We were born
and raised here, have our own little school, church, and cemetery,
and wish to remain here but times are so hard and jobs are so
scarce that we can hardly live.

—Jeff Abbey and Kinney Williams to John Collier, July 23, 1938

On September 2, 1919, Chief Jackson Langley and Vice Chief Alfred
John made the seventy-mile journey from the Bayou Blue community
north to Alexandria to meet with Robert C. Culpepper, a lawyer and
former Louisiana state senator, who held office from 1908 to 1912.[1] Over
three decades had passed since the Coushattas had settled into their new
home, and conditions were tough as the tribe faced severe poverty and
few prospects for relief. As a result, with the unexpected exception of
Sissy Robinson Alabama's homestead, which was held in federal trust,
Coushatta landowners, including Langley and John, struggled to retain
their land in the face of mounting property taxes and fraudulent attempts
by outsiders to acquire Indian-held lands. News that other tribes were
faring better by receiving federal appropriations and protected trust
lands in the early twentieth century reached southwestern Louisiana,
inciting hope and launching the Coushattas into action.

When he met with Culpepper, Chief Langley was no stranger to the American legal system. In 1911, just after becoming chief, he and a companion—appearing in documents as either "Sallie Celestine" or "Battice Celistine"—were struck by a freight train while walking in Kinder. According to one account, the woman was killed instantly, while "Langley was not seriously injured." Following the incident, Langley filed a lawsuit against the New Orleans, Texas and Mexico Railroad Company. He lost the case, but his action demonstrated his willingness to engage the courts, something he did with an equal fierceness on behalf of his people.[2] In fact, the Alexandria trip was the last straw in a long line of frustrated efforts to bring the tribe assistance from the federal government.

Upon arriving at Culpepper's office, Langley and John issued a joint statement declaring that the "tribe is desirious [sic] of being allotted a reservation or government land as other tribes have done."[3] Culpepper sent the statement to the commissioner of Indian Affairs, who promptly redirected it to the desk of James B. Aswell, a member of the U.S. House of Representatives and also Louisiana superintendent of education. The Office of Indian Affairs (OIA) was unwilling to consider the claims of the Coushattas, and Aswell was instructed to discourage them from continuing to agitate for their cause. The Department of the Interior was already overwhelmed by claimants and wanted to keep the Coushattas at bay until a proper review could determine whether they had a legitimate case.[4] Although it was a discouraging time, the tribe's work was not without purpose as multiple Coushattas joined the advocacy efforts over the first decades of the new century.

Ihoochakittap Aati Imintohnoọ

Advocating for a Better Quality of Life in the Early Twentieth Century

The Coushattas' decision to seek legal assistance was several years in the making.[5] They had observed the efforts of other tribes in the region that, like them, avoided removal in the 1830s, which left them without a tribal land base and erased nearly all interaction with the federal government. Before the turn of the century, a few tribes, such as the Eastern Band of Cherokees in North Carolina and the Seminoles of Florida, began rebuilding relationships with the federal government and securing reservation lands. By 1910 an investigation was launched to look into the conditions of the Alabamas and Coushattas who remained in Polk County, Texas. It wasn't long before this news reached the Louisiana Coushattas, prompting Paul Williams to ask Reverend Leeds for help in making sure they weren't overlooked. Having previously given some of his land to establish the Indian Church, Williams played an important role in securing the Coushattas' stability in the region. Leeds first wrote to Lake Charles attorney J. A. Williams, who sent a letter to the commissioner of Indian Affairs.[6] The reverend then enlisted the help of Arsène Pujo, a member of the Louisiana House of Representatives (in office from 1903 to 1913) and longtime resident of Lake Charles, to request clarification from the OIA on what could be done for the Indians residing within his district.[7] In less than a month Pujo received a thorough response from Commissioner Robert G. Valentine, who had conducted his own research on the Coushattas, looking through tax records and ethnographic studies. Valentine concluded that it would be a "reasonable inference" that they were descendants of those who were once part of the Creek Confederacy and then migrated westward, settling along the Red River in Louisiana before migrating farther into Texas. The problem, he wrote, was that "they have been less commented upon in recent years" because they failed to utilize benefits entitled to them through treaties and laws when they separated from "the main body of the tribe." A few months later, following a transition in leadership at the OIA, Acting Commissioner C. F. Hauke added to the claim, stating that as recipients of homesteads, the Coushattas had already received benefits from the government and had been absorbed into mainstream America. Both commissioners emphasized that the Coushattas had missed the opportunity to change their situation, stating that it was too late to be included among the Alabamas and Coushattas of Texas or to be added to the rolls of the Oklahoma Creeks, which had closed in 1907.[8] While the OIA rejected the request to extend federal Indian services to the Louisiana Coushattas, the Chitimachas of Charenton, located about one hundred miles to the southeast along Bayou Teche, received a drastically different outcome in 1916, when it was determined that they were eligible for federal Indian services, making them the only federally recognized tribe in the state. Unlike the Coushattas, the Chitimachas still occupied their traditional lands and for decades had disputed land claims that had considerably reduced their once vast holdings. Upon recognition, their remaining land was put into trust and made a reservation.[9]

The Coushattas were not deterred by the response they received. In fact, they approached their advocacy efforts with even more vigor. Yet it wasn't the Chitimachas' situation that energized them. The two groups saw little, if any, of each other.[10] Instead, the Coushattas were inspired by the Mississippi Choctaws' battle for services and land. As the first of the large southern tribes to sign a removal treaty, the Choctaws had compelled government agents to make concessions and address the deep divisions within the Choctaw Nation over ceding lands in the Lower Mississippi Valley and relocating to Indian Territory. As a result, in the 1830 Treaty of Dancing Rabbit Creek the federal government made a commitment that Choctaws who wished to remain in Mississippi could apply for land allotments and become citizens of the state while still retaining the privileges of a Choctaw citizen.[11] The local Indian agent failed to follow through, however, and denied land patents to several thousand Choctaws who turned up to register.[12] This betrayal prompted massive political agitation in the first decade of the twentieth century.

Like the Coushattas, the Mississippi Choctaws maintained a collective identity bound by a shared history, culture, and language. It was through this distinctiveness, and within a highly racialized context, that they were able to communicate their needs and leverage political alliances that helped them enforce treaty rights and secure resources.[13] This didn't happen overnight, however, and several approaches, including forming lobbying groups, were made to determine the best course. In the end, thousands of Choctaw claimants from all over the country emerged, looking to benefit from what they hoped would be a windfall of federal aid. The situation also attracted investment companies, attorneys, and crooks looking to cash in.[14]

In 1913 one such opportunist targeted the Coushattas. He arrived at the Bayou Blue community wanting to discuss the money they could receive if they claimed the right to Choctaw Nation citizenship.[15] Attorney Alexander P. Powell spent months traveling through the southern states, spinning tales about his own identity, sometimes proclaiming to be Choctaw and at other times falsely representing himself as a congressman from Oklahoma. He was scouting out "Choctaw" clients to pay him a fee and 30 percent of the proceeds if his firm won their case. While Powell had no difficulty finding willing claimants, he was particularly enthusiastic about the prospect the Coushattas afforded him, given their clearly identifiable Indian identity. He promised they could receive "monies from the federal government to the extent of over $4,000 per head."[16] Powell also tried to shape public opinion of the tribe, telling one reporter that "Coushattas are in reality Choctaws" and pointing out similarities in surnames of families of both groups.[17] Although his efforts may have been misguided and his motivations suspect, he wasn't altogether wrong about a connection between certain Coushatta and Choctaw families. Intermarriage had taken place between the groups over the years, particularly as Choctaws increasingly moved into Louisiana, which resulted in some Coushattas also speaking the Choctaw language.

In spite of his best efforts, the Coushatta people did not allow Powell to represent them. Instead, they pursued their own interests. That year Mark Robinson, the deacon for the Indian Church, wrote to the OIA looking to reignite the conversation about the tribe's plight, once again emphasizing how they were rapidly losing their private landholdings and hoped to receive protected federal trust land. Robinson received the same response as others had in previous attempts, that the Coushattas "have no claim against the Government for any reservation provided for them, and no appropriations have been made by Congress for their benefit."[18] Undeterred, Chief Jackson Langley assisted in continuing to pressure the OIA, and in 1916, the same year that the Chitimachas' reservation was created, he confronted Commissioner Cato Sells, following up with a series of letters to ensure that federal agents understood that the Coushattas didn't intend to give up.[19] This was a critical time. Because of what was transpiring in Mississippi, along with an increasing knowledge of the progress toward receiving aid among the Alabamas and Coushattas in Texas, the Louisiana Coushattas were inspired to continue their own aggressive lobbying efforts.[20]

Between 1913 and 1917, while World War I raged, the Mississippi Choctaws were in the throes of their own fierce battle. They rallied to be officially recognized as Choctaw, with their own tribal rolls separate from the Oklahoma Choctaws yet remaining treaty partners. They also demanded Mississippi trust lands, farming equipment, household items, and per capita payments.[21] Their efforts culminated in two hearings in the Mississippi towns of Philadelphia and Union in 1917, which were publicized in local newspapers to generate a large Choctaw attendance.[22] When a railroad strike prevented the congressional committee from reaching the Philadelphia courthouse, where approximately three hundred Choctaws had assembled for the meeting, the committee later met with Mississippi legislators who supported the Choctaw case at the second location in Union.[23]

Historian Clara Sue Kidwell declared that 1918 was a "momentous" year for the Mississippi Choctaws. Persistence paid off, and they gained the recognition they sought, along with some appropriations, land, and the establishment of an Indian agency housed in Philadelphia, Mississippi, which was staffed by a special agent, a farmer, and a field matron.[24] By the time the news reached the Coushattas, however, it was too late for them to send representatives to Mississippi to ensure that their concerns were also heard. "Why was I not notified of this meeting at Union, Miss. last March so that I might have been there to represent my people?" Chief Langley wrote to Louisiana representative Ladislas Lazaro, the predecessor of Representative Pujo. It appeared that the Coushattas' appeals weren't taken seriously enough for an invitation to the congressional hearings, and Langley entreated Lazaro to advocate for the tribe, an approach that the Choctaws had successfully employed in Mississippi.[25] The disappointment of missing a critical meeting emboldened Langley to stress the urgency of the Coushattas' situation, and he relayed how "quite a number of the older ones have died from shear [sic] want and attention."[26] Circumstances worsened as the Coushattas continued to be overlooked, a point that became increasingly frustrating when, in the same year, Congress made the first of several appropriations for the

Fig. 6: Jackson Langley, c. 1940. Courtesy of the Coushatta Tribal Archives.

approximately two hundred Alabamas and Coushattas living in Texas, giving them better access to education, health services, and dental care. No such benefits went to the Louisiana Coushattas. In fact, circumstances became even grimmer later in 1918 when Allen Parish was hit by a storm, which destroyed homes and left many destitute.[27] Also that year, an influenza epidemic infected communities throughout the region and shut down many Louisiana schools, businesses, and churches.[28] Worse still, tuberculosis swept through the area, killing nearly twenty Coushattas at Bayou Blue alone by 1920.[29]

Although relief didn't arrive during his time as chief, Jackson Langley's campaign to pressure the OIA not only contributed to and encouraged the efforts of other Coushattas working toward the same ends, but it shifted the trajectory of Coushatta leadership and survival strategies from focusing on more localized efforts to engaging officials within different levels of government. This was a remarkable feat. For Langley, who had been born in 1870, the census data reveals that he didn't learn to speak English or become literate until sometime between 1910 and 1920 (fig. 6). He lived to be seventy-seven years old, and details about him appear in five census reports throughout his life.[30] Known for his astute communication skills, he was a gifted storyteller and worked with anthropologists and linguists to record the Koasati language and traditional narratives.[31] His grandson Bertney Langley particularly appreciated the time he spent in preserving their rabbit tales and marveled at his grandfather's ability to "translate back and forth": "That would be hard. Even today, when I try to do some of his stories . . . It takes a little practice."[32] Jackson Langley's efforts still serve as a point of pride among his many descendants. Robin Langley recounted the role that her great-grandfather played in the survival of the Bayou Blue community: "He knew that we needed help [and] he took that initiative. He took his abilities, and he used them to his . . . advantage. Now we're [still] here."[33]

While Jackson Langley used his political visibility as chief to work for the betterment of the tribe, Mark Robinson ran a parallel campaign, drawing upon his respectable position as a leader in the Indian Church to generate a receptive audience of potential allies. The two men collaborated in their efforts, each reinforcing the message of the other as they sought the same types of resources for the Coushattas that they observed other tribes receiving.[34] By 1930 Robinson was named the tribe's chief spokesman as well as the head of one of the twenty-nine families represented at the Bayou Blue settlement when he, along with Reverend Leeds and sawmill owner Richard E. Powell, testified at a congressional hearing in Texas hoping to gain federal appropriations and land for the tribe.[35] Unfortunately, their expectations went unmet, and while no progress was made, in the years following World War I, the Coushattas' rising voice joined a chorus of others across the nation who contributed to what historian Francis Paul Prucha called "an atmosphere of tension" around an Indian bureau that had become "a bureaucracy of great size and complexity," which hampered its ability to effectively serve Indian people.[36] Reform at the OIA seemed imminent, and the Coushattas remained poised to seize opportunities that changes might bring.

Tatka Mikkok Akohchokchanaakato
Federal Resistance to Aiding the Coushattas

While the Coushattas were still many years away from receiving federal Indian services, their efforts to draw attention to their cause succeeded in getting the tribe on the schedules of federal officials looking to tour Louisiana Indian communities and document their observations.[37] In 1920 the special supervisor for the Department of the Interior, Frank E. Brandon, issued a report on the Coushattas, validating what Langley and others had claimed. Brandon wrote: "They live in poor framed houses made of scrap lumber from abandoned houses and such pieces of lumber as they can secure at the saw mills . . . They are very poor and are gradually decreasing in numbers . . . They are very much in need of medical advice and treatment."[38] Three subsequent reports written in the 1930s—by Nash (1931), Ryan (1934), and Reeves (1937)—added further details to the Coushattas' living conditions while also grappling with the question of whether the federal government had any responsibility to provide assistance, each issuing inconsistent suggestions on the matter.

The matter of health was particularly concerning. Nash reported that a local doctor saw Coushattas but that he charged $1.50 per appointment and $5.00 for a house call.[39] Indian doctors, such as Ency Abbey Abbott and Arzelie Roy Langley, regularly treated the ailing with great success, but many severe health problems remained.[40] Records from Reverend Leeds reveal that dozens of Coushatta people through the 1950s died not only from tuberculosis but from other illnesses like pneumonia, whooping cough, and dysentery.[41] Health records from the Alabama-Coushatta Reservation in Texas in 1928 offer additional insight into health conditions of the Coushattas at Bayou Blue, given the history and relationship between the two communities. Dr. Anderson of the Texas State Health Department examined eighty-eight Alabama and Coushatta adults, fifty-seven schoolchildren, and thirty-four preschool children. He found that "approximately 95 per cent of those examined had very bad teeth and gums, which may account for the many heart conditions discovered ... and the numerous complaints of rheumatism and kidney trouble." The report also revealed a high rate of infant mortality and cases of malaria.[42]

Although early government reports acknowledged the Louisiana Coushattas as a group of Indians in need of assistance, the OIA continued to find reasons not to extend services. Prominent among them was the claim that the Coushattas' history lacked the clarity of other tribes. In particular, their previous connection to the Creek Confederacy had been obscured over time, causing some government agents to claim that the Coushattas were not among those tribes that previously negotiated treaties with the U.S. government.[43] And those who acknowledged an earlier relationship with the federal government often claimed the Coushattas had forfeited their ability to receive services by hiding out while others received appropriations and federal trust land. Timing did not work in the tribe's favor. Throughout the 1930s the OIA staff were overwhelmed by Indian claimants, particularly from the Southeast and Northeast, and assessed all incoming claims with a healthy dose of suspicion. The commissioner was particularly critical of groups that, he argued, "have made their social and economic adjustments as human beings and as citizens not under the guardianship of the United States." Ever looming was the concern over the strain new groups could place on the OIA's budget that would "either jeopardize the work with those

Indians already under Federal guardianship or arouse hopes with newly-made guardians that could not be met."[44]

While the Coushatta people's history may have been shrouded in uncertainty, their racial identity was discussed in terms of "purity." Subscribing to the rule of hypo-descent, also known as the "one-drop rule," local white residents believed that any African or African American ancestry would automatically classify a person as black. Coushattas were both ascribed and self-identified as "full-blood" Indians, a racial composition that, in their particular location, admitted them into white schools and assured government officials that they had successfully assimilated into the local social environment without disrupting the racial caste system—thus not threatening white supremacy. A lack of racial clarity, on the other hand, placed other tribes in vulnerable positions. The Chitimachas, for example, were juxtaposed with the Coushattas in the 1920 Brandon report, which claimed that suspicions about the Chitimachas' racial origins had led St. Mary Parish to refuse them admission into white schools.[45]

The belief that Coushattas already had achieved all of the benefits of state citizenship also caused government officials to question the necessity of extending federal services to them. Coushattas held title to land, paid taxes, and were astute at navigating the local social and economic terrain. "I see no cause to disturb present conditions," Brandon wrote.[46] With assimilationist-based uplift perspectives shaping federal responses to requests for services, it was no surprise that Chief Langley was told the Coushattas "should take pride in making their own way, just like other people do, without calling upon the Federal Government for financial assistance."[47] Indian agents claimed the Coushattas had achieved economic independence—or, at the very least, they were no less disadvantaged as surrounding non-Indians. Nash wrote:

> The Coushattas in Louisiana are English-speaking Indians, recognized as full-fledged citizens, tax payers whose children are freely admitted to the public schools with white children. They have received no aid from either the state or Federal government. Without special consideration they maintain their economic independence. The day the rest

of the Indians in the United States attain the position already won by these Louisiana Coushattas, the Indian problem is solved. A pathetic problem of rural poverty remains, but it is something distinct from the Indian problem . . . these Indians are desperately poor, and dire poverty is pitiable. They are no poorer than thousands of their white and colored neighbors.[48]

The notion that Indians "should stand on [their] own feet" was a popular position, one echoed by Secretary of the Interior Ray Lyman Wilbur. In a 1932 letter to T. H. Harris, Louisiana superintendent of education, Wilbur argued against providing Louisiana tribes with federal aid, stating it would be best that they "exist free of the handicaps of wardship; to impose wardship upon them would be to turn the clock backward."[49] Against the backdrop of a national economic depression and with assimilation as the primary goal, federal officials argued that assisting the Coushattas would only thwart their ability to fully embrace their position as citizens. In spite of living in one of the most debt-ridden, impoverished states in the nation, the outspoken populist Governor Huey Long—who led the state from 1928 to 1932, then became a U.S. senator until his death in 1935—provided federal officials additional justification in letting the state address the Coushattas' needs through his boasting of efforts to assist the state's poor, which later culminated in his "Share Our Wealth" plan in 1934.[50] The case was particularly strong given that the state had already been funding Coushatta education.

Naathiihilka Inchaaka Hahpa Komachihbaachito
A New Deal and New Challenges

Despite having had a small schoolhouse constructed near Coushatta homesteads in the late nineteenth century, the first well-documented attempt to provide schooling for the tribe's children was in 1913, with instruction provided by Mr. and Mrs. H. O. Ensign. A short-lived effort, the Ensigns were succeeded in 1915 by L. L. Simmons, who taught there for over twenty years. He learned to speak Koasati and was the first teacher to hold class in a small one-room schoolhouse set back from the Indian Church (fig. 7).[51] One tribal member remembered what school

Fig. 7: Coushatta children with teacher, Mr. L. L. Simmons, in front of school, 1930s. Courtesy of the State Library of Louisiana Historic Photograph Collection.

was like during that time: "We didn't have any shoes, so even when it was cold and the ground was frozen we had to walk to school. Boy did our feet curl up! . . . We kids knew not to complain, so no matter how cold we were we just sat there . . . Mr. L. L. Simmons was our teacher, and if you didn't behave he would pinch you hard under your arm and bring you to stand by the window. He was really tall, so when he pinched you like that, you had to walk on your toes to get where you were going or it would really hurt!"[52]

Since the bayou divided the Coushatta settlement and often flooded during the rainy season, making it impossible to cross, the Allen Parish School Board funded two Indian schools by 1920. The first was in the western community, called the Lester Williams School, and remained in operation for only a few years. The second school, simply called the Coushatta School, was located near the St. Peter's Indian Church and was built on two acres donated by the J. A. Bel Estate.[53] Each school operated on a five- to six-month rotating basis so that Simmons could serve both with the limited parish funds. The schools went up to the fourth grade and offered English instruction in an attempt to prepare Coushatta children for transition into the public schools in Elton.[54] The modest funding that the Allen Parish School Board provided was one of several reasons that Coushattas were denied resources by federal officials, who argued that the tribe was already adequately being served.

By the 1930s attitudes toward Indian affairs began to shift. President Franklin D. Roosevelt launched the New Deal programs to bring economic relief to struggling American families, an approach that echoed the efforts already being employed in Louisiana by Governor Long, who criticized Roosevelt for not going far enough to alleviate poverty on a national scale. In 1933 John Collier was appointed head of the OIA, and as was hoped, he set out to reform it by reassessing past policies.[55] Under his leadership approaches and perspectives quickly changed, and soon new legislation encouraged many tribes across the country to reorganize their governments under prescribed constitutions and rules of membership and apply for federal economic development loans. The Alabamas and Coushattas of Texas followed suit when they incorporated under the Indian Reorganization Act (IRA), also known as the Wheeler-Howard Act, in 1938.[56] The Coushattas of Louisiana, on the other hand, were suspicious of a federally imposed tribal government and rejected it outright. One elder later recalled that an OIA agent had approached the community about adopting an IRA constitution, and the people had responded: "We don't want a constitution. We don't want anything on paper. Just work with us the way we are."[57] The tribe wished to maintain its existing political structure while simultaneously lobbying for federal Indian services. Access to services seemed out of their reach, however, following the Nash report's (1931) assessment, which argued that Indian groups, such as the Louisiana Coushattas, who appear "adjusted" within their present locales should not waste federal services. This wasn't an attitude shared by everyone, however, and this perspective was challenged a few years later by the director of Indian education, Dr. W. Carson Ryan Jr., who reviewed the status of southern tribes and concluded that "the Federal Government has an obligation to all people of at least one-fourth Indian blood . . . We sometimes refer to Indians as adequately 'adjusted' when what we really mean is that they are resigned to a discrimination that is neither fair nor socially desirable."[58] This renewed assessment was followed by Ryan's three-point program, which, among other suggestions, included developing federally funded schools within tribal communities—a prospect deemed more desirable than the increasingly scrutinized Indian boarding schools during this period.[59] For Louisiana Indians this shifting attitude signaled a new direction in their educational trajectory, evidenced by the moving of a single-room schoolhouse directly onto the Chitimacha reservation to offer instruction from first to eighth grade.[60]

For the Coushattas the first evidence of this transition came in 1935, when the Allen Parish School Board learned that the administration of the Indian school was to be assumed by the OIA's regional office, the Choctaw Agency in Mississippi, but the day-to-day operations still fell to the parish under government contract. The Indian school continued as before, running through the fourth grade, and Simmons was allowed to remain in his post as teacher. However, additional funding was provided to add a kitchen, providing a job for a Coushatta woman at forty cents a day, to prepare meals. Although the kitchen enhanced the school, it wasn't enough. At the tribe's urging, Simmons wrote to the Choctaw Agency, complaining: "I have been hoping the government may further aid these poor people. Especially I would like for them to have medical aid and the younger married men and women to have homes."[61]

In May 1937 the superintendent of the Choctaw Agency, A. C. Hector, traveled to Allen Parish to visit the Coushatta school, where he was met by Kinney Williams and several other Coushattas representing different families. They shared with Hector that the meager OIA educational funding provided to the Allen Parish School Board was scarcely enough to address their needs, and they requested additional land and farming equipment. It was clear that the tribe's vision of their needs encompassed a broader scope than what the OIA was equipped to address, as evidenced by Hector's follow-up report, in which he sidestepped the tribe's economic concerns and narrowly focused on their educational needs. He was particularly preoccupied with the transition of Coushatta children from the Indian school to the public school in Elton at fifth grade, reporting that they "usually fail," most commonly because of language barriers. This was a problem, Hector surmised, that could be addressed by expanding the Indian school to serve more grades, eliminating the need for students to transfer to the public parish school altogether. Hector's suggestion was met with resistance, however, by the principal of Elton's elementary school, who argued that it was the Indian school that should be closed instead so that Coushatta children could start in the white public school earlier. This was a curious proposition considering the school board's staunch position on maintaining segregated black schools in the district. When given an opportunity to draw bolder lines between white and nonwhite students, Elton school administrators protested the withdrawal of Coushatta children from their white schools. Perhaps they felt a vested interest in the tribe or, more pragmatically, an unwillingness to part with funding they received from the enrollment of Indian students. Regardless of the reasoning, Hector pushed back, writing, "The Government Day School helps to meet many social and economic needs of the Indians which would not be taken care of by sending all of these 50 or more children into the city schools." Instead, he recommended the OIA fully take over the operations of the Indian school and expand its instruction. The timing was fortuitous and the idea ambitious. Simmons had just retired after the 1937 school year, so a new teacher needed to be hired. Also, the U.S. Department of Education sought to improve the quality of instruction by increasing the rate of funding for Coushatta children from twenty-five cents to forty cents a day per pupil to secure a "more competent teacher" at a higher salary.[62]

In spite of the promise that the Coushatta school was on course for expansion, two months passed following Hector's visit without another word from the OIA. Anxious for news, Kinney Williams sent a letter asking for a progress update. "If you will not be able to do anything through the Indian Bureau," he wrote to Hector, "let us know so we will have to make other arrangements for next year."[63] If the Coushattas' educational situation was all the OIA was willing to address, the tribe intended to keep the federal agency accountable. It wasn't until later that year that Hector returned, accompanied by Edna Groves (superintendent of Indian education), and began to set plans in motion not just to take over the existing school but to acquire a tract of land that could be placed into federal trust and serve as the site of a new Coushatta Day School. It seemed the earlier assessments of the Coushatta people as already being served by the state no longer influenced the argument of whether they qualified for federal services. Within a decade the conversation had shifted significantly toward the notion that "these Indians are permanent and some effort should be made to help them."[64] Again, the assumed racial purity of the Coushattas played a large role in advancing this initiative because, as Klopotek argues, federal officials "were more willing to provide funds for groups that had not mixed much with other races."[65] Hector and Groves put forth recommendations, and the Coushattas were ready for the transition, but the months continued to pass without any further action on the new school project.

The tribe posed unique challenges to Allen Parish. The passing of new federal Indian legislation in the 1930s, coupled with the Coushattas' increased engagement with the OIA, created confusion on where funding and responsibility derived for local Indian education. With a new federal Indian school proposal seemingly in the works, the Allen Parish School Board was unclear on its continued role in the education of tribal children. The 1937–38 school year began without a transition plan, leaving school district administrators scrambling to get a new school year under way and Coushatta children to suffer the consequences of poor planning. With a promise that federal Indian funding was on its way, the Allen Parish School Board deferred the $950 revenue stream it would have received from the state for the Indian students. By the end of October, however, it became clear to Superintendent Thos J. Griffin that this had been a mistake, for no federal funds had been released, and the school started the year with a deficit.[66] In addition, without the new expanded Indian school in place yet, it was unclear how the continued education of Coushattas transferring to schools in Elton was to be funded. In the end the Allen Parish School Board covered the expenses for the tuition as well as the transportation of Coushatta children, despite Elton's location in the neighboring Jefferson Davis Parish.[67] It took until February 1938 before the OIA had finally reimbursed the Allen Parish School Board. However, a long-term, sustainable plan had yet to be developed moving forward.[68] Plus, Coushattas continued to be left out of a conversation that directly impacted the education of their children. While the rhetoric surrounding the Indian Reorganization Act claimed to involve Indians more in matters affecting them, there is no evidence that the Coushattas knew about the financial difficulties of funding their education.

In 1938 Jeff Abbey was elected chief of the Coushattas, and he soon joined the efforts of previous leaders in agitating for answers and change among federal officials. With no action on the new school, a frustrated Abbey, along with Kinney Williams who was then identified as his vice chief, sent yet another letter to Hector and then to Commissioner John Collier himself. Abbey stated, "We have heard that the government has aided other tribes of Indians in various states but so far we have not been given any help except a school kitchen." Abbey was confounded by the minimal efforts put forth at that point, particularly given the Coushattas' vast needs.[69] Increasing his aggravation further, Collier didn't respond directly. Instead, Paul L. Fickinger, the state associate director of education, wrote Abbey a noncommittal promise that "we have been thinking along these lines and will give your request further consideration."[70]

The primary delay with the proposed OIA Indian school was over the location. The plan required several acres that would be eligible to place into trust in order to function as a federal Indian school. Eager to accelerate the process, Abbey generously offered to donate three acres of his own land, a gesture that was particularly significant given that Coushatta landholdings were rapidly diminishing—dropping from over 4,000 acres within the first decade of the twentieth century to 1,050 by 1920.[71] By the 1930s landholdings had fallen by an additional 115 to 266 acres.[72] A 1941 assessment of Coushatta property by the Farm Security Administration showed that holdings had fallen even further, bottoming out at approximately 700 acres.[73] Several reasons contributed to this decrease in acreage. The land was rich in timber, and it was not uncommon for logging companies to pay Indian landowners for the timber, which left the land cutover and severely devalued. Some companies didn't stop there, however, and instead co-opted the land entirely. In one such case a Coushatta landowner told a government official that "[one family] used to have 160 acres as homestead, but one time one fellow came over here and [bought] the timber and he took it away. He took all the timber and the land."[74] J. Phillips, a neighbor to the Coushattas, explained that many Indian homesteaders were defrauded because they didn't read or speak English well. In a letter to the OIA, Phillips recounted how several Coushattas "were induced to believe that they were only selling a few of the best trees [on their land], when instead they signed deeds for all of their lands and timber."[75] Exacerbating the situation further, Ernest Sickey explained that many Coushatta homesteaders couldn't keep up with the taxes on their land, which led them to sell a portion of their acreage to companies such as the J. A. Bel Estate, which then paid the back taxes and secured title to the land.[76] The Bel Estate had acquired segments of Coushatta homesteads as early as 1909, inciting resentment toward the Bel family, whose landholdings increasingly engulfed the community.[77]

While Chief Abbey's offer to donate his own property for the new school demonstrated his dedication to advancing opportunities for his people, there were two major challenges with his proposition. Like many other Coushatta homesteaders, Abbey had previously issued mineral leases to Louisiana companies looking to drill for gas or oil on his property. These leases came with cash payments for the use of the land without actually giving up the land itself, which provided many Coushattas a viable opportunity to keep their property.[78] Although the terms of Abbey's leases are unclear, one can infer the details by looking at other tribal landowners who entered into similar agreements. For example, the seven leases that Ency Robinson Abbey Abbott had between 1924 and 1938 included contingency payments determined by drilling results as well as free gas use for her stoves and lights.[79] After oil was first discovered in 1901 in a rice field in Evangeline Parish, then gradually throughout the state, the petroleum industry played a pivotal role in shaping the area's economic landscape. By 1926 the state had more than thirty oil fields, and the yearly production of oil had surpassed 23 million barrels, with gas production of more than 150 billion cubic feet.[80] Louisiana's oil boom was akin to the gold rush in the West in that it lured hundreds of prospectors—from independent wildcatters to businessmen running both small and large companies—looking to strike it rich. The emerging Gulf Coast oil industry, with its sprawling petrochemical facilities in places such as Lake Charles or smaller operations in oil fields throughout the countryside, provided jobs for Coushattas and other locals. It also shifted residential patterns around Bayou Blue, in which landholdings gradually moved from families and into the impersonal coffers of companies such as the J. A. Bel Estate, which remained in the timber industry but also began drilling for oil and gas in Allen Parish by 1939.[81] For drill sites the company didn't already own, it convinced private landowners, including Abbey, to sell access, creating a challenge for the OIA to locate land that was devoid of legal entanglements to place into federal trust for the purpose of building an Indian school.[82]

Another challenge of building the new school on Abbey's land was that it wasn't in a centralized location but tucked away on the far end of the eastern part of the community. Given the importance of the Coushattas' community center, the tribe hoped to situate the school in the heart of the settlement, close to the Indian Church and old school. As a result, efforts to pursue Abbey's land soon ceased, and federal officials focused on purchasing a particular centralized plot of land owned by the J. A. Bel Estate that they had identified for the school. Confident that it would work out, a request for funds was placed in the 1940 Indian Office budget while the OIA waited for Congress to authorize the construction of the new school building by the Public Works Administration.[83] Soon it became clear that these plans would also be derailed when the OIA was informed that the heirs of the Bel Estate were willing to issue the Coushattas a ninety-nine-year lease for the land but would not sell it as long as it remained profitable with oil and gas.[84] This posed a problem because without obtaining clear title, "government funds cannot be legally expended to erect buildings on land to which title does not vest in the United States."[85] Reverend Leeds, who assisted the OIA with the negotiations, found the situation deplorable, stating, "Having made large sums of money from the fine pine timber which grew on this land, secured by the Indians from the government by homestead rights, this company will now make no concessions at all for the welfare of the needy Indians, although it reputedly bought the land from them at bargain prices."[86]

Despite this challenge, Superintendent Hector remained hopeful that a solution could be found, continuing to regularly meet with Bel family heirs and carefully studying maps in an attempt to locate alternative properties to pursue.[87] However, as was frequently the case with government agencies, staff turnover further stalled the project. Hector took a different job and left the new superintendents of the Choctaw Agency, first L. W. Page and then Harvey K. Meyer, to continue advocating for the Coushatta school. Regardless of administrative changes, Leeds remained determined to see a new school erected, even offering to sell the northern acre of land where the Indian Church stood for $300 for the new development.[88] Although this land was within the preferred centralized location, Willard W. Beatty, the OIA's director of Indian education, rejected the proposal, claiming the offer posed several problems. For one, a single acre wouldn't support the vision of the projected plan, which included multiple buildings, gardens, and grazing land for livestock. He had hoped to acquire no less than twenty acres. Second, he didn't want to construct a federally funded school so close to a church because, he explained, "there appears to be a tendency a great many times for the missionary to feel called upon to interfere in the school functioning which is neither to his advantage nor to ours."[89]

The new federal Indian school was never built. Additional land could not be secured, so the existing school continued to operate as a parish school funded by the OIA for the 1939–40 school year.[90] Frustrated efforts to secure land underscored the difficulties the Coushattas faced in holding onto their own land as well as the barriers that oil leases posed. Inspired once again to take action, in 1940, former chief Jackson Langley and Reverend Leeds enlisted the assistance of a Lake Charles land title company to investigate the alleged theft of Coushatta homesteads, hoping to reclaim some of the acreage that had slipped from tribal hands.

The claim hinged on the accusation that the federal government had failed to protect Indian lands from outside interests. The investigation concluded, however, that no "restrictions had been violated."[91]

In spite of the disappointments of the 1930s, the Coushattas did benefit from some New Deal programs. For example, the Civilian Conservation Corps (CCC) made the first government-built road within the community that provided an east-west passage. Its construction broadened the possibilities for movement beyond footpaths, easing horse and wagon travel and even accommodating vehicles in later decades. The road was named CC Bel Road, after "Conservation Corps" and the Bel Lumber Company, which owned the land north of the road. It remained gravel for many years, until the parish paved it with asphalt. The road's construction project provided jobs to Coushatta men, many of whom later enlisted in the CCC, working on other regional projects.[92] "That was a good experience," one tribal member said. "That was sometimes a gateway to the military . . . From there some of them went in the army and served in World War II."[93]

Naksaamoosip Komawiichito
The Increasing Presence of Federal Indian Services in the 1940s

While Jackson Langley sought recourse for the loss of Coushatta lands, Chief Jeff Abbey and Douglas John, who served as his interpreter, traveled to Washington DC to discuss the stalled school project and the need for additional financial relief for the tribe.[94] This was the same strategy employed by the Alabamas and Coushattas of Texas as early as 1928, when they sought appropriations.[95] A decade later the Tunicas also journeyed to Washington DC from Louisiana to make their case.[96] For too long federal and local officials had discussed the "Coushattas' situation" among themselves without seeking input from tribal leadership. Like Langley, Abbey became proactive in his advocacy and met directly with Beatty, identifying the Coushatta people as "a forgotten tribe" and demanding that something be done immediately to help.[97] Five months later, when the personal meeting didn't prompt the swift action the tribe had hoped for, Chief Abbey sent an agitated letter addressing the continued neglect, a message that was then reinforced a year later by

Douglas John. The correspondence reflected the Coushattas' frustration with the lack of response to their concerns.[98] In fact, John later declared the journey, as well as a follow-up visit a few years later, as unsuccessful. "We are fighting a lost cause," he told one newspaper. While Abbey was unwilling to stop fighting for a new school, John focused on preventing the continued pattern of tribal land loss. He encouraged other Coushattas to follow Sissy Robinson Alabama's example and turn their lands over to the federal government to be put into trust as a way of protecting it. This strategy, he believed, also would enable Coushattas to obtain additional land and federal funds for farming equipment. John argued: "We need about three or four thousand more acres . . . We want and need land for better farms and pastures." Despite his efforts, however, John couldn't convince other Coushattas to embrace this strategy. The OIA's seeming inability to keep its promises didn't instill confidence in the federal government. And while John's suggestions went unheeded, he understood their position: although the tribe lacked a reservation, he said, "we are free . . . free to go and come as we please . . . we are happy here."[99]

Although hopes of a new school were derailed, plans for a "rehabilitation project" to establish an agricultural enterprise within the Coushatta community were still on track. Joe Jennings, superintendent of Indian schools for the eastern area, and A. H. McMullen, the new superintendent of the Choctaw Agency, were intent on training young Coushatta men and women to become farmers and domestics.[100] Looking to examples of Indian vocational education across the country, Jennings stressed the importance of productive labor as a central tenant of the Coushatta school. He wanted Coushattas to settle into what Indian education scholars K. Tsianina Lomawaima and Teresa L. McCarty deemed "an American 'safety zone' of obedient citizenry and innocent cultural difference."[101] To do this, Jennings attempted to transfer the energy and reform efforts from the Southwest to the Southeast by distributing copies of a 1940 issue of *Arizona Highways* to the Coushattas and other southern tribes. The issue was a glamorized portfolio of economic activities among southwestern tribes that included agriculture, mining, and tourism.[102] As part of this new "Coushatta plan," in 1942 the OIA finally took control of the Indian school from the Allen Parish School Board and co-opted the existing school building. It was to continue providing grammar school instruction, with Coushatta children transferring to Elton for the upper grades. Since there was no additional land to sufficiently develop an agricultural training program, the plan was to look to the Farm Security Administration's (FSA) "Food for Freedom" program, which provided seed, feed, fertilizer, and canning supplies to rural and impoverished Americans to promote agricultural independence on their own private land. The FSA agreed to offer this program to the Coushattas if the OIA hired a full-time teacher to run the Coushatta Day School and help tribal families apply for federal loans and build an agricultural base.[103]

As was the case in previous years, government agencies discussed the Coushattas' future without first consulting the tribe about the plan. So, in March and again in July 1942, several families met with FSA representatives to assess the benefits of the Food for Freedom program. Coushattas were suspicious and vocal about their unwillingness to comply with a program that would cause them to generate debt. In order to get them to participate, the FSA had to relent, allowing Coushattas to receive funding in the form of grants, rather than loans. Nine Coushatta families submitted applications to the program as a result of this concession.[104] Other ideas from FSA staff were rejected outright, including a plan to relocate the tribe to a rice cooperative at another location—a notion that community members instantly protested.[105] Coushattas advocated for assistance on their own terms and on their own land.

Although the Indian bureau didn't fully take over the Indian school until 1942, teacher Elizabeth W. Lansden spent four years awaiting her termination as the OIA made clear its desire to replace her with a teacher with a background in agricultural education.[106] The day had finally come, and Lansden reluctantly packed up and left the school grounds.[107] Over the few years she taught, she had built strong relationships with the children, taking particular pride in her lessons in English and the domestic sciences.[108] Now under the OIA's administration, the Coushatta Day School hired agriculture teacher Kenneth McCoy, paying him an annual salary of $1,800. He worked with the tribe in farming operations in order to link its educational program with an economic one. His wife also became the school's housekeeper and oversaw the school lunch program in an updated kitchen, equipped with new gasoline burners and pressure cookers.[109]

With a teacher change and shift in focus, the old Indian school reopened anew. Although it was not what everyone had hoped for, the occasion was commemorated. The tribe hosted a barbecue, with Chief Abbey, Jacob Robinson, and Reverend Leeds giving speeches and inviting attendees to enjoy music and recreational activities. The invitation sent to Superintendent Joe Jennings even advertised "an exhibit of canned foods and field crops from the Coushatta Indian farms in the new kitchen-dining room."[110] A more prominent federal presence within the Coushatta community appeared to promise a future with less struggle. It was a sign that the Coushattas were no longer forgotten.

Since its inception, the federally run Coushatta Day School served upward of forty-seven children.[111] With agricultural training as the focus, as with other OIA schools across the country, Coushatta children were little prepared for careers or jobs outside of manual labor. "They didn't teach us how to go anywhere beyond [our] communities," said Ernest Sickey. In fact, even though Coushattas were permitted to attend the public parish schools in Elton and Kinder, many didn't continue on. English instruction was part of the curriculum at the Indian school, but farming and manual labor took primacy. "For a lot of them," Sickey explained, "their first language was Coushatta so they really had to play catch-up." In addition to the language barrier, many students didn't receive a substantial academic foundation to help transition to public schools. "I used to hear from the old people that all they did was learn how to make a garden," Sickey recalled. "There were no textbooks . . . It was mostly about life coping skills . . . how to farm, how to raise things, how to survive off the land."[112]

A report from a 1946 site visit revealed how poorly run and neglected the school was. Although it was a federal institution, the parish school board continued providing supplies to keep it running since the funds provided by the OIA weren't enough to cover the school's basic needs. The report indicated the building was dilapidated and the classroom "has tables and chairs but needs about everything else." Inadequate funding also meant that the school had to rely on the garden maintained on grounds to provide the necessary food for student lunches. By 1949 local newspapers had predicted the closing of the school altogether.[113] Despite all the lobbying to get the school turned over to federal jurisdiction, the outcome was disappointing. This wasn't the type of educational support the Coushattas had hoped for.

The medical services the tribe first received from the OIA allocations in the mid-1940s were also inadequate. The Indian bureau contracted with Dr. Otto Freeman to serve the tribe on a part-time basis. Freeman's office was based out of Basile, a small town east of Elton, and he was a "one-stop shop," providing both medical and dental services. "I've heard horror stories," one tribal member shared. The doctor "would extract teeth with pliers" using no anesthesia. Coushattas also jokingly referred to him as "Dr. Laxative" because Freeman freely dispensed laxatives to patients for a variety of ailments.[114] A few years after first contracting with the OIA, Freeman was arrested for abusing his narcotics license by selling drugs illegally.[115] Although fined for his crime, there is no evidence his contract with the OIA was revoked.

With the minimal care they received, it was difficult for the Coushattas of Louisiana not to notice the disparity between their medical services and what the Alabamas and Coushattas living in Texas received during the same period. A 1934 report from the Alabama-Coushatta Reservation provided the details of their medical services: "The State pays a Livingston physician $75 a month for medical attention to the Indians and pays the full-time salary of a nurse, who lives at the agency in quarters in a small hospital building. This building, in addition to the nurse's quarters, has two wards, each of which could accommodate three beds, a doctor's office, a dentist's office, and an enclosed veranda waiting room."[116] Sickey said, "They had things going on for them that we didn't have." As a child, he often visited the Texas community with his father and was shocked to see the differences between what the two communities had available to them. While the state of Texas specifically earmarked funding for the Alabama-Coushatta Reservation, the state of Louisiana lumped the Coushattas in with the rest of the state's rural and impoverished populations in determining the services they provided, which meant they received little to no assistance.[117]

The Coushattas of Allen Parish didn't have their own medical facilities, and a lack of transportation to doctors' offices posed an additional barrier. Most babies were born at home, although a few families utilized state charity hospitals in Lafayette and Alexandria.[118] The Charity Hospital System, an extension of Governor Long's "Share the Wealth" programs, provided immunizations and free medical care to those who lacked access to such care. Although controversial because it increased the state's public health care expenditures, the system vastly decreased mortality rates across Louisiana.[119] The tribe didn't share in this downward trajectory, however, with mortality rates remaining high. Between 1935 and 1953 Reverend Leeds recorded the deaths of forty-nine Coushatta people, nearly a quarter of the tribal population.[120]

Kommikkok Jeff Abbey-k Matkǫhachaalitǫ
Chief Jeff Abbey Took a Stand for Us

Poor transportation posed a problem in getting adequate medical services, but it also impeded older Coushatta children's ability to transfer to school in Elton, only a few miles away. As a result, by the late 1930s many of the older children stopped attending school altogether. Some stuck it out and successfully navigated their way through the system until graduation, but with transportation still a barrier, it became progressively more cumbersome. Students had to walk miles through the woods to catch the school bus to town, even during the cold winters or in the sweltering humidity of the warmer months.[121] Their white classmates, on the other hand, didn't face such challenges since bus routes were designed to ensure pickups close to their homes. While Coushattas were permitted to attend white schools, the busing situation highlighted the discriminatory practices the tribe faced that hampered their ability to obtain equal educational opportunities.

Chief Abbey never attended school, but he wanted Coushatta youth to have the opportunity. As Sickey recalled, one day Abbey, fed up with the transportation situation, gathered all of the kids who had to walk several miles to catch the school bus and said, "We're going to demand

Fig. 8: Jeff Abbey, c. 1935. Courtesy of the Coushatta Tribal Archives.

that a bus will come to this road to pick you up." Using the negotiating skills that he was known for, Abbey soon appeared before the school board, demanding that the bus be rerouted. "He fought for Indian kids to be picked up, like any other student, on a road closer to where they can catch a ride," Sickey recounted. "Finally the school board decided that they would come and make a circuit in our community and pick us up to take us to school."[122]

Like many Louisianans, Chief Abbey's perspective on the power of the state government was heavily influenced by the messages of Huey Long and the legacy he left behind. Although historians have documented Long's abuse of power and unethical practices—in some instances even comparing him to a "South American dictator"—the fact remained that Long had led impoverished Louisianans to believe that local government was their friend, and this trust extended to local parish municipalities.[123] Abbey subscribed to Long's perspective on taxes as "part of a sacred fund that is pledged by the people for their own care and to provide for their children and the generations that are to come."[124] Coushattas, by and large, were property-owning taxpayers who, Abbey argued, deserved identical services as their white neighbors. This belief encouraged Abbey and fueled his successful confrontation with the school board, an event that left a deep impression on Sickey. Abbey led the tribe during Sickey's formative years, and he identified the negotiations over the busing situation as "my first experience in [witnessing someone from my tribe] saying that we have some rights and we can do things as Indian people. That has stuck with me all of my life. We can do things on our own, but . . . we have to take [the] initiative, and we have to be heard."[125]

From the late 1930s, when Jeff Abbey first became the traditional leader of the community, until his death in 1951, he was tireless in his advocacy, leading the Coushattas with dignity and wisdom (fig. 8). He didn't relent in representing the tribe in Washington DC or in appearing before a locally elected school board. He wanted to ensure that the Bayou Blue settlement became the Coushattas' permanent home following decades of movement and uncertainty. As the largest landowner in the tribe, Coushattas looked up to him. According to Barbara Langley, Abbey was generous, sharing his livestock and the produce he grew with everyone. "Jeff was friends [with] everybody," Langley said. She was a young girl when Abbey died but knew about him from stories: "My grandmother used to tell me that if something needed to be told in the community, people would come to Jeff Abbey. He would ride his horse and go around the community [sharing the message]."[126] When Sickey was a child, Chief Abbey frequently visited his home and spent time with his father, Davis Sickey, and others who gathered, often talking for hours. Despite the ferocity with which Abbey advocated for his people, Ernest Sickey knew him as a gentle and soft-spoken man who enjoyed sitting with the tribal children, teaching them about the early days: "He was very wise and prophetic in what he thought would be challenges and issues that [we] would move on to confront."[127] Like other elders, Abbey prepared Coushatta youth, just as his own father had guided him, for the difficulties that he could see on the horizon.

The Coushattas' ability to thrive in Allen Parish hinged upon securing alliances and support outside of the community. Jackson Langley attempted this strategy in the early twentieth century, as did others before him who forged friendships with non-Indians who assisted the tribe in establishing themselves at the Bayou Blue settlement. The practice of building networks was also part of Jeff Abbey's strategy of promoting the future welfare of his people, even in the most precarious of times. Like other parts of the country, World War II prompted demographic shifts in southwestern Louisiana, and this, along with heightened wartime anxieties, contributed to increased racial and social divisiveness between different populations. Cajuns, for example, often found themselves at odds with outsiders arriving from other states to work alongside them in the region's oil fields because, with their distinct culture and language, they didn't fit the popularized vision of white America. As a result, historian Shane K. Bernard argued, "Cajuns became targets of ridicule in their own homeland."[128] Local law enforcement also felt compelled to keep a close eye on incoming populations, taking note of their race and nation of origin, as evidenced by the Jefferson Davis Parish sheriff publicly reporting that "there are no Japs in this parish" at the height of the war.[129] The war years also saw growing tensions between the area's African American and white residents. In 1943, for example, Allen Parish's Oakdale sheriff was shot and killed by an African American man, who claimed the shooting was in retaliation for a previous beating he and his fiancée had received at the hands of the sheriff. The case served to expose how commonplace racial violence was in the area as well as the ambivalent attitudes of local whites as the case went through the court system. Ultimately, the accused was found guilty and put to death.[130] While there is no evidence the Coushattas got caught in the crosshairs of the area's violent episodes, they nevertheless had to delicately navigate the racially contentious terrain. They walked a fine line between asserting their distinct tribal identity and displaying their willingness to be good neighbors and citizens by contributing to the war effort, as twenty-two Coushattas served in the military during World War II.[131]

Fig. 9: Chief Jeff Abbey, accompanied by Bel Abbey (middle), secures a tribal alliance by conferring an honorary title to Sen. Dudley J. LeBlanc, 1950. Courtesy of the Coushatta Tribal Archives.

By 1950 the Coushattas did become part of a highly publicized case that strained their relationship with some of the local white landowners. To address the tribe's continued loss of land, the Department of Justice instituted a suit in federal district court on the Coushattas' behalf against heirs of the J. A. Bel Estate and other residents of southwestern Louisiana in another attempt to recover land formerly held by Coushatta families. It was a tense time, and many of the tribe's neighbors, fearing seizure of their property, grew resentful. The land in question was connected to ten Coushatta families that each had representatives serve as witnesses in court, where they were asked questions through an interpreter.[132] The case lasted several months and was based on the notion that the named homesteads should have been taken into federal trust and protected from the start, appearing to have been an attempt by the federal government to correct an oversight from a half-century earlier. The complexity of the situation, not to mention the conflicting messages and contradictions surrounding the initial filings, doomed the case from the start, and once again, no landholdings were restored.[133]

Although the land case underscored the tense relationships between the Coushattas and some of the area's large-scale property owners, Chief Abbey strategically nurtured political alliances to ensure that the tribe was not socially alienated. During his last public appearance before his death in February 1951, Abbey participated in a symbolic ceremonial exchange in the gymnasium of Elton High School, conferring the title of "Honorary Chief" to Louisiana senator Dudley J. LeBlanc. Although this title held no actual power or responsibilities within the governing structure of the tribe, it represented an effort to secure friendships with politically powerful individuals in a quest to further secure a sense of goodwill toward the Coushatta people (fig. 9).[134]

This was a practice also encouraged among the younger generation, who were to become future leaders of the tribe. For example, in 1950, the same year as the land claims case, an eight-year-old Ernest Sickey was asked by his father, Davis, and Chief Abbey to write a letter to Senator Allen J. Ellender asking for assistance on behalf of the tribe.[135] Ellender was, as described by historian John Kyle Day, "the politician most responsible for returning the Longites to the Democratic fold" following Long's public feud with President Roosevelt and then his assassination in 1935. Ellender "supported local autonomy in social matters while simultaneously promoting an interventionist government for public welfare."[136] While his position on racial matters suggested he would not support the advancement of people of color, his favorable political stance on government assistance to the state's poor nevertheless encouraged the Coushattas to reach out to him.

Huddled next to an oil lamp one evening, with pencil in hand, the young boy wrote the senator a letter. The letter's details have faded from his memory, but Sickey said the overarching purpose was to alert Ellender to the Coushattas' severe poverty and unemployment. Sickey later recalled why the letter's timing was so critical. "Several of our men who fought in World War II came back to a community that was still the same . . . What few jobs were available were in the logging industry, which was fading fast. There was also some employment available to the tribal members in local farms, but farming is cyclical and these were only seasonal jobs. So, we had to survive through whatever means we could." In order to stave off hunger, many community members relied on fish and turtles from the bayous as well as shared yields from family gardens.[137]

Writing a letter to Senator Ellender was Sickey's first experience of being politically engaged. The action ignited an awareness within him that his father and other Coushattas had fostered since his birth, one he later identified as his first form of activism.[138] In fact, this was just the beginning of what would evolve into a half-century-long journey, adding to the work of previous Coushatta leaders looking to promote and improve the condition of their people by continuing to build networks and make the Coushattas' presence known in the area. Chief Abbey and others knew that the survival of the tribe hinged upon the ability of the younger generation to help navigate the new barriers that still awaited them.

3

Abandoned, Not Terminated

The Aftermath and Response to the Unilateral Withdrawal of Federal Services, 1951–1962

We went to bed one night in 1953 as Indians in the eyes of the Federal government, and the next day we woke up and were no longer considered Indians.

—Bertney Langley, July 12, 2018

In February 1951 Chief Jeff Abbey died from complications of influenza. A crowd of mourners piled into the Indian Church for the service before he was laid to rest at the nearby St. Peter's Indian Cemetery. Among the Coushattas who were present that day were also many local non-Indians who had developed longtime friendships with him. Well into his nineties, Abbey was the tribe's oldest citizen, and many saw his death, as well as those of Jackson Langley in 1947 and eight other significant leaders within the Indian Church around the same time, as the end of an era.[1] Abbey's death not only marked a transition in Coushatta leadership, but it also came during a period when the tribe was more vulnerable than it had been for some time. Post–World War II shifts in Indian policy began reversing some of the gains made in the 1930s and 1940s as the federal government began looking for opportunities to diminish its responsibilities to tribes. Like other tribes across the country, the Coushattas had no way to prepare for what was to come, but they knew they needed the next generation of leaders to emerge and help maintain the community's cohesion and continue to serve as the bridge between the tribe and its neighbors. A lot was at stake, and there was a great deal of pressure to ensure that the work of previous generations was carried on.

Mikko Hahpon Hohachaalihchin, Immaayasin Kommaayatikkoto Stathiiyato
Electing a New Chief and Increasing Public Visibility

The community mourned Jeff Abbey for nearly a month before regrouping and beginning the election process for a new chief.[2] There was no shortage of interest. Those who wished to be considered included Douglas John, Chief Abbey's former interpreter and travel companion to Washington DC; Bel Abbey, the nephew of Chief Abbey; and Martin Abbey, Chief Abbey's son. With so many viable candidates, an election was held at the Indian Church, where thirty-three representatives from different clans and families showed up to cast their votes with Assistant Pastor Solomon Battise moderating the election. To mark its importance, the event began with gospel hymns and a prayer in Koasati, before each candidate delivered a speech explaining why he was the most suitable to take on the role of tribal chief. Slips of white paper were carefully cut and distributed to the voters, who, after thoughtful consideration, wrote the name of the candidate they most supported for the position. Battise read the names aloud, while a teenage assistant kept a tally on the church blackboard for all to see. There must have been great anticipation in the church that day as Martin Abbey was declared the winner with twenty-six of thirty-three votes.[3]

Both the process and outcome of the election piqued the interest of the tribe's neighbors. Accompanying voters that day were Elton mayor, C. L. Marcantel, and Police Chief Oday Herbert as well as Jennings sheriff R. L. Thompson. Joining them were newspaper reporters who wished to cover the election; "choosing a chief for an American Indian tribe," one wrote, "no longer is a ceremony of barbaric splendor, it is more like an American town meeting."[4] Although still a child then,

Ernest Sickey recalled how members of the media found the election interesting because they didn't know how a tribal government worked: "They didn't have any idea that the Coushatta tribe was a community in itself in Allen Parish." By permitting the election to be attended by outsiders, the Coushattas helped the public understand them in terms of their political identity, rather than just their cultural one. The attendance of two law enforcement officers is particularly interesting and suggests an effort by town officials to better understand the jurisdictional roles of local municipalities in tribal affairs.

Martin Abbey became chief during a transitional time in the Coushattas' history. While he maintained some continuity with the tasks carried out by previous leaders, he also embraced a more symbolic role for himself. Just as previous leaders did, Abbey advised and brokered communication within the community. Sickey remembered meeting with him on several occasions, just as he had with his father. The difference was, Sickey believed, that attitudes about a chief's function changed following Jeff Abbey's death. "I think the community was ready for [something different]," he reflected, particularly as they confronted new challenges.[5] Outside reports, based on observations and interviews with Coushattas, further reinforced the sentiment that Coushatta leadership underwent an evolution as old positions were realigned to better address modern needs. Not fully understanding that such shifts didn't indicate an abandonment of traditional values, some reports claimed that Jeff Abbey's death began the erosion of "the traditional leadership of the tribe." Others pointed to Martin Abbey's temporary relocation to Texas for work as a sign that the position of "chief" was "without a function."[6]

While Abbey negotiated his new responsibilities within the tribe, he also leveraged his position as chief to become the public face of the Coushatta people. Strategically opting to fit non-Indian expectations of what Indians should look like, he made many public appearances wearing generic plains-style "Indian" clothing and regalia. Donning these "costumes" Abbey marched in local parades and at festivals in what newspapers identified as "full ceremonial dress," each time drawing crowds of curious onlookers.[7] One of his first acts as chief was to follow his father's alliance-building strategy by securing the loyalty of Elton's mayor, C. L. Marcantel, by naming him "assistant chief and advisor" and then frequently appearing publicly with Marcantel in order to substantially increase the Coushattas' media exposure.[8] In March 1951 alone, local newspapers featured the Coushattas on four different occasions, an unprecedented level of coverage during a time when the tribe was all but ignored by the media. In addition to covering Martin Abbey's election, the papers fed into a growing curiosity about these "forgotten Indians" of Bayou Blue, describing how they lived in "small houses in the woods [where they] are very poor and undernourished."[9] Journalist Dorothy Seals painted the Coushattas' situation with particular flair, writing that they "reside deep in the festering dripping swamps of Louisiana's Allen parish."[10]

Newspapers also reported on a growing interest with the tribe by a Boy Scout troop in Lake Charles, which gave Chief Martin Abbey a "ceremonial" feather headdress as a gesture of friendship, also inviting tribal artisans to sell their "wares" on the courthouse lawn.[11] Although Coushattas previously made "seasonal appearance[s]" in Lake Charles to sell baskets and other handcrafted goods, the public election of Chief Abbey heightened interest in the "Coushatta village near Elton," described as "the only tribe in the state today that has remained a cohesive group, marrying within their own tribe and retaining the old language."[12] Abbey's election also coincided with—and perhaps even sparked—the beginnings of local efforts to develop a tourism industry. By 1958 the Elton Businessmen's Club had established a tourism program that relied on the Coushattas' proximity to the town. Area merchants looked to leverage the growing attention to the tribe to boost the local economy by inviting out-of-state guests to Elton for tours, culminating with gifts of locally grown rice and souvenir baskets acquired from Coushatta weavers.[13]

The intense focus on the Coushattas was led primarily by Boy Scout leader Tim Dugas, who, according to Barbara Langley, "loved the Indians out here in the woods."[14] With a shift early in the twentieth century among the ranks of the American boy scouting movement, transitioning away from a militaristic persona to one that appropriated and romanticized Indigenous ways of life and lore, the close proximity of the tribe offered Dugas an opportunity to create an "authentic" experience for scouts.[15] Dugas worked with Coushattas, such as Bel Abbey, to plan "Indian dances" and then led groups through the Coushatta community for "sight-seeing tours."[16] He even enlisted Chief Abbey to present awards and badges at scouting ceremonies.[17] Dugas continued to develop his "Indian displays," using Coushatta participants through several generations of Boy Scouts and forged long-standing friendships within the tribe along the way. Sickey felt that Dugas was sincerely concerned for their welfare: "He really came out and tried to help the Indians. He used to bring used clothing and have little parties during holidays . . . He did what he could."[18] Despite the meager resources allotted by the Bureau of Indian Affairs (BIA)—the Office of Indian Affairs was renamed in 1947—Dugas found the Coushattas' conditions appalling. Many lived in tiny tar-paper–covered wood-framed homes, and none had indoor plumbing.[19] In 1948 the first Coushatta homes got electricity, but a majority didn't acquire it until many years later.[20] Intent on assisting the tribe to improve their conditions, in 1952 Dugas wrote to the BIA regional office in Mississippi insisting that more aid be provided.[21]

Other local residents joined Dugas's efforts in taking up the "Coushatta cause." The Louisiana Federation of Women's Clubs, for example, raised money to buy books for the Indian school and establish scholarships.[22] The nearby Society of Children of the American Revolution chapter also held charity picnics to benefit the tribe in which Coushatta children provided the entertainment by singing in Koasati.[23] Teachers at the Indian school collaborated with Dugas, organizing and advertising basket shows so Coushatta weavers could generate additional income.[24] Information cards were also created to be included with the baskets as a way of educating purchasers about Coushatta history.[25] To further increase exposure, weavers entered arts and crafts competitions in which their baskets were assessed alongside other handmade crafts produced by local non-Indian artisans. In 1954 Ency Robinson Abbey Abbott made news by winning four blue ribbons for her basket work in an event emphasizing floral designs.[26] Just as the tribe gained momentum in befriending many in the surrounding area who rallied to help improve their living conditions, the federal government had begun a slow shift away from continuing to support tribal programs. In fact, Congress was looking to end federal responsibilities toward Indians altogether.

Palaaki Nokchoobaachito Komawiichilka
An Abrupt Halt to Coushatta Services

In the years following World War II, there was a call to repeal the 1934 Indian Reorganization Act (IRA). This was in part due to new political anxieties during the Truman administration that served to reshape policies and attitudes toward Indians. Mounting wartime expenses, coupled with Truman's Fair Deal philosophy based on American middle-class hegemony, reignited the idea that Indians fare better without the supervision or services of the federal government.[27] Also, following resignations of key officials who had encouraged tribal rehabilitation and economic development under the IRA, namely BIA commissioner John Collier (1945) and Felix Cohen of the Interior Department (1948), few who remained in positions of power wished to continue advocating for New Deal–inspired policies. The Hoover Commission on Indian Affairs formalized this attitude shift in a 1949 report, calling for the complete integration of Indians into mainstream society with little regard for the preservation of tribal cultures and lifeways.[28] The report's conclusion crossed party lines but gained momentum with the presidential election of Republican Dwight D. Eisenhower in 1953, whose party carried the majorities in both houses of Congress. Concerned with dangers from big government, the new Republican majority strongly felt that removing the federal government's role in Indian lives was a form of "freedom" for Indian people. As Senator George W. Malone of Nevada put it, the BIA should be discontinued, for although it was "originally established to improve the status of individual Indians and prepare them to take the responsibility of citizenship—after 125 years this still has not been accomplished" and Indians would be best left to their own devices.[29] Severing federal relationships with tribes also addressed Cold War fears, which viewed tribal communal living as un-American.[30] The most pragmatic arguments, however, focused on the benefits to the national budget if federal Indian programs were defunded.

On June 9, 1953, the House Concurrent Resolution 108 was introduced

in Congress. Eventually known as the "termination policy," this resolution was embedded among a series of minor bills, easily passing
without as much as a debate.[31] It de-emphasized the unique status of
tribal peoples, removing the special government-to-government relationships, and foregrounded the status of Indians as citizens under the
jurisdiction of their respective states. It called for an end to the federal
government's trust relationships with tribes and for the elimination of
federal benefits, support services, and trust lands.[32] Deeply troubled by
this turn, many tribes sent representatives to Washington DC to oppose
the legislation, waging arguments that cited financial concerns, the loss
of rights and privileges established by treaties or previous legislation, the
anticipated implications for tribal-state relationships, and the disregard
for the emotional ties tribes had to their lands.[33]

The Coushattas didn't send anyone to Washington DC to argue against
the legislation. In fact, there is no evidence that Chief Abbey was aware
of what was happening enough to communicate the situation to the rest
of the tribe. There are indications that tribal allies were given signs that
Indian affairs was in transition when the year before passage of the Indian
termination policy, Tim Dugas received a response to one of his letters
from Robert M. Cullum of the BIA Muskogee Area Office in Oklahoma
stating that the agency wasn't obligated to help the Coushattas. "There
is always a question," he wrote, "whether a group would have its situation bettered by being more closely tied to the Government." Given
that Coushattas already attended white schools, Cullum argued that this
posed "a more favorable opportunity" for the federal government to save
the expense of Coushatta education. Cullum's attitude diverged significantly from BIA officers of only a few years earlier, who had dreamed of
a large, federally funded Coushatta day school with its own agricultural
land and livestock. Since this plan never came to fruition, over time
it became convenient to leverage the Coushattas' "friendly" relations
with local whites to justify decreasing the already meager federal funds
directed to the existing Indian school. Plus, as Cullum pointed out, the
Coushattas could access the same resources as other citizens, such as
the Louisiana State Employment Service, "which one might hope might
lead to independent self-support."[34] This likely wasn't the response

Dugas had expected. In fact, this rhetoric harked back to responses Coushatta leaders had received to requests for assistance before 1935. Here they were again—eighteen years later—essentially back to where they had started.

Although bureaucracy moved slowly as new programs and resources were allocated, the process seemed to accelerate when they were slated to be shut down. Immediately following passage of the termination policy, area BIA officials began identifying tribes they believed were able to handle their own affairs without further federal assistance, a process of identification that happened in a haphazard fashion.[35] The Menominees of Wisconsin were first in line because of a perception of economic independence and evidence of relationships with local non-Indians, so federal officials set to work convincing the tribe that termination was in their best interest. The Menominees gradually succumbed to the pressure and voted to approve it, which impacted 3,270 tribal members and 233,881 acres of land.[36] Other tribes identified as candidates for termination didn't necessarily fit the same profile. The Seminoles of Florida, for instance, seemed to have been targeted "without reason," argued historian Donald Fixico: "The majority of the 870 members were inexperienced in handling their own business affairs and lived under extreme substandard living conditions."[37] Seminole leaders were able to redirect the termination gaze away from them by successfully convincing federal officials of their situation in formal testimony, during which they argued that they weren't well positioned to develop an economic base without at least twenty-five more years of assistance from the federal government.[38] By 1957 tribal leaders had drafted a constitution and formally created the Seminole Tribe of Florida, Inc., as a nonprofit organization, to pursue economic development opportunities. Similarly, the Mississippi Choctaws also were assessed for a "withdrawal program" under the guise that despite rampant racism and Mississippi's segregation statutes, the Choctaws could be made acceptable to local whites and forcibly assimilated into their institutions. Once bureau officials fully realized how entrenched Mississippi's racial politics were, however, the Mississippi Choctaws also managed to avoid falling prey to the termination legislation.[39]

No tribe was safe from being made a candidate for termination, regardless of size or level of federal investment. It wasn't long before the Chitimachas and Coushattas also came under consideration. In fact, Louisiana was among the initial list of states for which authorities proposed eliminating all federal Indian services.[40] Historian Jay Precht argued that for the Coushattas, in particular, their "history of homesteading and private landownership made them a prime candidate for termination, just as it had made them a model of assimilationist policy."[41] As early as 1940, federal officials had expressed a desire to stop paying for Indian education in Louisiana. Although the conversation at the time primarily focused on the Jena Band of Choctaws, there was a growing sentiment that Indian education in total should be turned over to the state.[42] As World War II began, fiscal reallocations shifted money away from domestic programs. The budgetary constraints led to drastic reductions in many appropriation bills, and the Coushattas' school budget felt the immediate impact.[43]

The wheels were in motion, and on October 2, 1953, BIA officials had planned to meet with the Coushatta community. Paul Vance, from the Choctaw Field Office in Mississippi, and Marie Hays, from the Muskogee Field Office in Oklahoma, traveled to Allen Parish to discuss the new legislation with the tribe, but the community received almost no notice of these plans. In fact, Vance didn't even notify Chief Abbey; instead, he first discussed the matter with Reverend Leeds, who supported the termination of BIA services to the Coushattas. Growing up, Ernest Sickey was told that Leeds had changed his views about the role he felt the federal government should play in the Coushattas' lives, gradually adopting the position that the tribe was better off without BIA assistance.[44] It is difficult to decipher why his perspective shifted, but it may have stemmed from difficulties the tribe had faced in first receiving federal Indian funding, beginning with education funding in 1935 and contract health care in the 1940s, and then witnessing what little impact the meager budget for health care had made as well as the state of the poorly funded Indian school. Leeds himself had dedicated great effort toward the plans to build a new federal Indian school for the Coushattas, only to face bitter disappointment when land couldn't be acquired to carry out the vision. Leeds likely was unimpressed with the BIA's presence in the community, and he may have felt that Coushatta leaders would have a better chance of meeting their community's needs if energies were directed elsewhere. The decision was not his to make, however. Just a week before his trip to Allen Parish, Vance wrote to Martha John, the tribal custodian and librarian of the Indian Church and school, asking that the school building be opened for his visit and to "give the meeting publicity amohg [*sic*] the Indians." The meeting seemed to be organized in haste, and there was urgency in Vance's mission to begin termination proceedings immediately. "It is my hope," he wrote, "that something can be worked out at this meeting whereby the part of the building belonging to the government can be turned over to the Indians to be used in such a manner as they desire."[45]

Only eighteen Coushattas showed up to hear what Vance and Hays had to say.[46] Although a few families attended, they were by no means fully representative of the tribe. Even Chief Abbey was absent. Vance explained that the termination policy would free the Coushattas from federal oversight. He then gave the group a written resolution that he had prepared and asked them to discuss and "thoroughly endorse" it. The one-page document was full of inaccuracies, such as that the Coushattas had not entered into treaties with the federal government. It also stated that "Congress has not adopted legislation recognizing responsibility for the Coushatta Indians or made any special provisions for them."[47] These claims were troublesome on several fronts because the tribe had indeed entered into treaty agreements in its early history as part of the Creek Confederacy. The federal government also acknowledged its responsibility to the Coushattas when taking 160 acres of land into trust for them in the late nineteenth century and then providing special provisions through funding for health care and education in subsequent decades. Nevertheless, Vance saw an opportunity to break away from the Coushattas during a time when BIA officials were pressured to clear up their rosters. He further justified his efforts in a letter a few years later, writing that terminating the Coushatta tribe was a "constructive move" since their children had already integrated into white schools.

To do otherwise, Vance reasoned, would reinforce school segregation by maintaining a separate Coushatta school.[48]

With the Coushatta termination resolution in hand, "the old people met at the school and decided that they didn't even know what all that meant," Sickey said. "They didn't understand termination, and they didn't understand what it meant to be released from federal wardship. So they decided not to sign it."[49] Seven days after the meeting, Newton Williams sent a handwritten letter to Vance on behalf of the tribe:

> Mr. Vance,
> We have read it over and decided not to sign the papers
> you left for us to talk over among the Indians. Over half
> of them rather not sign it.
>
> > From,
> > Newton Williams

Vance neither expected nor accepted this response.[50] In a message to the BIA's Choctaw Agency Field Office, he reported that the Coushattas "will not give their wholesale endorsement to withdrawal at this time." Their position evidently was sufficiently firm that Vance left southwestern Louisiana a day earlier than he had initially planned, rather than attempt to convince the tribe to reconsider. "I sincerely hope that you find the report adequate and will not feel that it was handled too badly," he wrote his supervisor.[51] Without the Coushattas' consent on the resolution, Vance couldn't officially submit it for legislative action. Nevertheless, he moved forward with it anyhow, and the Coushattas were unilaterally and without statutory authority terminated from federal Indian services.[52] No official announcement was made on this decision or action. "They just walked off," Sickey explained. "They shut the school down and cut off the few dollars that they were giving toward health care, and they left without an explanation and never came back."[53] For most terminated tribes, the transition was gradual, with a period that ranged from a few months to seven years, depending on the number of federal programs to be phased out.[54] For the Coushattas, however, it was instantaneous.

The Coushattas' experience offers insight into how decisions and actions (or inactions) of individual federal agents impacted the trajectory of tribal affairs. The power afforded individuals within the BIA proved to have damaging consequences, especially when necessary time wasn't taken to ensure their actions were in the best interest of tribes. Addressing this issue, Mississippi Choctaw leader Phillip Martin gave a biting critique of BIA staff in 1960, writing to Interior secretary Fred Seaton that they "are average human beings, timid but not bad, and it is pitiful that their fate put them in a job they do not have enough courage to do."[55] Vance's early departure from the Coushatta settlement, along with his subsequent note about his inability to effectively communicate with the tribe, demonstrated a lack of interest in considering their needs or even offering them the opportunity to ask questions. A pattern of similar hasty actions by federal officials in handling termination nationally prompted the American Civil Liberties Union (ACLU) and other advocacy groups to issue a statement on the ethics of obtaining tribal consent, compelling the BIA to improve its practices.[56]

Although the flow of federal funding to the Coushattas ceased following the October meeting with Vance, efforts had been under way for months in preparation for terminating the federal government's trust obligation to the Coushattas. In fact, plans were first set in motion as the tribe recovered from one of the largest natural disasters it had faced since settling at Bayou Blue. Although the area had a history of flooding, in May 1953 officials declared a state of emergency after twenty-two inches of rain in two days forced the northwestern and southern portions of the Coushatta community to evacuate. Bayou Blue is only thirty feet above sea level and slopes only two feet per mile, according to a 1952 geological survey, which contributed to poor drainage.[57] Residents struggled to evacuate, and children living in the area couldn't attend school until the water receded.[58] Red Cross volunteers in motorboats evacuated 131 Coushattas, who had to live temporarily in the Indian Church, the Elton Negro Dance Hall, or the American Legion Hall. They were fed at the nearby black school and received bedding and clothing from the Red Cross.[59]

A few weeks after the flood but prior to the Coushattas' meeting with Vance and Hays, Sissy Robinson Alabama's land, 160 acres that had passed to her heirs, Emily Alabama and Jane Battise, was released of its federal trust status.[60] The BIA concealed this development from the tribe while attempting to convince members to sign the termination agreement. In fact, the resolution presented to them even addressed the status of the 160 acres of trust land, stating it would be transferred to fee patents upon the community's agreement.[61] Without the tribe's consultation or consent, however, the land had already been transferred out of a federal trust status, a move that the family was likely first made aware of when property tax bills were distributed.[62]

While the Coushattas were left stunned and confused following the abrupt cessation of federal services, the Chitimachas fought a similar fate. The first Louisiana tribe to receive federal services, the Chitimachas were singled out for termination under the guise that they were an already "semi-acculturated population."[63] Like the Coushattas, the Chitimachas resisted the withdrawal of federal Indian services and rallied to keep their tribal school open. Unlike with the Coushattas, however, BIA officials sent a termination bill to Congress rather than unilaterally terminate the Chitimachas "off the record." Yet timing favored the Chitimacha tribe, and the termination policy fell into disfavor before the bill was even considered.[64]

Not only did the BIA discontinue services to the Coushattas, but the impact of the policy became obscured as the tribe also was consistently left out of follow-up reports as well as later scholarship on the termination period. Between 1953 and 1966 Congress terminated its trust relationship with 109 tribes.[65] Because federal services weren't withdrawn from the Coushatta tribe through congressional action, however, they weren't counted among those officially terminated. Yet the impact was the same. The Coushattas and the Chitimachas were both omitted from a 1954 BIA document that reported whether different area agencies believed tribes within their jurisdictions were "ready to handle their own affairs."[66] Several southeastern tribes were listed, including the Cherokees of North Carolina (marked no), the Catawbas (yes), the Mississippi Choctaws (no), the Florida Seminoles (no), and the Alabamas and Coushattas of Texas (yes).[67] Following the suggestions included in the report, the Alabamas and Coushattas of Texas and the Catawbas of South Carolina were terminated through congressional acts in 1954 and

1959, respectively.[68] Both communities voiced opposition but couldn't stall the legislation.[69] As a result, their reservations were released from federal trust status, and BIA services ceased.[70] In contrast to Louisiana, the state governments of both Texas and South Carolina stepped in to ensure the continuation of some of the lost services. Texas, for example, created a state Indian commission "to protect the legal status, land and property, resources, and lives of the tribes and its members."[71] As a result, the Alabama-Coushatta Reservation was maintained under state jurisdiction, and Texas assigned a state-appointed agent to work in the community.[72]

The termination years were full of discord and suffering and, on all accounts, seen as a great disaster across the country. In 1968 Robert F. Kennedy said the legislation had "'poisoned the well' of meaningful dialogue among government officials, legislators and Indian people."[73] Many tribes never fully recovered, and others required decades to rebuild an infrastructure that had been swiftly demolished. Although the Coushattas didn't lose as much land or resources as other tribes, they suffered similarly. Throughout the 1950s the Louisiana Coushattas maintained a population of around two hundred people, with about fifty of them moving back and forth between Lake Charles and Texas for work, and contrary to Vance's claim that they would be "better off" securing state resources instead of continuing to draw from federal Indian funds, the community's situation visibly worsened.[74]

Maamin, Yaamito
The Aftermath

The suspension of federal Indian funding immediately impacted the Coushatta community. Of particular concern was the loss of medical services. Although the services provided by the contract doctor were limited, he did offer members of the tribe antibiotics when needed.[75] An absence of health records prevents an assessment of any potential medical care Coushattas may have received from state-funded programs in the twenty years following termination, but cemetery records show that the tribe lost over twenty people between 1953 and 1973.[76] Tuberculosis cases were common, and without a doctor, the community relied on the parish schools to vaccinate children. "As a group," one report documented, "the longevity of tribal members is a great deal less than the non-Indian population. Doctors, nurses and medicine are all needed badly but the economic level is too low to afford such luxuries."[77]

As medical care soon became an indulgence, so did having an Indian school nestled within the community. After the BIA school closed, the Allen Parish School Board refused to reinstate funding previously provided for the Indian school, as it had done earlier in the century. The school simply shut down. Coushatta children, some as young as six years old, began riding the bus to Elton to attend the public elementary school without the transitional preparation in English instruction that the Indian school provided. These children had little exposure to English, and the majority spoke only Koasati.[78] The only remaining opportunity for Coushatta children to have bilingual instruction was in Sunday school at the Indian Church, which was often taught by Solomon Battise. Battise's own son Leonard, who was seven years old when the BIA discontinued services to the tribe, found the transition to parish schools difficult. "We didn't know a bit of English when we went to school," he shared. "All we talked at home was our language . . . We didn't know what the teacher was saying."[79] Barbara Langley also found it difficult to navigate the parish school and remembered the advice of older Coushatta children, who suggested she simply say "Yes ma'am" and "No ma'am" to get her through most situations. The problem was that she didn't understand when to appropriately use these words. She told of a teacher who tested the children's English comprehension by holding out a long stick and instructing them to follow her commands to "jump over it, hop over it, [or] skip over it":

> I didn't know which one I was supposed to do . . . [so] I just jumped over it and the teacher grabbed me and pulled me down to where she was sitting. There was this one little white girl, who was always there by my side helping me . . . When we lined up to jump over that stick, she was behind me. She knew exactly what the teacher was telling her to do, but she did exactly what I did . . . [The teacher] grabbed her, pulled her down to her side. She was a delicate little girl. I think she

injured her arm . . . We didn't know the English language. We was just kids that were lagging behind. We were having a hard time. The teachers overlooked us because it seemed like their thought was . . . that we are not going to amount to anything. When I realized how bad we were treated, I was determined to make something out of myself.[80]

The language barrier also created difficulties between generations because many Coushatta parents couldn't read their children's report cards. Loretta Williams remembered: "My mom didn't know too much English. My daddy knew a little bit, because he went to the war . . . [So, when] report cards [came], it would have to be him to sign our report cards, because my mom wouldn't . . . have even known what grades we got."[81]

The educational challenges faced by Coushatta children at times developed into a source of camaraderie with Cajun children, who also found difficulty adjusting to the English-only environment. Historian Marian Patterson discussed the resentment between the French-speaking Cajuns and the English-speaking "Yankees" in southwestern Louisiana, which grew because the Cajuns internalized the prejudice against them. The pressure to speak English in parish schools influenced many Cajun families to opt against teaching their children French so that they wouldn't be ridiculed or targeted as poor "barefoot Cajuns."[82] While Cajun heritage never ceased to be a point of pride, many Cajun families recognized, in the years following World War II, that emphasizing differences from their English-speaking peers would deny their children certain opportunities afforded other white residents in the state. This was not the case among the Coushattas, however, who may have been afforded entrance into white institutions but had never been considered part of the area's white population or compelled to conform to speaking only English. As a result, the Koasati language maintained a prominent place in their homes and in defining Coushatta identity. "If we lose our language," Ernest Sickey said, "we're just like anybody else on the planet."[83]

In the years following the federal government's withdrawal of services to the Coushattas, the Indian Church continued to serve as a unifying force. Yet its role, too, underwent some changes when, in 1958, Reverend

Paul Leeds died, fifty-seven years after holding his first service for the tribe. Pastoral duties soon fell to Rev. Donald K. Johnson, a graduate of the Congregational ministry from Cedar Rapids, Iowa. Johnson's wife, Wanda, was from the nearby town of Kinder and grew up under the mentorship of Reverend Leeds, spending much of her childhood around the tribe. One report romanticized her connection to the Coushattas, stating that as a young girl, Wanda Kuntz was "frequently seen at the side of Rev. Leeds as he made his rounds of the Indian settlement . . . Whether going about her studies at school or saying a bedtime prayer, Wanda was not to realize until years later why the plight of the Indians tugged at her conscience so. She would often stop and whisper a short prayer for 'her people.'" From a young age she saw herself as a dedicated friend of the tribe with an intense interest in their welfare—one that continued to grow after her husband was assigned to supervise the ministry at the Indian Church.[84]

Settling into their new roles, the Johnsons were disheartened by the scope of the tribe's needs and sought external assistance from a New York–based advocacy group dedicated to working with Indian tribes around the country. The Association on American Indian Affairs, Inc. (AAIA) was founded in 1922 and promoted the idea that it was "a national responsibility to protect our Indian tribes as long they need protection."[85] According to historian Daniel M. Cobb, the organization had approximately twenty-five thousand members by the 1950s and "carried considerable influence in national Indian politics."[86] Reverend Johnson contacted the AAIA in 1959, seeking guidance and support for what seemed a monumental task given his inexperience with tribes. AAIA field secretary Claude H. Heyer was soon sent to the Bayou Blue settlement to assess the Coushattas' situation. Heyer later wrote that their "history seems to be a story of sad neglect." He toured the community and met with several Coushatta families as well as several local non-Indians. The resulting seven-page report of this visit painted a depressing picture of unemployment, poverty, and rampant alcoholism. The owner of a local lumber company even admitted to Heyer that "sometimes whites have paid the Indians for labor with liquor, paying with a very cheap grade so the Indian will not get his full pay." Heyer also observed "excessive overcrowding" in Coushatta homes. Despite these problems, however, Heyer was impressed by their strength and community spirit. Serving as a guide and host, Solomon Battise spent a generous amount of time with Heyer, even showing him the house he was building for his family. At the end of his visit, Heyer made nine recommendations to assist in "raising the social and economic status of the Coushatta." Among these recommendations he suggested leveraging state and federal funding to repair homes, build a community center, repair the old Indian school, and launch a tribal tourism enterprise. Heyer commended the Johnsons for their interest in the tribe's welfare, stating that with some assistance "there is considerable possibility that things will begin looking up for the Coushattas for the first time in history."[87]

The Johnsons were pleased with such optimism and were further encouraged by a follow-up response from the AAIA's executive director, LaVerne Madigan, who wrote that she was "moved by the description of the Indians' problems" described in the report. Noted for her interest in working with tribes at the local level, Madigan offered to tap into the AAIA's own pool of allies that spanned the nation. She also suggested that the Johnsons build their own advocacy group by "stimulating the organization of a citizens' committee . . . which could interest itself in the Coushattas' problems." This, Madigan reasoned, would persuade Louisiana to begin helping the tribe "if a group of non-Indians began to show interest."[88] On the Coushattas' behalf Madigan also contacted the Race Relations Department of the Congregational Christian Churches Board in New York and requested help locating people to serve on a Louisiana Citizens' Committee to improve the welfare of the Coushattas.[89] The creation of such committees was a common strategy of the National Association for the Advancement of Colored People (NAACP) in places such as New Orleans and Baton Rouge to support the political and social needs of African Americans, and the AAIA thought the Coushattas would benefit from following suit in forming a group to look out for their interests.[90]

There is no evidence that the Johnsons followed Madigan's suggestion to organize a Coushatta-focused citizens' committee. Yet evidence does indicate that they wasted no time in generating greater public awareness about the tribe. Wanda Johnson, in particular, spoke at numerous local and statewide events about the origins of the Indian Church and the Coushattas' contributions to Louisiana's unique cultural history. She also regularly gave tours around the Bayou Blue settlement and requested that Louisiana newspapers report on Chief Abbey's public relations activities.[91] With Johnson's guidance journalists painted a deplorable picture of a neglected people. She also helped revive characterizations of racial purity from earlier decades, emphasizing that Coushattas were the only full-blooded Indians in Louisiana. Like previous government reports, newspapers compared the Coushattas to the Chitimachas, who had avoided termination and remained the only federally acknowledged tribe in the state. One article proclaimed the injustice of the situation, stating that "unlike the Koasati, the Chitimachas do not speak their native tongue, have intermarried, receive government aid, have their own school on the reservation and are composed of about 180 members."[92] Through the 1950s and 1960s the preservation of the Coushatta bloodline became a matter of public interest. Aligning this mission with the movement toward maintaining American exceptionalism and heritage, various officials and media sources called for concrete actions to ensure that the tribe continued to thrive. For example, one publication stated:

A recent scientific report disclosed that not only did the Indian arrive on the American scene thousands of years before the birth of Christ; but his blood is the purest of type "O" known to science. The Coushattas' blood line is said to contain less alien types than most tribes on the American continent today. Thus, if the Coushattas allow themselves to be usurped into the white mainstream, or marry into other Indian tribes, a beautiful and vastly valuable part of our American heritage will be lost. The only solution to the problem seems to be the establishing of industry at or near the Indian settlement. This would not only bring back those who left, seeking jobs in other parts of the country; but provide employment for those "soon-to-be adults," the younger generation.[93]

The Johnsons played a large role in the increasingly venerated status the tribe came to hold in the region. An about-face from the termination rhetoric prevailing just a few years earlier, the Johnsons' work at the Indian Church came at an opportune time, when national public opinion once again shifted toward supporting the integrity of tribal cultures.

Ischoba, School-ka Stoklo Paataliboolito
Rebuilding the Indian Church and School

As the Johnsons worked to generate public interest in the Coushattas, Solomon Battise reignited negotiations with the Bel Estate, seeking more land for the church. In the 1940s Reverend Leeds and BIA officials failed to convince the Bel heirs to donate land for a federal Indian school, largely because the donation would have meant relinquishing all oil, gas, and other mineral rights in order to place it into federal trust. However, with that concern no longer dictating the terms of land acquisition, Battise found a more agreeable audience, one that was also willing to put aside any lingering hard feelings over previous legal attempts to reclaim land. In 1960 the Bel Estate donated about five acres to the Indian Church to be used for a parsonage and cemetery.[94] Attorney David L. Garrison Sr., the land manager of the Bel Estate who also married into the family, represented the eight heirs, who agreed to donate the land with the stipulation that they keep their oil, gas, and mineral rights.[95]

With the church's property slowly expanding, the Coushattas initiated a rebuilding program. Tribal leaders began searching for building materials, asking their "wide circle of white friends," as one newspaper put it, to help acquire abandoned buildings for the community to repurpose.[96] Both the church and inactive school had fallen into disrepair, and without funds to purchase new supplies, creative measures were sought. The Johnsons supported these efforts and joined the tribe to lend a hand. Newspaper reporter Betty LaFleur later described the situation: "As word filtered into the mission that abandoned buildings could be had, providing they were torn down and removed from the site, Rev. Johnson and his following undertook the task of refurnishing their church and school. As the lumber was hauled in by any means available, the Indian women carefully removed the nails while the men constructed new Sunday School classrooms, two classrooms, a small neat kitchen and dining area and two bath rooms." It was a community-wide effort, and before long the refurbished school building was renamed the Leeds Memorial Indian School and relocated closer to the church, reopening its doors in the early 1960s to offer kindergarten through fourth grade. Wanda Johnson and Rose Vilardi served as the first teachers of what they called a "preparatory school" aimed at helping Indian children transition into the mainstream parish schools.[97]

Reestablishing the Indian school was a huge commitment. As one of the recommendations in the Heyer report, the AAIA supported the school and even solicited manufacturers to donate supplies.[98] The Allen Parish School Board soon re-recognized and accredited the school but didn't commit to funding it as it once had. As a result, it was forced to operate as a charity school, supported by donations and "free will offerings" from other Congregationalist churches and local organizations, with the Johnsons only receiving $100 a month for their work, much of which paid for student lunches.[99] Although difficult times still lay ahead, many Coushattas were glad to see their school reopened.

Ittimoklalahok-kohchok Ittimoklato
Developing Unlikely Friendships

While the 1950s was a decade of federal neglect, it also was an important time in the Coushattas' progress toward developing local political alliances. Chief Martin Abbey embraced his role as the tribe's ambassador to the public, and while he worked to maintain the Coushattas' local visibility, his efforts were complemented by the advocacy work of other Coushattas who had also grown up under the mentorship and guidance of Jeff Abbey. Davis Sickey, for example, didn't aspire to hold a formal leadership position within the tribe, but he did feel a deep sense of responsibility to contribute to his community by working behind the scenes building alliances and identifying points of intersection between Louisiana politics and the Coushattas' needs. Despite his limited English and a fifth grade education, Sickey became a student of government, observing the power structures from the local to national levels. He read a newspaper daily, studied public policy, and carefully searched for ways to assist his tribe in making critical connections with influential people.[100]

Sickey was unimpressed with the BIA's promises and questionable actions. He kept a cautious distance from the federally funded Indian school before it closed, opting not to send his own children there. Instead, he saw greater value in connecting with local and state governments to build a strong foundation of allies who were better able to assist the Coushattas. In fact, in 1942 Davis and Daisy Sickey named their only son after one of Louisiana's "master politicians."[101] Ernest S. Clements was a senator who represented Allen, Beauregard, Calcasieu, Cameron, and Jefferson Davis Parishes from 1936 to 1944 and was deemed one of the most powerful men in the state. He was a Democrat who was heavily influenced by Huey Long Jr.'s response to the poverty and destitution of the 1930s by calling for a program intended to redistribute wealth to the state's rural and poor populations. His approach gave hope to Sickey, who looked to benefit from state-funded programs, such as the Lafayette charity hospital where his children, Ernest and Bernetta, were born.

Senator Clements was part of a group of Louisiana politicians dedicated to carrying out Long's legacy, one that also included Long's younger brother, Earl, who had served as governor for three nonconsecutive terms.[102] In a 1937 letter to the *Weekly Town Talk*, an Alexandria newspaper, Clements exhibited his nostalgia for the Huey Long years, writing that under Long's administration the tensions between urban and rural citizens had dissipated: "Let's keep that ill feeling destroyed by sharing the wealth of the state in equal portion."[103] Addressing the urban-rural split by distributing state resources equally served as the cornerstone of Long's platform—one that also resonated with Clements, who lived in the small town of Oberlin, the seat of Allen Parish and approximately seven miles northwest of the Coushatta community.[104]

Davis Sickey supported the call to reach across the state's class divides and bring more services and opportunities into the economically disadvantaged corners of rural Louisiana. Although race often complicated the class-based rhetoric of politicians advocating for assistance to poor whites, Sickey looked for opportunities to integrate the Coushattas into the discussion by emphasizing their economic status as a rural, overlooked, and underserved group of Louisiana citizens. This mission led him to Clements's Oberlin office to introduce the tribe and convey their needs. The two men quickly became friends, and within a political environment that relied on a system of patronage, Sickey secured this alliance by naming his son after the senator.[105] Clements enjoyed his relationship with the Sickeys, and the younger Ernest remembered: "I used to go see him even as a young kid . . . and he would always express gratitude that my dad named me after him. He said [to me], 'Anything that you need in life, come see me.'"[106] The senator may not have known it at the time, but his namesake would one day take him up on the offer, just as the younger Sickey also would continue nurturing the many other relationships his father had developed.

Nestled in the eastern part of the Bayou Blue community, near the Bel Oil Refinery station, Davis and Daisy Sickey lived a short walk from the Abbey residence and a four-mile walk through the dense woods to the central part of the settlement. Like many Coushatta men, Davis worked in the logging industry and as an agricultural laborer. Woodworking was his passion, however, and he became known for his beautiful wood carvings, many of which were effigies of significant Coushatta animals and symbols. He also kept a robust garden, contributing to the tribe's supply of produce.[107] His was one of the first Coushatta families to purchase a vehicle, and the Sickeys' truck helped improve the community's mobility. Barbara Langley tells how Sickey brought people to town to shop: "He was always there, whoever needed a ride; he would take them." Sickey also drove Coushattas to Texas to visit relatives or attend funerals. They would pack lunches for the journey, with several riding in the back of the truck, and make their way down the gravel road to their destination.[108] In addition to shopping and social visits, the truck expanded the tribe's political reach.

Sickey boldly sought the attention of local civic leaders whom he thought could help the tribe and was known to appear unannounced at their offices to introduce himself. He also monitored the schedules of state officials and frequently drove to Lake Charles to meet with them. For many elected and appointed officials, Sickey was the first Indian they had ever met, and they were surprised to learn that the Coushattas lived in Allen Parish. Unlike Chief Martin Abbey, Sickey didn't appear in Indian regalia with the intent of bestowing honorary titles. His message was more somber. He wished to expose the BIA's unjust actions and recruit advocates for the Coushattas who could help them access resources and services from either the federal or state governments.[109] Sickey also frequently met with journalists of the *Daily World* newspaper in Opelousas, looking for what one reporter explained was "some help in the form of publicity . . . which would show the outside world the plight of this tiny segment of a once proud race."[110] During his travels, and when the opportunity arose, Davis brought his son, Ernest, along for the ride. Ernest jokes that his father "introduced me to every politician he could find . . . I was pretty much raised in the courthouse . . . As a little boy, I knew all these political [people] that my dad knew in Oberlin and Jeff Davis Parish." Davis Sickey studied the local political climate by befriending judges and attorneys and making frequent stops at the sheriff's office to learn about recent developments that may impact the tribe. The connections that he established became quite useful to the tribe. Ernest remembers that people often asked Davis for assistance with legal matters or in arranging funeral services.[111]

One friendship Sickey forged with an Oberlin judge became particularly important to the Coushatta people. Minos D. Miller was a World War II veteran who, as a fighter pilot, was shot down and held prisoner in a Japanese prison camp.[112] He later became a lawyer, married Ruth Means Loyd, who was among the first wave of female attorneys in the state, and started a family. In 1953 he was elected as the first judge of the Thirty-First Judicial District Court for both Allen and Jefferson Davis Parishes, the same year that the Coushattas were cut off from BIA services. He served in this capacity for nearly sixteen years, during which time he received special appointments to the Louisiana Supreme Court and to the first, third, and fourth circuits of the Louisiana Court of Appeals. Judge Miller had generated an impressive résumé of accomplishments, including many significant contributions to the evolution of the state's judicial system.[113]

As a frequent visitor to the Oberlin courthouse, Sickey shared with Judge Miller his concerns about the future of his tribe. Miller was sympathetic but unable to assist the Coushattas in regaining federal funding. Miller did, however, collaborate with Sickey on developing a work-release program for Coushattas who got into legal trouble. Typically, this was related to public intoxication, resulting in offenders being ordered to jail. As Ernest Sickey explained, "These crimes were nothing serious . . . but some [of these men] had jobs that they didn't want to mess up . . . so my dad and Judge Miller worked out a deal where . . . the Indians can work all week, and then go back [to jail] on weekends . . . until their sentence is completed." This program, the first of its kind in the area, helped many Coushatta families and prevented a possible period of unemployment from exacerbating an already dire economic situation.[114] A tragic cycle of poverty and substance abuse took its toll on the tribe, but in a unique partnership, Judge Miller and Davis Sickey created a strategy for mitigating the impact of legal troubles on Coushattas.

Judge Miller and his wife, Ruth, were politically connected. Their connections derived primarily from their professions as attorneys but also extended into local business dealings in the natural gas industry as well as through family lines. Their daughter, Bonner, for example, was named after her great-aunt Ethel "Bonner" Baker and also the mother of James A. Baker III, the White House chief of staff under both Presidents Ronald Reagan, from 1981 to 1985, and George H. W. Bush, from 1992 to 1993.[115] Sickey's friendship with Judge Miller afforded him recognition and credibility within political circles because, as Ernest put it, the Millers were a "family that nobody wanted to mess with."[116] In fact, the friendship between Miller and Sickey grew to have local political implications as the two men frequently discussed how the tribe could secure the most favorable representation by leveraging their votes. Like other southern states, Louisiana had a long history of disenfranchising African Americans through such means as literacy tests, poll taxes, and land ownership requirements.[117] In an attempt to exempt poor whites from such restrictions, Louisiana became infamous for enacting a so-called grandfather clause, which was a provision that protected the rights of poor white men to vote if their fathers or grandfathers had voted prior to 1867.[118] In spite of being considered citizens since the late nineteenth century, when they began acquiring allotments and serving in the military, the Coushattas were also disenfranchised in their early years at the Bayou Blue settlement. In fact, Indians were systematically disenfranchised across the country until as late as 1965, when the Voting

Rights Act reaffirmed their citizenship and prohibited states from denying their votes.[119] The first known mention of the Coushattas' voting status appears in a 1913 letter to the Indian bureau from the tribe's neighbor, Richard Powell, who wrote in support of the tribe receiving federal Indian services. He argued that the Coushattas were "good citizens" who obeyed Louisiana law despite being unable to vote.[120] According to Solomon Battise, the tribe didn't have much interest in "town politics or elections" in the early twentieth century anyway.[121] Instead, they focused on their shared form of internal governance and interacted with American government officials on a piecemeal basis when addressing specific issues. It is difficult to pinpoint exactly when Coushattas first participated in elections, but Ernest Sickey recalls the designation of a voting booth at the BIA school sometime in the 1940s.[122] By the late 1950s the Coushatta community was counted among those voter registration sites (located at the "Indian Church") listed in an election itinerary.[123]

Although small in number, the Coushattas became an increasingly visible constituency as racial tensions began sharply rising in the years following the *Brown v. Board of Education of Topeka* (1954) ruling, which outlawed states from continuing to operate segregated schools. "Something very much like a panic seized many parts of the South toward the beginning of 1956," writes historian C. Vann Woodward. "Race relations deteriorated in many areas, and as both [the black and white] races recoiled, old lines of communication between them snapped or weakened." The White Citizens' Council movement spread across the region, growing to some 500,000 members intent on maintaining the racial order of Jim Crow, and by July 1956 the Louisiana legislature had approved twelve new segregation bills.[124] Louisiana senators Allen J. Ellender, to whom Sickey had written in 1950, and Russell B. Long, the son of Huey J. Long, played important roles in the writing and dissemination of the *Declaration of Constitutional Principles*, commonly known as the *Southern Manifesto*. The *Manifesto* reaffirmed the Southern Democratic Party as a white party and publicly contested the *Brown* decision and emerging civil rights movement.[125] In addition to reflecting racial anxieties, the document also expressed state defiance of federal oversight, a sentiment that had gained a renewed momentum years earlier, following President Truman's executive order establishing the Commission on Civil Rights, which incited hostility toward the federal government among much of Louisiana's white population. These mounting resentments, in part, provided Davis Sickey a sympathetic audience when sharing the Coushattas' story about neglect and deceit at the hands of the Indian bureau. While the federal government appeared to impose itself on behalf of African Americans, it shirked its responsibilities when it came to American Indians, a point taken up by one of the *Manifesto*'s primary authors, North Carolina senator Sam Ervin. Ervin played the role of constitutional expert during congressional debates on civil rights, and he fought to defend racial segregation while simultaneously arguing for the protection of American Indian rights under the Constitution—a peculiar position that earned him the moniker of "Dr. Jekyll and Mr. Hyde" from Lawrence Speiser of the ACLU.[126]

Louisiana is touted as one of the most politically complex states in the South. Historian Alan Brinkley calls it "a morass of warring factions" in which politicians contend with divisions based not only on race and class but also between those from urban and rural settings and those with contrasting cultural and religious identities.[127] As the Coushattas engaged in the electoral process, they learned to navigate this political environment carefully. Generally speaking, they supported the Louisiana Democratic Party.[128] Although it was the party that protected white privilege, to the Coushattas it also was the party that echoed Long's rhetorical legacy of economic justice. For all intents and purposes the Coushattas had subverted the color line, so desegregation was not their battle, although local representatives from the African American community occasionally rallied the tribe around particular candidates who ran on platforms of racial equality. The Coushattas' votes were primarily informed by their immediate need for economic relief and services. Davis Sickey and Judge Miller consulted on which politicians could best elevate the Coushattas' standard of living. "My dad would run around the community and say, 'This is who we're going to vote for,'" Ernest Sickey said. Dewith Carrier, a longtime neighbor and friend to the tribe, confirmed this point, adding that "if you went to [Davis], you'd probably get 90 percent of the Indian vote." Davis wielded the tribe's collective political voice to generate an audience for the Coushattas' message. "We didn't have much," Ernest offered, "but we all got together and made do with what we had."[129]

Imanihta̱ Imittahobaachilk
Preparing the Next Generation

Davis Sickey had grand expectations for his son. Not only did he name him after a senator and instruct him to write letters to prominent politicians; he also sought to educate Ernest about the inner workings of Louisiana politics and the American legal system. By the time he could read, Ernest began accompanying his father to Oberlin for court proceedings to learn about the judicial process. The two also drove to Baton Rouge for legislative sessions. The experience demystified the political process, and Ernest quickly realized that by "knowing the system first" it would reveal itself as a "workable one." The two frequently joined Oberlin judges and attorneys at legal conferences and workshops in New Orleans, Houston, Atlanta, Boston, and other places around the country. They were always the sole Indians in attendance, and Ernest was the only child. While Davis Sickey was on a mission to help the tribe, Ernest admits, "My father and his friends were maybe in some way grooming me." And as their circle of friends widened within the local and state government and Ernest demonstrated increasing interest and potential, many began to hope that the young boy would grow up to help the whole area, both Indian and non-Indian. Although Sickey did, indeed, develop a deep interest in government, he recalled the pressure brought upon him. He found himself overwhelmed yet empowered by all that he learned and witnessed and thought, "Maybe I can do that one day."

In addition to learning about the legal system, Ernest Sickey also studied social interactions and communication styles. This education taught him to effectively cross cultural boundaries and function within the American political system—knowledge that proved invaluable in his adult years. "Those experiences gave me a tremendous [insight] on the possibilities," he explained. "I learned right away how to be effective, and that's where I learned how to relate to people and [the] social etiquette

[I needed]."[130] Unlike many of their peers, Ernest and Bernetta Sickey became fluent in English at a young age. At home they spoke Choctaw, Koasati, and French. Because of the geographical location of the Sickey property in the eastern portion of the Coushatta community, they were neighbors not only to Cajuns but also to many white, English-speaking families. "The white kids used to come to my house and we all played," Ernest recalled, "and I used to go to their houses . . . so I had a good knowledge of the English language when I went to school, as opposed to other [Coushatta kids] who didn't have that opportunity." Because Davis Sickey refused to send his children to the BIA-run Indian school, they started school in Elton with their neighbors. Davis's friendships with local politicians and merchants influenced the decisions he made for his own children, whom he wanted to see grow up on equal footing with their children. His goal was not to encourage his kids to shed their identities as Coushattas but, rather, to position them within the local power structure. It was a balance that Sickey was keenly aware of as he frequently warned them, "Never lose your language, never lose your identity, and get the best education possible."[131]

Ernest also built his language skills by negotiating with his white neighbors to secure part-time jobs. To earn his own spending money, which came in handy during trips with his father, he started taking care of Ruth Jenkins's lawn when he was ten years old. Ms. Jenkins was a retired schoolteacher whose family owned hardware stores in Elton and Oberlin where Coushattas frequently shopped. "They were very good to the tribe [and] very good to me," Ernest said.[132] For several years he worked for Ms. Jenkins, until he got a job taking care of the property around the Bel Oil refinery station. By 1953 Bel Oil operated six out of fifteen producing wells in the North Elton Field and flourished over the next few decades.[133] Growing up a short walk from the station, Sickey had watched the operation grow and practiced his English with the workers. The quiet existence that once defined life in the northeastern part of the Coushatta settlement had erupted with a steady flow of traffic as tanker trucks containing oil and natural gas regularly made their way up the road. A thriving operation, the refinery ran twenty-four hours a day and employed both locals from Elton and Kinder and technical specialists from places such as New York. Sickey became a frequent visitor. "I was this little Indian kid that showed up," he explained. "They had a big soda machine there, and they would treat me. It was probably a nickel at that time. They had a snack shop. So I would hang out, and then they would pay me for hauling trash and keeping the offices clean. Then, later on, I mowed the yards right there at the refinery." By the time he was fifteen, he had steady employment there after school, on weekends, and during the summer. Sickey continued to work at the refinery station until he graduated from Elton High School in 1960.[134]

His exposure to people and places outside Allen Parish, paired with the insight he regularly received from the tribe's elders, profoundly shaped Sickey's thinking. He developed a perspective that broadened his vision from the everyday activities most youth were concerned with and occupied his mind with different scenarios of how the Coushattas' future might play out. Grappling with his own future, he felt the dual pressures of not wanting "to live in a community where there was no running water" yet never wanting to leave his people. Ultimately, however, he couldn't ignore his desire to leave the community, so he set out to pursue a career in broadcast journalism. Sickey attended the University of Houston for two years, earning an associate's degree and training as a broadcaster. Upon reflection he realized his education could have led "to the halls of corporate America," but he couldn't escape the feeling that he was progressively leaving behind "the people that needed help." "In the back of my mind I knew that I wanted to focus on what I could do for my people. It became very important . . . that the children [get a] proper education . . . I saw people . . . hauling water from bayous and creeks and rivers nearby and so when I went [home] . . . I saw that there were opportunities [to improve things by] . . . communicating our needs . . . So it became personal for me." Still intending to have a career in broadcasting one day, he also focused on learning skills in public relations, hoping to acquire techniques useful for the Coushattas in communicating with the public. "That training really . . . [helped me] master what needed to be said," he explained.[135]

After two years in Houston, Sickey took a hiatus from school to join the U.S. Air Force. It was 1962, and U.S. involvement in the Vietnam War had escalated. Because he was selected to receive technical training as a supply specialist, he never had to serve overseas. Instead, he contributed to the training of airmen and officers who were preparing for deployment.[136] As a result, Sickey spent six years of active duty stationed in Baton Rouge and Alexandria. "I lucked out," he acknowledged. He was able to serve but also remain close to his community.[137] Upon leaving active duty, he moved back to the Bayou Blue settlement and lived with his parents while determining what to do next. Upon his return a group of Coushatta elders approached him and requested that he stay and help the tribe: "Several of the older people who inspired me and taught me about the ways of the Coushatta life were still around . . . And by that time I felt like I had some worldly views and [ideas about] outreach . . . I also had connections in the political world . . . So I thought maybe if I stayed, maybe I could . . . get something going . . . towards the re-recognition of the tribe and maybe getting the Department of Interior back on the scene . . . because we still had the same problems we had when I was a kid. Nothing had improved; nothing had changed. We still had the same poverty-stricken community." Sickey postponed pursuing a potential career outside of the community in order to reestablish himself within the tribe. It was a sacrifice he thought would be temporary. But he simply couldn't leave without attempting to use his skills and knowledge for the betterment of his people. "I have always been proud that the community never gave up and wandered off," Sickey shared. "They stayed together. They fought together. They died together, and they went to their graves hoping for a better day for [our] people. That really touched me."[138]

The years after the federal government severed ties to the tribe were difficult ones. Although the nation's economy was on an upswing, experiencing a post–World War II boom, the Coushattas had sunk into a deeper economic depression than in previous decades. Tribal unemployment rates remained high, and insufficient access to health care was the norm. The termination era became a critical point in the tribe's history, stirring a new sense of urgency to shape the next generation of leaders who would help reclaim lost services while navigating a legal system that historically had dismissed the Coushattas as a people on the margins.

4 Poor but Not Hopeless
Relentless Advocacy Efforts and the Opening of the First Tribal Enterprise, 1962–1969

We didn't have the resources. No one understood anything about
what was going on around them, even around the parishes . . .
because they were so concerned about how to even survive . . .
They were just worried about their next meal. It was very difficult.
—Ernest Sickey, November 16, 2015

"There is no single group of Americans whose distressed plight is more
real and visible than the Coushatta Indians," wrote journalist Elvin Reed
in a 1964 issue of the *Opelousas Daily World*. "This band of Indians lives
closely huddled together in the backland and waste of Allen Parish . . .
Their death rate is three times that of the United States at large." At a
time when the newspapers were generally flooded with coverage of the
war in Vietnam, the investigation into President Kennedy's assassination, and civil rights activities, stories about the Coushattas occasionally
appeared in Louisiana news. Their living conditions were described in
great detail to remind readers of "the hard facts of poverty in this so-
called rich land." A decade had passed since the Coushattas were cut
off from federal Indian services under the rationale that they would be
better off drawing aid almost exclusively from the state. Yet their situation continued to deteriorate, which was a point of deep frustration for

Davis Sickey, who had spent years working with parish and state officials to improve the economic outlook of his tribe. There simply weren't enough opportunities to make a difference. As a result, he told Reed that he was so frustrated with the situation that he was contemplating a move to Oklahoma "unless help for his people comes soon."[1]

Stintolihnoto, Naasok Konnaahotok
Working with What We Had

In the early 1960s Allen Parish's unemployment rate was among the highest in Louisiana.[2] The timber industry was the driving economic force, but it failed to fill the area's employment needs and progressively worsened as unsustainable logging practices caused a steady decline.[3] Within the Coushatta community the unemployment rate was as high as 50 percent, and many households lived on less than $2,000 a year.[4] Families cobbled together a living in a variety of ways. Solomon Battise, the Indian pastor and a World War II veteran, was among those who managed to find work in the timber industry. His son Leonard recalled how low his father's wages were and that although he supplemented them with disability checks, the family struggled.[5] Coushatta men who didn't work for timber companies took jobs where they could as welders, service station attendants, mechanics, and seasonal laborers on rice farms. Women and children also continued to contribute to family incomes by working in agriculture and selling baskets on roadsides and at fairs.[6] Since most members of the community had no transportation, they couldn't venture far from Allen Parish unless they chose to move farther away. Crystal Williams explained, for example, that her father, Rodney Williams, "moved to Houston for more opportunities. It was easier to get a job [there and] my dad was needing to work. [As] Houston evolved into more of a city . . . They moved to Livingston, [Texas]." Although the Williams family relocated in the early 1960s, they never severed their connection to the Bayou Blue community and frequently traveled back to southwestern Louisiana to visit relatives and stay informed about tribal issues.[7]

The Coushattas' conditions were further exacerbated by their isolation. During the wet season gravel roads were impassable. Neighboring communities also often used the location as a makeshift dump, and it was not uncommon to see rusted-out appliances in roadside ditches.[8] Indian families generally lived in small-framed houses, many of which were wrapped in tar paper and set off the ground to prevent flooding, and by 1959 only thirty-five of the roughly fifty Coushatta homes surveyed in Allen Parish had electricity.[9] All homes lacked plumbing, so families used outhouses and collected water from nearby wells. Darlene Langley Dunnehoo remembered how she and her siblings took turns collecting water from a neighbor's well. For her the task was an adventure because it required sneaking by the neighbor's geese and chickens, which chased anyone who came nearby. Although she laughed during the retelling, she recalled a day when she was about eleven years old and didn't quite make it to the well: "I remembered one [time] I went . . . to go get the water with two buckets in my hand. I went to the edge of the woods, but I could see the geese . . . So I stopped there and thought . . . 'I can't do it.' I turned back around [and] came back through the woods. I knew I was going to get in trouble or get sent back if I didn't have my water . . . But there was a pond, an old pond, a dirty pond, right between [the neighbors'] house and my house so I stopped right there, skimmed off the top of the dirty stuff and filled up my buckets and brought [them] home. [My family] never realized what I had done, and I never told anybody."[10]

Like her brothers and sisters, Dunnehoo contributed to the household in various ways. One of her primary chores was to help her mother, Loris Abbott Langley, an accomplished basket weaver, sort the longleaf pine needles needed to create baskets as well as bundle and dry them. Because baskets played a significant economic role in supporting the family, Loris often worked late into the night, using only a kerosene lamp for light (fig. 10).[11] Her grandson Eli Langley also described how she supported her family by driving a horse and buggy, transporting Coushatta children to the Indian school before the BIA withdrew funding.[12] Loris was the last person to hold this position, which paid a mere sixteen dollars a week, income that was not only intended to cover the transporting of children in the early-morning hours but also the upkeep of the horses and wagon.[13]

Fig. 10: Loris Abbott Langley and her children (from left to right), Darlene, Bertney, Bobby, Timmy, and Melissie, 1961. Courtesy of the Southwest Louisiana Photograph Collection, Archives and Special Collections Department, Frazar Memorial Library, McNeese State University.

Newspapers relished the opportunity to paint a picture of distress and hopelessness as they detailed the poor economic conditions of the tribe. One reporter claimed that Coushatta children were lethargic and malnourished and told of a starving community on the cusp of extinction.[14] While these types of descriptions made for interesting reading, it was a gross exaggeration. Yes, Coushattas were frustrated with their circumstances as Indians overlooked by the BIA, but they weren't without hope. Even Davis Sickey's threat about moving to Oklahoma was more a critique on the Coushattas' treatment than a sign of resignation.

Despite what observers assumed, Bertney Langley insisted that no matter how difficult things became, they were never at risk of starving because community members looked out for one another. "Everything was provided for us," he shared. "If we were hungry, we'd go fishing . . . My uncles would hunt and bring back game, and we'd have food. Sometimes, when they had to work, they'd work for some of these rice farmers around here, and . . . the rice farmers would give them milk and meat."[15] Government commodities further subsidized their diets. Ernest Sickey talked about how powdered milk, cheese, peanut butter, and boxes of raisins were sometimes distributed to impoverished families of Allen Parish. "They'd give it away in Oberlin, behind the courthouse on the fairgrounds," he said. "The Indians were like a parade going to Oberlin to pick up commodities."[16]

While the tribe's isolation created some economic barriers, it also was a strength that contributed to its cohesion and cultural maintenance. Everyone spoke Koasati, and there was little to distract children from learning from their elders. Langley recalled vivid details about his childhood in the 1950s and early 1960s: "Sometimes on winter nights we'd put wood in our wood stove and just sit there and my uncle, Bel Abbey, would tell us stories that were told by his grandmother. We call these stories 'rabbit tales.'" Abbey would frequently retell the same stories as a way of training young people to become storytellers themselves. "It made them learn the Coushatta language," Langley said. "It taught them what it meant to be a tribe, to be a people—how we are supposed to work together and how to respect the animals and the earth."[17]

There was great comfort that came with growing up in the Coushatta community, one that Ernest Sickey felt when he returned to his parents' home to finish his stint in the Air Force Reserves. The Sickeys were glad to have their son back. Davis, in particular, was eager to resume their routine road trips. "[Ernest] and his dad used to ride around, and they would go buy . . . RC Cola or something like that," recalled Barbara Langley. "I know they used to drive around the community and into different towns. They traveled together a lot."[18] One frequent stop was at St. Peter's Indian cemetery, where the Sickeys had buried several children who died in infancy. Ernest was particularly somber as he stood near the tiny graves: "I used to . . . see all kinds of little babies buried there [and asked] what caused that. [The elders] would say, 'Well it could be a bad cold.' They just died for hardly any reason because of lack of health care."[19] To compound matters, diabetes among older Coushattas was increasing. Preventable illnesses were the leading cause of death, and without intervention this trajectory was not likely to improve. Like Davis Sickey, other Coushatta elders also compared their level of health care to that of tribes in Oklahoma, and they lamented, "We should be getting the same thing."[20]

Bassi-tilka, Ittihaplitilkato
The War on Poverty

On January 27, 1963, Davis Sickey read his newspaper, as he had done every day, and was greeted by hopeful news.[21] Segments of a speech by President Lyndon B. Johnson were reprinted, outlining his antipoverty campaign and including a passage that spoke directly to Native people. Johnson had said "Indians suffer more from poverty than any other people . . . [and] the neglect of our Indian population is a disgrace." The president further explained that "Indian[s] would be in the forefront of his anti-poverty program."[22] This was the message Coushattas had longed to hear—one that offered a first inkling that the termination era mentality was falling into disfavor and that the old guard's power within the BIA was being decentralized.[23] The 1960s became what legal scholar Philip S. Deloria called "the Office of Economic Opportunity (OEO) decade." Following the passage of the Economic Opportunity Act (EOA) in 1964, "Indian Desks" were formed throughout federal departments so that funding streams came to Indians from multiple sources, paving the way for greater access to resources and providing opportunities for tribes to administer their own programs.[24] While this shift toward a more self-determining future for Indian people was a result of several coalescing factors—including the steady efforts of Native and non-Native activists—the Coushattas remained far removed from the conferences and position papers that influenced the Kennedy and Johnson administrations' perspectives on Indian affairs.[25] Nonetheless, the news generated a fresh surge of hope among the Coushattas. Not everyone shared this enthusiasm, however. Tribal leaders across the country responded differently, with some arguing that Johnson's position didn't go far enough to address the concerns of Indian people as distinct nations and, instead, favored a message that portrayed them as a homogeneous group of impoverished minorities.[26] In spite of such critiques, the Coushattas saw it as an opportunity, and soon several heads of families congregated to formulate a response, marking a renewed surge in the tribe's advocacy efforts. They wondered whether it was possible that they were being presented with a chance to rebuild their relationship with the federal government—one that had barely gotten off the ground in the first place.[27]

Together, Chief Martin Abbey and Davis Sickey devised a plan. After years of fostering and nurturing friendships locally, they wanted to expand their reach. To start, the two asked attorney Paul C. Tate for guidance in accessing the new federal programs. Tate practiced law in Mamou, located in Evangeline Parish east of the Coushatta settlement, and became a strategic partner to the tribe.[28] He was a fearless critic of political posturing and publicly demanded that Louisiana's elected officials remain accountable to their constituents. He was particularly vocal about his disdain for politicians who used segregation as a platform to secure popularity, such as Mississippi governor Ross Barnett, who, Tate argued, "sold the state of Mississippi out for personal gain" by orchestrating clashes around the segregation issue, just as Alabama governor George Wallace and Arkansas governor Orval Faubus did.[29] Tate's reputation and acquaintance with Coushattas whom he had invited to his ranch the previous year for a two-day Veterans Day fête, made him an ideal ally.[30] He also maintained an active agenda, including appointments on state and national committees and positions in civic, fraternal, and veterans' organizations. More important, however, he knew influential officials within the federal government, people such as R. Sargent Shriver Jr., director of the Peace Corps, a Kennedy in-law, and the director of the Johnson administration's antipoverty programs.[31] Following Tate's meeting with Abbey and Sickey, newspapers reported he had "assumed the responsibility and leadership to obtain help for the Coushatta Indians," prompting him to travel to Washington DC to meet with Shriver on their behalf. There was a great deal of pomp and circumstance surrounding this meeting. The Coushattas supplied Tate with gifts for Shriver, including a pine needle basket and blowgun, to express gratitude for considering their case. A newspaper even printed a picture of the meeting in which Tate and Shriver intently reviewed the tribe's petition for assistance. The petition outlined how the Coushattas' plight was a human rights issue because of their severe economic condition, which made them the quintessential "neglected" population that Johnson had addressed in his speech. Tate also shared that the Coushattas were not just Indians but American citizens entitled to preserve their identity and culture, something that could only be achieved with assistance in improving the quality of their lives.

Tate may have delivered the petition, but it was drafted by the Coushatta people themselves. They knew a solution to their situation was "not simple" but had hoped the new antipoverty programs could assist them in maintaining their school and developing tribal residential grounds. Plans to launch a tourism enterprise had been brewing since the early 1950s; however, the petition to Shriver provided the opportunity to formalize the tribe's intention to establish such an industry, along with a commercial market for their baskets. And although a copy of the document hasn't survived to the present, fragments of its contents were captured in newspapers, offering important insights into the Coushattas' evolving vision for their future.

Accounts indicate that Shriver was impressed by the Coushattas' petition and promised to send someone to study their situation.[32] For the first time in a long time, the tribe was hopeful that federal resources might reach them again. This optimism appeared justified, given that Indians nationwide had effectively leveraged opportunities presented by the EOA, but it soon became clear that matters wouldn't progress so easily.[33] Without a reservation or clear-cut legal tribal status, the Coushattas were not viewed as a distinct tribal community eligible for direct federal funding. Instead, they were seen as part of the larger population of Allen Parish, many of whose residents also lived in poverty. Within a year of Tate's trip to Washington DC, local civic leaders had created the Allen Action Agency, Inc., and conducted a study on the needs of the parish, counting the Coushatta people among the parish population. As expected, Allen Parish qualified for multiple EOA programs through the Louisiana Antipoverty Office. Some of these programs included

Head Start preschools, legal aid services, adult education classes, and a work-study program aimed at curbing steep high school dropout rates.[34]

Unfortunately, the Allen Action Agency failed to serve equally all the parish's residents who met eligibility requirements. This was a common complaint associated with other antipoverty programs across the state in which discriminatory practices reigned.[35] Although the tribe's low economic standing contributed greatly to Allen Parish qualifying for funding for its programs, Coushattas complained that they benefited very little. Ernest Sickey noted that "all of the statistics included the Indian people, but we never got a nickel out of it."[36] Dewith Carrier, a neighbor of the tribe, reaffirmed this position, stating, "They used [the tribe's] poverty to their advantage."[37] Tribal representatives even confronted members of the Allen Action Agency staff, who consistently remained unwilling to broaden their service scope to incorporate the tribal population. This was a betrayal, particularly considering the Coushattas' efforts to reach out to Shriver and the role they had played in alerting the surrounding community to the antipoverty programs in the first place.[38] This was yet another example of how the Coushattas' existence outside of the federal umbrella continued to pose challenges for them. They simply had to find another way.

Komistilkạ, At-hichaachilkatọ, Bayou Blue-ka-fạ Biniiliha-stillatọ
Promoting Distinctiveness and Bringing Tourism to Bayou Blue

Since his election in 1951, Chief Martin Abbey had contributed to the Coushattas' local visibility. Serving as tribal ambassador, he marched in parades and was an honored guest at various festivals, all while wearing a headdress and other "Indian-styled" regalia. His costume did not reflect Coushatta culture, but it certainly generated interest in the "Indians in the woods." By the mid-1960s, however, Abbey's fading health prevented him from being as active as he once was. He appeared in a wheelchair in a 1965 news photo, but he continued periodically to attend events throughout the state in the 1970s and 1980s. He died in 1991.[39] Throughout his time as chief, Abbey was not the only Coushatta to engage the public. Others also participated in local events and accepted invitations to speak in front of groups about their culture and history.[40] The 1960s marked a pronounced shift in the community's activities as the Coushattas increasingly embraced their cultural distinctiveness as a tool to generate support and lay the groundwork for economic stability.

The Boy Scouts further helped this development. Under the guidance of Tim Dugas, who had been a loyal ally of the tribe since the early 1950s, local scouting groups teamed up with the Louisiana Indian Hobbyist Association, a group of non-Indians dedicated to preserving Indian heritage as something uniquely American.[41] According to Philip J. Deloria in *Playing Indian*, there are two types of hobbyists: the "object hobbyists," who are interested in Indian artifacts and costumes as relics of a distant past; and "people hobbyists," who enjoy interacting with Indian people within an imagined "authentic" context.[42] The Louisiana Indian Hobbyists belonged to the second group. Members jumped at the opportunity to put on Indian programs, charging twenty-five cents for children and fifty cents for adults, featuring Boy Scouts performing "Indian dances in full costume." Coushattas were honored guests at these events, both to observe the displays and participate. The gatherings brought visitors to the area and raised awareness of the Coushattas' existence, with the proceeds from the programs being donated back to the tribe.[43] Although "playing Indian" was part of the Boy Scout experience, and therefore some might assume Coushattas received little actual benefit from participating, many in the tribe viewed it as a lucrative employment opportunity. Bel Abbey, in particular, participated in Boy Scout events throughout the 1950s and 1960s, staging "Indian dances" or the "mock saving of an Indian maiden" for the boys' enjoyment. While he knew such activities lacked authenticity, he also knew that Boy Scouts had resources and organizational capabilities that could help generate the needed publicity to jump-start a tribal tourism venture.

An Indian Princess contest was one outcome of Bel Abbey's partnership with the Boy Scouts. The first contest was in Lake Charles in 1961, a day Barbara Langley remembers well. She was wearing her best dress, one with purple flowers that her grandmother had bought her, for what she thought was to be a tribal picnic. Upon arrival she was directed to stand in a line with other Coushatta girls. "They said, 'We're going to pick a princess today.' They call[ed] us to move up front and back . . . I think it was the Boy Scouts that voted. They voted for me. I got to be the princess for that day. They had planned a boat ride for the princess and the others that were involved . . . [and] they gave me roses, a pretty bouquet of roses." The second year involved more planning and incorporated additional categories, such as interviews. The event was bigger and more publicized, so judging was conducted by prominent Lake Charles community leaders, who voted Langley as the winner for a second year. "This time," she recalled, "the mayor of Lake Charles presented me with the bouquet and my crown."[44]

The Indian Princess pageant gained momentum, becoming a much-anticipated public yearly event. In 1966 a carnival had grown up around it. Touted as the first "tri-racial event" in Lake Charles, it became a daring celebration of racial integration—a progressive move given resistance to the recent overturning of a 1914 Louisiana law outlawing racial integration at parks, circuses, and festivals. The Indian Day Festival featured not only Coushattas but the Tunicas from Marksville and the Alabamas and Coushattas from Texas. Attendees enjoyed concessions, entertainment, and sales of Indian-made items. The day culminated with the Coushatta pageant, and Caroleen LeJeune took the crown that year. In addition to successfully raising awareness of the Coushattas' presence in the area, the event also generated donations of clothing, shoes, and toys for the tribe.[45] Although Indian Princess contests waned as the years went on, only to be revived years later by the tribe, they were critical in generating Coushatta visibility and promoting public interest, placing pageant winners into roles as ambassadors and contributing to the tribe's early efforts to get its tourism endeavor off the ground.[46]

While Coushattas joined other Native people across the country in giving the public what they expected by embracing the vanishing people persona, they also increased the demand for Coushatta baskets. Weavers had been a common sight locally, selling baskets in the early decades of the century at roadsides and festivals.[47] The 1960s marked a turning point, however, when the community strategically leveraged its growing public Indian identity as a way of bringing its authentic Coushatta identity into focus. Pageants and staged "war dances" brought in curious crowds, which then allowed Coushatta weavers to showcase their talents through demonstrations that ultimately initiated sales. It gave them the exposure and support that they had previously lacked. In 1963 three Coushatta weavers were invited to the State Exhibit Museum in Shreveport to demonstrate their basket weaving skills for an audience in front of a television crew, who aired the demonstration on local stations.[48] The following year Coushatta weavers appeared at the annual Lake Charles Rodeo for the first time. The advertisement claimed their presence was a special feature since "the Koasati [were] one of the few remaining Indian tribes in the South."[49] Within months Coushattas received additional invitations to events as interest in their weaving grew and the baskets transitioned from items of curiosity to fine art. They were even invited to an Arts and Crafts Festival in 1964, which was attended by more than fifty painters, sculptors, and other artisans from a four-state area. The Coushattas were the only tribal community invited, and their baskets were among the specially featured items.[50] These opportunities encouraged weavers to become increasingly more creative, incorporating more decorative details and different materials, such as dyed raffia, and styling their baskets in the shapes of animals and handbags.[51]

For over a half-century the selling of baskets was a transient endeavor. Weavers shaped their lives around building inventories and traveling to a large range of events. But with families to care for and travel expenses to cover, it was not a sustainable practice. As a result, tribal leaders began to strategize how to attract customers and tourists to them, but this proved difficult, for the Bayou Blue community was hard to reach given substandard roads. By 1966, however, the situation began to change, when Allen and Jefferson Davis Parishes launched road projects, adding blacktop to existing gravel roads. These upgrades made the central segment of the Coushatta community more accessible to the public and helped improve the potential of establishing a tourism enterprise within the community.[52]

The tribe had to overcome several hurdles first. The main challenge was money. Two years had passed since Shriver received the Coushattas' petition for assistance from a federal antipoverty program, an opportunity that was usurped by the parish. As a result, Coushattas began looking beyond federal programs to fund the launching of a tribal enterprise. By this time Ernest Sickey had been home for several years. In 1965 he married Ena Mae Robinson, who was the daughter of Harry and Vera Robinson and came from the western portion of the Coushatta community, and the two settled into their own home near Sickey's parents. He had also acquired a full-time job in Lake Charles. Things were progressing well for him personally, but he continued to struggle with how he could best use his knowledge and skills for the tribe.[53]

It wasn't long before Sickey joined forces with Solomon Battise and Rosabel Sylestine to hatch a plan to open a store, called the "Trading Post," to sell baskets and other Coushatta-made art. Because the road improvements were made near the Indian Church and school, that seemed an ideal location. Also, it was determined that because the Coushattas lacked a legal status as an Indian tribe, the enterprise would have access to more funding if it were organized as a nonprofit, 501(c)3 endeavor, a path already taken by many non-reservation and terminated tribes.[54] Legal scholar Philip S. Deloria argues that to spur development, many tribes felt that the only choice was to embrace the awkwardness of state chartered tribal nonprofit corporations.[55] The Coushattas certainly saw it as their only viable option and, as a result, petitioned Louisiana for nonprofit status under the name "the Coushatta (Koasati) Indians of Louisiana, Inc."[56] Much like the Indian Church's governing board, the nonprofit organization created formal leadership positions, naming Solomon Battise president and Ernest Sickey vice president. Rosabel Sylestine was named secretary and treasurer, and Deo Langley, Davis Sickey, Nora Abbey, and Ruth Poncho were made board members. The tribe soon received a donated building for the Trading Post and convinced the Bel Estate to allow use of nearby property. The land, adjacent to the Indian Church, was offered to the Coushattas at no cost for ten years. This was a major turning point in the trajectory of the Coushattas' development and what Sickey described as their "first organizational effort."[57] While Chief Abbey retained his position and title, the new tribal enterprise created a dual governing framework and signaled the beginning of a gradual shift toward the current tribal council structure. For their efforts the Coushattas received great support from their neighbors, who gathered at the Indian Church to acknowledge the significance of the tribe's plan to launch a new venture. In July 1966 the Coushattas' nonprofit charter even made the front page of the *Opelousas Daily News*, further marking the historic occasion.[58]

In the weeks leading up to the Trading Post's opening, Coushattas worked diligently to get the building ready and made an inventory of baskets and other items to sell. Ernest Sickey focused his efforts on starting a public relations campaign to ensure its success. He wanted to send a clear message about the unique culture and identity of the Coushatta people that was reflected in their baskets and other art forms. "These baskets were made by the tribal people, which gave them an identity as great artisans, great basket-makers," Sickey said. "These were actual Coushatta baskets, not made in Taiwan or Japan." Their authenticity and beauty were already appreciated among a small circle of academics and collectors, but Sickey wanted to broaden the audience and transform this message into one that would have a larger impact. He started by asking the Louisiana Tourist Commission for an endorsement of the Trading Post, which it readily gave, before going on to promote it as the "first Indian trading post since frontier days [operated by] perhaps the last full-blooded tribe in this state."[59]

The Trading Post opened on February 1, 1967, and was run by volunteers from 1:00 to 4:00 p.m., Tuesdays through Fridays.[60] Sickey proudly shared with the newspapers that "tourists visiting the Trading Post will find that it is operated by the women of the tribe, who demonstrate fine basketry work right on the premises for those who have never seen the art of pine needle craft. Members of the tribe donate their time in an effort to reach a greater market for their baskets."[61] The Trading Post carried an assortment of items intended to appeal to curious tourists and "object hobbyists." It featured baskets and other Coushatta-made items, such as wood carvings, ornamental pieces made of pine cones, blowguns, dolls, and necklaces. However, to satisfy visitors looking for the "brand of Indian" they saw in western films, the Trading Post also stocked souvenir items, such as postcards with Coushattas posing in costumes and headdresses.[62] Ronnie Petree, a friend of the tribe who grew up in Elton, said many visitors came looking for "classic teepees," which prompted the tribe to build a massive teepee-like structure by the building's entrance. This landmark became a gathering point for Boy Scouts, Camp Fire Girls, and school groups that frequently met for field trips and events. Coushatta hosts, such as Solomon Battise or Chief Martin Abbey, greeted guests and shared stories or told of the tribe's history.[63] It was a delicate dance between fiction and reality. Tribal leaders felt it necessary to emulate similar efforts of other tribes, such as the Seminoles of Florida or the Cherokees of North Carolina, by selling a commercial form of "Indianness" to ensure a steady stream of visitors.[64] They saw it as the only way to protect Coushatta culture and traditions. "What we had [was] very special," said Sickey. "[We were] determined to protect it and . . . to help preserve it."[65]

After the Trading Post opened, it continued to get prominent coverage in newspapers, advertised more than 150 times between 1967 and 1971.[66] It hosted visitors from across the United States and from as far away as Thailand. In December 1968 Coushatta weavers had received such acclaim for their skills that they were invited to display sample pine needle baskets at the Smithsonian Institute in Washington DC.[67] Demand for Coushatta baskets became so great that the Alabama-Coushatta Reservation gift shop in Texas, which opened in 1965, purchased them from the Trading Post for resale in its own gift shop. In 1970 it made an unprecedented request for one thousand small pine needle baskets, the largest order the Trading Post had received; it took the daily labor of twenty weavers for three months to fill the order.[68]

The Coushatta Trading Post's success not only boosted the tribe's economic situation; it also impacted the surrounding area. For years Elton had searched for ways to leverage its proximity to the Coushattas, so the town's residents were excited about the possibilities the Trading Post brought. The timing was particularly significant given that in 1965 the town was in the midst of a transition. That year the Voting Rights Act was passed, paving the way for African Americans to enjoy the same franchise rights that whites and Coushattas already enjoyed.[69] Also that year, a federal district court ruled that African Americans be integrated into the Elton public schools, which brought African American, white, and Indian students together in the same schools for the first time.[70] Although similar rulings incited violence, boycotts, and other extreme measures in places such as New Orleans, resistance to desegregation was much more subtle in Elton.[71] According to Sickey, the most visible repercussion of school integration was when Elton High School closed its band program down because white parents and school officials "[didn't] want black people in the band."[72] Whether the level of resistance resembled that of other areas of the state, there is no denying that Elton underwent a social evolution during this period. As the status quo was disrupted, the Coushattas' tourism venture helped remake the town's identity. Suddenly Elton became an actual destination spot and not just a place that motorists passed through. Earlier efforts to capitalize on the tribe's distinctiveness were ramped up as the Trading Post became a popular draw for school groups and those looking to satisfy their curiosity from all over the state.[73] More broadly, the Trading Post contributed to a growing emphasis on Louisiana's identity as home to Indigenous peoples. "No matter where you go in the state, you'll find evidence that the red man was here first," printed one newspaper in 1969. The article featured a long list of place names in Louisiana with Native roots and even encouraged readers to visit tribal communities "scattered here and yon throughout the state."[74] Residents of Elton enjoyed the frequent mentions they received because of their Coushatta neighbors, and the town's elementary and high schools adopted generic "Indian" mascots to draw additional attention to their connections to the tribe.

Because of the publicity the tribe received, a group of Creeks who were loosely unified across Alabama, Georgia, and Florida, learned about the Coushattas in the late 1960s. Sickey recalled his surprise upon receiving a letter announcing an upcoming visit by Creek representatives. The group, the Creek Nation East of the Mississippi, Inc., was endeavoring to bring the scattered descendants of the former Creek Confederacy together. Knowing the Coushattas were once part of the Confederacy, six Creek representatives traveled to Louisiana to ask Coushatta leaders about their willingness to cooperate in unifying efforts. "They were trying to get recognition," Sickey explained. "They had no idea where to start [and] they were getting a lot of backlash from the people in the state of Alabama." Although the Coushattas opted not to join the Creek unification movement, wishing instead to focus on their own independent efforts, they supported the mission. Sickey remained an ally and consultant to what later developed into the Poarch Band of Creek Indians, a fragment of the original group, which became federally recognized in 1984 and whose members reside in Alabama.[75]

The Coushatta Trading Post had several dedicated boosters and patrons. Eloise M. Fruge of Lake Charles, for example, published a letter in the *Lake Charles American Press* in 1967 encouraging people to make the trip to Elton to "lend moral support to our Indians" by purchasing a basket or touring the Indian school.[76] Hosea Herbert from Basile also contributed, donating funds to the Trading Post and writing to the Indian Arts and Crafts Board, which was administered by the U.S. Department of Interior, requesting support for the tribe's efforts.[77] The coverage in the *Opelousas Daily World* was perhaps the most effective means of generating support. It ran stories such as one asking why "many Louisianans will go out west to see some Indians when we have Indians right here in southwest Louisiana." The paper noted that "invariably, after a story about the Elton Indians is published, we get scads of telephone calls asking how to get to the settlement. Once there was a campaign to get articles of winter clothing for poorer members of the tribe. Judging from the phone calls we got about this, Opelousas area people responded most generously."[78]

The portrayal of Coushattas as a neglected people was effective, making them one of the area's most popular charitable recipients of books and used clothing. Assisting the tribe even became a "special project" for several civic and religious-based groups, such as the Lion's Club and the Women's Society for Christian Service.[79] Schools also held charity drives, culminating in field trips in which students personally delivered packages of goods so they could meet, according to one newspaper, "real live Indians."[80] While the tribe benefited from the donations it received, Coushatta leaders questioned whether this support was enough to address the tribe's actual needs. They had their own vision about what they wanted for their future but just needed the opportunity to implement it in their own way and on their own terms.

Naksofon Stamaahilkaahi̱? Himaak Stamaahilkaak
Naksaamin Komaatik Ho-aalo̱
Where to Begin? Taking the First Steps in Implementing the Tribal Vision

Since his return to the community, Ernest Sickey had been urged to do more to help the tribe. The Trading Post was a promising start in addressing poverty, but the tribe's needs far exceeded what the small operation could provide. The community needed to improve its members' quality of life and build a future for the next generation. By the late 1960s Sickey realized he would not return to college or follow a career in broadcasting or the air force. He made the decision, definitively, to put all his energy into continuing the work of his father, Davis, Jeff and Martin Abbey, and other Coushattas before them who had fought for the community's survival. The problem was that he didn't know where to start.[81]

Sickey did what he had seen others do throughout his childhood; he went to the elders for insight. They were, as he described, "the people who kept the tribe together. The people who kept the culture and the history and the tradition together . . . in spite of all of the tragedies, in spite of all the oppression." Sickey wished to take on the role of translator and facilitator of the elders' vision. "In listening to the older people talking about how we can help ourselves," he remembered, "that gave me inspiration to say . . . 'We should build our own community, with our own people . . . [with] what little bit of resources we had. We can build on that . . . We don't have to be influenced by outsiders. We don't have to be told that this is what you need to do because we're the only ones who know what our conditions are, we're the only ones that can fix what our problems are if we work together.'"[82] The charge to be self-sufficient and for the tribe to take control of its own development was a powerful message. As Coushattas became among the most popular recipients of charitable donations in the area, the elders became increasingly concerned about the broader implications of such an arrangement. There had to be a balance. There had to be a way to maintain these relationships while still exercising self-advocacy aimed at addressing all areas of the Coushattas' needs.

Sickey worked closely with Solomon Battise, who ran both the Trading Post and Indian Church, to develop a strategy for the tribe's next move. "People like Solomon," Sickey said, "were very encouraging to me about what we should be doing. I looked to him as a leader in [the] community." He also saw Battise as a friend that he "could call upon because of his knowledge of history, traditions, and the values that he was promoting." Leonard Battise spoke about this friendship, remembering that his father and Sickey were "inseparable." Sickey "would come ask my daddy [his] opinion [on different issues]," he recalled. While the Coushatta pastor played a key role in guiding him, he wasn't Sickey's only mentor. Sickey also consulted others who represented different clans and who trusted his emerging leadership. Sickey explained: "It was an art to work with every family in the community . . . I would hold community meetings at the church to bring them up to date because we [didn't] have any place to meet. It gave the community an opportunity to ask questions and be informed. Afterward, because they were shy or afraid to ask questions, I would say, 'Come to my house and let's talk.'"[83] He found himself in a position of great responsibility during a time of transition in the tribe's developmental journey. His education, paired with his insight into how different levels of government worked, uniquely situated him to traverse different institutional and organizational spheres. Previous Coushatta leaders and advocates had built a foundation from which Sickey was able to work, leaving him a rich inheritance. But because times had changed, he had to tread into unknown territory and incorporate additional resources and strategies into his efforts.

With an overwhelming list of needs to contend with, Sickey began with the communication challenges facing the tribe. While electricity had reached Coushatta homes by the mid-1960s, telephone services had not, and this lack of access contributed to their continued isolation. It also slowed business at the Trading Post, making it difficult to receive orders or schedule school groups. Previously, Coushattas working or traveling away from home had relayed messages to their families by calling Pastor Johnson's home, but the system soon became problematic.[84] As a first step in addressing this need, Sickey called the closest phone company in the town of Welsh but soon learned that getting service for the Coushattas wouldn't be an easy process: "They put me off [and] gave me the run-around, [saying,] 'Not many people [have phone lines out that way]. We have to have so many people on the line to get service down there.'" Sickey then went around the community asking different families about whether they could afford a phone line at approximately five dollars a month. A few families, including his own, agreed to have one installed in order to compel the phone company to service the area. However, it still wasn't enough to entice the phone company. As a result, a determined Sickey reached out to one of his father's longtime friends, the politically powerful man for whom he was named, former senator Ernest Clements. Clements was at the time the Louisiana public service commissioner for the area, and Sickey had maintained a relationship with him since childhood, frequently making social calls to his office in Oberlin. This time, however, Sickey intended to take Clements up on his repeated offer to come see him if he ever needed anything and told him about the struggle with the phone company; as expected, all it took was one phone call from Clements to the manager of the phone company. "The next day," Sickey said, "I had people in my yard [installing the line]." Phone lines were installed in a handful of Coushatta homes as well as two at the Trading Post: one inside to conduct business and a pay phone outside of the building. As the primary community gathering point, the Trading Post pay phone received a lot of traffic. "That was a very, very busy pay phone," Sickey recalled. "Even the white people in that community didn't have phones . . . At two or three in the morning you'd see a family talking on the phone . . . Logging companies [and] oil field people . . . would stop and use that phone . . . [Even] farmers . . . would come and use the phone." Soon the Coushattas were able to profit from this traffic when the Trading Post began selling snacks and sodas.[85]

With phone services installed, Sickey and Battise looked to further develop the Trading Post (fig. 11). They collaborated, each tackling different challenges. Sickey set his sights on persuading the Allen Action Agency to share its resources with the tribe by granting access to funds provided by the National Youth Corps Program. Since the Trading Post was run by volunteers, the hope was to create a paid position for a

Fig. 11: Solomon Battise stands in the doorway of the Trading Post as two weavers, Adeline Battise (in sweater) and Lycia John, work on sewing baskets. The payphone on the side of the building was among the first telephones to be installed in the community, c. 1970. Courtesy of the Coushatta Tribal Archives.

tribal member. Although the job placements through this program were generally with schools, hospitals, libraries, and other public facilities, the tribe managed to gain funding for a position in the Trading Post. In 1967 Caroleen LeJeune, the previous year's Coushatta Princess winner, was hired to manage the Trading Post for thirty-two hours a week while she also attended night school.[86] While Sickey worked on tapping into funding through the local agency, Battise focused on his own initiative. As the president of the Coushatta (Koasati) Indians of Louisiana, Inc., he wanted the Trading Post to be more than a place for tribal weavers and artisans to sell their work. He wanted it to be a community hub to educate the younger generations. Being near the Indian Church and school, it was already the heartbeat of the community that brought together Coushattas from across the settlement. As a church leader, Battise promoted and preserved the Koasati language, and he wished for the Trading Post to serve a similar function for the Coushattas' material culture. So, just months after opening the facility, he expanded it to serve as more than just a store when he incorporated displays to showcase historical items. Battise wanted to educate the public as well as younger Coushattas about the tribe's long tradition of creating art and handicrafts. He gathered vintage baskets sewn by previous generations of weavers and other items contributed by the community. He also wanted to reclaim significant historical items that had left the tribe, and in 1968 he negotiated with a local white family for the return of an old bow and arrow made by George Abbey (brother of Chief Jeff Abbey) that had been given to the family in the 1920s. Battise invited newspapers to report on the repatriation effort, using the opportunity to make a wider public plea for the return of other significant items to the tribe.[87]

The Trading Post's success wasn't measured solely by sales and number of visitors. It also had value in preserving culture and traditions among the younger Coushattas. Sustaining the community meant raising a new generation of weavers and storytellers. The Trading Post provided teaching and mentorship opportunities for elders to pass on knowledge and help younger Coushattas develop skills and talents in what was described as "open air classes under the shade of tall pines."[88] It was also where people from other tribes taught workshops to help the Coushattas revive different art forms, such as beadwork and cane weaving. Without the resources to cover travel expenses for workshop teachers, Sickey researched different funding sources and tried grant writing for the first time. Quickly developing his skill in this area, he secured a small grant from the Louisiana Office of Tourism and a few others from local foundations connected to Louisiana's oil and gas industry.[89] This funding fueled the crafts program, while Sickey refined his message, expanding beyond an economic needs-based approach to promote tourism to one emphasizing the community's educational need to retain and enrich its culture. The Coushattas had much to share, yet they also had much to lose. Inviting Native artisans from other southern communities, Sickey posited, was one way to reinforce and expand Coushatta knowledge and practices. His argument was convincing, and in 1968 the Louisiana Department of Education funded a five-day workshop at the Trading Post, paying the travel expenses of Elsie Jim, a Choctaw weaver and member of the Choctaw Craft Association of Mississippi. Coushattas eagerly awaited her arrival, and the workshops were well attended. The event's success led to several subsequent workshops conducted by Mississippi Choctaw weavers, who found a welcoming host in Daisy Sickey who enjoyed conversing with them in Choctaw, the language of her mother. The workshops drew Coushattas from across the settlement to learn techniques for creating new items to sell in the Trading Post and further supplement their families' incomes.[90]

Faikilkot, Intohnoot, Nas-hahpoot Akostiniichit, Kobassitik Stamaahilkato
Tribal Advocacy Work: Creative Solutions and Sacrifices

Writing grants for the Trading Post was just the beginning. Armed with ideas shared by people from all over the community about the tribe's needs, Sickey made regular trips to libraries in Jennings and Lake Charles to study foundation directories. He focused on organizations with missions that looked most likely to support grant proposals from the Coushattas. "I would come back loaded with a legal pad [full] of addresses and then I would sit . . . all night writing to them or calling them and getting their guidelines and application packages." He also carefully studied contribution patterns of religious organizations, looking for those that raised funds specifically for Native populations. Although the Coushatta Indian Church was Congregationalist, Sickey expanded the scope of his search and investigated opportunities from the Presbyterians, Episcopalians, Methodists, and Catholics. As the state's dominant religion, the Catholic Church seemed the most promising. One day he walked into a nearby church and asked to speak to a priest. The priest was gracious and expressed support of the tribe, suggesting that Sickey subscribe to the Bureau of Catholic and Indian Missions newsletter to learn more about funding opportunities on a national scale. The priest also shared how the local diocese organized an annual collection earmarked for Indian communities and guided Sickey on how to apply for funding. Over the years the tribe received small grants from the diocese, encouraging him to continue searching for funding and support from a variety of sources as he pushed on in his advocacy efforts.[91]

And push he did. The more Sickey learned about potential funding opportunities, the longer his list of tasks grew. In any given week he researched dozens of grants and spoke with even more people. Grant writing was a new skill he worked to develop, and he relied on his background in communication and his lifelong interest in writing to help him progress in this area. Outreach and alliance building, on the other hand, was something he already knew well. He had been trained in it since first crafting a letter to Senator Ellender at the age of eight. He had witnessed many of his elders, particularly his father, do it time and time again since he was old enough to understand. Sickey's childhood was unlike anyone else's in the area, Indian or non-Indian. While many children of his generation spent most of their free time in the woods or swimming in the bayous, a large portion of his youth was spent by his father's side at court hearings, legislative sessions, or lectures given at law conferences. These experiences cultivated in him a deep understanding of how government worked at different levels, so he didn't enter into his tribal advocacy work naively. He knew things would not be easy.

The Coushatta people have always united in times of need, and Sickey knew he could count on this sense of commitment. "He would find people who had special talents" and ask for assistance, said Bertney Langley.[92] Early on, Sickey needed help typing letters to foundations and politicians. He approached Darlene Langley Dunnehoo, who was known for her typing skills. "He came to the house [and] asked if I could type up some papers," she recalled. "So, I said, 'Well, if he wants me to do it, if he has confidence in me to do it, I'll do it.' He brought me a typewriter . . . and a [large] stack [of handwritten papers to type] . . . so I would stay up late at night, and I got it [done] . . . I don't know how many papers it was . . . I know that [they were addressed] to [state] representatives and people like that . . . At that time there was no mention of pay, which was okay. I was just willing to help him. Later on . . . he found a grant to pay me . . . It was very early [on, when] there was nothing. There were no offices. There was nothing."[93] While Dunnehoo diligently typed late into the night, Sickey also worked at home in the evenings after long days at his paid job. This arrangement grew increasingly more difficult, for as the stacks of paper grew, so did the Sickey family. The first of his six sons was born in 1969.[94]

Eager to find an office to call his own, Sickey had to be resourceful. Along CC Bel Road, just past a clearing and behind some refinery equipment, was a square office building nearly camouflaged from roadside view. This was where he established his first office, where he spent many nights hunched over stacks of paper until well past midnight, writing grant proposals and letters seeking financial and political support for the Coushattas. After working late into the night, he shared, "I drove home [to] get up at four fifteen . . . and go to Lake Charles again to go to work. That was my life."

In its heyday the office was part of the bustling refinery station operated by Bel Oil Company. Located just up the gravel road from where Sickey grew up and where he continued to live with his own family, he spent a lot of time there. As a child, it is where he practiced his English with the workers and earned money mowing the grass. Although no longer functioning around the clock as it once did, the refinery was still operational when he moved back into the community to finish his tenure in the U.S. Air Force Reserves and, later, to dedicate himself to tribal advocacy work. But because it was then only open during the day, he thought that perhaps the company might allow him to use the office at night. Luckily, given his history with the refinery and the friendships he maintained there, the owner agreed and gave him the key to the building. Sickey worked nights and on weekends in that office for several years. He did the hard work that, he admitted, not all of the tribe understood, and he found himself lonely at times. "I was [doing it] for the tribe, [but sometimes] I would get so frustrated," he stated. There were occasions when Coushattas would drive by late at night and blow their horns when they saw the lights on in the office. "They [were] probably out . . . having a good time," Sickey recalled, "[and] I would think oftentimes, 'Why am I doing this?'" However, as if to prevent him from giving up, the lights also attracted visitors from the tribe, who stopped in to offer their encouragement and support for his efforts.[95]

As necessary as the support from the broader community was, Sickey could not have engaged in this type of work if it wasn't for the sacrifices of his wife, Ena Mae. She took care of the household and raised their children while Sickey was, as one of his sons put it, "in the trenches" working on behalf of the tribe.[96] "I gave everything I had," Ernest stated. "I spent thousands and thousands of dollars of my own money doing the things that I needed to do to get the tribe going . . . I gave it all: my life, my health, my finances. Everything that I had went to the tribe in those days." Sickey's dedication also meant that Ena Mae had to be resourceful, a quality that she had developed as a child who grew up in a very different situation than her husband (fig. 12). "She had a rough life," Sickey stated. Her mother died when she was nine years old, and her father left the children and moved to Texas. David Sickey continued telling his mother's story, sharing that "she raised her siblings in the woods in a shack with rotting floors and rain coming through the roof. Scrounging the woods for food . . . she grew up with literally nothing . . . her inner strength came from [that] . . . adversity in her early childhood. I think that sustained her [while my dad was gone]."[97]

And Ernest was gone a lot. He worked two full-time jobs, one paid and one unpaid. Through his paid work he brought in a steady income, working for different companies throughout the region in various

Fig. 12: Ernest and Ena Mae Sickey with sons, Durwin, Kevin, and Brock (listed from oldest to youngest), early 1970s. Image from Princeton University, William Byler Collection. Photograph by Sam Guillory.

administrative roles. Given the unemployment rate in the area, he thought of himself as fortunate to be able to provide for his family. Their basic needs were always met; however, any surplus in their household budget went directly to his tribal advocacy work. He paid for paper, postage, and other office supplies out of his own pocket. As the years went on and his commitment intensified, so did his mounting travel expenses. He began doing more than writing letters, regularly traveling throughout the state and even to Washington DC and New York.[98] In some instances he drove his own car, but more often, he was spotted catching a bus to his next destination. Linda Langley shared, "Do you know how many people have told me over the years . . . 'I would see Ernest catch the bus.

I didn't know what he was doing . . . [but I] would give him a quarter.' This was big money to them."[99] The willingness of many Coushattas to support Sickey's travels, even without knowing just where he was going or what he was planning to do, speaks to their confidence that he was working to carry out the tribe's vision.

The 1960s was a transitional decade for the Coushatta people. While the rhetoric and intentions behind the termination policy gradually fell into disfavor and tribes across the nation enjoyed the impact of the Great Society programs, the Coushattas still found themselves unable to benefit from federal funding earmarked for Indians. They even faced challenges accessing resources made available to the nation's impoverished communities when Allen Parish became the gatekeeper of the area's programs. Although blocked at every turn, the Coushattas didn't allow their self-advocacy efforts to be stalled. Instead, they maneuvered their way through the politics of poverty within Louisiana, working outside the federal system by leveraging the resources they had: their friendships and marketable distinctiveness as Indigenous people. They followed a similar trajectory of other tribes across the country whose situation, for one reason or another, disqualified them from federal funding unless they formed as nonprofit corporations chartered by their respective states. The Coushatta (Koasati) Indians of Louisiana, Inc., helped launch the Trading Post as the first tribal enterprise to develop a formal market for the sale of baskets and other tribal-made items, provide the platform for the Coushattas to jump-start tourism, create opportunities for youth to learn and engage in cultural art forms, and lay the groundwork for an emerging tribal infrastructure. There were still many struggles ahead, but the Coushatta people were committed, and their efforts would pay off in the first years of the next decade.

5

An Unusual Road to Recognition
Uncovering Administrative Oversights and Drawing Louisiana into Indian Affairs, 1969–1973

Because he dreamed of better things for his people, a young Coushatta Indian has become the first of his race in Louisiana's history to take part in planning Indian affairs at the governmental level.
—"Coushatta Indian Named to Governmental
   Agency," *Shreveport Times*, July 12, 1972

In the early 1970s the Bel Oil station office north of Elton grew progressively vacant an increasing number of nights. The facility had become Ernest Sickey's twilight base camp for tribal advocacy work long after the refinery workers clocked out for the day. But the light emanating from the office within the darkness of the woods, a sight that Coushattas living in the eastern part of the community had grown accustomed to seeing, had frequently been off. Those who didn't know otherwise may have thought Sickey's absence a sign of discouragement or retreat from efforts to improve the tribe's living conditions. Those who knew better, however, were aware that he had taken his work directly to the offices of legislators, lawyers, and Indian advocacy organizations. He drove across Louisiana and temporarily traded his typewriter for a suitcase as he endured long bus rides to Washington DC and New York.

Letters and phone calls to procure small grants or lobby legislators were tedious and on their own didn't yield the results the tribe had hoped for. Sickey made headway, but it wasn't enough. As a result, he once again sought guidance from elders in the community, who encouraged him to take a more aggressive approach, one that focused exclusively on getting the Coushattas back onto the federal government's radar.[1] At this point it had been nearly twenty years since the government had unilaterally withdrawn federal Indian services. Since then, times had changed. Civil rights activities had created reforms on a national level, and southern legislators felt tremendous pressure either to ardently defend positions that had been deemed "outdated" or to build careers on platforms of racial equality and social justice. In addition, the nationwide visibility of Indian activists, along with a critical reassessment of federal Indian policy, indicated that new opportunities for Coushattas were on the horizon.

Nashahpạ Komponaak, Stintoliinolahọ
Leveraging the Changing Tide in Federal-Indian Relations

On July 8, 1970, President Nixon issued a statement asking Congress to address "the historic and legal relationship between the Federal government and Indian communities" that had been "oscillating between two equally harsh and unacceptable extremes": paternalism and termination. Nixon's request echoed concerns of the Johnson administration but adopted language that was less about addressing poverty through managing Indian affairs and instead encouraged support of Indians to identify their own needs and respond accordingly.[2] Delivered amid mounting pressure from Indian activists, ranging from moderate to radical in their demands and actions, Nixon's message both reflected and contributed to the evolution of Indian policy toward supporting tribal self-determination. As a result, over the next several years a series of bills were enacted reinstating tribal lands across the country.[3] Then, in 1973, the Menominee Restoration Act marked what many deemed the official end of the termination era, when the Menominee tribe's status was restored after nineteen years. These targeted pieces of legislation culminated in the 1975 Indian Self-Determination and

Education Assistance Act, which set a new course in Indian affairs and paved the way for the development or redevelopment of tribal nations.

Within months of Nixon's speech, the Coushattas took strategic action in accelerating their efforts to lobby the federal government to reinstate them as a recognized tribe. To do this, they sought support from two important sources. First, they met with a few other Louisiana tribes to discuss the potential of fostering intertribal relationships among the state's unrecognized tribes. Meeting in Baton Rouge, tribal leaders talked about how they might help one another by opening up channels of communication and putting an end to tribal isolation.[4] Next, the Coushattas looked to address their strained relationship with the Allen Action Agency, which had consistently overlooked the tribe for locally administered services since its inception. Sickey was intent on convincing the agency's staff to use their authority to advocate for the tribe, giving the Coushattas' case more validity.[5]

In a demonstration of goodwill, the Allen Action Agency's director, R. E. Weatherford, agreed to leverage his position by writing to the federal Indian Health Services (IHS) office, asking for sanitation services for the Coushatta people. "Most of these people are of a very low income bracket," he wrote. "We find that many are without water wells or bathrooms, and do not possess the finances to obtain these necessities. This tribe does not live on an Indian Reservation, so therefore, they do not receive funds from the Federal Government as many other American Indians do." To reinforce his point, Weatherford attached a list of twenty-seven Coushatta households and their monthly incomes, which averaged $147 a month.[6] As the tribe had hoped, Weatherford's letter soon prompted an investigation into their status, reviving a case that had been buried for decades and generating a flurry of correspondence between agencies seeking clarity on the claim's legitimacy. A representative from the IHS even made a trip to the Bayou Blue community to spend a few days with the tribe to see for himself whether the Coushattas were really Indian people, as Weatherford had claimed. Sickey recalled that "he was impressed with who we were and . . . said, 'Maybe in due time [the BIA] will do something but, meanwhile, I am going back and telling my superiors that you are, indeed, a tribe qualified to receive health services.'"[7] A review of the Coushattas' history proved they had previously received BIA services, which qualified them for IHS programs under new, broadened policies.[8] A more thorough investigation, headed by BIA commissioner Ernest Stevens, supported this conclusion. Stevens wrote that although all federal aid had ceased by 1953, "there is no Federal Act either specifically terminating the special relationship which exists between this Indian group and the Federal Government or prohibiting special Federal services to the Coushattas." As a result, he recommended that "in the absence of such legislation, and in consideration of the possibility of a treaty relationship," aid should be reinstated. The tribe was assured that it would be placed back into the IHS budget.[9] This was the outcome the Coushattas had hoped for, with the anticipation that full federal reinstatement would easily follow. It soon became apparent, however, that this wasn't going to be the case, nor was the IHS funding going to be released so readily.

In November 1970 the first needs assessment report in decades was conducted in the Coushatta community. The Office of Environmental Health reported on the tribe's living conditions, examining thirty-eight of the forty-four identified Coushatta homes in Allen Parish, and determined that they were in great need of assistance since they were "very small and in an advanced state of deterioration." In spite of this finding, however, the conclusion of the report was noncommittal and its summary vague. Although it acknowledged need, it didn't outline a plan for future services or make a commitment to the tribe. Instead, it issued the suggestion that the Coushattas should establish a more concrete definition as "a legal entity within the State."[10] A few months later the BIA reinforced this suggestion, telling the Louisiana district attorney, "It would be at least presumptuous for this Bureau to suggest any means that the State of Louisiana might employ in recognizing the group . . . we merely wish to say that the Federal Government could have no objection to such recognition."[11] This carefully worded statement was interpreted as an invitation to the state to get involved in Indian affairs. It also served as a point of encouragement to the tribe that the state could provide a pathway to federal acknowledgment. The challenge was that there was no precedent, for Louisiana had had little formal contact with its Native populations since the colonial period.[12]

If the Coushattas were to follow this path in reaching out to the Louisiana government to initiate the first tribal-state relationship, they would need legal assistance. So, they drew from the local resources they had available and sought the help of J. Daniel Rivette, the former attorney for the town of Elton. Rivette was from Mamou, where Paul C. Tate practiced law and had worked with the Coushattas in the early 1960s. Rivette had long been aware of the tribe's presence in Allen Parish. By 1971 he was a staff attorney for the Southwest Louisiana Legal Service, Inc., a nonprofit organization created in 1966 to assist low-income residents with civil legal issues, which was an ideal situation for the Coushattas.[13] Without the benefit of an example to look to, Rivette drafted a bill to present to the Louisiana legislature that would extend state recognition to the Coushatta tribe; however, his approach didn't take the tribe's wishes into account. Instead, it focused on the concerns he anticipated legislators might have, particularly the fear of losing jurisdiction over Coushatta people and potential legal entanglements between the tribe and federal government that would complicate matters for the state. As a result, the draft legislation downplayed tribal sovereignty, explicitly empowering the state with "jurisdiction . . . over the people of the Coushatta Indian Tribe."[14] Rivette's strategy to reassure Louisiana legislators wasn't what the Coushattas intended to put forward, so they never submitted the bill. The stakes were too high. The tribe wished to represent the case on its own terms and with transparency about its intentions to seek state support to further its goal of being federally reinstated. To accurately represent the tribe's intentions, Sickey determined that it was time to seek new assistance, and he knew precisely where to turn.

Komoklahą, Hahpą Komawiichihą, Ittoiyat Intolihn
Old Friends, New Allies, and the Art of Political Persuasion

Sickey called two of the most politically connected people he knew: his father's longtime friends Judge Minos D. Miller and his wife, Ruth Loyd Miller. Judge Miller had previously worked closely with Davis Sickey to help the Coushatta people with local legal matters. Ruth, who in 1957 became the fifty-second woman admitted to the Louisiana Bar Association, was deeply committed to social justice and lent her wisdom and political connections to the mission Ernest presented them with. "She just jumped right in with both feet," he recalled.[15] Miller's interest in helping underserved populations, up to that point, had focused on gender inequality in the courts, sports, and labor. She soon expanded her focus to incorporate Indian affairs and later claimed she found herself "spending more time on Indian affairs than on [her] law practice."[16]

Sickey was impressed by the intensity of Ruth's commitment, and the Millers' home in Jennings quickly became like a second home to him. At the end of the workday, Sickey often spent a few hours strategizing with Ruth. He dined there and even spent a few nights on their couch. Later he brought his sons to the Millers' home to play in their den while he and Ruth met. "We were determined to make something happen," Sickey said. Together, they generated a list of potential political alliances at all levels within Louisiana. To her this simply meant a few phone calls to friends and acquaintances. As someone heavily involved in the Democratic Party of Louisiana, she was well positioned to raise the Coushattas' profile among the state's most powerful figures. Miller arranged meetings for Sickey with people such as Allen J. Ellender (state representative, 1932–36, and U.S. senator, 1937–72), Russell B. Long (U.S. senator, 1948–87), Bennett Johnston Jr. (state representative, 1964–68, state senator, 1968–72, and U.S. senator, 1972–97), and John Breaux (U.S. representative, 1972–87, and U.S. senator, 1987–2005). This group was a combination of Louisiana's old political guard and a new generation of legislators who emerged on the scene to tackle the state's challenges with a fresh outlook. Although Sickey had already corresponded with many of these men on his own, Miller brought him a new level of exposure. With Senator Long, the son of former Governor Huey Long, she took matters a step further than a mere phone call and invited him to her home for a private meeting. Sickey recalled her directness in telling the senator: "You need to support this tribe. You need to support . . . legislation to get them recognized."[17] Long had previously shown a willingness to engage the state's tribes when he backed the Tunicas' unsuccessful attempt to gain federal recognition in the early 1950s.[18] Senators Long and Ellender also had histories of supporting the Allen Action Agency's antipoverty programs, so they were keenly aware of the economic struggles of the area's residents.[19] It didn't take much convincing to entice them to extend support to the Coushattas' efforts. Miller's outreach produced commitments for support from additional influential people in the state. "People respected her," Sickey said. "If she called somebody, they better call her back."[20]

Miller also lobbied business leaders to assist the Coushattas. The oil and gas industry was the state's major economic driver, so this seemed like a logical place to start. Plus, the Millers were themselves involved in this industry. Ruth was on the State Mineral Board, which gave her access to many industry executives.[21] To further build alliances, Miller and Sickey turned to the oil company that held the most influence around Bayou Blue and whose own history was intricately connected to the Coushatta people: the Bel Oil Corporation. The tribe had a complex relationship with the company as well as with the Bel Estate, its sister company, which had for decades logged the area around the Coushatta settlement. While the company donated to the tribe small parcels of land around the church, school, and Trading Post, some Coushattas had distrust and resentment because of a pattern of land loss to the company over the years. Nevertheless, Miller was intent on securing Bel Oil's support to further strengthen the Coushattas' case. As she wrote to Governor-Elect Edwin Edwards, "Without Bel family interest and cooperation the Elton [Coushatta] settlement would be handicapped in all development programs."[22]

Coincidentally, she didn't have to look beyond her own family for a connection. The Millers' son-in-law, Edwin Kidd Hunter, was a lawyer and had married their only daughter, Bonner. He also was a good friend of Bel Oil heir and executive David Garrison Jr., who was the great-grandson of founder J. A. Bel and the son of David L. Garrison Sr., Bel Oil president from 1950 to 1963 and board chairman until 1978, who had earlier been involved in making a land transfer to the Coushattas. The younger Garrison became involved in his family's business at a time when its profitability was steadily increasing.[23] So, when Hunter, at his mother-in-law's urging, approached Garrison about getting involved in Indian affairs, he found himself in a position to pursue other side interests and agreed to join Sickey and Miller in their mission. Plus, he had a growing interest in learning more about the history between his family's business and the Coushattas, expressing that the "economic and sociological advancement [of Indians] has been of deep concern to me for some time." This made the prospect of getting involved more intriguing for him.[24] Sickey stated: "David was really a fun guy to work with . . . He didn't know anything about Indians, even though they owned the property all around us. He would laugh about it [saying,] 'The only thing I know about Indians is we stole all your land.' You got to love him." Sickey appreciated Garrison's openness and grew to respect him as the two fostered a close friendship of their own. Later Sickey even named his fifth son after David Garrison Jr.

Garrison wasn't the only one Sickey had to educate. He found many legislators "had no idea what a tribe was." Wishing to extend his reach even beyond what Miller had orchestrated, he went to the public library to pore over the Louisiana directory of elected officials. While Miller helped target support, Sickey used the directory to expand his reach, explaining:

> There's this tremendous need [for] educating the people of Louisiana because there's very little . . . knowledge of Indian tribes . . . I would start the education process [with], "The Coushatta Tribe has been in Allen Parish for [nearly] one hundred years," and just [go] through the whole thing. Surprisingly, they would be curious, and they wanted to know more. My next step was [to] invite these people, legislators, both the Senate and House members, to come to the tribe. I would actually take them on a tour of our community, where they see rundown houses, no water, nothing . . . They had no idea that we had a government or could . . . have this relationship with the federal government.

Before hosting visitors, Sickey selected Coushatta families who "could speak and present the same picture that I was presenting on their behalf." He chose different families each time and focused on topics that he wanted to emphasize, such as education, health care, and housing. "I was able to [present] a complete picture of what our needs were so that [visiting public officials] could understand." It was important that Sickey didn't simply ask for support without justifying the specific needs the tribe had. "I wanted them to know what our concerns were. I gave them as much . . . facts and statistics that I could gather among the tribe."[25]

With a background in broadcasting and a lifelong interest in communication, Sickey was skilled at articulating his tribe's needs. Plus, he had good community role models. They laid the groundwork for what became his particularly inclusive message regarding the benefits of supporting the Coushattas. "I spoke the language of what [legislators] understand, and that's economics," Sickey explained. "If [the] Coushattas got recognition, [the future boost to] the economy would benefit everybody. Everybody would have jobs, not only Indians . . . That was the message I preached . . . it was very successful, but it took a lot of talking." He didn't ask for handouts: "That was the wrong approach. When I talked to the chamber of commerce in Jennings or Lake Charles . . . I wanted to make my position a win-win for everybody."[26] One newspaper commentator wrote that Sickey was "one of this state's, perhaps the world's, most effective spokesmen for causes, especially those in support of minority viewpoints."[27] Sickey had to tread lightly, however, so that the tribe's economic status didn't overshadow its political one. As anthropologist Robert L. Bee explained about the complexity of tribal advocacy during that period, "Antipoverty enthusiasm tended to ignore the special legal status of Indian tribes as distinct from minorities."[28] Although Sickey focused on fiscal concerns initially, he also talked about the extraconstitutional relationship tribes have with the United States as preexisting sovereign nations.[29] While this concept proved difficult for some to understand, Sickey kept making speeches with simple messages, telling a story of the Coushatta people that was deeply entrenched within the Louisiana narrative. "You have to be a great storyteller," he stated. Tribal leaders who couldn't speak effectively about their community's history and make it relevant to others found it difficult to inspire people to support them. Sickey had observed other tribal leaders who found themselves paralyzed by anger and "started blasting white people . . . [describing] how they stole their land [and] how they were discriminated [against] in schools . . . [They] hurt the community more than [they] helped over time." Keeping it simple, Sickey chose to emphasize the tribe's perseverance and focus on a message he had frequently heard growing up: "The struggle has made us stronger."[30]

The Coushattas did experience some resistance. A few legislators thought the tribe could threaten businesses and landowners. One senator, in particular, challenged Sickey, asking "Why should we recognize Indians? Why don't they want to be a part of the whole American lifestyle?" Those who exhibited reluctance in supporting the Coushattas were in the minority, however. Several legislators, such as Russell Long, felt morally obligated to help the tribe. Sickey remembered Long stating that he believed that "Indians didn't get a fair shake . . . [so] we should do something."[31] Regardless of the attitudes of whom he faced, Sickey didn't avoid asking for help, and he wasn't intimidated by those in powerful positions. He described his thought process when meeting with a public official: "I would think to myself: 'How can you help me? How can we be partners?' That is the approach that I took because they are no better than I am. I just come from a different culture . . . I would go in there and sit down with different people and know that we were on an equal basis. I did not want to be threatened or to be told 'You're just an Indian.' I wanted to be treated as an equal who just happens to be Indian."[32] After these meetings Sickey followed up with handwritten notes expressing gratitude, reasoning that this gesture "shows the appreciation from a personal standpoint . . . and I think that's really important."

The Millers helped Sickey translate his message into one that resonated with the political environment of the early 1970s. To do this, Ruth Miller showed Sickey how to communicate using legal language. As an exercise, she brought him into her professional world by asking him to write letters to oil companies on her behalf. The two also practiced debating significant issues to prepare for any pushback Sickey might receive. As Sickey spoke with legislators and state committees, Judge Miller edited his speeches and helped sharpen his points, crafting them to generate greater appeal with a particular audience. Sickey recalled occasions when Ruth, during several drives to Baton Rouge, coached him on the details of those he was to meet with, how he should talk, and even what body language to use. Her instructions were always followed with encouragement. "You have the skills, you can do this," she would tell him. "You're intelligent . . . You cannot afford to quit."[33]

Sickey's upbringing, paired with this mentorship from the Millers, was an invaluable asset to his advocacy work. He learned to hone his listening and communication skills within different contexts and to portray the Coushattas' perspective in a genuine and impactful manner. "I've always looked at myself as just a messenger representing a group of people who desired change in their community's [circumstances] but yet retain . . . their values and their heritage and . . . culture." The tribe's basket weavers helped him reinforce this message by providing baskets to give away as part of a practice he coined "basket diplomacy."[34] While the Coushattas had a long history of gift giving when encountering public officials, Sickey credited the weavers themselves for his adoption of the practice. He described how one day, when he was first preparing to travel on behalf of the tribe, a Coushatta woman visited him: "She gave me a basket and said 'When you go to Baton Rouge or Washington, wherever you go, take this basket and give it to that person [you meet with]. That will be our identity.'" The baskets were powerful symbols that represented a people who had maintained their culture in spite of centuries of hardship and dispossession, and by gifting them, Sickey brought the strength of his whole community into those interactions. The first basket he gave away was to Senator Russell Long.[35] In the years that followed, the community's weavers continued to provide him with a steady supply of baskets to accompany him as he built a network of Coushatta allies. Solomon Battise made cane baskets to hand out, and other weavers made pine needle baskets (fig. 13). Heather Williams proudly shared that her grandmother, Leona Francis, was one of the weavers who sewed baskets for Sickey to use as gifts in those days.[36] "That was a joint effort from everybody that got involved," Sickey said. "When I would go out on my little treks to talk to people . . . I didn't have a business card, but I [had] a basket, and I would leave a little miniature, maybe four-inch, basket on a congressman's desk or a senator's desk, and they would be happy. Then sometimes their wives would call and say, 'We'd like to order some' . . . The local politicians would say,

Fig. 13: Ernest Sickey collecting a basket from Maggie Langley, widow of Jackson Langley, to include as part of his outreach plan to promote the talents of Coushatta weavers, 1972. She is seen standing here in front of her tar paper–covered home. Image from Princeton University, William Byler Collection. Photograph by Sam Guillory.

'We didn't know that Coushattas even live here or even made baskets.' That was my marketing tool."[37] The baskets that Sickey distributed to public officials over the years left enduring impressions. They not only advertised the talents of the Coushatta people but also raised awareness about how far away from Bayou Blue the tribe was willing to reach in order to initiate change within their community.

As dedicated allies, the Millers were gifted several baskets over the years as a demonstration of the tribe's appreciation for their support. According to their daughter, Bonner, they treasured the gifts, bestowing them to their children. In fact, she received three of these baskets from the collection and later learned the story behind them when she met Sickey forty-five years after he first collaborated with her parents.[38] The baskets endured as remnants of a friendship that shifted the course of the Coushattas' history as it accelerated their progress toward reestablishing a relationship with the federal government.

Edwin Edwards-ka̱: Mikkok Komawiichi̱
Edwin Edwards: The Right Governor at the Right Time

In 1972 Edwin W. Edwards was elected governor of Louisiana. Born of French and Catholic ancestry in rural Avoyelles Parish, Edwards was referred to as the "Cajun governor," whose historic election was largely determined by heavy support from Cajun and African American voters. He positioned himself as the champion of the underdog at a time when emotions over class and race divisions in Louisiana were raw. Historian Adam Fairclough argued that his political platform propelled him to success by creating a "coherent 'bloc'" among black voters.[39] Many Cajuns believed Edwards gave them the visibility they had lacked within the state's political machine and gathered by the thousands after the election in New Orleans to celebrate with the new governor, who waved a banner donning the words *Cajun Power* from his hotel window in a demonstration of his victory.[40]

Even with significant support from Louisiana's Cajun and African American populations, Edwards still relied on endorsements and assistance from the Democratic Party's elite, including the Millers. In fact, Ruth campaigned for Edwards in the months leading up to his election, and he later appointed her to the constitutional convention alongside state legislators and some of Louisiana's leading civic and business leaders.[41] In March 1972 she approached Governor-Elect Edwards and asked him to become the first Louisiana governor to take a primary role in Indian affairs and promote the "preservation of the culture, heritage and ethnic identification of the Indian nations of Louisiana and for their economic and sociological advancement." This request resonated with his campaign message, which emphasized embracing the unique cultural heritage of Louisiana. In her straightforward style Miller told Edwards that he should personally address the marginalized status of the Coushattas and the state's other Native populations, for they had "been static for hundreds of years."[42] He didn't need any further convincing and soon incorporated Louisiana's Indians into his larger platform, which, he argued, cleared the pathway for "various minority groups which have not yet enjoyed the full benefits of the American dream."[43]

Miller made it easy for Governor Edwards to support the Coushattas' initiative by methodically laying out the steps for him to take. First, she presented him with a newly drafted resolution to formally recognize the Coushatta tribe. Since the legislative bill initially prepared by Elton lawyer J. Daniel Rivette didn't reflect the tribe's perspective on the type of relationship with the state they wished to pursue, Sickey and Miller crafted a new document, opting to present it as a resolution. It explicitly stated that recognition was a means to "urge the [federal] government, particularly the Bureau of Indian Affairs, to give assistance" to the Coushattas by taking "appropriate executive and/or congressional action." In fact, the new resolution's final statement required that copies of the document also be sent to the president, Senate, House of Representatives, and the Department of the Interior's BIA director. Rather than position the tribe as a "subdivision" of the state, as the initial House bill draft did, the resolution made the state a tribal partner, not a jurisdictional overseer. Instead, Louisiana's special place in the relationship was as the only "state in the Union" to formally recognize the Louisiana Coushattas, acknowledging their rights to receive BIA services and entering into a federal-Indian relationship like "that of other Indian Tribes in the United States." Within weeks of the start of

Edwards's term, Senate Concurrent Resolution No. 38 was introduced in the 1972 regular session and passed, making the Coushatta tribe the first to be formally recognized by the state of Louisiana. As mandated, a copy of the resolution was then promptly sent to President Nixon and the Department of the Interior.[44]

State recognition was an important first step, but it lacked tangible benefits. Anticipating this, Miller's lobbying of the governor had also included a request for the creation of a Louisiana Office of Indian Affairs (LOIA) by executive order.[45] Signed by Edwards on May 30, 1972, the order gave the agency the "responsibility of coordinating and spearheading all programs and projects necessary to assist the people of this unique ethnic group . . . in achieving a complete sociological and economical advancement."[46] This was a similar trajectory followed by other southeastern states that also began creating state Indian agencies in the 1970s to secure federal funding.[47] Given the historically contentious relationship between tribes and states that had long characterized United States federalism, dating back to the early American Republic, this was a relatively new trend. It was one that not only provided tribes with fresh opportunities but also complicated the legal definitions of *Indianness*, as states developed criteria independent of the federal government's standards, which were formalized in 1978 with the establishment of the Branch of Acknowledgment and Research (BAR). Tribal recognition, whether at state or federal levels, became a politically charged issue that came to dominate Indian affairs in the years following the Coushattas' state recognition. Federal recognition, in particular, has many implications and provides important political, financial, and psychological benefits to federally recognized tribes.[48]

Miller not only made it easy for Governor Edwards to support the creation of the LOIA; she also suggested its first commissioner. This nomination, she argued, was part of the governor's authority under the Louisiana constitution and previous attorney general rulings. She reasoned, "Considering that initially these are volunteer services . . . and will probably involve developmental programs requiring leadership rather than legislative authority, there can be no possible strain even on discretionary authority of the Governor."[49] Eliminating possibilities for protest, she pushed further and suggested that Edwards appoint David Garrison Jr. as the first commissioner. Not only was Garrison "immediately excited and enthusiastic about such an undertaking," Miller argued, but "he is refreshingly rich, generous, [and] out-going in relationships. I am confident he will spare no personal expense or effort to assure [*sic*] the success of the project . . . [and] the program he develops will be a credit to your administration."[50] Confident that the governor would comply, Miller pre-drafted a letter to Garrison on the governor's behalf with the terms of appointment, which also included the additional appointments of Ernest Sickey as deputy commissioner and consultant as well as Miller herself and her son-in-law, Edwin Hunter, as legal advisors. Just as with every other request Miller presented him with, Edwards supported Garrison's appointment, giving him office space and inviting him to start immediately.[51]

Based on correspondence, Garrison had begun his efforts even before his official appointment. According to one account, he "plunged into the job . . . [and] set an example for anyone who wants to serve the public."[52] He started by defining the commission as a technical assistance program, with hopes of securing funding to provide vocational training and medical services. He also immediately extended the commission's purview beyond the Coushattas by reaching out to the Chitimachas and Houmas, even hiring the Gulf South Research Institute for a needs assessment to determine how the new state agency might best serve them.[53] Garrison later included the Tunicas and Jena Band of Choctaws among "tribes which are recognizable entities."[54] To help him do well in this new role, he sought advice from John Gordon, superintendent of the Choctaw Agency, at the BIA's regional office in Mississippi. Garrison also arranged meetings with the Louisiana Economic Development Office and the Louisiana Tourist Commission to learn how they might assist the Houmas in developing a shrimp co-op and the Coushattas in further developing their Trading Post.[55] He thought tourism held the most profit-earning potential for tribes, citing the Alabama-Coushatta Reservation of Texas as a model, for it displayed impressive results, earning a profit of $50,000 in both 1971 and 1972. "Their needs are great," Garrison wrote Governor Edwards.

"The average education of 2,300 Houma Indians is 2.9 years . . . In a survey of 38 Coushatta families, 33 had income below $3,000 a year and none above $5,000."[56] Though likely overwhelmed by the position he had eagerly volunteered for, within the first year of his post, Miller declared, Garrison had "accomplished more for our Indian people than has been accomplished in the history of our state."[57] Garrison, however, credited Sickey. In a 1972 interview he recounted that "the new agency was initiated largely through the efforts of a progressive young Coushatta Indian, Ernest Sickey of Elton, who 'reads a lot—and dreams a lot' and has a propensity for parlaying his dreams into action."[58] Garrison generally viewed himself as a facilitator of Sickey's vision (as it was informed by the tribe), which he mostly shared, but the two men didn't always see eye to eye.

One of Garrison's biggest hopes for the LOIA was to build an intertribal coalition within Louisiana.[59] This was Sickey's goal as well, but there were differences in how each wanted to approach such an undertaking. As a newcomer to Indian affairs, Garrison's experiences were limited, and his exposure to increased news coverage of national pan-Indian activism informed his general understanding of Indian rights issues. Between 1968 and 1972, for example, the Louisiana newspapers covered the reclaiming of California's Alcatraz Island by Indian activists more than 130 times. Likewise, Louisiana papers ran articles about the occupation of the BIA headquarters office by members of the American Indian Movement (AIM) in 1972 more than a dozen times and about the intense standoff at Wounded Knee in 1973 more than 50 times.[60] The overriding theme of this coverage was that Indians were angry and willing to engage in public protests to reclaim land and other resources. Therefore, when the activities of a Louisiana-based pan-tribal organization called the Indian Angels, Inc., began receiving news coverage, it appeared that the "Red Power movement" had reached the Deep South.

The Indian Angels, Inc., was founded in 1969 with the broad mission to "aid in the welfare of the American Indian." The organization drew membership from across the state, including from the Houma and Tunica communities, and often made public statements drawn from the AIM-inspired rhetoric of the time.[61] While Garrison supported the group's efforts and credited the Indian Angels for being "instrumental in gaining early recognition and opening doors for Louisiana Indians," the leadership of the Coushatta and Chitimacha tribes, on the other hand, strongly disagreed. Although Chief Martin Abbey had hosted a meeting with representatives from the Indian Angels before retiring as chief, Coushattas generally agreed that the organization was too "radical" and that the group's message presented a false sense of homogenization among Louisiana's tribes, which was not in their best interest.[62] The Coushattas' public education efforts emphasized their own unique attributes, and they had no interest in conflating their identity with that of a pan-Indian organization. In fact, the Coushattas formally denounced the broader American Indian Movement, releasing a tribal resolution condemning a "grave error in their philosophy" that resulted in "scandalous action."[63] Sickey even issued statements distinguishing the Coushattas' advocacy efforts from those of "Indian militants." In a 1973 letter to the editor in the *Shreveport Times*, he wrote: "It has always been the expression of the Coushatta Tribe to seek ways to benefit the tribe in a peaceful manner and through the system set forth by the government of this country . . . It is my feeling the new Indian of today should be the type to sit down and negotiate in a businesslike manner and present himself as a competitor in today's society, fully capable of managing his own affairs."[64] While Sickey's words resonated with many other tribal leaders in the state, the Indian Angels, according to Brian Klopotek, "balked at the Coushatta tribe's apparent willingness to work with white authorities in the established power structure, and read their disapproval of radical activism and public demonstrations as a lack of outward pride in their Indian ancestry."[65] Even with differing perspectives on what the composition of the LOIA should be, Sickey ultimately convinced Garrison to support his position that the agency should be comprised of not intertribal organizations but leaders of tribal nations, each with its own distinct cultural identity and needs.[66] This, Sickey believed, was the only way to be taken seriously by legislators and to strengthen the Coushattas' case as well as future attempts by other Louisiana tribes to gain federal recognition.

Wihhilito Naasinchaaka Tatkak Aththaamooli Kosobbaayaalilahon
Lobbying for Federal Recognition

Following passage of the state resolution granting Coushattas recognition, the tribe reset its mission, now aiming to exert pressure on the Department of the Interior to acknowledge its tribal status and fully reinstate BIA services. The first step was to refine its message so that it underscored the injustice of the situation and could easily be adopted and repeated by others willing to advocate for them. Instead of continuing to focus on the tribe's contributions to the cultural richness of Louisiana, the Coushattas began emphasizing the message that the BIA was "morally bound" to reinstate services, which were initially established as a result of treaty obligations and then were unilaterally halted.[67] This was an effective argument that was also used by Garrison and Edwards in advocating on behalf of the tribe.[68] It also was language shared with legislators invited to the Trading Post in June 1972 for an intimate introduction to the Coushatta settlement. The Coushattas had already received their support toward recognition at the state level. Now these politicians were asked to elevate their efforts further as they underwent training to be vocal advocates for the tribe in Washington DC.[69]

As part of his efforts in advocating for reinstatement, Sickey also monitored the activities of other tribes looking for models to emulate and even joined the regional intertribal organization, the United Southern and Eastern Tribes, Inc. (USET). Established in 1969 as the United Southeastern Tribes, Inc., the USET was cofounded by the Eastern Band of Cherokees in North Carolina, the Mississippi Band of Choctaws, and the Miccosukee and Seminole Tribes of Florida. The organization gave the Coushattas the opportunity to broaden their information network and resources beyond Louisiana. It also gave Sickey access to other tribal leaders who understood his struggles, such as Buffalo Tiger (Miccosukee), who provided valuable mentorship as the Coushattas navigated the federal system. The Miccosukees already had a contentious history with the BIA, which refused to recognize them as a distinct tribe following their separation from the political umbrella of the Florida Seminoles. As a result, Tiger made the provocative move to lead a tribal delegation to

Cuba in 1959 to meet with Fidel Castro and gain international recognition as a tribal nation.[70] This move asserted Miccosukee sovereignty while also playing into Cold War anxieties. Sickey argued that "the pressure that the Miccosukee put on the federal government resulted in their 1962 recognition through administrative channels, forging a pathway for a similar process for the Coushattas a decade later." Tiger was a tremendous influence on Sickey, helping to shape his thinking about tribal sovereignty and diplomatic pursuits and the manner in which he applied this understanding to his own advocacy work.[71]

The Coushattas' efforts additionally led them to rekindle a friendship with the Association on American Indian Affairs (AAIA), a New York–based advocacy organization that provided tribes with legal and technical assistance. The AAIA had been in contact with the Coushattas thirteen years earlier, at the request of Reverend Johnson, when the organization conducted a survey and made a series of recommendations on how to jump-start tribal development. Without tangible resources or support for the recommendations, the Coushattas saw little progress come out of the report, and it soon became a distant memory. In fact, Sickey was unaware of the AAIA's previous contact with the tribe when he encountered the association independently. In light of a steady shift in federal Indian policy and the well-publicized recognition of such tribes as the Passamaquoddy of Maine, the Coushattas sought the AAIA's help once again in hopes of accelerating the process. Sickey wrote several letters and later visited AAIA executive director, William Byler, to explain the nuances of the Coushattas' case. "He found it interesting enough because of the lack of legislation that terminated us," Sickey recalled. "He was very curious about how that happened, why it happened . . . and why nothing was done for the past two decades."[72] Byler exhibited enthusiasm for the case rivaling that of Miller and Garrison, and the AAIA began work immediately by assigning a staff attorney to research the tribe's history. Byler was so interested in achieving a quick resolution that he personally joined the research efforts.[73] In the meantime, however, the AAIA recommended Garrison request funding from the Louisiana legislature through the State and Local Fiscal Assistance Act, commonly known as the Revenue Sharing Act. This act was intended to revitalize state and local governments through congressional appropriations of federal tax revenues, a practice that was in effect from 1972 to 1986, until it was replaced by federal block grants. The plan's crucial provision made tribal governments eligible to receive funds directly from the secretary of the Treasury for a host of programs. The Chitimachas had already participated in revenue sharing, and the Coushattas also wanted to join in with the hope of being able to launch some much needed programs while awaiting reinstatement.[74]

Further enhancing the support they received from the AAIA, the Coushattas also enlisted the assistance of the Native American Rights Fund (NARF), an interest group dedicated to protecting Indigenous rights on major legal policy issues. The NARF legal staff collaborated with the AAIA in compiling the Coushattas' dossier, stating that they thought the tribe had a strong case.[75] The National Council on Indian Opportunity (NCIO), another Indian rights group established by President Lyndon B. Johnson in 1968, also intervened on the Coushattas' behalf and plotted out a long-range strategy to access federal funding sources with great confidence that their status would soon be reinstated.[76]

While things were moving forward, there were a few setbacks. For one, BIA superintendent Gordon of the Choctaw Agency was transferred to another office. This news upset Coushatta leaders, given Gordon's support of their efforts and, in Garrison's words, that he had "'stuck his neck out' on more than one occasion" on behalf of the tribe. The news of his impending transfer prompted the tribe to pass a resolution to demonstrate support for retaining Gordon in his post, stating that his "continued presence in the Southeastern part of the United States is essential for the well-being of the Coushatta peoples." There was little that could be done, however, and Gordon soon left Mississippi for another office.[77] In addition to Gordon's departure, the tribe was also challenged by BIA officers, such as Deputy Commissioner John Crow, who felt the Coushattas had a weak case. Despite support from Louisiana as well as optimistic positions from the AAIA, the NARF, and the NCIO, Crow wrote, "Quite frankly, we are confronted with a difficult problem in view of the cloudy history of the Coushatta descendants."[78] The crux of this confusion, Byler maintained, "was the belief that the Coushattas were the same people as the Alabamas and that the Alabama-Coushatta Tribe of Texas represented the surviving Coushatta tribal entity." As a result, the AAIA set out to clear up this confusion and prove to the BIA that "the Coushattas are a distinct tribe, with a distinct history, language and culture."[79]

In spite of these barriers, Sickey was unwilling to get discouraged and, instead, expanded his lobbying efforts. A report on Sickey's activities from September 11 through November 20, 1972, reveals dozens of phone calls, four meetings in Lake Charles, six meetings in Baton Rouge, two at the Coushatta Indian Church, and three in Washington DC. While some of these meetings were to discuss education and cultural programs for all of the serviced tribes in his role as consultant to the LOIA, much of these efforts were focused on generating support for the reinstatement of federal services for the Coushattas.[80] This was a full-time job in itself, which was why Sickey increasingly had to take time off his wage-earning job to travel to Washington DC for days at a time. Garrison informed Governor Edwards of this issue, emphasizing that Sickey "sacrificed a $10,000 year salary to dedicate himself to this work."[81] Once in DC, Sickey met with the Louisiana congressional delegation, BIA officials, the Indian Press Association, and numerous lawyers, such as S. Bobo Dean and Arthur Lazarus Jr., who worked for the AAIA to prepare documentation to support the tribe's case. Dean and Lazarus researched congressional records, while Sickey inquired about Coushatta records housed at the BIA Choctaw Agency in Mississippi, which were eventually turned over after repeated requests. According to Sickey, those files "explained everything from A to Z about what took place [when the BIA walked away from the tribe] . . . It was interesting who signed off and who did what and who didn't do anything. It was a blame game up the line." The documents were critical resources for the AAIA lawyers in building the Coushattas' legal case.[82]

The AAIA funded several of Sickey's trips, but that wasn't his only source of support when in Washington DC. On several occasions he met with Senator Russell Long, who, since being introduced to Sickey by Ruth Miller, had kept informed of the Coushattas' progress and gave Sickey an office to work from. The senator was "a very powerful [person] in Washington," Sickey said. "To me he was just a very nice individual who wanted to help . . . The timing was just right for us to have people in seniority [positions] like him in Congress to be able to do the things that we needed to do." Even with support from individuals such as Long, however, Sickey had his work cut out for him. "I had to demonstrate that Coushatta people needed help and [explain] . . . the kind of help we needed," he said. "I didn't go to Washington and say, 'Well I need help' [and leave it at that]. I went there [having done] my homework." In choosing his words wisely and being cognizant of the image he presented within the political arena, he made an impression that allowed his message to gain traction: "Image was important because I was walking into foreign territory. [These were] people who didn't know me, people who knew nothing about my cause or my mission . . . I wanted to present an image that they felt comfortable with. I ran around in suits when I could because that's what white people understand. [I] learn[ed] that early on. How you present yourself is what they remember." Sickey wore secondhand sport coats given by friends and even bought a fake Rolex watch for ten dollars from a street vendor. His sartorial choices reflected how he adapted to the environment he was in, which was not unlike the survival skills employed by Coushattas who came before him.[83]

Naasachihbạ Paathopotlit, Kaanohchon Stonthatọ
Overcoming Skepticism and Reaching Compromise

There were two audiences Sickey regularly had to address. In addition to those within the political realm, he also had to return to Allen Parish and inform his people about how things were progressing. He had several strong supporters, including Loris Abbott Langley, who, he said, "would encourage me with kind words . . . of support . . . and thanked me for what I was trying to do for the people."[84] Roy Abbey, one of Martin Abbey's sons, also was a vocal supporter of Sickey's efforts. Abbey's daughter Paula Abbey Manuel recalled that her father "was very appreciative of all the things that [Sickey] brought to this tribe." She also made her own observations about Sickey: "He's not afraid to talk to anybody. I know that he makes friends wherever he goes [and] that he was more of an outspoken Coushatta than any other that I knew, especially . . . in that generation . . . [As a result,] he was able to go out and do a lot for this tribe."[85]

While Sickey already had the personal trust of many Coushattas, he found that he frequently had to meet with different segments of the community and dispel misunderstandings about what a reinstated relationship between the Coushattas and federal government would mean. "A lot of the older Coushatta people had no love or trust for the federal government," Sickey explained. "One of the threats that they were all so concerned about was, 'Well, if we got recognition, if we got the BIA involved in our tribe, will they take our land away? Or, [will] they move us to Oklahoma?' . . . It took a while to assure them that everything will be okay."[86] These long-standing fears were rooted in the historical trauma the tribe experienced, which resurfaced in their encounters with the BIA since settling around Bayou Blue. The Coushattas were intent on protecting their private landholdings, which were assessed at about one thousand acres by 1973. Their property was part of a collective inheritance and set of values that reflected their resilience as a people.[87] As Sickey made his way around the community, addressing concerns and answering people's questions, his efforts were joined by a group of respected elders, "the ones," he said, "who talked me into doing this in the first place." They helped explain to the others what federal recognition meant and why Sickey had to take the approach that he did to generate the necessary trust and respect among outsiders.[88] In reflecting back on what the generations before him must have thought, Pratt Doucet stated, "I think Mr. Sickey had a bigger . . . view for the future that a lot of people didn't understand . . . he [was] working to get there, and it was probably just a little bit of a struggle to get people to understand."[89] It wasn't surprising that many Coushattas felt hesitant to invite the federal government back into their lives, given their previous experiences with the BIA. Moreover, Sickey's frequent absences from the community and his shift in attire to suits was cause for speculation.[90] Barbara Langley recalled that he was often seen boarding a Trailways bus heading to Baton Rouge: "In the evening, he would hop back on and come on home. There's a lot of people [who don't] know what really went on for him to get the tribe recognized . . . He sacrificed his time [and] his family . . . When he would come home late at night, his wife would have food prepared. She would get up and heat his meal."

Langley personally saw the sacrifices Sickey made, for she played a critical role in supporting his efforts as his administrative assistant. Before this time, however, the former two-time winner of the Coushatta Indian Princess pageant had left Louisiana for a brief time to attend college in Dallas. Upon her return, she married J. D. Langley, who was another leader in the tribe who worked closely with Sickey. Barbara held different jobs over the years, such as with the telephone company and the Allen Parish Head Start program. She recalled her husband asking her one day in 1972 about working with Sickey, just after Edwards signed the resolution declaring the Coushattas a state-recognized tribe. Langley agreed and, like Darlene Langley Dunnehoo years earlier, began typing stacks of handwritten notes onto formal letterhead pages Sickey provided. Since he traveled extensively during that period, Langley recalled her difficulty in understanding the specifics of his work. "I was just doing the day-to-day thing until I caught on," she said. Sickey soon requested Langley accompany him on trips to provide administrative assistance. She recalled how intimidated she felt the first time she went to Washington DC. During one trip, before meeting with Sickey and the AAIA lawyers, she recalled sitting in the lobby of the hotel "watch[ing] people go up the elevator. Finally, I got brave enough to get up [and] got in the elevator. I ran down the hall [to where] my room was way at the end."[91] Leonard Battise also frequently joined Sickey in Washington DC as another Coushatta representative for meetings with legislators and lawyers. The two traveled frugally, riding buses, sharing hotel rooms, and surviving on homemade sandwiches. Battise was an emerging community leader in his own right, and despite his discomfort with traveling hundreds of miles from home, he did it out of friendship. "We were just like brothers," Battise said, recalling all the time Sickey spent with his father, Solomon Battise. "I let him do the talking. He wanted me to do some talking too, but I just wanted to sit back and listen to how he operates . . . He can stand on his own." Battise fondly remembered his adventures traveling to Washington DC as "good experiences," which later inspired and prepared him to serve on the tribal council.[92]

In preparation for federal reinstatement, the Coushattas were encouraged to reorganize their governing structure. S. Bobo Dean of the AAIA, in particular, encouraged them to develop a constitution and bylaws and assisted them in this process by creating a draft version based on criteria outlined by the Indian Reorganization Act (IRA). An IRA form of government, Dean argued, would provide for an easy transition for the Coushattas into the federal fold and make the tribe eligible for certain funding sources.[93] The Coushattas first had encountered this rationale in the 1930s, when they were approached about organizing under the IRA. They resisted the notion then and continued to express reluctance in the 1970s. Sickey explained: "For centuries the Coushatta tribe had traditional leadership . . . When I talked [with the community] about an organization under the BIA, that's one thing they didn't want. They were hesitant about having an un-Indian . . . organizational structure on paper . . . I proposed many times . . . that we come up with a constitution . . . and they all said 'no' . . . That's where it was left."[94] A new governmental structure didn't make sense to them, given that they already had one that worked, with an elected chief and heads of families who deliberated on behalf of the tribe. Over the years additional processes were established to manage different aspects of the community's social and economic interests, such as the Indian Church's governing board (1906) and the Trading Post's nonprofit Coushatta (Koasati) Indians of Louisiana, Inc. (1966). Confronted with the pressure to further organize the tribe around a constitution that would require formal approval by the Department of the Interior raised concerns. In particular, Coushattas wanted to know if it would lead to more federal oversight in their lives. Despite reassurances, reinforced by the national trend toward tribal constitutional development, the Coushattas remained reticent. Even though many saw the adoption of a constitution as a stabilizing factor for tribes such as the Mississippi Choctaws (constitution ratified in 1945, revised in 1975), the Florida Seminoles (1957), the Miccosukees (1962), and the Chitimachas (1971), the Coushatta people feared the opposite would be true for them.[95]

Looking for a compromise, the AAIA eventually convinced the tribe that in order to continue progressing toward federal reinstatement, they had to develop an interim governing organization until the community's concerns could be addressed. On March 10, 1973, over 85 percent of the adult members of the tribe met at the Indian Church to elect a board of trustees for a newly formed 501(c)3 nonprofit entity called the Coushatta Alliance, Inc., to function as the tribal council and assume responsibility of the business enterprise.[96] Because the initial Coushatta (Koasati) Indians of Louisiana, Inc., nonprofit was created prior to the 1969 Tax Reform Act, the new Coushatta Alliance, Inc., was an updated organization, one that reached beyond the management of the Trading Post and focused more broadly on tribal self-determination and the socioeconomic advancement of the community. A few reporters attended the election, and Dean and Garrison were on hand to answer any legal or administrative questions. According to Garrison: "The election was done in a democratic manner. Nominations were accepted from the floor. The members voted for five persons from a total of nine nominations on the slate." Sickey was elected to three prominent and interlocking roles: chairman of the Coushatta Indian Tribe of Louisiana, chairman of the Board of Trustees, and president of the Coushatta Alliance, Inc. "Sickey's support from the rest of the community was overwhelming," Garrison later told Byler. "Everyone is very proud of working together towards realizing [their] goals." Others elected for different positions that day included J. D. Langley, Solomon Battise, Leonard Battise, and Roland Sylestine (see appendix).[97]

Running "Coushatta Choose Corporate Chiefs" as the headline, the *Alexandria Town Talk* alerted the public to the shifting nature of the Coushattas' administrative structure following the election.[98] According to an LOIA press release, "The new board of trustees were authorized to act for the Coushatta Indian Tribe of Louisiana in all tribal matters in addition to the Coushatta Alliance Corporation." The dual leadership roles were intended to temporarily address a long-term strategy. The tribe not only wished to qualify for donations as a nonprofit entity; it also wanted to discern the most acceptable form of governing authority, one that didn't bind the Coushattas to decisions made by the Department of the Interior but one akin to those the BIA was familiar with. Under the Coushatta Alliance, Inc., the tribe created a governing document with election rules and procedures, voted to limit tribal membership to those with at least one-quarter Coushatta blood, and began holding regular meetings to tackle a robust agenda. The tribe also formalized diplomatic efforts that Sickey and others had started by establishing an awards committee "so that those who assist the tribe can be recognized."[99] While both BIA agents and AAIA staff continued to pressure the Coushattas into following the standard tribal government development route by adopting a constitution, the creation of the Coushatta Alliance, Inc., was the largest step many tribal members were willing to take. Anything more, they thought, would compromise their ability to govern themselves away from external interference.

Tatka Mikkok Thoiliichit Hokomawiichito
Reinstating Federal Services to the Coushatta Tribe

On April 30, 1973, after eight months of exhaustive work—clocking thousands of miles of travel as well as thousands of hours of phone conversations, time spent lobbying, and researching and drafting correspondence—the efforts of the Coushattas, the AAIA, the NARF, David Garrison Jr., Ruth Miller, Governor Edwin Edwards, and others who had exerted energy toward the Coushattas' case culminated in an eight-page letter, drafted by S. Bobo Dean and delivered to Marvin Franklin, assistant to the secretary of the Department of the Interior. It presented "the request of the Coushatta Indian Tribe of Louisiana for formal recognition . . . [by] the Federal Government qualifying it to receive services from the Bureau of Indian Affairs and eligible for other Federal assistance which the Congress has made available to Indian tribes." The letter had two primary objectives: to clarify the validity of the claim that the Coushattas were a historically rooted tribe with its own culture, language, governing structure, and deep connections to the U.S. government through treaties; and to provide details of the "federal blunders" resulting in the government abdicating its responsibility to the Coushatta people despite "contemporary instances in which the Federal Government recognized and acted upon its obligations to these

Indians." In the letter Dean accused federal agents of a lack of professionalism and consistency in the Coushattas' case over time, which resulted in confusion and negligence. The argument was simple: the Coushattas were never terminated. The evidence, Dean stated, made it "abundantly clear that the Federal Government did not proceed with this idea after failing to obtain Coushatta consent." While some federal agents had ignored the Coushattas for nearly two decades afterward, others, upon reexamining the case in 1970–71, acknowledged the procedural discrepancies. Yet even they failed to reestablish the tribe's access to federal Indian services, forcing the Coushattas to turn to the state of Louisiana for help.[100]

The prominent role that Louisiana played in furthering the Coushattas' case generated a vocal cadre of supporters who pressured the Department of the Interior to reach a decision. Confident of the outcome, a Louisiana newspaper reported that reinstatement was imminent, noting that "thirty years of inexcusable neglect of a legal and moral trust could end at any moment with the U.S. Bureau of Indian Affairs formally acknowledging that the Coushatta Indians [are] . . . a bonafide American Indian tribe."[101] Louisiana legislators monitored the situation closely. Senator J. Bennett Johnston, in particular, was persistent, sending two letters to the Department of the Interior, urging it to "act favorably on the Coushattas' request at the earliest possible time." He then rallied others within the Louisiana government to send similar letters of support (fig. 14).[102] Congressman John Breaux also offered to speak about the Coushattas on the floor of the House of Representatives to have his remarks captured in the congressional records. "He wants to do the right thing," Sickey shared with Byler, "and also wants to be sure that the Coushatta issue is in the minds of his peers at all times."[103] It is difficult to determine the level of influence the lobbying surrounding the Coushattas' case had on the Department of the Interior's decision-making process, but the level of support the tribe received from different levels of government was unprecedented.

On June 27, 1973, the Department of the Interior issued its decision to fully reinstate services to the Coushattas to be administered by the BIA on behalf of federally recognized tribes. The letter, curiously addressed

Fig. 14: Ernest Sickey and Barbara Langley presenting Louisiana senator J. Bennett Johnston with a crawfish effigy basket, early 1970s. Courtesy of the Sickey Family.

to LOIA commissioner Garrison and not Coushatta leadership, states, "In view of the research conducted in conjunction with clarifying the status of the Coushatta group in Elton, we have concluded that it constitutes the identifiable remnants of the historic Coushatta Tribe."[104] After twenty years the BIA had officially redefined the Coushattas' status as a federally acknowledged tribe. One local newspaper boasted that this was only the "second tribe (after the Miccosukee of Florida) in U.S. history to gain recognition through administrative channels [within the Department of Interior] without an act of Congress or an executive order of the President."[105] The AAIA newsletter declared the tribe had "won from the United States at long last fulfillment of their ancient treaties."[106] It became a day that the Coushatta people celebrate as their formal recognition as members of a sovereign nation. A tribal publication emphasized that this "single action put an end to the long years of hopelessness," paving the way for new opportunities to address the community's largest economic, social, educational, and health needs.[107]

The Coushatta "drama"—as deemed by scholar Daniel Jacobson—was not over, however.[108] Celebrations were tempered by stipulations attached to receiving many of the services offered by the BIA, creating further delays in the tribe witnessing any progress. "No one will ever know what a mighty effort that was," Ruth Miller complained, "every time we took one step forward, the U.S. Bureau of Indian affairs set us back three."[109] The two main issues were that the Coushattas no longer had a land base held in trust (a frustrating critique given that the BIA took Sissy Robinson Alabama's land out of trust in the 1950s) and hadn't organized their tribal government under the terms of the IRA. Both conditions were necessary, BIA staff claimed, "to receive the full compliment [sic] of Bureau services." Disheartened, Sickey distinctly remembers thinking: "What? We [still] have to do more?"[110]

"Ihaani Komiksoop, Komawiichilkak Iksohchi"
"No Land, No Services"

Harry A. Rainbolt, BIA director of Southeast Agencies, was assigned to assist the Coushattas in their transition. A citizen of Arizona's Gila River Indian Community, Rainbolt managed the region's office from Washington DC, generally attending to his administrative duties from afar and sending locally based field agents to work with tribes directly. Understandably, the Coushatta people had questions about what they should expect and the timeline for when services would begin rolling out. Sickey, in particular, sought clarity on stipulations placed on the tribe's status and insisted that Rainbolt make the trek to southwestern Louisiana himself, instead of sending someone from the Choctaw Agency in Mississippi. Based on his experience with the American political system and his awareness of problems caused by misinformed field agents, Sickey was unwilling to meet with anyone but Rainbolt during such a critical transitional period.[111]

Only a week after the Department of the Interior's decision, Rainbolt joined Sickey and Garrison at a community meeting at the Indian Church to share details about what the tribe should expect with federal reinstatement. The agenda allocated fifty minutes for the presentation and sixty minutes for "questions from the floor." As expected, a large crowd turned out, which "[gave] every indication the Coushatta tribe means business," Sickey later wrote to Byler. Rainbolt started by commending the tribe's "remarkable achievement" of involving Louisiana's governor and congressional delegation in its case that, as a result, was pushed through "in a small amount of time." He also explained the programs and services provided by the BIA. However, the mood of the meeting took a sudden turn when Rainbolt made it clear that the tribe didn't have access to these resources just yet. Sickey recalled him saying: "'You're not Indians yet until you get a piece of land . . . You [have] a long ways to go.'"[112] This message was disappointing and unexpected. When pressed for more details, Rainbolt was initially vague on the number of acres required to satisfy the criteria, claiming simply that it should be substantial. "Don't come in and say 'we've got a couple of acres, because you'd be barking up the wrong tree; that would be tokenism,'" one reporter quoted him.[113] Later, after Byler pushed the issue further, Rainbolt said he would be satisfied with "at least 25 acres." His colleague at the BIA, Les Gay, offered more by explaining the importance of a land base, noting that "BIA services are rendered to tribes on a priority basis, and without a land base, the Coushattas would be so far down on the priority list that they would receive little or nothing." He claimed that tribes were ranked by priority, listing tribes with a reservation at the top, then Indians living near a reservation, and last, the category in which he placed the Coushattas, "Indian individuals of one-quarter blood or more, without regard to where they live."[114]

There was great irony—cruelty even—in the situation in which the Coushattas were placed. To categorize the Coushattas as a people "without regard to where they live" simply because they no longer held federal Indian trust lands disregarded their long and proud history of private land ownership, a factor that allowed them to grow roots around Bayou Blue while maintaining their sense of peoplehood. Tribes such as the Menominees, whose circumstances paralleled the Coushattas in timing, had nearly all of their former reservation lands restored when they were re-recognized in 1973, but the 160 acres of Coushatta lands that had initially been placed into trust and removed from this status in 1953 were not restored.[115] And since Coushattas were unwilling to turn over their private property to the federal government to place into trust, they were pressured to raise money to purchase additional land for that purpose before they would be eligible for services.

Fortunately, months before this stipulation was made, the Coushattas had already been working with the AAIA on a land acquisition plan with the intention of securing acreage for a future reservation. As early as September 1972, the AAIA priced some of the Bel family's land surrounding the Coushatta homesteads, finding that it ranged from $100 to $200 an acre. By January the AAIA had committed a $2,000 donation toward the purchase of ten acres for the tribe. At the time, however, there were no available Bel Estate properties that weren't already tied up with oil leases. So, Byler and Sickey kept looking until they found ten acres that had been previously owned by a Coushatta family before being foreclosed on.[116] Since the tribe was still months away from federal reinstatement at that point and the AAIA would have had to incorporate in the state of Louisiana to purchase the land, Byler acted as a private trustee and made the land purchase in his name until the property could be transferred to the Coushattas.[117] "I hope this land acquisition is the beginning of many," Byler wrote to Sickey, "and that the day will come when the Coushatta people once again enjoy secure tenure of sufficient land to preserve the integrity of their community, their values, and their way of life."[118]

As Byler arranged for the purchase of the initial ten acres, Garrison and Lake Charles–based attorney Leonard Knapp Jr. met and drafted a Coushatta land acquisition plan. They presented three ideas for consideration: (1) determine whether the land where the Indian Church was located, donated in 1960 by the Bel Estate and legally transferred to Solomon Battise, could be put into a trust status; (2) request that Bel heirs donate additional land; or (3) research whether the ten acres could be traded for a larger parcel elsewhere. Each of these suggestions seemed reasonable in contributing to a broader strategy of land acquisition over a twenty-year period, with the ultimate goal being to acquire one thousand acres of reservation lands. This plan specifically included identifying desirable foreclosure property close to land already privately owned by Coushattas. Given that many of those foreclosed properties once belonged to Coushatta people, the plan also served as a hopeful source of empowerment as tribal members worked to reclaim what was once theirs. Sickey recalled the excitement around these discussions as several of them gathered in Byler's New York office, standing over maps and plotting out an acquisition strategy.[119]

Rainbolt's insistence that the tribe acquire twenty-five acres prior to any BIA action created an urgency that dominated conversations for several months, even inhibiting other areas of development to progress. The AAIA had already purchased ten acres for the tribe, and it wasn't long before it purchased an adjacent five acres from Martin Abbey's family. This future reservation soon became known as the "15 Acre Circle," located along CC Bel Road, near the North Elton Gas Field in the eastern part of the Coushatta community.[120] In an attempt to act swiftly, plans were under way to acquire the remaining ten acres needed to fulfill Rainbolt's expectation, when the BIA informed Byler that, upon reconsideration, ten acres was sufficient "to qualify the Tribe for all BIA services."[121] Frustrated by this news, the Coushattas and the AAIA also soon discovered that "there is no 'land base' requirement for the tribal development program and that the Bureau has repeatedly made . . . contracts with Indian groups for which land has not been held in trust by the Secretary of the Interior." In addition, Sickey learned that despite all of the pressure put on the tribe about conforming to a particular governing structure, the Coushattas also didn't need a tribal constitution to qualify for services.

The arbitrary nature of the BIA-imposed restrictions was puzzling and became more so when Rainbolt delayed the transfer of the fifteen acres into trust by refusing to approve it until additional stipulations were met. The AAIA adamantly condemned his behavior, writing: "In our discussions of this matter you have not given us a single explanation of your action which bears the scrutiny of reason. We are forced to the conclusion that your action is wholly arbitrary and discriminatory, completely without rational foundation and constitutes a flagrant abuse of administrative discretion." Sickey explained, "We had to fight like hell to get that put into trust because the very same agency and office that is supposed to be helping Indians . . . put every kind of barrier in front of you." The Coushattas navigated one difficulty after another, from clearing mineral rights to correcting improperly recorded title documents, before they submitted an official resolution to the secretary of the interior to take the fifteen acres into trust. Sickey found this last delay particularly difficult because he had to communicate it back to the tribe. "It was very frustrating because here I'm facing a community of people [saying,] 'Okay, now we're recognized.' [Then I had to say,] 'No, [we're] not recognized yet.' [I tried] to explain the bureaucracy. They didn't understand that. They wanted to know, 'When can we get health services?'"[122]

After months of legal hurdles, the Coushatta Tribe of Louisiana once again had federal Indian trust land and was declared a reservation tribe on March 14, 1975.[123] It had been nineteen months since the process began, which was a frustrating time that could have been shortened if multiple mistakes and repeated delays hadn't occurred. The 15 acres were only the start, however, and within a month the tribe received an additional 20.8-acre donation from the Bel Estate.[124] "That's all I can get from my family," a disappointed Garrison told Sickey. Although the acreage was smaller than Garrison had hoped to offer the Coushattas, the property's location wasn't predetermined, generating many possibilities across the Bel Estate's vast landholdings. With the initial 15 acres located in the eastern part of the Coushatta community, Sickey strategically selected acreage in a centralized segment of the settlement to become the future tribal administrative hub.[125] Barbara Langley, who continued as Sickey's administrative assistant following the tribe's reinstatement, was touched by Garrison's desire to help and called his donation a "friendship gift."[126]

In 1977 Senator Johnston helped increase the tribe's land base further, appropriating $100,000 in federal funding for the purchase of about 100 acres so the tribe could expand its reservation and accelerate development.[127] This move was unprecedented; according to two administrators within the BIA, "Congress has not seen fit to appropriate such monies [for tribal land purchase] since about 1940."[128] However, Johnston directly entreated Senator Robert C. Byrd, chairman of the Subcommittee on the Interior of the Senate Appropriations Committee, who then personally introduced the Coushatta land acquisition request to the committee and ensured that the appropriation was approved for adding to the 1978 budget.[129] By 1980 Coushatta trust lands had grown to 134 acres and continued to expand, reaching 151 acres by 1982.[130]

"[We had] incredible timing," reflected Sickey, regarding all that had transpired in the years leading up to the tribe's reinstatement in 1973. The Coushattas had "escaped the horror [of the BIA petition process] that other tribes had to go through" and at a historically rapid pace.[131] "The politics were working right too," attorney Leonard Knapp Jr. said. "It was an unusual coalition that came together because of the various connections" among politically powerful people who dedicated themselves to the Coushattas' case.[132] The Coushattas had entered a new era in their developmental journey, and while there was much excitement around the introduction of new resources and opportunities, they approached the transition cautiously. Representatives from multiple generations, hailing from different families and clans, frequently gathered to plan the tribe's future. Speaking in Koasati, people shared thoughts on which programs the tribe should pursue. "Everybody had a voice in the government [and] the programs that we [wished to implement]," said Crystal Williams.[133] This is how things had always been done, and it was the reason the community had persevered. Even after the tribe adapted its leadership roles and titles following the formation of the Coushatta Alliance, Inc., the democratic process by which decisions were made remained stable. Alliance officers were also tribal board of trustees members, representing Coushattas in a variety of arenas to advocate for their interests. According to Leonard Battise, discussing the vision and "what it would probably be like for the tribe in the next two . . . [or] five years," there was no need to change because "it was running smooth . . . [they] were always together."[134] Even after it was revealed that the tribe didn't have to reorganize under the IRA to receive services, the AAIA continued to pressure the tribe to develop a constitution. While the intent was to be helpful, the Coushattas still wouldn't entertain the idea. "We are one of the few tribes in the country that does not have a constitution," Sickey said. The goal was "to have an organization so strong that no one would bother Coushatta people . . . This is how they wanted to live and enjoy the benefits of federal recognition . . . We have to adapt . . . but we don't have to lose . . . who we are."[135] As the first years of the 1970s attested, the Coushattas navigated the state and federal systems on their own terms. They crafted poignant and timely arguments, strategically gifted baskets, and hosted dozens of public officials who visited the Bayou Blue settlement. The friendships the tribe forged with powerful allies provided the opportunity to mobilize its mission to a successful conclusion, all while protecting the Coushattas' cultural and political integrity as the community laid the groundwork for the next chapter in its developmental efforts.

6

Controlling the Conversation
Reshaping the Narrative and Building a Tribal Nation, 1973–1984

It has been a constant and daily ritual in delivering our message to those who are not aware of the issues and concerns which confront us daily . . . We have begun a new day in determining our own role and I feel that because of our own ideas we have carried a message forward that has much more of a lasting meaning.
—Ernest Sickey, "Chairman's Report,"
   Coushatta Smoke Signal, 1977

On a temperate May afternoon in 1982, hundreds of spectators joined Coushatta representatives in the parking lot of the Baton Rouge City Municipal Building for a ceremony to name the Louisiana Office of Tourism's hot air balloon, considered the state's "high-flying ambassador." One of only ten state-sponsored balloons nationwide, the tribe named it "Ohtokombinil"—meaning "Come over and visit with us" in Koasati. It was a colorful spectacle, with "Louisiana—a Dream State" emblazoned across it, and became a fixture at sporting events and festivals statewide.[1] It also represented the high level of visibility the Coushattas received in the years following federal reinstatement. Their active political lobbying and marketing of their baskets had drawn a great deal of attention. So, in spite of their small population and remote location, they were invited to be part of a larger effort to bolster the state's image and tourism potential. In fact, the inclusion of Coushattas in such an event was the result of a decade-long tribal effort to saturate local news with their story.

"One of my many dreams for the tribe," Ernest Sickey wrote William Byler in 1973, "was to get as much exposure to the public and to center as much as possible on the tribe . . . Once the news gets around that Coushattas exist . . . I feel the non-Indian will want to see what we have to contribute."[2] In order to achieve this objective, the tribe initiated an aggressive media campaign, regularly sending press releases and story ideas about their events and activities to Louisiana and Texas newspapers. Sickey wrote his own letters to the editor addressing significant issues about American Indians. In one he urged the public to "look beyond used clothing in assisting the first Americans [since] the kindness of used wares is only temporary while respect for Indian people would enhance if the long-range issues were properly addressed."[3] He also contacted television stations in Baton Rouge and New Orleans, requesting airtime to promote this message.[4]

As the Coushattas' political status shifted, so did the tone in their representation by the media. Rather than focusing on their plight as a forgotten or economically disadvantaged people, stories about them began drawing from human rights discourse and emphasized the injustice of their situation at the hands of the federal government.[5] By 1973 articles about the tribe reflected great disdain for the "years of inexcusable neglect of a legal and moral trust" and described how "the Coushatta story is another in a long series of broken promises."[6] While these shifts were in part indicative of the changing times, they can also be attributed to the Coushattas' successful reframing of how the media represented them not simply as a cultural island or muted minority but as a tribal nation with a unique socioeconomic and political status. Stanley Leger of the *Kinder (LA) Courier News* said Sickey frequently sent him updates to publish: "When he saw an opportunity to educate people about the tribe, he always [emphasized that] . . . 'we are a nation.'"[7] Sickey also invited the public to help celebrate the tribe's achievements. Because tribal sovereignty was an unfamiliar concept to most Louisianans, the Coushattas, in the years following reinstatement, educated them on the implications of federal recognition. They also shaped the terms by which the public understood and interacted with them by sharing messages that encouraged others to embrace the depth of the Coushattas' culture, history, and vision for the future.

Himaakap Akohichaachichootohook Hinaap Ittohyat Intolihnohchi
From Research Subjects to Partners

Bel Abbey (1916–92) and Nora Williams Abbey (1920–84) had grown so accustomed to outside visitors that they were always prepared for whomever turned up next. They initially welcomed guests in their original home and later at a new two-room, gable-roofed house constructed in 1948. Although the Abbeys used a water pump and outhouse, they were among the first wave of Coushatta families to get electricity.[8] Bel was the great-nephew of Chief Jeff Abbey and held different tribal leadership roles. He was a friend to the local Boy Scouts and Camp Fire Girls, represented the tribe at festivals, and worked with multiple anthropologists, linguists, and folklorists. Like most Coushattas of Abbey's generation, he spoke Koasati as his first language, and the English he acquired came from the few grades he completed at the Indian school and his years in the army during World War II. He was called a generous and patient man who enjoyed woodworking and storytelling. In fact, the Abbeys "shared their culture with anyone willing to watch and listen," according to the Louisiana Folktale collection *Swapping Stories*.[9] This view was supported by Abbey's nephew, Bertney Langley, who said his uncle loved to talk to people.[10] Dozens of Abbey's stories, ranging from traditional animal tales to personal hunting stories, were recorded over the years. He recalled that researchers and university students would "come find me in the fields" and sit until late into the night recording stories.[11] In 1982 the Abbeys were inducted into the Louisiana Folklife Center's Hall of Master Folk Artists at Northwestern State University because, as one article explained, "Bel Abbey and his family have helped train anthropologists from across the nation . . . They have also patiently taught young linguists how to interview."[12]

The Abbeys shared their time and knowledge with people such as Daniel Jacobson, who, as a graduate student and later as a professor, traveled to the community many times between 1951 and 1972.[13] While working on his doctorate at Louisiana State University, Jacobson was initially introduced to the Coushatta people by Fred Kniffen, a geography and anthropology professor who had often sent students to the Bayou Blue settlement for fieldwork training. He instructed them to record the life stories, tales, and songs of Coushattas as a way of building upon previous research produced by scholars, such as Mark Harrington, John Swanton, and Mary Haas, who collected folktales and linguistic data in the early decades of the twentieth century.[14] While many students didn't produce substantial studies or publications, Jacobson wrote his dissertation on the tribe, calling it "Koasati Culture Change." He completed it in 1954, a year after the Coushattas were cut off from federal Indian services, and his assessment of their future was bleak. He argued that what he observed was a tribe on the decline, saying, "There are forces at work which may ultimately lead to the abandonment of the community."[15] His conclusion was later echoed by historian Edwin Adams Davis in *Louisiana: A Narrative History* (1961). Davis wrote that "within a few years the Louisiana Indian will have disappeared as a racial group; he will have become an American."[16] Both assessments reinforced the hopeless image seen in newspaper coverage of the Coushattas in the 1950s and 1960s. While it is unclear how Davis made his determination, Jacobson relied heavily on an economic analysis of the tribe and its impoverished situation, leading him to de-emphasize the community's cultural resolve and ability to adapt. Using this line of thinking, Jacobson suggested that changes in the tribe's living situation would result, almost assuredly, in the loss of its Coushatta identity.

Several years after Jacobson's grim assessment, Kniffen sent another student, Hiram F. Gregory, to assess the tribe's situation. Gregory, who later became an anthropology professor at Northwestern State University, took a different perspective on the tribe. Although he acknowledged the poor living conditions, he was impressed by the Coushattas' ability to maintain their culture. He explained how they were of particular interest to researchers because they had retained their language: "That was like a magnet because it was very hard to find a tribe that had a language . . . where you can sit for hours and nobody would speak English, nobody speak French, they're all talking Koasati, it was wonderful. Linguists went crazy."[17] As a result, by the mid-1980s the tribe held starring roles in dozens of studies on linguistic analysis, ethnobotany, and folklore.[18]

Although surviving recordings of the Koasati language and stories later benefited the tribe in its own preservation and education efforts, the volume of researchers and their approaches to gathering information were problematic. Some were respectful, but others arrived uninvited and with a sense of entitlement. Sickey remembered how college students "used to roam around the community, visiting houses and pestering people."[19] Not everyone shared as willingly as Bel Abbey, although he also had his limits. In an interview with historian Jay Precht, Wallace Stroud, a neighbor to the Coushattas who worked for the Bel Oil Company, recalled that once when he asked Abbey to teach him some Koasati words, Abbey taught him words one shouldn't repeat in polite company.[20] Gregory called this "an old Coushatta trick" that also was played on him the first time he visited the community. One woman asked him to repeat a phrase to a group of Coushatta men. "They were just rolling on the ground [laughing] . . . I don't know to this very day what she told me . . . I said, 'Oh God, I've been had.'"[21] Although many Coushattas found humor in tricking visitors, this was also a form of resistance. Others were more reserved in encounters with researchers, as noted by Swiss linguist Emanuel Drechsel, who wrote that he found Coushattas "hesitant to answer my questions until they had an opportunity to get to know me better . . . I believe . . . [they] wish[ed] to keep their native language to themselves."[22] Similarly, Gregory recalled that early communication with Sickey was tense, and when he asked on several occasions in the early 1970s whether he could work with the tribe, Sickey avoided him. In fact, Gregory nicknamed him "Ernest *Ikso*"—the Koasati term for "I'm not here," which was what he often overheard Sickey yell when told that Gregory was on the phone asking to speak with him.[23] Sickey explained his evasiveness: "I would get complaints from tribal members [about] students who invaded their houses and poked microphones in their faces asking all kinds of weird stuff . . . simple things like, 'What do you eat?' . . . [or]

'What do you wear?' . . . It made them uncomfortable."[24] Researchers also asked invasive questions about medicine or dreams. On one occasion two students arrived with shovels, poised to "take samples" from the Indian cemetery. Sickey told them to leave and never return. "We would all laugh when they would leave in their beautiful cars and go back to their campuses," Sickey remembered. "They were so disappointed that I wasn't sitting in my office with my face painted and feathers all over." Sometimes researchers contradicted Coushattas, claiming they were mistaken about a detail from a story they had shared or a Koasati word they had used, and asserted that their own expertise superseded the Coushattas' knowledge of their own culture and language. Equally frustrating, scholars often published misinterpretations or factually inaccurate information about the tribe.[25]

With the opening of the Coushatta Trading Post in 1967 and the tribe's increasing role in public education, they also began to take a more active part in defining the terms by which researchers interacted with them. Coushattas had no interest in simply being "informants" to researchers. Instead, they pushed to establish partnerships. Sickey explained: "[We] wanted some kind of product that was going to help reinforce what [we were] doing or, at least, advance what [we were] interested in promoting twenty-five years from now . . . I've said many times [to researchers] . . . 'I want help with something that can contribute to my tribe . . . information to advance their education [or] their health care.'" By the 1970s Sickey believed most of the academics who continued to arrive in Allen Parish understood "what the true feelings of the Koasati people were and how they should . . . respect their turf." This perception, in part, reflected the approach of the tribe in asserting authority over its own history and culture. Coushattas even began conducting community tours specifically for researchers to temper their inclination to wander aimlessly.[26] These efforts created boundaries and implied that the researchers were guests, a shift that coincided with national conversations regarding problematic methodologies employed by academics within tribal communities. The publication of Vine Deloria Jr.'s *Custer Died for Your Sins* in 1969 influenced Gregory, for example, who, after reading the chapter on "Anthropologists and Other Friends," thought that perhaps "Ernest could have wrote this chapter" because it so closely echoed his complaints.[27] Gregory didn't see himself as the type of anthropologist described by Deloria, however. He credited years of working closely with tribal people all over the state for sensitizing him to their concerns. In spite of earlier rocky interactions, Sickey later identified Gregory as an example of a scholar who fostered sustainable and mutually respectful relationships with tribes. Although Gregory never did get an opportunity to conduct an in-depth study on the Coushattas, he collaborated with them on multiple projects ranging from efforts to revive artistic techniques to conducting archaeological research to identify grave sites. Additionally, in 1974 Gregory organized a conference for more than thirty anthropologists to meet leaders of Louisiana tribes in order to better coordinate anthropological research with tribal needs in mind. This approach carried over into his teaching. "I have to tell my students about Indian country," he explained. "You got to have a little patience. It takes a lot of time. People have to know what you are doing [and] they have to all agree that it's worth doing. You're going to have to wait until *they* decide." In addition to training a new generation of researchers on how to conduct themselves respectfully in Indian communities, Gregory also became an advocate for Louisiana tribes by organizing arts and crafts fairs, testifying in court on their behalf, and assisting with grants and petitions for federal recognition.[28]

By the mid-1970s southern tribes generally saw a positive shift in their relationships with academics.[29] Historian Theda Perdue explained that this was a reflection of a changing political environment: "Many American Indian peoples were taking control of their own pasts. They were increasingly regulating access to their reservations and to their intellectual resources, or those over which they had control. The kind of participant observation that anthropologists had been able to do a generation earlier was becoming less and less possible as Indians began to say, 'Wait a minute. We don't want to be the mere subjects of your academic research . . . We want control over what goes on in our communities.' Tribal self-determination meant that both historians and anthropologists had to do things differently."[30] Fewer Coushattas felt invaded by researchers, who were less frequently portraying them as a static people swiftly moving toward extinction. Even Jacobson, whose early work anticipated the demise of the Coushattas, changed his perspective. In a 1973 letter to William Byler, Jacobson admitted that "the notion of the [Coushatta] chieftainship has been carried right up to the present day . . . such men as Ernest Sickey, Solomon Battise, J. D. Langley, and R. Sylestine were elected to important tribal positions—shades of the old chieftainship, of the old viability of the Coushatta."[31] Gregory explained how Jacobson's assumptions had been challenged. "He had this whole idea that Indians should never change . . . If they changed, they couldn't be Indians."[32] Confronted with roles that Coushatta leaders played in the years leading up to federal reinstatement, Jacobson couldn't deny he had missed the mark in his previous argument and chose to share his new perspective in educational materials he authored for primary and secondary schoolchildren years after writing his dissertation.[33]

By and large coverage of the Coushattas remained marginalized within mainstream literature. In 1968, for example, a BIA publication, *Indians of the Gulf Coast States,* provided an overview of southeastern tribes but contained only a passing mention of the Coushattas.[34] By the early 1970s, however, the tribe's relationship with the AAIA provided the first real opportunity to showcase its story. In preparing the research for their case toward federal reinstatement, Sickey helped Byler and his staff develop the Coushattas' historical narrative by drawing on their collective memory and other resources that were woven together to explain the tribe's early migration history and the circumstances that led the community to settle in southwestern Louisiana. This narrative was included in the dossier shared with the Department of the Interior, and it also formed the basis of a 1973 article published in the AAIA newsletter. "Red Shoes' People: Coushatta Victory" reached a national audience, calling Sickey the "architect of the Coushatta victory" and claiming that "the Coushattas played an important role in the shaping of the history of the southeastern United States."[35]

To share more details of the tribe's story, Sickey planned to have a book written about the Coushattas. He wrote to John Griffin, a consulting editor for the Indian Tribal Series, a publication in Phoenix, Arizona, that was first conceived in 1970 to help the Havasupai Tribe raise money.

The books in this series were written by academics, but tribes ultimately approved the content and received 50 percent of the net profits from sales. Tribal leaders were asked to autograph each of the books, which were stamped with special medallions issued by the Franklin Mint and marked with serial numbers. The series became quite popular among collectors and was displayed at coin shows across the country.[36] When Sickey contacted Griffin, the series was already scheduled for thirty-eight issues on tribes from across the United States. While the Coushattas were not among the selected tribes, Sickey's letter piqued Griffin's interest, given that editors had recently returned from a coin show in Lake Charles.[37] Soon the Coushattas were added to the lineup, and editors began looking for a historian to write the book. The AAIA supported the endeavor. "I think you will agree," Byler wrote to Griffin, "the Tribe has had an extraordinarily interesting history . . . [It] will have to fight long and hard to get its place in the sun and to get the kinds of programs it has been denied for so many years. The Indian Tribal Series can be an important part in achieving this goal."[38]

After looking for some time, Bobby H. Johnson, a professor at Stephen F. Austin State University in Texas, was hired to write the history of the Coushattas. Although his scholarship mostly focused on the American West, he agreed to the assignment and soon began traveling to Allen Parish to work on the new project. *The Coushatta People* was published on April 1, 1976, with fifteen thousand copies printed. Each book featured an imprint of a medallion with the words *Sovereign Nation of the Coushatta* wrapped around an image of two women. The publication's narrative was unlike any other work published about the tribe to date. Instead of a sad tale of a tribe losing its culture and identity, *The Coushatta People* painted a picture of resilience and tenacity. It concluded by explaining several factors that worked in tandem to secure the Coushattas' survival into modern times, such as the elevated value they placed on their language, the prevalence of community cohesion, their geographic isolation, and the region's racial and ethnic diversity. Johnson added that "the Coushatta will survive because they have the potential leadership necessary for continued existence. With educational opportunities now open to Indian youth, the supply of future leaders should not suffer."[39]

The Coushatta People represented a turning point for the tribe as it actively collaborated in the production and publication of its own history.[40] The next year, with funding from the BIA's Bicentennial Project, the tribe self-published its own account, which was a pamphlet titled *The Struggle Has Made Us Stronger*. As Sickey wrote at the beginning of the pamphlet, its purpose was not just to tell the tribe's history but also to highlight "efforts to alleviate the social, economic, health and educational problems of the tribe." This was a critical message at a significant time as Coushattas positioned themselves as members of a tribal nation who were determined to continue plotting out their own future developmental path.[41]

Koasati Asaala Achoolihak Ommiifookon, Aatohyak Hokosobbaalito
Coushatta Weavers Bring Tourism to the Heart
of Elton and Gain National Notoriety

Since the opening of the Trading Post, the town of Elton had enjoyed the publicity the tribe brought to the area.[42] Elton reaped significant economic benefits from tourists and school groups who frequented the town's gas stations, stores, and restaurants. While many visited intentionally, others came by happenstance, led by signs guiding them along rural roads to the heart of the Coushatta community. By 1969, though, a shift in transportation patterns through southern Louisiana threatened to reduce traffic into the area. While this change adversely affected the Trading Post, much of its business was already being conducted through mail orders. Elton businesses, however, had come to rely on the patronage of motorists traveling along Highway 190 and saw the most devastating impact. Although Interstate 10 didn't traverse southern states until the late 1970s, it began disrupting travel routes much earlier. As more drivers found the I-10 to be a quicker and easier route, dozens of towns along a 180-mile strip of Highway 190 between Baton Rouge and Beaumont, Texas, experienced a noticeable decrease in their gasoline sales and overall economic bottom lines. Fearing the worst, mayors of those towns met to discuss how to make Highway 190 more appealing by marketing the towns' attractions. Creating the Acadiana Trail Association, town businesses joined civic leaders to promote a scenic route through southern Louisiana as an alternative to the expanding interstate.[43] Multiple attractions, including outdoor camping and recreation areas, museums, and festivals were identified as possibilities. Elton offered the Coushattas as the town's main attraction, making the tribe the only specific group of people singled out as something travelers might stop to see.[44] While Elton had previously benefited from the Coushatta Trading Post, suddenly the store had a critical stake in the town's success as it became fastened to the mission of Elton's joint tourism endeavor.

The tribe became more than just an attraction for Elton. It also came to bolster tourism efforts in the broader area when the Lake Charles Tourist Bureau began selling Coushatta baskets, beadwork, and picture cards.[45] In 1972 Wade O. Martin Jr., Louisiana secretary of state, reaffirmed the prominent role the tribe had come to play in the state's tourism industry in a speech he gave at the Indian Church during an event to renew the Trading Post's charter. He spoke of the growing impact he anticipated the Coushattas' tourism efforts would have on the state's economy and employment prospects, claiming that "tourism will eventually replace oil as the number one money maker in the state." He called the "Coushatta Indian tribe a valuable asset to the state not only for the potential as [a] tourist attraction but for the heritage as well."[46]

Coushattas felt this increased attention from local and state officials was a long time coming. For nearly a decade they had watched the Texas Alabama-Coushatta Reservation's tourism venture grow rapidly, while the Trading Post at Bayou Blue continued to operate with limited outside assistance and on a primarily volunteer basis. This difference stemmed from the Texas Tourist Council's investment in tourism on the Texas reservation since the early 1960s.[47] Like in Louisiana, the Texas community was in dire economic condition following federal termination, and it considered several avenues of economic development before settling on tourism as the most viable option. Walter W. Broemer, superintendent of the Alabama-Coushatta Reservation, explained that "if we had gone into manufacturing our people would have been further isolated as the language spoken on the reservation is the native tongue. Agriculture was not the answer either because the land is poor sand. Tourism brings people to the reservation and helps the state as well."[48] Around the time the Louisiana Coushattas opened the Trading Post, the Alabama-Coushattas opened a gift shop and, with assistance from the state, created a long-term tourism plan.[49] In 1973 they were awarded a $2.4 million grant from the Economic Development Administration (EDA) to further expand their tourism efforts and repair infrastructure. This funding went partially toward construction of an amphitheater, which hosted an outdoor drama portraying tribal histories during the Texas War of Independence from Mexico. The play received much attention, becoming one of four official plays of Texas in 1979. The EDA grant also funded a "living Indian village" and museum, with newspaper headlines touting "White Man Welcome in Indian Country."[50] A disparity obviously existed between the Texas and Louisiana communities' tourism operations, both in scale and funding. However, the differences didn't end there.

Six months after federal services were reinstated to the Louisiana Coushattas in 1973, Sickey attended a gathering of Elton's businessmen and rice farmers, who met to discuss the town's future. The Missouri Pacific Railroad Company had just announced that it planned to eliminate a stop in Elton and wished to donate the train depot building to the town to repurpose for its own use. Seizing the opportunity, Sickey asked Mayor Mildred "Millie" LaFleur and other town officials to consider contracting the building to the tribe for expanded tourism efforts. Considering how this agreement met the objectives of the Acadiana Trail Association to make towns along Highway 190 more attractive for passing motorists, they agreed. Sickey said that LaFleur recognized that "whatever we did as a tribe helped the town too . . . She was happy to do what she could to help us to bring people into town."[51] The assembly of town leaders lent a prime opportunity to announce the intent to renovate the train depot to house a new space to sell Coushatta baskets and other handmade items in town (fig. 15). Congressman John Breaux, one of the tribe's strongest advocates for reinstating federal Indian services, was the guest speaker at the meeting, where he praised the town, stating "Elton is on the map [now,] let's keep the ball rolling." Sickey also

Fig. 15: Solomon Battise, Ernest Sickey, and Elton mayor Millie LaFleur pose in front of the old train station, 1973. Courtesy of the Coushatta Tribal Archives.

spoke, labeling Elton a "natural place to be declared an Indian Capitol [*sic*] of Louisiana."[52]

The Elton Train Depot was much more accessible to tourists than the Trading Post, which was several miles from town. As Sickey explained, the tribe had big plans to transform the building into a Coushatta Cultural Center that would reach "a tremendous traveling audience . . . as well as those who are interested in the many varied aspects of Indian history." As with the Trading Post, the Coushatta Cultural Center proposal had two goals. The first was to sell works by Coushatta artisans, with a particular emphasis on pine needle baskets. The second goal was to create a museum that would support educational programming and the organizing of a small dance and speaking group composed of Coushattas who could be called upon by schools or for public events.[53]

Fig. 16: Darlene Langley Dunnehoo with son, Shane Robinson, near an impressive display of baskets in the Coushatta Cultural Center, late 1970s. Courtesy of the Coushatta Tribal Archives.

The Coushatta Cultural Center became a point of pride. With the assistance of various funding sources, the structure took two years to refurbish, and although it was in operation much earlier, it was officially completed in 1977. It was very inviting, with cedar shelves stocked with pine needle and river cane baskets and one case displaying beadwork and other handmade items. In all the center contained more than one thousand items (fig. 16).[54] According to Johnson, in *The Coushatta People,* tribal artisans sold approximately $42,000 worth of baskets and other crafts in the first year.[55] As revenue allowed, the tribe hired community members to run the center. At one time Sickey's sister, Bernetta Baker, managed the facility and supervised three sales clerks.[56] Bertney Langley was a manager at another time. The son of renowned weaver

Loris Abbott Langley and nephew of Bel Abbey, he knew how to further generate cultural awareness among the public. He also secured a grant from the Louisiana Arts Council to prepare a public educational program to promote the tribe's basketry and maintained enthusiasm within the tribe itself by holding basket weaving contests.[57] At another time the center was managed by Claude Medford Jr., a weaver of Choctaw descent from Texas who had married Rosalene Langley, a daughter of Edna Lorena Abbott Langley, another master weaver and also one of the last known Coushatta potters. Medford earned his own reputation as a skilled split river cane basket weaver. He published works on Louisiana's Indigenous material cultures and also consulted and taught basket weaving workshops around the state. During his brief stint at the Coushatta Cultural Center, Medford helped write grants and marketing materials for Coushatta basketry as the tribe further expanded its audience.[58]

Through the 1970s the Coushattas also received greater attention from the Department of the Interior's Indian Arts and Crafts Division. The southeastern field representative at that time, Stephen M. Richmond, was particularly interested in Coushatta material culture. Sickey said: "[He] was just so taken aback by the quality and the traditions and the history that went with it . . . He said, 'I want to work with your tribe.' He came and he took tons and tons of photographs of people going out into the woods to gather pine needles and then the drying process . . . It was very good exposure for us."[59] Richmond, a field representative since 1963, had a good reputation with tribes throughout the Southeast. In addition to photographing and collecting traditional art forms, he served as a liaison so tribes could share knowledge and helped them develop thriving economic markets to sell their work. Once he began working with the Coushattas, Richmond purchased many of their baskets for the Indian Arts and Crafts Division collection and gave suggestions for the train depot's renovation.[60] As with other tribes he had worked with, Richmond encouraged Coushatta artisans to not undervalue their work and recommended against displaying it alongside inexpensive souvenirs and trinkets.[61] During the transition from the Trading Post to the new Coushatta Cultural Center in Elton, Richmond also assisted in revising the pricing of baskets and other items. Sickey was pleased with the updates, telling Richmond, "I feel with a new approach and outlook we can further expand our craft sales and support even greater benefits to our tribal members."[62]

Richmond offered a new platform for Coushatta weavers to expand their audience, and his praise of their talent further increased their work's attention and stature. In 1973 he began working with weaver Rosabel Sylestine and planned the Coushattas' first traveling basketry exhibit. Born in 1922, Sylestine was considered "one of the most resourceful, creative basketweavers among her people." A Trading Post founder, she was deeply committed to her craft. Recalling her childhood, she stated: "Around seven years of age, I became interested in the pine needles by playing with my mother's gatherings. Then I grew to love the art my mother was creating with the straws. I would constantly be by my mother's side when she was doing baskets, and I began to learn the art by beginning to feel the working of the straw . . . As I became more involved in the craft, I saw the potential of sales, as did my mother with her work. My education is limited to the sixth grade and I felt this training would help me to provide additional income for me and, later, my family."[63] Sylestine honed her work as Richmond, Sickey, and Garrison—the Louisiana commissioner of Indian affairs—collaborated to launch the exhibit. The Louisiana State Historical Museum in New Orleans reserved six weeks at summer's end to dedicate to the event. Unable to veil his excitement, Richmond wrote to Sickey, "They want as many baskets to sell as possible, so you had better get prepared as I have a feeling this is going to be a big attraction."[64] Garrison helped to market the event, emphasizing the "unusual quality" of the Coushattas' work that was of a "regional nature." The timing of the exhibit could not have been better; it opened right after the Department of the Interior reinstated the Coushatta tribe's federal status. Sylestine's exhibit offered a convenient opportunity to celebrate with the tribe's advocates and friends, who gathered from near and far to view her work, which embodied the traditional knowledge and values that the Coushattas had worked to protect.[65]

The exhibition opening was "outstanding in every respect," wrote

Richmond. He reported that "attendance was much greater than it had been for the opening of much more extensive exhibitions [and] press coverage was the best that [the Arts and Crafts Division artisans] have had on any exhibition."[66] Museum staff also admitted that interest in Sylestine's exhibit was "more than even we had anticipated . . . We get calls daily inquiring about the length of the exhibit, additional demonstrations, and baskets for sale." Within the first few weeks, Sylestine had sold thirty-five of eighty-three items she brought to display. By the exhibit's end, she had made more than $1,000 in basket sales.[67] Because of high demand, she was asked to continue holding demonstrations at the museum even after her exhibit closed.[68]

Pleased with Sylestine's success, a few months later Richmond also began working with Edna Lorena Abbott Langley on plans for another exhibit. The marketing materials revealed a purposeful effort to draw even broader audiences by framing the exhibit as an "educational opportunity" to view a "way of life, much of which remains hidden from mainstream America."[69] Like Sylestine's work, Langley's also was well received, prompting her to write Richmond that she was "anxious to have another showing."[70] Throughout the 1970s Langley exhibited her work many times, even making it a family affair when she included work produced by her husband and children. As Langley's work received more exposure, she began experimenting with different designs and media. She had perhaps her most memorable exhibits in Texas and Louisiana during 1977, when she incorporated traditional Coushatta designs into clothing.[71] The National Endowment for the Arts recognized her with a Craftsmen's Fellowship grant to continue working on designs, along with her daughters, who had worked in the garment industry.[72] Langley was more than just an artistic visionary; she generated a deeper appreciation for the fluidity of Coushatta culture by demonstrating how traditional aesthetics had a place in a modern context.

Marian John was the third Coushatta weaver Richmond worked with to implement a traveling exhibit. Born in 1938, she first learned to weave at the age of seven, a skill that helped her support her siblings after her mother died. She was among those weavers who first sold pine needle baskets on roadsides and later at the Trading Post, earning a reputation as a "master designer and craftswoman." John said, "I love doing my basket weaving and would like very much to continue and encourage others in the tribe and especially young people."[73] Like the others, her exhibits also received a warm reception. She initially showed her work at the Louisiana State Museum in New Orleans and then at Houston's Contemporary Art Museum in the summer of 1974.[74] "Few people in the Houston area had any previous knowledge of this Native American art, to say nothing of their knowledge of Indians being in the state of Louisiana," Richmond said. The show was so successful, in fact, that John also received a National Endowment for the Arts grant.[75] In 1975 she was selected by the Smithsonian American Art Museum to display her baskets, and she launched a two-year traveling exhibition with the Louisiana Council for Music and Performing Arts, offering a series of public demonstrations. Crowds gathered to watch John's skillful fingers shape longleaf pine needles into tightly bound baskets and animal shapes. People were particularly drawn to what one photographer called "the whimsy and humor of the effigy baskets."[76] Each exhibition was expertly executed, and Sickey wrote to Richmond: "I assure you that without your professional expertise and guidance, the tribe would not be in [the] advanced stages we are now enjoying. The current program provides more outlets [and] more income."[77]

The rising fame of Coushatta weavers was a statewide point of pride. In 1976 the Louisiana State Arts Council awarded the tribe a grant to cover multimedia costs for additional showings. Governor Edwards wrote to congratulate the tribe, stating, "The programs you sponsor provide much to the overall wellbeing of Louisiana."[78] The Coushattas' efforts also contributed to the rising popularity of Louisiana folk art and traditional crafts. Eager audiences frequently invited Coushattas to participate in conferences and new exhibitions, and the tribe's artisans were often profiled in literature on Louisiana art. A 1980 publication, *Louisiana Traditional Crafts*, for example, featured baskets by Coushattas and Chitimachas alongside Louisiana folk crafts, such as quilting, All Saints' Day wreaths, and corn husk mats.[79] Richmond also raised the profile of Louisiana's Indigenous arts by connecting the Coushattas' and Chitimachas' work to other well-known southeastern tribal artisans. In

1980 he organized a *Southeastern Indian Basketry* exhibit, which displayed their work along with pieces from Mississippi Choctaws, Cherokees of North Carolina, Seminoles of Florida, and Catawbas of South Carolina. This combined show was to "provide far-reaching benefits for the Indian Tribes of the Southeast" and was the final exhibition Coushattas collaborated on with Richmond before he retired in 1983. It appeared across the region, and according to Richmond, the Coushatta baskets were the "highlights of this show [and] people have been eager to find out where these baskets might be purchased."[80]

While baskets elevated the Coushattas' visibility, they also provided the tribe with opportunities to lobby for improvements within the Bayou Blue community. For example, when Louisiana senator A. John Tassin Jr. was unable to attend a basketry exhibit in New Orleans that the tribe personally invited him to, he sent his regrets, stating he found the Coushatta basketry "intriguing and interesting" and promised to speak personally to the governor about improving roads in Allen Parish.[81] The publicity also attracted the attention of other influential people in the state, such as Lucille Blume, New Orleans socialite and president of the Louisiana Council for Music and Performing Arts. She circulated among Louisiana's elite and regularly visited the tribe to buy baskets.[82] Blume shared her experiences with her art-loving friends throughout the state and told a reporter that "there is something in American Indian art which is viable, exciting and relevant to Americans today."[83] Her love of Coushatta basketry, in particular, inspired her to advocate for the tribe within the political realm. Sickey remembered Blume making demands to "some bureaucrat in Baton Rouge [that] 'I want this done for the tribe . . . my Indians.' She would harass them and get right in their faces about how the state has mistreated Indians." Blume's efforts may have taken a possessive tone, but she exhibited some influence in paving another way for Coushatta baskets to find prominence and yield triple the price they had once received.[84]

The Coushattas harnessed art to promote social and economic change, creating what education scholar Darlene E. Clover called "pedagogic contact zones" to effectively engage the public.[85] From their localized economic ventures to the various exhibits throughout the state, the tribe controlled the discourse of their narrative by showcasing the talent of some of their finest weavers and using the opportunity to share a compelling story of a people who survived seemingly insurmountable odds to make significant contributions to the cultural and economic vitality of Louisiana.

Komaatik Stibachasakato Im-iltolihnok
Building a Tribal Nation

While the Coushattas' tourism enterprise and basket exhibitions progressed quickly, programs to improve health care, housing, education, social services, and employment opportunities didn't come as easily.[86] The wheels of bureaucracy were slow moving, and federal reinstatement didn't bring the immediate relief the Coushattas had anticipated. In fact, it took two years after reinstatement before the tribe was placed on the BIA's budget cycle. There were immediate concerns, however, and the Coushattas were unwilling to wait before taking action, driving Sickey back into a rigorous program of grant writing and advocacy work. The combination of the Coushattas' high-profile allies and their own increased role in the state's evolving public image aided their pursuits. By 1974 Sickey had developed a plan for land acquisition and use, along with strategies to boost community and economic development. "I believed in the art of planning," he said, "because I didn't want the tribe, or myself, just wandering around hoping and guessing." He met with dozens of people throughout the tribe to assess their greatest needs. "It wasn't my dream," Sickey emphasized. "It was their vision" that shaped the tribe's "road map" for the next ten years. As this master plan grew in complexity, committees had formed to share the efforts in overseeing such broad areas of need such as recreation and health care, encouraging community-wide participation in the development process.[87]

In 1975 the tribe received a $100,000 grant from the U.S. Department of Housing and Urban Development (HUD) to construct an administrative building on federal trust land in the center of the community.[88] The grant covered expenses for building materials, but the labor was primarily provided by Coushattas, who volunteered to erect the building and pour concrete for the sidewalks leading to what became the nerve center for tribal programs and services. Rodney Williams, Sickey's contemporary and friend, told his daughter Crystal, "It was a huge thing for the community to experience . . . Our people were living in poverty. They barely had jobs, and there was hardly any income . . . To see actual buildings going up, I think that [had] a big impact."[89] In documenting this period, Johnson wrote, "The Coushatta have entered a new period of prosperity symbolized by the sound of saws and hammers of workmen constructing a new tribal headquarters."[90] The tribal administrative building drew a lot of outside attention, and Sickey enjoyed the chance to demonstrate publicly that the Coushattas were more than just a source of tourism to the area. They were part of an emerging tribal nation. As a result, they invited friends and neighbors to the dedication celebration, which was a milestone event that attorney Leonard Knapp called "very special."[91]

With the new building in place, the Coushattas needed resources to launch their operation. "I wasn't shy about going and asking for help," Sickey said, "[because] we didn't have a dime." Like before, he continued meeting with civic organizations, such as the Lions and Kiwanis Clubs. He also regularly visited the Oakdale Rotary Club, which was how he met the Rush family, who, he said, were "instrumental in the early days of helping me out and encouraging me."[92] Howard Rush was an influential businessman in the area who, according to his children, Ray and Kelly Rush, respected Sickey and "did whatever [Ernest] asked him to do . . . He helped him because of their friendship."[93] While the Rush family expanded the Coushattas' support network in Allen Parish, the tribe already enjoyed long-standing friendships with businesses in Elton. These relationships proved helpful when seeking a bank to extend the tribe credit prior to the release of BIA funding. Local businesses wanted to see the tribe succeed, so Elton American Bank ensured that tribal projects and programs could proceed at a steady pace. Also, a local office equipment store allowed the tribe to furnish the administration building on credit and even donated an old copy machine to get it started.[94]

As the tribe gained momentum, Sickey realized he needed assistance with planning and grant writing. Plus, the leadership overlap of the nonprofit Coushatta Alliance, Inc., and the Coushatta Tribal Council, which had previously given the tribe latitude to maneuver different funding requirements, progressively complicated matters as donors expressed concern about the commingling of funding.[95] The Coushattas faced a critical juncture about whether to mentor and prepare other tribal members to step into important administrative positions or hire professionals from outside the tribe. Ultimately, they did both. To assist with strategic planning and grant writing, the Coushattas worked with several people on a part-time basis, including an AAIA intern, graduate students from Louisiana State University, and employees of a local planning organization.[96] However, it soon became clear that the scope of their needs required a dedicated full-time person, so the tribe hired Roderick "Rod" Bertrand, the son of a Cajun rice farmer whose family lived next to the Coushattas and had a long-standing relationship with them. Bertrand attended school with tribal children and had fond memories of swimming in irrigation wells during the summers with his Indian classmates. He had also spent a lot of time with Bel Abbey as a young child. A former teacher, Bertrand started working as the tribal planner in 1978 and stayed for several years, before leaving to attend law school. Sickey credited Bertrand with helping to guide the tribe's early development by preparing assessment reports, researching how to acquire more land, and administering funding received from federal agencies for different programs. Despite a lack of experience with government contracts, grants, and compliance requirements, Bertrand learned quickly and collaborated with Sickey to creatively find ways to fund large-scale projects by piecing together different grants. The two also strategically diversified the tribe's funding sources so the Coushatta people wouldn't become overreliant on federal programs.[97]

The reservation was buzzing with activity. While outside help was necessary for some positions, the tribe focused on hiring Coushattas for critical jobs in community development. People such as George Abbott were pivotal in building tribal infrastructure in the early years. Lovelin Poncho also made important contributions as the first director of maintenance and housing. He oversaw HUD grants for rehabilitating existing homes, building new ones, and transporting prefabricated houses. By 1976 Coushatta private landownership had increased to approximately thirteen hundred acres, with rough roads linking the homes of tribal citizens. At its peak there were about ten families living on or near the original fifteen acres of trust land in the eastern community. As the tribe acquired more reservation land, twenty-five to thirty families established homes in the western community. Much of the new development, however, was in the central community where many families moved into clustered homes that took on a somewhat suburban character. Like other reservations in which more than 90 percent of Indian housing, by 1982, was financed by HUD, the Coushattas' residential patterns had shifted. And while Coushattas had resisted this trend in previous decades, they soon embraced the transition as federal trust lands expanded without sacrificing private landholdings.[98]

There are many stories circulating throughout the community about the important impact of the housing program. The tribe was able to repair homes with two $150,000 community development block grants—one in 1978 and another in 1980.[99] Other funding allowed the tribe to build new homes for those in need and those whose names were placed on a list, with priority given to the elderly. Barbara Langley estimated that through 1985 two to three homes were built each year, and even more were repaired or remodeled with new bathrooms or roofs.[100] Loretta Williams recalled how happy her family was the first time they received running water in their three-bedroom home.[101] The housing program not only improved the Coushattas' quality of life; it also permitted some tribal members who had left years earlier to return home. Heather Williams told how her great-grandmother, Ivy Thompson, one of many weavers who supplied Sickey with baskets during his advocacy work, had left Allen Parish for a period. In the late 1970s she wished to return, so a home was built for her at the end of the fifteen-acre circle in the eastern community. "She didn't have anywhere else to go," Williams said, and the housing program allowed her to reunite with the tribe until her death in 1989.[102] Lelia Battise's family also lived within the fifteen-acre circle, and she remembered when her mother's home was built through the program. Years later Battise had a home of her own built right next door. "I think that was the most important thing to us because we lived in an old run-down house [before that]," she recalled. "My new home was so clean, and it was mine."[103] In addition to the housing program, by 1977 twenty-one Coushatta families also began receiving assistance with covering the costs of utility bills through the Energy Crisis Intervention Program. "We just kept on striving for a better environment for the community," said Leonard Battise.[104]

As the housing program took off, the need for health care was also central to the tribe's advocacy efforts. While some Coushattas used state-funded services, medical care remained largely inaccessible. According to Ronnie Petree, a banker who worked closely with the tribe and also held a position on the rural health clinic board, Elton didn't have a doctor in the mid-1970s, so residents—Indian and non-Indian—had to travel to other towns for service.[105] This lack of local care particularly hurt the Coushattas, given the enduring gap in life expectancy compared to white Americans, who lived an average of ten years longer, according to a 1985 study among the Mississippi Choctaws.[106] The unavailability of health care drove several Coushatta families to the Alabama-Coushatta Reservation in Texas. Crystal Williams explained how her grandmother was among them, even transferring her tribal membership so she could access the Texas reservation's health services.[107]

When the Coushattas first received funding from Indian Health Services (IHS) in 1974, it was for an initial contract of $25,000. The funding was to pay staff salaries and medical bills incurred by the tribe, but its members weren't given guidance on how to set up such a program or keep records to comply with reporting expectations. To further frustrate matters, Sickey explained, "there wasn't even a hint of money for a building to house the medical center." So, space had to be made in the new tribal administration complex for the health program, and the tribe was left to search for funding from private foundations to adequately cover its needs. It wasn't long until the Jennings-based Zigler Foundation agreed to assist the Coushattas by awarding them $10,000 for the medical center. The funding was enough to pay for construction materials, but the tribe had to design and build the one-story health services building, equipped with offices and examination rooms, itself.[108]

In spite of the challenges of getting the medical building erected, the reintroduction of health services to the tribe after nearly twenty-five years inspired hope. While many Coushattas continued to practice traditional medicine at home, the new health facility provided an extra level of care. Contract doctors gave on-site examinations, and Coushattas could fill prescriptions as well as participate in prevention and health education efforts. While these services gave the Coushattas greatly needed relief, the funding didn't stretch very far. Just a few months into the fiscal year, much of the annual budget was already spent on salaries and hefty medical bills. In 1976 Bertney Langley became the first tribal health services director. He began as a forester but later took accounting courses at a vocational school. As tribal development accelerated in the mid-1970s, Langley found himself taking on multiple roles. Initially, he was the tribe's finance director and Coushatta Cultural Center manager. He also raised money for youth activities and recreation programs. When Sickey asked him to manage the tribe's health services and get the program on track, Langley was reluctant but soon relented. He had to make tough choices to prevent the tribe from running a deficit and instituted a strict expense approval process. The process was not popular, but he knew it was necessary to save the program. Sickey's support softened the community's response, but Langley explained that "it didn't go over too well with the tribe . . . We got hollered at by aunts and uncles . . . [but] Ernest held his ground and slowly but surely, after two years, they accepted what I was talking about."[109]

Sickey came to rely on Langley as a strategic collaborator. The two discussed at length which new programs to pursue. "It seemed like we worked day and night," Langley said. "I was young . . . and I really didn't want to work all those hours, but when I saw him working late at night I said, 'God, I feel sorry for the guy.' If I could help, I would help . . . We'd stay all night writing proposals." Sickey mentored Langley, asking him to read letters and attend meetings to observe how he represented the tribe. Langley said Sickey "didn't have time to sit down and explain [everything] to you. He said, 'Here it is. I know you can do it. Go do it.' That was a good training model."[110] The friendship endured through the years, and Langley's daughter Eleyna vividly recalled her father's long conversations with Sickey: "My dad and Ernest were always very close . . . Even now when they speak on the phone, they laugh a lot. They speak quickly in Koasati . . . [they] were often talking about fighting for the people . . . and allowing us as a tribal community to be able to be seen [and for] other people to have an understanding of who we were, what we were about, and what we are capable of."[111] Sickey tried to emulate the mentorship he had been provided through his life by supporting the efforts of Langley and other Coushattas who were committed to the tribe's development. It was a joint effort, which helped ease the struggle. Yet these leaders learned many tough lessons along the way.

Setting the health care program on the right course was a huge victory. Even the national IHS office commended the Coushattas for their savvy use of such a small budget. Although the budget later increased, it never fully covered their needs, which encouraged the use of creative measures. For example, Sickey met with the public affairs division of the nearby Fort Polk military base and convinced its medical and dental staff to provide the tribe with medical exams and dental care on a rotating basis for several years. He also invited medical students from the University of Houston to the reservation to conduct eye exams, and he later secured donations of eyeglasses for the children. Langley's efforts brought additional resources to the tribe. To supply the children's dental program, he wrote letters and sent pictures to the makers of both Colgate and Crest, asking for donations. A month later he received a call from Procter & Gamble, saying: "'We got your letter, and we want to help. We'll be sending you some supplies' . . . [In] two or three weeks . . . here comes an eighteen-wheeler full of supplies—floss, toothpaste, and toothbrushes . . . everything that we could possibly use . . . We had enough supplies for a year or two. Not just [for] the little kids but the whole tribe."[112]

Coushatta education and employment also were among the top priorities following federal reinstatement. The correlation between educational attainment and income were well documented. A 1976 report published by the Louisiana State Planning Office claimed that this association transcended race, noting that "the man who . . . has more education makes the most money in Louisiana. And it matters very little whether he is black or white." The report extended its claim to Indian communities, whose "members suffer from the disadvantages associated with poorly educated people . . . and even today the school dropout rate is extremely high."[113] While this study downplayed race-based employment discrimination, it reinforced other data that identified a trend of low educational attainment among the state's tribal communities. A 1978 survey among Louisiana's rural Indian populations offered more details, identifying a 32 percent illiteracy rate, with 38 percent surveyed not having a high school education and 19 percent having never attended school.[114] Coushattas who completed high school had few opportunities to further their educations in college or trade schools. As Leonard Battise explained, "After they finished school, some wanted to go to college . . . but they couldn't. They didn't have the funds. They just had to go in the world and start working." Even then, however, they faced disadvantages, as another study revealed, given that Coushattas generally earned well below the state median income.[115]

The founding of the Louisiana Office of Indian Affairs (LOIA) in 1972 offered tribes an opportunity to curb this trend through job training and educational resources. This was one of the motivating factors that encouraged tribal leaders to negotiate, for the first time, the terms of tribal-state relationships. It was a delicate process, however, because the parameters of these relationships remained uncertain due to the evolving roles of states in implementing economic policies and social programs within the federal system. The relationships between tribes and states have historically been characterized by mistrust, frustration, and anger. Yet tribes and states also shared overlapping concerns in protecting the health and welfare of their people. The challenge, as tribal leaders discovered, was how to balance these interests with the budget.[116] Although budgetary constraints always seemed to be a prohibitive factor in state government, the executive order creating the LOIA carried significant promise in merging the efforts of Louisiana Indians, as a group, to qualify for financial assistance reserved for larger populations. Through Sickey's efforts the Coushattas were involved with the LOIA from the beginning. He first served as a consultant to the LOIA and then as its director from 1973 to 1975. He was the first Indian hired by the state to coordinate Indian affairs, which he did while serving as chairman of his tribe.[117] Sickey's mission was to make the LOIA a resource for helping Louisiana tribes improve their job prospects and quality of life. It appeared as if things were on track when the agency secured a Comprehensive Employment Training Act (CETA) grant for vocational education and job training.[118] To administer the grant, Sickey hired Jeanette Alcon Campos, who was of Ute and Pueblo descent and had been working for the Council on the Aging in New Orleans. Campos and Sickey set right to work building the infrastructure needed to support a growing intertribal coalition and a strong base by which grants could be managed. Campos described how the two of them complemented one another. While she dedicated herself to building intertribal collaboration and communication, "He was the visionary in the state for Indians."[119]

The CETA program promised to fill a great need among the state's tribes. Yet it soon became apparent that the LOIA's effectiveness was compromised by a series of bureaucratic woes, including delayed budgets, rigid regulations, and complicated approval and reporting systems.[120] Frustrated that the administration of the CETA grant was stifled, Campos explained: "We couldn't get [it off the ground] because of state regulations . . . And we couldn't put trainees on because there was no process for that within the state."[121] Ultimately, the only way to effectively administer the program was to circumvent the barriers the state imposed by not running the grant through the LOIA and, instead, establishing a nonprofit, 501(c)(4) organization. Initially called the Indian Manpower Services, Inc., the organization was later renamed the Louisiana Inter-Tribal Council (ITC) as it took over the CETA program. Incorporated in 1975, the ITC became the state's prime sponsor of the CETA grant, providing temporary employment, vocational training, and career information.[122] An ITC board of directors supervised the organization, comprised of representatives from four Louisiana tribal communities, including the Coushattas, the Chitimachas, the Jena Band of Choctaws, and the United Houma Nation.[123] These tribes, along with others who joined in subsequent years—including the Tunica-Biloxis, who joined in 1979—regularly convened as the ITC took shape. As the CETA grant coordinator, Campos transferred from the LOIA to the ITC and became executive director, a position she held until 1986. Sickey also left the LOIA (as Garrison had earlier), telling a reporter that he "couldn't abide the bureaucracy" since the state seemed to be working against Indian interests in spite of earlier hopes and promises. Furthermore, he felt his role at the LOIA took too much time away from his own tribe.[124]

From its inception the ITC administered CETA funds for job training and emphasized industrial electronics, welding, nursing, auto mechanics, and drafting. Twenty-four Coushatta adults and youth participated in the first year, with sixteen more the following year.[125] As the ITC's vision evolved, so did the nature of the grant, which was renamed the Job Training Partnership Act (JTPA) program and grew to support different kinds of programming. One example was a salary-matching program in which participants received on-the-job-training for which employers and the grant split the costs. Once training was complete, the employer could permanently hire the trainee. According to a 1982 report, this program saw several Coushattas successfully hired into jobs following a training period.[126]

The vocational training and job experience many Coushattas received were often strategically planned so they could later contribute to tribal development. As Sickey explained: "There was always a purpose for everything we did, like teaching them bookkeeping, how to start a business, and help each other as they go . . . We wanted the Indians to be the first priority . . . because other places wouldn't give them a chance to advance."[127] Plus, many Coushattas preferred to work for the tribe so they could be a part of its advancement. Paula Abbey Manuel described how her father commuted for years to a job in Lake Charles but later retired from the job to start working for the tribe.[128] Lelia Battise also sought tribal employment after learning to become a receptionist. As a young mother, she had commuted to Jennings for work. Then she took advantage of the CETA program to attend a trade school.[129] Loretta Williams had a similar story. Her two brothers worked offshore in the oil industry, but she stayed at home and gained job training through a program she entered as a sophomore in high school in the early 1980s. She first worked in the Coushatta Cultural Center and then as an aide at the local library. Following graduation, the tribe sent her to a trade school to learn secretarial skills, and when she finished, she returned to work for the tribe.[130]

The CETA grant (and subsequent versions) also funded programs to educate and train tribal youth for future leadership roles. The ITC

Summer Youth Program, for example, connected adolescents from different tribal communities each year. "These are the future tribal leaders," Campos said. "They are starting out with the advantage of having had a chance to deal with one another as young people, which will build a strong trust relationship [between their different tribes]." As the executive director, Campos looked to this program as a way of securing the intertribal collaborations that many had worked so hard to build and which were critical for the future of the ITC. The program also supported the future career paths of those such as Leland Thompson, who became the Coushatta Tribal Fire Department chief, and Kevin Billiot of the United Houma Nation, who later became the executive director of the ITC.[131]

Once job training programs were established, Coushattas began working on an adult learning program for tribal citizens in need of credits toward earning their high school diplomas. Working in collaboration with the ITC and the Allen Parish Adult Education office, the program received money from several sources. Elton schoolteachers, who had long observed the difficulties Coushattas faced, saw the tribe's efforts and wanted to help. As a result, the adult education classes were run by local educators, some of whom volunteered and others who were paid through Indian education funding. If the tribe couldn't find a math teacher in Elton, they would use the funds to pay mileage for someone to come from Jennings. Kenneth Bruchhaus was a teacher in the town of Kinder in 1975, when Sickey approached him about teaching weekly classes on the reservation for a small salary. Bruchhaus accepted and remained there for nearly ten years, giving him a critical perspective on the program's progression since its inception. He developed curricula using guidelines established in the parish school system and regularly attended conferences in Baton Rouge on running adult education programs. "We just had a really good thing going out there," he said. With his wife and a few Coushatta assistants, Bruchhaus held class every Tuesday evening; an average of ten tribal members working toward their GED attended each week. Loris Abbott Langley brought food to entice greater participation from the community, and soon she became the first to complete the program and earn her GED.[132]

A critical part of the tribe's developmental efforts was the creation of an education department to serve the tribal children. Sickey credited the Elton school system for working cooperatively with the tribe to devise ways to improve Coushattas' educational experiences and to encourage their retention through high school. Extra effort in this area was important, Sickey pointed out, because "many parents had very little education themselves, so they weren't able to encourage their own children."[133] Sickey's years working with the LOIA and the ITC provided him with the opportunity to secure funding for Indian education that benefited not only the Coushattas but also other tribes in the state. During the 1974–75 fiscal year, for example, nearly $400,000 was distributed to parish schools for approximately twenty-two hundred Indian children throughout Louisiana—fifty of whom were Coushattas.[134] A few years later Sickey helped found a Louisiana Indian college fund to encourage the pursuit of higher education among Indian youth.[135]

With work under way in housing, health, job training, and education, the tribe also focused on maintaining community cohesion by plotting out ways to use reservation land for recreation and to support tribal gatherings (fig. 17). While many Coushattas still planned social events around the Indian Church, the hope was to expand upon this foundation by establishing a tribal park where both Indians and non-Indians could congregate. Allen Parish contributed labor and equipment to the plan, and in 1976 this collaboration received a boost when the tribe started a Youth Conservation Corps (YCC) program funded jointly by the U.S. Department of the Interior, the U.S. Agriculture Department, and the Louisiana Parks and Recreation Department. The program allowed the tribe to hire sixty-five teenagers from the tribe and surrounding towns to clear land, plant gardens, repair houses, and address other community development needs. Sickey explained, "This was a black, Indian, and white program," which was one of fifteen YCC programs in Louisiana providing summer employment. Principals and teachers made hiring recommendations, and the teens were clustered into teams to engage in friendly competitions to create projects to improve the reservation. This was a productive approach that helped launch a tribal beautification program. Participants planted shrubbery and flowers and cleaned up one of the tribal cemeteries, even making crosses to adorn the grave

Fig. 17: The community regularly came together for picnics and to celebrate holidays. Here Coushatta children gathered for an Easter egg hunt, 1970s. Courtesy of the Coushatta Tribal Archives.

sites. The Coushattas' YCC program ran for several summers and also employed local teachers to supervise teens. The program not only helped tribal development efforts but provided the surrounding non-Indian community with a new perspective on the tribe as a thriving community with a vision to improve their lives and those of their neighbors. Coushattas further encouraged this message by hosting a Parents' Day barbecue as the program concluded in August, which served as the tribe's gesture of appreciation for the contributions the participants had made to improving the reservation as well as an invitation to consider the Coushattas their friends. The experience left a lasting impression on a whole generation of the area's youth, who became loyal allies to the tribe. "Some of the people I run across still talk about it," Sickey said. Additionally, the program filled a great need in the area, so "the local politicos were very happy . . . because they didn't have the resources to hire kids for the summer, but the tribe did. It was a win."[136]

By 1978 the Coushattas had expanded their recreation area to include a baseball diamond that became known as the best in the area. The idea began when the tribe tried to enroll children in a nearby town's Little League program but discovered that it wasn't inclusive and showed favoritism toward certain players. As a result, Coushattas created their own teams, which were open to everyone. They couldn't host games without their own field, however, so they went looking for funding. Within months the tribe secured grants from the BIA, Louisiana's Land and Water Conservation Fund, and the Zigler Foundation, allowing them to begin clearing land and installing lights. Bertney Langley described how volunteers brought their own lawnmowers: "We would all pitch in and finish cutting the ball park." To install fences and a backstop, they called on Cajun friends who were welders. Because they were willing to do much of the work themselves, the Coushattas constructed the ballpark for only $60,000, and it was, according to Sickey, the "the pride and joy of the community." They developed both youth and adult athletic programs, and in its prime there were ten to twelve tribal baseball and softball teams at play. Almost everyone in the community was involved in some way, either as a player or coach. Local businesses supported the tribal athletics programs by donating uniforms and equipment and sponsoring tournaments. The ballpark was also used for the Coushatta Olympics, in which tribal members gathered for friendly competitions that involved running and even children's tricycle races.[137]

In addition to the recreational benefits, the ballpark provided an impetus for the tribe to continue outreach efforts and earn additional revenue. The adult fast-pitch softball leagues, in particular, drew many spectators who had never before ventured down the rural roads to the Coushatta reservation. Public invitations were extended via newspapers to those interested in participating or attending tournaments.[138] One visiting reporter wrote of a game he had witnessed "in which young blacks and whites are competing under the watchful eyes of Indian umpires and scorekeepers. A culturally diverse crowd fills the bleachers, people of French, English and Indian descent. It would be an unusual gathering were it not for the fact that the people of Louisiana are an unusual lot."[139] By 1984 travel into the reservation had become easier, for many of the roads were finally leveled and blacktopped, and so the number of people from all over southwestern Louisiana and southeastern Texas who journeyed to play at the Coushatta ballpark grew.[140] Gene Paul, a lifelong resident of Oakdale who later served as mayor, fondly remembered tournaments on the Coushatta reservation: "I played softball on an independent team [and] . . . that's how I got to know . . . a lot of tribal members." The friendships developed through softball endured, and many of those visiting players, including Paul, were later hired by the tribe as its economic enterprises continued to expand. Hosting tournaments, Sickey explained, was a perfect way for the tribe to "showcase what we've done. We still didn't have much, but we had the best ballpark in the region . . . People could bring their barbeque pits out there and cook . . . The ballpark was a big hit for many, many years." It also provided a revenue stream for the tribe, which early on ran a concession stand and later a convenience store and gas station.[141]

The rapid pace at which Coushattas developed their community left onlookers in awe. It seemed liked "a lot of things were done in a short period of time," said Bruchhaus.[142] Among these developments were the establishment of a tribal fire station, police force, and court. "I was amazed at what we did with very little money," Sickey said. "It was really a volunteer spirit that we had, [and the people] were so proud of what they saw." Ernest's father, Davis Sickey, died in 1983, but he lived to see the tribe's early efforts come to fruition. His own sacrifices and advocacy, along with that of others such as Martin Abbey, Solomon Battise, and those who came before them, undoubtedly laid the groundwork for the successes the tribe saw in the years following reinstatement.[143]

With such rapid growth came the need to keep the community updated on developments and opportunities, inspiring the founding of a tribal newspaper in 1976. *Coushatta Smoke Signal* was an internal means of communication, not circulated outside the tribe, which published birth and graduation announcements, advertisements for tribal job training and youth summer programs, and an extensive segment devoted to the "chairman's message." In each issue Sickey encouraged and praised the community while updating readers on his activities as he continued to advocate for the tribe. In the February 1977 issue he

Fig. 18: Raising the tribal seal on the Coushatta Cultural Center, late 1970s. Courtesy of Bertney and Linda Langley.

reminded the Coushatta people that, in spite of progress, "we must continue the aggressive and organized approach we continue to rely on . . . to move ahead collectively."[144] This message of self-determination and community cohesion was woven through each issue. Although the newspaper didn't survive beyond the 1970s, a few issues have been preserved by the Coushatta Heritage Department and offer important insight into this critical period of the tribe's development. They reveal how the Coushattas handled such a quickly changing environment with a community-centered sensibility, which was grounded in the values that had sustained them through the generations. The means of communication may have changed, but the core message never wavered.

Konnaathiihilkaak Kolkafihliichito
The Language of Sovereignty

By 1977 motorists traveling through Elton on Highway 190 were greeted by a large, colorful sign.[145] It was the new official emblem of the Coushatta Nation featuring an alligator garfish across a circle of colors representing the daily cycle from sunrise to sunset.[146] The emblem was affixed to the front of the Coushatta Cultural Center, and it soon appeared on tribal stationery, business cards, and price tags of items sold at the center and in newspaper articles covering the tribe's activities (fig. 18). The image offered a glimpse into significant cultural symbolism with deep historical roots, and it carried a strategic purpose of declaring the Coushattas' status as a sovereign nation—one with an unquestionable foothold in a region it had called home for a century.

Gone were the days when Coushattas were referred to as "Elton's Indians" or an "orphaned" or "lost" people. Their rapid progression in the years following federal reinstatement influenced the development of the entire region and particularly attracted the attention of their Cajun and African American neighbors, who also held precarious positions within the area's economic and racial hierarchy. Dewith Carrier, the brother of two Oberlin mayors and a former mayor pro tem himself, explained the impact of the Coushattas' development on the outlook of Cajuns: "We were never involved in government, not many Cajuns at all . . . [My brothers] got involved with Ernest [Sickey] because they were new leaders that people didn't think could lead. Ernest was the . . . first [Coushatta person] that would come out dressed in a suit and actually . . . speak the way he did. Here came a leader for the Indians and the Cajuns . . . It was kind of along the lines of Edwin Edwards [who] showed people that Cajuns could be smart . . . I really think that Ernest and a few others made it easier on people like me to be able to succeed even though we were Cajun people."[147] While the political and social struggles the Coushattas faced were framed by their status as a tribal nation, Sickey's message of empowerment resonated with their Cajun neighbors, who shared some overlapping experiences and were also looking to find their political voice in Allen and Jefferson Davis Parishes.

Such connections didn't necessarily define the historical relationships between Coushattas and African Americans. During the Jim Crow years, Coushattas were permitted to attend white schools, while the status quo was upheld when it came to the African American population. Elton's black families resided in segregated neighborhoods and attended separate schools until 1965. While both populations were among the most impoverished and underserved in the area, the two groups interacted informally. As black civil rights activities increased in the area, Coushattas generally avoided involvement because the tribe's mission emphasized asserting self-determining rights as a tribal nation instead of individual civil rights. Nevertheless, following reinstatement, Sickey contacted African American organizations with an invitation to lend mutual support for their advocacy efforts, which landed him invitations to speak at several black churches about important issues facing tribal nations. He recalled: "I was never asked to publicly join a protest, but they would ask for my support for their cause with the legislators that I knew. When there was a need, I was there for them, and when I needed them, they were there for me." Over the years Sickey wrote letters, made phone calls, and testified on special issues regarding race relations in Louisiana.[148]

By the mid-1970s the Coushattas' developmental efforts permanently redefined the local power structure in Allen and Jefferson Davis Parishes. The tribe occupied a unique position within the political arena because of relationships Sickey had fostered with members of the state legislature. He had direct access to the governor's office and influential people, something that many local elected officials lacked. This access often proved valuable in negotiating with surrounding towns for resources in exchange for assistance in lobbying state representatives. "We're quite proud of what we accomplished back then," Sickey said. "As a smaller tribe almost unknown to the world, surrounded by non-Indians, [we] managed to be a cooperative entity among the people and have this excellent relationship with neighboring communities." This reciprocity not only let Coushattas continue emphasizing their responsibility as "good neighbors," but it also helped to position them as an emerging agent of change, a particularly appealing message in an economically depressed area. As Coushatta developmental efforts took off, the tribe made donations to local events and festivals and was a valuable customer to surrounding businesses as it purchased large quantities of building supplies. Sickey preached a consistent message that the success of the Coushatta tribe would benefit the entire region. He argued that people's livelihoods and quality of life would improve if they all worked together.[149]

While the tribe's local influence continued to grow, it also emerged as a significant force in a region-wide Indian movement. In 1973 the tribe joined the United Southern and Eastern Tribes, Inc. (USET), during a critical time in the evolution of federal Indian policy. Sickey had been on several USET committees, and he had testified in Congress and collaborated on resolutions to influence federal legislation.[150] As a newly reinstated federal tribe working on infrastructure, Coushattas benefited from their involvement with the USET, which also facilitated the support they received from Chairman Phillip Martin of the Mississippi Choctaws. Martin was recognized as a visionary because of his approach to tribal self-determination through business and industry. According to one article, he was the "Lee Iacocca of the Choctaw reservation," for he brought economic stability to his tribe through multiple enterprises. The tribe also created thousands of jobs, bolstering Mississippi's economy.[151] "I was truly impressed with what he did . . . [and] what he brought to the people," Sickey said. Like Buffalo Tiger of the Miccosukees, Martin provided Sickey with mentorship and inspiration on the possibilities that savvy tribal development could bring. The Mississippi Choctaws had a history of assisting the Coushattas, which continued into the 1970s, when Martin sent them help in establishing a tribal accounting system and organizing trainings on the complexities of different government program reporting processes. The technical assistance provided by the Mississippi Choctaws during those formative years was invaluable.[152]

Being at the forefront of Louisiana's Indian movement, Sickey wished to use his experience and knowledge to support other tribes throughout the state, many of which sought to follow a trajectory similar to the Coushattas'. The Jena Band of Choctaws was one of the first communities Sickey assisted by soliciting help from the AAIA in the tribe's preliminary steps toward its bid for federal recognition, which it achieved in 1995.[153] Also, Donna Pierite of the Tunica-Biloxi Tribe, which was federally recognized in 1981, said that "Ernest has inspired us and encouraged us" over the years.[154] Anna Neal of the Clifton Choctaws, which was recognized by the state in 1979, noted that Sickey "really bent over backwards to help my tribe," particularly in grant assistance.[155] As the Coushattas' developmental efforts were under way, Sickey reached beyond southwestern Louisiana and began approaching other legislators with Indian populations in their districts to ask for their support of Indian affairs. What he encountered was different than the relative ease with which he had advocated for the Coushattas years earlier; he discovered that many politicians from other parts of the state were more difficult to ally with. "Some didn't really care to help," he remembered. "Some were kind of . . . scared, [asking], 'If the Indians get all this power, then where do the rest of us reside, what happens to us?'" Many responses were fueled by lingering anxieties from the black civil rights movement that prompted questions about whether Indians might pursue legal action for land or civil rights violations. Also, educating state policy makers about the distinctions between individual civil rights and tribal sovereign rights sometimes led to questions about whether these efforts might "wreak havoc on our economy." The confusion and suspicion over the implications of tribal self-determination were enough to keep Sickey alert to "legislation that would impose any restrictions or start interfering in tribal affairs . . . I knew at that point to defend tribal sovereignty . . . I was determined not to get the state involved in anything that would hurt the tribes." Cognizant that the Coushattas had first brought the state into Indian affairs, Sickey felt a responsibility to carefully monitor the political environment. He feared that any lapse in public education efforts, further challenged by frequent turnover among elected officials, could adversely impact Indian communities.[156]

The strategy to set Louisiana tribes on a positive course was to forge a united, statewide, intertribal front. Tribal leaders hoped that the LOIA and the ITC would advocate in tandem, with the LOIA focusing on legislative matters and the ITC fostering intertribal communication and providing services through grant funding.[157] Unfortunately, this partnership didn't evolve as was hoped, and the LOIA became increasingly ineffective and "too paternalistic," according to Larry Burgess of the Chitimacha Tribe.[158] Plus, competing visions regarding state tribal recognition criteria made for some heated debates. While ITC membership was limited to the five tribes that fit a particular set of guidelines, the LOIA served a broader base that had gradually formed and sought state recognition over the years.[159] The two organizations were on separate trajectories. The LOIA continued to work with a few state agencies, distributing small scholarships and fielding citizens' questions about Indian history and genealogical resources. The ITC, on the other hand, administered the CETA grant and a variety of other social service programs. Although it was not the first attempt to achieve such cooperation, it was the first to achieve a formal level of intertribal organization at that scale. In its early years the ITC reinforced cooperation among its member tribes in a variety of ways. In 1978, for example, it created the Louisiana Indian Women's Task Force to "improve the interrelationship between tribes in Louisiana," with its first conference hosted by the Coushattas.[160]

By the 1980s there was a significant need to accelerate the cohesion and unified voice of Louisiana tribes following the election of President Ronald Reagan and the fiscally conservative turn of the nation.[161] This shifting political environment reached Louisiana when the tenure of Edwin Edwards, governor since 1972, was interrupted by the election of David Treen for one term, from 1980 to 1984, making Treen the first Louisiana Republican governor in more than one hundred years.[162] The transition between administrations had a disruptive rippling effect across state agencies, including the LOIA, where operations were halted for months with no director. Under the Treen administration there were massive state budget cuts in response to the more than $50 million in tax cuts at the federal level. These cuts affected many programs that served underrepresented populations and came when funding was already on a downward slide. Medicaid was scaled back, and other programs, such as the Youth Conservation Corps, were eliminated entirely. By September 1981 tribes were informed that twenty-five programs previously run by the Louisiana Department of Urban and Community Affairs (DUCA), which many of them had relied on, had been consolidated into seven, with a 70–75 percent cut in funding from previous years. The scholarship program that the LOIA managed was slashed, and by 1983 many of the thirty-one students receiving the diminished funding had to quit school.[163] Moreover, the federal funding distribution process was reorganized toward a block grant system, positioning states as the central authority in distributing certain funds to tribal communities, a change that generated anxiety and tension between tribes and states nationwide.[164] In Louisiana decreased funding also stunted any gains made in forging relationships between tribes and parish agencies. A 1983 poll of representatives from eighty parish community action agencies confirmed that not a single one served Indian communities directly.[165] It seemed that within a few short years resources that tribal leaders had fought so hard to obtain were in peril.

With so much at stake, Sickey argued for the increased mobilization of Louisiana's tribes, encouraging them to speak up and join in broader national conversations. He advised other tribes to lobby state legislators and create alliances, as the Coushattas had done for generations. Sickey also pushed for a new state subcommittee on Indian affairs, in which both federal- and state-recognized tribes could have a voice within the state government.[166] The subcommittee never gained momentum, but Louisiana tribes did rise to the challenge and voiced their intent to protect themselves. In 1981 six chairmen representing the Coushatta, Tunica-Biloxi, Houma, Jena Band of Choctaw, Clifton Choctaw, and Choctaw Apache tribes convened to draft and sign a "Declaration of Unity." Representatives from the Chitimachas and Louisiana Band of Choctaws were unable to attend.[167] This meeting was followed by another several weeks later, when the same six chairmen drafted a position paper, identifying themselves as the "Undersigned Sovereign American Indian Tribal Governments of Louisiana." The document was a direct response to the federal government's expanded use of block grants and "the attitude of the Reagan administration toward returning many of the federal powers and responsibilities to state governments." "It can be assumed," the document declared, "that portions of the federal responsibilities towards the American Indian people and tribes will be delegated to the state for administration . . . a matter of deep and immediate concern to the tribal governments." The paper explicitly outlined how tribal governments were unlike other "minority" or "ethnic" groups and should be provided subsidies, just as local governments were, for road and school construction, education, public transportation, urban renewal, human services, and other projects and services. It also asked the state to appoint Indians to all state boards and commissions impacting them directly.[168] While the declaration did little to reshape the actual relationship between Louisiana tribes and the state, as was hoped, it set a tone and identified the shared intention of the state's tribes to be dealt with as distinct polities.

The Coushattas may have had a strong voice in both the regional and statewide Indian movement, but the tribal council remained steadfast in its efforts to meet the community's specific needs. Real progress had been made, but much was still yet to be achieved. By 1983, 83 percent of Coushattas continued to be considered economically disadvantaged. Funding for programs and services never seemed adequate to cover the full scope of their needs, so tribal leaders continued looking for ways to defray costs.[169] Motivated to secure a positive economic future, the Coushatta people entered the 1980s with a willingness to explore new opportunities. As Sickey explained to Senator John Saunders, "The tribal administration has several plans to . . . combat cuts and inflation through development of its resources and the introduction of business development." The tribe's leaders leveraged Reagan era policies, such as the gas tax, to improve federal roads on the reservation and build a concrete bridge over a creek leading to the 15-acre circle portion of the Coushatta trust lands.[170] They also looked to further expand their economic enterprises. Sickey wrote Governor Treen in 1982 that "we are ready . . . to gain self-sufficiency and exercise self-determination and we need your full support [through seed funding] to move ahead in the future." In the same year, the request was granted, and the tribe built a coin-operated laundry with a modest $15,000 budget. Moreover, of the 151 acres of reservation land held by 1982, 76 acres of it was set aside to use for an agriculture program that continued to expand throughout the decade.[171] As the tribe gained momentum in building its infrastructure, it also took further steps toward establishing a solid economic foundation by following in the footsteps of the Florida Seminoles to push the boundaries of tribal sovereignty and reaffirm the limits of local and state jurisdiction over tribal lands by opening a bingo hall in 1984, paving the way for full-fledged Indian gaming in later years.[172]

A decade after federal reinstatement, the Coushattas never relented in their pursuit to make a better life for themselves. The community continued to work together to run programs, educate the public, and make plans for the future. Likewise, Ernest Sickey never ceased nurturing, building, and strengthening the Coushattas' network of advocates to ensure the tribe's ongoing political and economic stability. His two youngest sons, David and Clark, have vivid memories of their home being a "revolving door" of visitors. Clark described how "we'd clean the house . . . [and] my mom would cook," then the family would sit with guests around a salvaged conference table in the family's dining room to visit and make plans.[173] David remembered that he and his five brothers "were always around the table, just overhearing, listening, watching and learning. It was a part of our lives, ever since we were little . . . We probably didn't fully grasp all the details . . . I just remember knowing that what . . . [was happening] was big." They were witnesses to the building of a nation. As they grew older, they learned more about why their father was often away from home or bringing visitors into their house. "I remember being proud," David recalled, "because even at a young age, I knew that our lives [were] . . . being improved . . . My dad and others took risks . . . not even knowing that there would be rewards."[174]

The sacrifices made by generations of Coushattas in traveling hundreds of miles and then learning new languages and navigating foreign political, social, and economic systems enabled subsequent generations to build a life for themselves in southwestern Louisiana. It was because of them, Ernest Sickey affirmed, that they stand here today. Now it is up to the next generation to "share that same journey with the same drive and determination . . . [because] it must be carried on."[175] The Coushattas' story is about overcoming one hurdle after another by adapting to challenging situations while carefully maintaining the integrity of their culture and internal governance. They achieved this success on their own terms by working together to engage the public, build lasting and productive relationships, and position themselves to take on increasingly significant roles in the region. The invitation from the Louisiana Office of Tourism to be part of the naming of the state's hot air balloon in 1982 was just one example of this—an indication of how far the Coushattas had come not only as contributors to the vitality and image of Louisiana but as partners in building toward the future.

Epilogue

Chairman David Sickey

In 2018, forty-five years after the reinstatement of Coushatta federal recognition, which my father, Ernest Sickey, and others worked so hard to accomplish, the Coushatta Tribe of Louisiana is alive and well and poised to realize even greater achievements. The publication of this book so close to the forty-fifth anniversary of reinstatement was not deliberate but does provide a welcome opportunity for me and others to reflect on our "Journey of Progress." It's easy to lose an appreciation for these kind of reflections amid the urgency of meeting daily needs of the community, so I was particularly honored and glad to be invited to write this epilogue.

As a young man, I grew up watching my father work on behalf of the tribe. He took long bus rides to attend meetings with people whose importance I didn't understand. It seemed that he spent every waking moment on tribal affairs, and it has taken me a long time to fully appreciate how much I have benefited from his efforts. Now, as an adult, a father myself, and the current chairman of the Coushatta Tribe of Louisiana, I have an entirely different perspective. I understand the drive that my father as well as other Coushatta leaders who preceded him had to selflessly devote themselves to our people. I hope to emulate their spirit and courage and allow their vision to guide my own efforts.

Previously, my father was reluctant to tell the story of how he helped guide our tribe along the pathway to reinstatement of federal recognition. I understand why. In our Koasati language the word for boasting (illakasaamo̱) always has a negative connotation; self-promotion, even to tell of one's hard-earned accomplishments, is simply not the Coushatta way. Following these teachings, my father worked hard to be "illakasaamotikko" (humble, not boastful); accordingly, he never told anyone the details about his decades of work, not even his own family. In that regard this book, and the written history of our tribe's journey of progress over the last century, would literally not have been possible without the hard work and dedication of Denise Bates. She was, and still is, the only person whom my father ever allowed to hear, and record, this history. We Coushattas are grateful to her and to all of the people who made this book possible. We appreciate all of their contributions to telling the story of our people with dignity and grace, in a manner consistent with how we view ourselves—as peaceful and diplomatic but with a tremendous tenacity and determination to survive and succeed against all odds.

This book describes the ways our Coushatta people worked together to ensure our survival over the past century, forging key alliances and engaging the public in order to navigate the racial and social class issues endemic to the Deep South, a region we chose to call home. Dr. Bates addresses the federal policies and legal mechanisms by which our tribe was marginalized and officially "disappeared" or removed from the government's requirement to recognize and honor treaty obligations. In doing so, she provides a window to understand not only our tribe's history but also the actions our people took to protect our language, culture, and traditions in perpetuity. This book is about the many Coushatta tribal members who participated in activism toward our self-determination, from the most visible chiefs to those completely behind the scenes, like the weavers who provided my father with baskets for his "basket diplomacy."

We Coushattas have always identified ourselves as having a "traditional" form of government, in which decisions are made collaboratively by the heads of families or representatives from each of the clans gathered together, accompanied by prayer. This book also details the processes by which our elders continued this traditional form of governance while navigating the demands of the larger society through venues such as nonprofit corporations and advisory boards. The vision and determination of our elders to ensure our survival comes through clearly in every chapter.

In the three and a half decades that the book leaves off this chronicle of our tribe, we have continued to grow and expand as a nation. From an initial reservation base of fifteen acres in 1973, the tribe now owns over seven thousand acres in trust and fee simple lands, including almost six thousand acres in Allen Parish. Our tribe now has over nine hundred enrolled members and operates over twenty departments to provide services to members, including the Health Department and Clinic, the Education Department, the Social Services Department, and the Recreation and Wellness Center. We also have our own tribal police, fire departments, and a tribal court.

Following a landmark federal court decision in 1985, which confirmed that the Coushattas' lands were "reservation lands" and that the State of Louisiana had no jurisdiction over activities on such lands,[1] coupled with the passage of the Indian Gaming Regulatory Act in 1988, we opened a tribal casino in 1992. Coushatta Casino Resort has now grown to become the largest land-based casino in the state of Louisiana, employing nearly three thousand people, which makes it the third largest private employer in the state. From our early history to our current status as an economic, social, and cultural leader, the Coushatta Tribe of Louisiana has played an increasingly important role in the local, state, and national communities. We have also been able to leverage this economic strength into programs to teach and revitalize our Koasati language, basket making, and other cultural traditions.

In addition to detailing our tribal history, this book also provides a model for mutually beneficial and successful collaboration between an academically based scholar and an Indian tribe. Dr. Bates worked closely with the Coushatta Heritage Department to gather and share resources, Koasati translations, and feedback on this manuscript. In turn she donated copies of all of the interviews and resources collected for this book to the tribal archives. I believe that the final result is a story with far broader reach and impact than even we had hoped for. This narrative of our Coushatta journey speaks to Indian tribes and other Indigenous groups, and ultimately to marginalized peoples everywhere, as a testament to the incredible power of cultural resilience, coupled with the collective strength and determination of elders to survive against all odds.

From my dual vantage point as the current tribal chairman and my father's son, I can hope for no greater legacy to leave future generations than that they continue this "Journey of Progress" by maintaining our Coushatta traditions of strategic alliances, collective decision making, and prayer in all situations. With the blessings of Aba Chokkooli (the One Who Sits on High) and the guidance of our elders, future tribal members will continue to build on these foundations for generations to come.

APPENDIX

Traditional Chiefs in the Modern Era

-1910   John Abbey

1910-38   Jackson Langley

1938-51   Jeff Abbey

1951-72   Martin Abbey

Early Coushatta Leadership in the Church
Reproduced from records kept by Reverend Leeds. The spelling of names reflects the original records.

1906   Deacons: Mark Robinson, Boyd William, and Alex
          Johnpierre
          Treasurer: Mark Robinson
          Sunday school clerk: Paul William
          Church clerk: Man William

1908   Deacon: Mark Robinson
          Church clerk: Man William
          Sunday school superintendent: Jacob Robinson
          Sunday school secretary and treasurer: Man William

1909   Deacons: Mark Robinson, Man William, and Paul William
          Trustees: Gossett Robinson, George Abbey, Doc William,
          Henry Thompson, Alex Johnpierre, and Jimmy John
          Sunday school superintendent: Gossett Robinson
          Sunday school secretary and treasurer: Sissy Alabama

1910–11   Deacons: Mark Robinson, Mann William, and Doc William
           Sunday school supervisor: Doc William
           Janitor: George Abbey
           Trustees: Paul Williams, Mark Robinson, Henry Thompson,
           and Jimmie John
           Clerk: Man Williams
           Sunday school superintendent: Jacob Robinson
           Sunday school treasurer and secretary: Man Williams
           Clerk and treasurer of church: Mark Robinson

1912   Sunday school superintendent and treasurer: Jacob
           Robinson
           Sunday school secretary: Jacob Robinson
           Church clerk, treasurer, and sexton: Mark Robinson
           Deacons: Mark Robinson, Jacob Robinson, and Jim John
           Church librarian: H. Thompson and Jim John

1913   Deacon: Ed Wilson
           Church clerk and treasurer: Mark Robinson
           St. Luke's Church
           Deacons: Ed Wilson and Henry Thompson
           Trustees: Charlie Boatman, Bennie John, and Alexander John
           Clerk: George Willie
           Treasurer: Ed Wilson

1919   Assistant pastor: Mark Robinson (licensed)

1921   Deacons: Mark Robinson and Gossett Robinson
           Deaconesses: Lucy John and Susie Robinson
           Church clerk: Mark Robinson
           Church treasurer: Ency Abbey
           Trustees: Jacob Robinson, Gossett Robinson, Doc Williams,
           D. L. Stafford, and Jeff Abbey
           Sunday school superintendent, clerk, and treasurer: Jacob
           Robinson

1930   Deacons: Mark Robinson, Luke Robinson, and Doc
           Williams
           Deaconesses: Annie Poncho and Vera Robinson

1934 Deacons: Doc Williams and Jacob Robinson
Trustees: Kinney Williams, Douglas John, and Ellison
Battise
Deaconesses: Vera Robinson and Annie Poncho
Church clerk: Lycia Robinson
Church treasurer: Baker Williams
Sunday school superintendent, secretary, and treasurer:
Jacob Robinson
Church leader: Jacob Robinson
Cemetery sexton: Doc Williams
School director: Ellison Battise

1939 Deacons: Doc Williams and Jacob Robinson
Trustees: Alfred John, Ellison Battise, Houston Williams,
and Charlie Sickie
Deaconesses: Nora Williams, Biney Williams, and Annie
Poncho
Clerk: Solomon Battise
Treasurer: Kinney Williams
Sunday school superintendent: Jacob Robinson

1940 Deacons: Doc Williams and Jacob Robinson
Trustees: Houston Williams, Charlie Sickie, Kinney
Williams, and Alfred John
Clerk: Houston Williams
Treasurer: Kinney Williams

1941–42 Deacons: Doc Williams and Jacob Robinson
Trustees: Doc Williams, Henry Thompson, Charlie Sickie,
Houston Williams, and Kent Sylestine
Deaconesses: Annie Poncho and Ency Abbott
Church clerk: Douglas John
Church treasurer: Jacob Robinson
Sunday school superintendent: Jacob Robinson
Sunday school treasurer: Emmy Abbott

1943   Deacons: Doc Williams and Jacob Robinson
Deaconesses: Annie Poncho and Ensie Abbott
Trustees: Houston Williams, Charlie Sickie, Doc Williams,
Hogie Wilson, and Kinney Williams
Treasurer: Jacob Robinson
Clerks: McKinley Williams and Marie Abbott
Sunday school superintendent: Jacob Robinson
Sunday school treasurer: Emmy Abbott
Sunday school secretary: Margaret Williams

1944–46   Clerk: Douglas John
Sunday school superintendent: Jacob Robinson
Sexton: Houston Williams

1947   Treasurer: Jacob Robinson
Sexton: Houston Williams

1948   Deacons: Jacob Robinson and Ed Wilson
Deaconesses: Ensie Abbott and Ethel Williams
Trustees: Bel Abbey, Douglas John, and Kinney Williams
Clerk: Marie Abbott
Church treasurer: Douglas John
Sexton: Houston Williams
Sunday school superintendent: Solomon Battise
Sunday school treasurer: Ethel Williams

1949   Deacons: Bel Abbey and Ed Wilson
Deaconesses: Ency Abbott and Nora Abbey
Trustees: Bel Abbey, Houston Williams, Kent Sylestine,
Kinney Williams, and Solomon Battise
Clerk: Marie Abbott
Treasurer: Bel Abbey
Sexton: Kinney Williams
Sunday school superintendent: Solomon Battise
Sunday school secretary: Savana Mae John

1950   Deacons: Bel Abbey and Kent Sylestine
        Deaconesses: Rosabel R. Sylestine and Fern Williams
        Church clerk: Douglass John
        Church treasurer: Kent Sylestine
        Trustees: Bel Abbey, Kent Sylestine, Davis Sickey, Douglas
        John, and Abel John
        Church sexton: Davis Sickey
        Sunday school superintendent: Solomon Battise
        Sunday school secretary and treasurer: Fern Williams

1955   Sunday school superintendent: Solomon Battise
        Sunday school secretary: Marian Robinson
        Deacons: Bel Abbey and Kent Sylestine
        Deaconesses: Margaret Williams and Martha John
        Church clerk: Nora Abbey
        Church treasurer: Kent Sylestine
        Trustees: Ed John, Douglas John, Davis Sickey, Houston
        Williams, and Jameson Poncho
        Sexton: Houston Williams

1956   Deacons: Kent Sylestine and Douglas John
        Deaconesses: Adaline Battise and Ruth Poncho
        Trustees: Davis Sickey, Ed John, Bel Abbey, Kent Sylestine,
        and Jameson Sylestine
        Church treasurer: Ed Wilson
        Church clerks: Norah Abbey and Rosabel Sylestine
        Sunday school superintendent: Solomon Battise
        Sunday school secretaries: Marion Robinson and Ina Estelle
        Abbey

The Coushatta (Koasati) Indians of Louisiana, Inc.

1966   President: Solomon Battise
        Vice president: Ernest Sickey
        Secretary-treasurer: Rosabel Sylestine
        Board members: Deo Langley, Davis Sickey, Nora Abbey,
        and Ruth Poncho

Tribal Council (Board of Trustees) and Coushatta Alliance, Inc. (dual positions)

1973–82   Chairman of the board of trustees, president of the
           Coushatta Alliance: Ernest Sickey
           Vice chairman of the board of trustees, executive vice
           president of the alliance: J. D. Langley
           Trustee and secretary: Leonard Battise
           Trustee and treasurer: Roland Sylestine
           Trustee and councilman: Solomon Battise

NOTES

INTRODUCTION

1. For the purpose of this book, the word *Koasati* is used to refer to the tribal language, and *Coushatta* is used to refer to the people. In some of the sources and personal narratives, the words are used interchangeably to reference the tribal people.

2. Population estimate found in "Coushatta Indians Struggle to Earn Tribe Recognition," *Rural Louisiana* (Jeff Davis Electric Co-op Edition) (April 1974): 8.

3. Ernest Sickey, interview with author, December 15, 2015. Although the Coushattas came to settle in multiple places, the use of the identifier *Coushatta* in this book, unless otherwise indicated, refers to the Bayou Blue community in Louisiana.

4. For more on how Coushattas used basketry as a symbol in asserting economic self-sufficiency and Indigenous identity, see Precht, "Coushatta Basketry and Identity Politics." The work of Daniel H. Usner also reveals how the Chitimacha Tribe of Louisiana used baskets in a similar fashion, positioning weavers as cultural mediators who made significant contributions to the promotion and visibility of their community. See *Weaving Alliances with Other Women*.

5. Coushatta storyteller Bertney Langley shared the story "How the Koasati Got Their Name" with Pat Mire and Maida Owens, who recorded it on September 18, 1993. The story was reprinted on the Louisiana Public Broadcasting site at http://www.lpb.org/index.php/programs/program2_episode/how_the_koasati_got_their_name_bertney_langley.

6. Coushatta Tribe of Louisiana, *Red Shoes' People*; "'Forgotten' Craft Revived as Indians Learn Weaving," *Opelousas Daily World*, May 28, 1973, 10.

7. The Coushattas' migration story is discussed as part of the larger narrative of Mississippian groups living in the "shatter zone" of the sixteenth and seventeenth centuries American South. See Shuck-Hall, "Alabama and Coushatta Diaspora and Coalescence in the Mississippian Shatter Zone," in *Mapping the Mississippian Shatter Zone*. For other retellings of the Coushatta migration story, see May, "Alabama and Koasati," in *Handbook of North American Indians, Southeast*; Howard N. Martin, "Coushatta Indians," in *Handbook of Texas Online* http://www.tshaonline.org/handbook/online/articles/bmcag; Johnson, *Coushatta People*, 1–46; Jurney, "Diaspora of the Alabama-Coushatta Indians."

8. According to Swanton, the Coushattas first appeared in the de Soto narratives (1540) under the name of "Coste, Acoste, Costehe, or Acosta," while living on an island in the Tennessee River. See Swanton, *Indians of the Southeastern United States*, 145.

9. To better understand the political complexity of the Creek Confederacy, see Steven C. Hahn's study of the Creek Nation from 1670 to 1763 as the tribe contended with external colonial pressures and internal factionalism while struggling to develop a unified force within the region. See *Invention of the Creek Nation, 1670–1763*. Regarding later settlements, Sharon O'Brien reported that "thirty-four organized rural and small urban communities of the once-powerful Muscogee Confederacy are scattered throughout the towns and rural areas of central Oklahoma. Two groups still inhabit the Muscogees' aboriginal homeland, the area that now encompasses the states of Georgia, most of Alabama, and the panhandle of Florida . . . Other groups formerly in the confederacy include the Seminole tribes of Oklahoma and Florida, the Coushatta of Louisiana, and the Alabama-Coushatta of Texas." *American Indian Tribal Governments*, 119.

10. The Creek Confederacy entered into treaty relationships with France, England, Spain, and the United States. The Treaty of Augusta (1783) was the first major one the Confederacy signed with the United States that ceded hundreds of square miles of land. See Swanton, *Indians of the Southeastern United States*, 145. For an account on the Coushattas during this period, see Debo, *Road to Disappearance*. Also, for a compelling argument that Alexander McGillivray, the renowned principal chief of an upper Creek Confederacy town, was actually Coushatta and not Creek, as he is frequently purported to be, see Langley, "Tribal Identity of Alexander McGillivray."

11. One group of Coushattas pushed westward toward the Tombigbee River and another to Spanish Florida for a short time before also changing course westward. See Swanton, *Indians of the Southeastern United States*, 87; Rushing, "Promised Land of the Alabama-Coushatta," 49.

12. Coushatta Tribe, *Red Shoes' People*.

13. See Flores, "John Maley Journal" and "Red Branch of the Alabama-Coushatta Indians"; Hudson, *Southeastern Indians*; McCrocklin, "Red River Coushatta Indian Villages of Northwest Louisiana."

14. See Langley, "Koasati (Coushatta) Literature," 263.

15. For more on the Coushattas as a "buffer population," see Haggard, "Neutral Ground between Louisiana and Texas."

16. This period of Coushatta history was captured by John Sibley, who in 1805 was asked to serve as a U.S. agent tasked with keeping the tribes in the vicinity of Natchitoches allied with the United States in order to keep the Spanish at bay. See Sibley, "Historical Sketches of the Several Indian Tribes

in Louisiana," 48–62. For a nuanced historical examination of the migrations and diplomatic efforts of the Alabamas and Coushattas, see Shuck-Hall, *Journey to the West*.

17. Letter, Jorge Antonio Nixon (commissioner) to Frank Hardin (land surveyor), January 8, 1835, reprinted in Trammell, *Seven Pines*, 26.

18. See Johnson, *Coushatta People*, 34–46; Martin, *Myths and Folktales*; Smither, "Alabama Indians of Texas"; and Winfrey and Bryant, *Indian Tribes of Texas*, 5–14.

19. The "Act for the Relief of the Coshattee [*sic*] Indians" was presented to the Texas legislature on February 6, 1854. See letter, General Sam Houston to Ashbel Smith, December 8, 1855, box 2G224, Ashbel Smith Papers, Dolph Briscoe Center for American History, University of Texas at Austin (hereafter cited as Smith Papers). Some Alabamas joined the Coushatta families who moved to Louisiana, and both appear in records compiled by Rev. Paul Leeds in *St. Peters Congregational Church Records, Bayou Blue, Elton, Louisiana* (1901–58) and *St. Luke Congregational Church on West Side of Bayou Blue* (1913–21).

20. The Alabama-Coushatta community in Texas has been the destination for many researchers interested in their economic and cultural history. See Bounds, "The Alabama-Coushatta Indians of Texas"; Jacobson, "Alabama-Coushatta Indians," 1–255; Rothe, *Kalita's People*; Fox, *Winding Trail*; Hook, *Alabama-Coushatta Indians*. Given all of the accounts that have been written about the Alabama and Coushatta peoples of Texas over the years, an effort to promote a closer—more critical—look at their history was launched by Gelo and Morales in an annotated bibliography that assesses published sources, theses, and dissertations through 1991. See "Alabama-Coushatta Indians: An Annotated Bibliography."

21. Ernest Sickey, interview with author, July 28, 2015.

22. While living at Indian Village, many Coushatta men found work on nearby farms. The 1880 census from Calcasieu Parish lists every reported Indian male over the age of sixteen as a "laborer" or "farm laborer," indicating that they had already transitioned into a semi-wage-based economy. See 1880 census records for Hickory Flat, Calcasieu, roll 449, film 1254449, p. 458C, Enumeration District 006, image 0680, U.S. Federal Census. In 1883 James Nevils purchased the land, becoming "the first white man to settle in Indian Village," according to his granddaughter, Hattie Nevils Nixon. See Angela Wendell, "A Country Coffee Break in a Village without Indians," *Alexandria Town Talk*, June 23, 1985, 38. While the majority of Coushattas were pressured to relocate, a few, such as Alec Robinson, stayed and bought land along the Calcasieu River. See Jacobson, "Origin of the Koasati Community," 106.

23. "Louisiana Retains Old World Flavor," *Lake Charles American Press*, October 23, 1955, 2.

24. See, e.g., Harrington, "Among the Louisiana Indians"; Swanton, "Animal Stories from the Indians of the Muskhogean Stock," "Indian Language Studies in Louisiana," in *Indians of the Southeastern United States*, 145–46, 167, and "Myths and Tales of the Southeastern Indians," 275.

25. Although official termination actions often took years before tribes felt the impact of the policy, the Coushattas saw an abrupt end to their relationship with the federal government. Studies that have been consulted as a point of comparison include Ulrich, *American Indian Nations from Termination to Restoration*; and Peroff, *Menominee Drums*.

26. In my previous work I detail the formation of the Southern Indian Movement as it evolved across the region, but with a particular emphasis on Alabama and Louisiana. See Bates, *Other Movement*; and "Reshaping Southern Identity and Politics." The role of Indigenous activism and political engagement in the 1970s supports Jacquelyn Dowd Hall's argument that the civil rights movement—and all of its parallel resistance movements—were not on the decline by the 1970s but still very much a part of the American political arena. Hall, "Long Civil Rights Movement," 1254.

27. "Sickey Appointed," *Basile Weekly*, December 27, 1972, n.p., Coushatta Tribal Archives (hereafter cited as CTA).

28. This figure derives from the 1970 United States census, which is a 47.6 percent increase from the reported 3,587 documented Louisiana Indians in 1960. Figures reprinted in Roy and Leary, "Economic Survey of American Indians in Louisiana," 11. Both figures have been called into question given the knowledge of multiple Indian families who were not counted by the census during those years, according to the Louisiana Health and Human Resources Administration, "Elderly Indians of Louisiana and Their Needs," 7; and Gregory, "Louisiana Tribes," 162. The 1980 census recorded approximately 12,000 Indians living in Louisiana, making it the third largest Indian population in the Southeast. The population broke down as follows: Chitimacha (520), Coushatta (360), Tunica-Biloxi (233), Houma (8,000), Jena Band of Choctaw (150), Clifton Choctaw (250), Louisiana Band of Choctaw (150), and the Apache Choctaw (1,500). See Inter-Tribal Council of Louisiana, "An Overview of the Present Status of the Indian Communities of Louisiana," May 1988, Inter-Tribal Council of Louisiana Records (hereafter cited as ITC); Margrett Fels, "Liberty and Justice for All?" *Baton Rouge Magazine*, November 1986, 15.

29. Since a formal federal recognition process wasn't established until 1978, there were a variety of approaches taken to acknowledge tribes. Between 1962 and 1974 other avenues that tribes had been extended recognition were through congressional statute (e.g., Yavapai and Tonto Apache Tribes of Arizona in 1972 and the Menominees of Wisconsin in 1973), solicitor's opinion (e.g.,

Burns Paiute Indian Colony of Oregon in 1967, Nooksacks of Washington in 1971, and Original Band of Sault St. Marie Chippewa Indians of Michigan in 1974), and a special request letter of the deputy commissioner (e.g., Upper Skagits and the Sauk-Suiattle Indian Tribe of Washington in 1972). Hearing before the U.S. Senate Select Committee on Indian Affairs, 95th Cong., 2nd sess., on S. 2375 (Washington DC: U.S. Government Printing Office, 1978), 65–66.

30. Policy shifts toward tribal self-determination were a result of the interplay between the attention generated by Indian activists on a national scale and the reassessment of the role of institutional actors, such as the Bureau of Indian Affairs, in the lives of Indian people. See Cobb, *Native Activism in Cold War America* and *Say We Are Nations*; Cobb and Fowler, *Beyond Red Power*; Josephy, Nagel, and Johnson, *American Indians' Fight for Freedom*; Peters and Straus, *Visions and Voices*; Shreve, *Red Power Rising*; Britten, *National Council on Indian Opportunity*; and Clarkin, *Federal Indian Policy*.

31. The Coushattas' approach to nation building aligns with what is described by Stephen Cornell and Joseph P. Kalt, as an assertion of decision-making power that is strategic and complements the tribe's political culture. See Cornell and Kalt, "Two Approaches." Also see Calliou, "Culture of Leadership"; and Wickman, *Warriors without War*.

32. At one time there were at least ten clans, each of which represents an animal or element. Traditionally, the clan system was used to determine political positions and ceremonial rights. Today seven clans have survived—Deer, Panther, Beaver, Daddy Long Legs, Bear, Turkey, and Bobcat—and the practice of passing clan affiliations to children through their mothers is still very much a part of the Coushattas' culture. For a discussion of the Muskogean matrilineal clan system, see Ethridge, *Creek Country*, 109–11. To focus more specifically on the Coushatta clan system, see Kniffen, Gregory, and Stokes, *Historic Indian Tribes of Louisiana*, 225–26.

33. David E. Wilkins argues that scholars who write about abrupt shifts from traditional tribal governments to constitutional governments (or organized tribal councils, as was the case with the Coushattas) without discussing the role of decision making and transition in between denies the part of the narrative that demonstrates "a strong measure of self-determination." See *American Indian Politics and the American Political*, 126–27.

34. Adams, *Who Belongs*, 214.

35. The term *interlocking leadership roles* was borrowed from James Clifton in *Prairie People*, 59.

36. Gregory A. Cajete's work provides the basis for understanding Indigenous forms of education as providing "foundations for dynamic and multi-contextual processes."

See "Indigenous Education and the Development of Indigenous Community Leaders."

37. Evans, *Power from Powerlessness*. Also, Kevin Bruyneel's work has shaped my thinking about how Native people have contested the external limitations placed on them to develop economically and politically. See *Third Space of Sovereignty*.

38. Cobb, *Native Activism*, 2.

39. For scholarship on how racial discourse shaped the boundaries of Indian identity, see Klopotek, *Recognition Odysseys* and "Indian Education under Jim Crow"; Usner, "'They Don't Like Indians around Here'"; Blu, *Lumbee Problem*; Lowery, *Race, Identity, and the Making of a Nation*; Sider, *Living Indian Histories*; and Coleman, *That the Blood Stay Pure*. In addition, Theda Perdue's work provides a foundation from which to better understand the significance of Native peoples in the construction of southern historical narratives. See, e.g., "Indians in Southern History" and "Native Americans, African Americans, and Jim Crow."

40. This point builds upon the work of J. Anthony Paredes who argues that "mastery of white institutions depends to a significant degree on the success of Southeastern Indians in 'marketing' their distinctiveness." See "Paradoxes of Modernism and Indianness in the Southeast," 341. It also draws upon the emerging scholarship focused on Indigenous arts leadership as a way of contesting and reshaping public space and identity. See Evans and Sinclair, "Containing, Contesting, Creating Spaces." Finally, I would like to acknowledge the insightful work already published on Native weavers in Louisiana and the roles that they played as cultural brokers and leaders within the Chitimacha and Coushatta tribes. See Usner, *Weaving Alliances*; and Precht, "Coushatta Basketry and Identity Politics."

41. Katherine Osburn's study on the Mississippi Choctaws looks at a similar phenomenon in how tribal leaders leveraged class and race in order to secure political allies, see *Choctaw Resurgence in Mississippi*.

42. Opponents of Coushattas receiving federal Indian services in the early decades of the twentieth century argued that by making them "wards" of the federal government, they would be taking a step backward from becoming successful citizens. For a discussion on the federal assimilationist agenda, see Hoxie, *Final Promise*.

43. Paredes, "Paradoxes of Modernism," 334. Here Paredes builds upon Nancy Lurie's description of "contact-traditional cultures" in "Contemporary Indian Scene." Raibmon, "Meaning of Mobility on the Northwest Coast."

44. Shuck-Hall, *Journey to the West*.

45. Tribal federal acknowledgment is a highly contentious and subjective issue. Native perspectives are not consistent, nor are the experiences of tribes who went through the process of petitioning or, like the Coushattas, sought recognition through other avenues. With such a large percentage of the petitioners hailing

from southeastern states, I have found the scholarship focused on this region to be particularly insightful. See, e.g., Klopotek, *Recognition Odysseys*; Roth, "Federal Tribal Recognition in the South"; M. Miller, *Forgotten Tribes* and *Claiming Tribal Identity*; and B. Miller, *Invisible Indigenes*.

46. A "strength-based" approach, as described by Voyageur, Brearley, and Calliou, is a way of emphasizing the "wise practices and successful leadership in Indigenous communities." It also is a response to the "deficit paradigm" that has been applied in past scholarship that has positioned Indigenous leadership models as ineffective in comparison to European- and American-based models. See *Restoring Indigenous Leadership*, 3. Also see Kenny and Fraser, *Living Indigenous Leadership*; and Gipp, Warner, Pease, and Shanley, *American Indian Stories of Success*.

47. By 2002 the Coushatta Tribe employed just over twenty-eight hundred people from the five-parish area of Allen, Calcasieu, Evangeline, Jefferson Davis, and St. Laundry. In addition, between 1999 and 2002 the tribe's gaming operation purchased goods and services from Louisiana vendors for upward of $41 million. See Coushatta Tribal Economic Impact Report (2002), 2, CTA.

48. Interviews were conducted between April 2015 and July 2018.

49. Scholars have a responsibility to the tribal communities they write about and work with. For more of a discussion on this issue, see Kievit, "Discussion"; and Mihesuah, *Natives and Academics*.

50. For an overview on the historiography of the Native South, see Saunt, "Native South"; and Frank and Ray, "Indians as Southerners." This will be the first book-length work published on the history of the Coushatta Tribe of Louisiana since 1976, when they were among a handful of tribes featured in a trade publication as part of the Indian Tribal Series. Johnson's *Coushatta People* provided a basic overview of their history without much detail or citations. To date the majority of publications in circulation focus on the Coushatta language and traditional tales. Historical accounts are limited to book chapters, articles, and broader collections covering tribes across the region. I am particularly grateful for the scholarship of anthropologist Linda Langley, the Coushatta Tribal Preservation Officer, who has published articles and book chapters on the Coushatta language, basket weaving, and homesteading, and historian Jay Precht, who has published articles on the Coushatta gaming enterprise, the role of baskets in their identity politics, and homesteading. Their work has been invaluable to the development of this book.

51. According to Goldsmith and Mueller, "Remarkably, of the 175 Indigenous languages remaining on the entire continent, only 20 are spoken by people of all ages as vigorously as the Coushatta language." *Nations Within*, 66.

Langley, "Koasati (Coushatta) Literature," 264 and 266. In 2006 the Koasati Language Project began to grow conceptual roots after Bertney Langley (director of the Coushatta Heritage Department) and Dr. Linda Langley (his wife and

Coushatta tribal preservation officer) attended the University of Arizona's American Indian Language Development Institute and received training in language documentation. Through the Langleys' efforts, along with the support of Susan Penfield, they received funding from the National Science Foundation for five years of funding. Acquiring more than thirty volunteers from the Coushatta tribe to work on the project, they set to work in reversing the trend of language loss. See Langley, "Koasati (Coushatta) Literature," 264–65. In the summer of 2007 the Koasati Language Committee and the Coushatta Heritage Department began collaborating with linguist and Muskogean specialist Jack Martin to create a new writing system for Koasati and build a digital linguistic archive. A description of this ongoing endeavor is provided in Hasselbacher, "Koasati and 'All the Olden Talk.'"

52. Koasati translations and transcriptions were provided by Bertney Langley, Linda Langley, Raynella Thompson Fontenot, and Loretta Williams.

1. "DON'T FORGET YOUR GUMBO BOWL"

EPIGRAPH: Barbara Langley, quoted in Mueller et al., *Nations Within*, 99.

1. The Colfax massacre occurred in Grant Parish on Easter Sunday, April 13, 1873. It was the result of the contested governor's race of 1872, which generated a confrontation between white Democrats and Republican freedmen and members of the state's black militia. While three white republicans were killed, upward of 150 African Americans were executed and their bodies thrown into the river. See Foner, *Reconstruction*, 437.

2. Usner, *American Indians in the Lower Mississippi Valley*, 124. Usner also discussed the development of the Creole Wild West Tribe and Mardi Gras Indians, 125–27.

3. Although there were Alabamas who moved to Bayou Blue, and in many cases intermarried with Coushattas, the two never converged and should not be addressed as a single tribal entity. While many of the historical experiences detailed throughout this work also impacted the Alabamas living in southwestern Louisiana, the focus of this book is on the Coushattas. Report, Ernest Cushing, "Investigation of Alleged Loss by Koasati Indians of Louisiana of Lands Acquired by Them under Homestead Patents," March 14, 1941, 6–7, exhibit K-37, box 4C335, Richard Yarborough Collection, Dolph Briscoe Center for American History, University of Texas at Austin (hereafter cited as Yarborough). For a published list of Alabama and Coushatta Homesteaders from 1887 to 1920, see Precht, "Coushatta Homesteading in Southwest Louisiana," 115. Of note, the list only includes eight of the nine Alabamas mentioned by Cushing given the availability of homestead records provided by the U.S. Department of the Interior, Bureau of Land Management, General Land Office Records, https://www.glorecords.blm.gov/search/. Coushatta Tribe, "Struggle Has Made Us Stronger," 3. For additional details, also see Johnson, *Coushatta People*, 47–48, 85.

4. What was more formally called "Imperial Calcasieu" had itself evolved from its previous designation as part of St. Landry. Reaching even further back in time, southwestern Louisiana was known under French and Spanish dominion as the "Opelousas District" since it was part of the Opelousas Indians' hunting grounds. See John Berton Gremillion, "Allen Parish," transcribed by Leora White and held by McNeese State University, 2008, http://ereserves.mcneese.edu/depts/archive /FTBooks/gremillion-allen.htm.

5. Cole served as a witness for multiple Coushatta homesteaders to verify that they complied with the regulations of continuous occupancy and land cultivation. Multiple "Homestead Notices" found in the *Lake Charles Commercial*, February 17, 1883, 3; March 10, 1883, 4; and March 17, 1883, 4. See also Jacobson, "Koasati Culture Change," 13. Powell was among the transplants to southwestern Louisiana from Nebraska. He acquired a homestead in Allen Parish under the terms of the original 1862 Homestead Act and advised many Coushatta families in obtaining legal land titles. Ernest Sickey, interview with author, July 28, 2015.

   The Homestead Act of 1862 and later the Southern Homestead Act of 1866 were championed by northern reformers and boosters of westward expansion to encourage independent farming and discourage the continuation of large slave-holding plantations. With an eye toward reform in the South, Radical Republicans looked to homesteading as a means to secure African Americans property as they transitioned from slavery to citizenship—a goal that was widely regarded as a failure due to bureaucratic hurdles and insurmountable discriminatory practices. See Lanza, *Agrarianism and Reconstruction Politics*, 54, 97, and 113; and Pope, "Southern Homesteads for Negroes," 201–12. Although Indians were excluded from the initial legislation requirements, later statutes aimed at assimilation authorized the allotment of land to individual Indians who did not reside on a reservation; were settled on public domain; or occupied national forest lands. See Getches, Wilkinson, and Williams, *Cases and Materials on Federal Indian Law*, 166.

6. Banner, *How the Indians Lost Their Land*, 257; McDonnell, *Dispossession of the American Indian*, 10. For a more detailed analysis on how the politics of land intersects with race, tribalism, kinship, class conflict, and nationalism, see Chang, *Color of the Land*; and Stremlau, *Sustaining the Cherokee Family*.

7. Debo, *And Still the Waters Run*, 91.

8. Precht, "Coushatta Homesteading," 120.

9. The terminology of emerging from the "legal shadows" was also used by Winfrey, "Civil Rights and the American Indian," 58.

10. It was discovered that four other Coushatta land patents also were recorded under the authority of later homesteading laws, but unlike Alabama's patent, they were amended to fall under the authority of the Homestead Law of 1862. Case, *United States v. Mrs. Della Bel Krause et al.* (Civ. A No. 2497, 92 F. Supp. 756), U.S. District

Court, Western District of Louisiana, Lake Charles Division, September 6, 1950, folder 3, box 246, Association on American Indian Affairs Records, Seeley G. Mudd Manuscript Library, Princeton University, Princeton NJ (hereafter cited as AAIA).

11. Sissy Robinson married Jackson Alabama two years after first filing her petition, and the two had eight children together. Her homestead was initially placed under a twenty-five-year trust patent in 1898 and then was extended by another twenty-five years in 1920 by executive order. See "U.S. Sues Allen Parish for Taxes on Indian's Land," *Times*, November 13, 1939, 7.

12. *United States v. Mrs. Della Bel Krause et al.*

13. Langley, Oubre, and Precht, "Recognizing the Contributions of Three Generations," 164.

14. This civil suit offers insight into the lack of understanding by both the Allen Parish tax assessor's office and Sissy Robinson Alabama's children on the unique privileges of federal trust land. Alabama died in 1914, and when her heirs were sent property tax bills in 1916 and 1917, they paid them. "U.S. Sues Allen Parish."

15. Langley et al., "Louisa Williams Robinson," 155, 162, 164.

16. Roth, "Federal Tribal Recognition," 56.

17. Africans first arrived in Louisiana around 1719, when they were forcibly transported during the slave trade. With the Code Noire (1724), Louisiana slaves had the ability to win their freedom in both French and Spanish Louisiana, which was a marked difference from slaves in the Anglo-American colonies, the result being a complex class system differentiating between free blacks, free persons of color, and slaves. Although there were scattered pockets of black communities in southwestern Louisiana in the late 1800s, more African Americans began to move into the region with the advent of rice farming and increased employment opportunities in the timber industry. Louisiana's African American population has left a significant imprint on Louisiana folklore and broader cultural identity. See Kein, *Creole*; and Fabre and O'Meally, *History and Memory*.

The Acadians or Cadiens (Cajuns) are descendants of the French who during the seventeenth century settled Acadia (Nova Scotia), where they created a close-knit cultural enclave. They soon came under attack by English colonists and were exiled from their home. By the mid-eighteenth century a group of Acadians first appeared in Louisiana, where they established isolated settlements intending to preserve their culture, religion, and language. It is important to point out that Louisiana's French population is diverse and doesn't all derive from Cajuns, a term that has until recently been considered derogatory. See Brasseaux, *Acadian to Cajun*; and Trepanier, "Cajunization of French Louisiana," 161–71.

Louisiana has been home to German immigrants since colonial times; however, the influx of immigration accelerated in the 1870s, when German Catholics felt compelled to flee their home nation when Chancellor Otto Von Bismarck instituted a *Kulturkampf* (war of cultures) against the Catholic Church. As a result, a group followed a Benedictine priest, Father Thevis, to Indiana and then Louisiana, where they settled in the southwestern prairie around Robert's Cove. See Merrill, *Germans of Louisiana*.

18. Johnson and Leeds, *Patteran*, 23; Post, "Rice Country of Southwestern Louisiana," 574–90; *Cajun Sketches*, 46; and Jacobson, "Origin of the Koasati Community," 109–10.

19. Jacobson, "Origin of the Koasati Community," 110; Ernest Sickey, interview with author, November 17, 2015; and letter, Frank E. Brandon to U.S. Commissioner of Indian Affairs, January 12, 1920, and report by Roy Nash, "The Indians of Louisiana in 1931," 4, box 48, folder 7, ser. 4C, Joe Jennings Bureau of Indian Affairs Records, Archives of Appalachia, East Tennessee State University, Johnson City (hereafter cited as Jennings).

20. Hartman, "Calcasieu Pine District of Louisiana," 65; quotation from Millet, "Lumber Industry of 'Imperial' Calcasieu," 53.

21. "John Albert Bel: Pioneer Lumberman," *Lake Charles American Press*, December 30, 1918, n.p.

22. Dewith Carrier, interview with author, November 17, 2015; Ernest Sickey, interview with author, November 19, 2015; Giovo, Turner, and Langley, *Jefferson Davis Parish*, 6; Milton Turner, no title, *Beaumont Enterprise*, September 16, 1951, scrapbook 4, ser. 1 (MR4-48), Maude Reid Collection (hereafter cited as MRC), Archives and Special Collections Department, Frazar Memorial Library, McNeese State University, Lake Charles LA.

23. Leeper, *Louisiana Place Names*, 138 and 179.

24. Leeper, *Louisiana Place Names*, 90; Giovo et al., *Jefferson Davis Parish*, 8–10.

25. Julia Truitt Bishop, "Is Child of the Frisco: Elton Thriving Little Town Surrounded by Farms," *New Orleans Times-Democrat*, September 1, 1912, 37.

26. Data retrieved from "Historical Census Information, Louisiana State Census Data Center," http://louisiana.gov/Explore/Historical_Census/.

27. Solomon Battise, quoted in Giovo et al., *Davis Parish*, 13.

28. Quotation from Langley, LeJeune, and Oubre, *Les Artistes*, 53; Sickey interview, November 17, 2015.

29. Stanley Leger, interview with author, November 18, 2015. These perspectives were also captured in Turner, no title, *Beaumont Enterprise*, September 16, 1951, scrapbook 4 (MR4-48), MRC.

30. Harrington, "Among Louisiana Indians," 656–57 and 660. During his visit Harrington also collected multiple Coushatta-made items, including armbands, hair ornaments, rings, brooches, shoulder sashes, earrings, and necklaces, which are now housed at the National Museum of the American Indian in Washington

DC, inventoried under thirty-two acquisition records (some reflecting multiple items). It wasn't until two years later, in 1910, that Harrington made his way to the Alabama and Coushatta community in Texas to continue acquiring items for the collection. See http://www.nmai.si.edu/searchcollections/results.aspx?catids =0&cultxt=Coushatta&src=1-1&size=75&page=1.

31. Turner, no title, *Beaumont Enterprise*, September 16, 1951, n.p., MRC; Johnson and Leeds, *Patteran*, 18; Dorothy G. Seals, "Forgotten Indians Long for Their Own Land," *Lake Charles American Press*, January 28, 1951, 11, CTA. For a discussion on "vulnerable spaces" where Indians traded and sold their work, see Usner, *Indian Work*.

32. Battise, "How We Survived Long Ago," 276.

33. Loris Abbott Langley, quoted in Langley et al., *Les Artistes*, 59; Loris Abbott Langley as relayed to Bertney Langley and recorded in Giovo et al., *Jefferson Davis Parish*, 20.

34. Langley et al., "Louisa Williams Robinson," 159. For more on this subject, see Mihesuah, "Commonality of Difference," 15–27; and Shoemaker, *Negotiators of Change*.

35. For more on the "basket craze" of the late nineteenth century as well as the rise in tourism in the early decades of the twentieth century, see Smith-Ferri, "Development of the Commercial Market," 15–22; and Hutchinson, *Indian Craze*.

36. Trump, "'Idea of Help,'" 60.

37. For scholarship on the Indian arts and crafts market among western tribes, see, e.g., Mullin, *Culture in the Marketplace*; Cahill, "Making and Marketing Baskets in California," 126–49; and Wilkins, *Patterns of Exchange*. For scholarship focused on southeastern tribes, see Hill, *Weaving New Worlds* and "Marketing Traditions," 212–35; and Usner, "From Bayou Teche to Fifth Avenue," 339–74, "'They Don't Like Indian around Here,'" 96, 104, 116, and *Weaving Alliances*.

38. Rosabel Sylestine, quoted in marketing materials for "Coushatta Pine Needle Coiled Basketry" by Rosabel Sylestine, 1973, CTA.

39. Loris Abbott Langley, "Getting Started: Collecting and Sorting the Pine Needles," in Langley et al., *Les Artistes*, 54.

40. Sandra Lantz, "Coushatta Indians: Basket Weaving Trade Changes," *Opelousas Daily World*, June 18, 1978, 17; Doris Robinson Celestine Battise and Jamison "Jimmy" Poncho, "How We Survived," 275–80.

41. Usner, "'They Don't Like Indians around Here,'" 96; and "From Bayou Teche to Fifth Avenue," 339.

42. Giovo et al., *Jefferson Davis*, Parish, 37.

43. Bates, "Reshaping Southern Identity," 129; Taylor, *Reconstructing the Native South*, 96–99; Perdue, "Indians in Southern History," 136.

44. Statement of Raymond Gibbs in Hearing before the United States Senate Select Committee on Indian Affairs, 95th Cong., 2nd sess., on S. 2375 (April 18, 1978), 127.

45. Cook, *Monacans and Miners*, 85.

46. Klopotek, "Indian Education under Jim Crow," 63. In a 1938 report on Louisiana, Ruth M. Underhill reported that the Houmas living in Mauvais Bois, Bayou Dularge, Bayou Grand Caillou, Bayou Terrebonne, L'Isle Jean Charles, Bayou Point aux Chenes (or Chien), and Bayou Lafourche were denied access to quality education and, as a result, have it worse "than the negro and White population of the bayous chiefly because of their illiteracy which leaves them unable to get the best economic advantage out of their situation." Ruth M. Underhill, "Report on a Visit to Indian Groups in Louisiana, Oct. 15–25, 1938," 9–10, 15, folder 9, box 43, ser. 3C, Jennings.

47. Hiram F. "Pete" Gregory, interview with author, November 19, 2015. According to Klopotek, the Choctaw-Apaches' primary school was designated a "white school" by the parish and provided with white teachers, but they weren't admitted into white high schools in the parish until 1970. "Indian Education under Jim Crow," 63.

48. Ernest Sickey, interview with author, April 6, 2015.

49. Klopotek, "Indian Education," 52.

50. Precht, "'Lost Tribe Wanders No More,'" 50.

51. Dominguez, *White by Definition*, 25–34; and Jolivette, *Louisiana Creoles*, 17–25.

52. Solomon Battise, quoted in Giovo et al., *Jefferson Davis Parish*, 13.

53. Loris Abbott Langley as relayed to Bertney Langley and recorded in Giovo et al., *Jefferson Davis Parish*, 20. Portions of this interview are also in Langley et al., *Les Artistes*, 59.

54. Carrier interview, November 17, 2015.

55. Sickey, interview, November 17, 2015.

56. Ernest Sickey, interview with author, September 20, 2016.

57. Charley's mother was Coushatta, and his father was part of a Creek group that previously migrated into southeastern Texas to live with the Alabamas and Coushattas. Mary, like Sissy Poncho Abbey, was born into the Poncho family, and all accounts indicate that her parents were both Coushattas. Both Charley (b. 1871) and Mary (b. 1872) were born at the Indian Village along the Calcasieu River. The name *Si key* appears in the 1832 Parsons and Abbott Creek census, which is likely the earlier used version of the *Sickey* name. See the Cus se taw Town 1832 census at https://www.accessgenealogy.com/native/1832-creek-census-cussetaw-town .htm. In an interview conducted by James Sylestine in 1956 with Charley Sickey's sister, Alice Sickey Sylestine, more details on the family history unfold. Alice shared: "We lived at a place called 'Chikapoo' until my mother and my father were

dead, then my uncle took me to Shepherd, Texas, near 'Coley Creek' . . . Majority of my people at 'Chikapoo' migrated to Oklahoma and scattered out while I was taken to Shepherd, Texas and then to here." Alice lived on the Alabama-Coushatta Reservation in Texas at the time of the interview. See interview with "Alice Sicky [*sic*] Sylestine" in "Kossati tribe," James Ludwell Davis Sylestine Papers, folder 25, box 1990/106, Archives and Information Services Division, Texas State Library and Archives Commission, Austin. Interview was transcribed from the original thermal paper by attorney Victor Alcorta, who has conducted extensive research on the early migration of the Coushattas, with a particular emphasis on their Texas presence.

58. Other details from the 1910 census about Charley Sickey indicate that he was employed on a farm and his native language was "Indian." U.S. Federal Census, 1910, Police Jury Ward 1, Calcasieu LA, roll T624_510, p. 22B, Enumeration District 0030, FHL microfilm 1374523, Ancestry.com. Also see Leeds, *St. Peter's Congregational Church.*

59. Charley Sickey appears in the records as being back in Louisiana by the late 1930s as a trustee for the St. Peter's Church. Leeds, *St. Peter's Congregational Church*, 69. His grandson, Ernest Sickey, was told by Solomon Battise that Charley became very active in the Indian Church, even becoming a song leader and music teacher, where he remained until his death in 1943. See Sickey interview, September 20, 2016. The 1920 census places Davis and Gladys in the Abbey household, where they lived with Jeff, Sissy, and five other Abbeys. See U.S. Census, 1920, Police Jury Ward 2, Allen LA,

60. Leeds, *St. Peter's Congregational Church*, 49; U.S. Federal Census, 1910, Police Jury Ward 1, Calcasieu LA. According to records left by Reverend Leeds, Alcide Langley was the son of Joe and Silia Langley, whose children included Jackson, Alcide, Lillie, and Louisa. See "Indian Families on Bayou Blue, near Elton, La." (1941), CTA; United States, World War I Draft Registration Cards, 1917–18, Ancestry.com. Daisy Langley was born in Idabel, Oklahoma, during her family's short-lived move there. United States, Social Security Applications and Claims Index, 1936–2007, Ancestry.com. According to Kniffen, Gregory, and Stokes, Choctaws living in Louisiana and other nearby states were encouraged to move to Oklahoma starting in 1900 under the guise that they would receive allotments. Many of them walked to Idabel and Broken Bow, only to discover that no allotments had been secured for them. *Historic Indian Tribes of Louisiana*, 98.

61. For more on Choctaw migrations into southern Louisiana, see the report of John Sibley, an Indian agent in Natchitoches in the early nineteenth century who captured some of the early migration patterns of multiple groups. Sibley, "Historical Sketches," 48–62.

62. Levine, "Arzelie Langley and a Lost Pantribal Tradition," 191 and 268; Ernest Sickey, interviews with author, April 6, 2015, and October 5, 2016.

63. Sickey interviews, April 6, 2015, and September 20, 2016. U.S. Federal Census, 1920, Police Jury Ward 1, Allen LA, Ancestry.com.

64. This information was provided by two of Abbott's daughters, Loris Langley and Elizabeth Marie Thompson, in an interview with Linda Langley, April 14, 2006. Referenced in Langley et al., "Louisa Williams Robinson," 166.

65. Linda Langley's special notation following "Grandmother and the Nail," 282–83. The Harrington plate can be found at the National Museum of the American Indian, Smithsonian Institution, negative no. 2739.

66. Crystal Williams, interview with author, April 5, 2016.

67. In a 1972 testimony geographer Daniel Jacobson acknowledged that, "even now there is a great deal of movement between the two communities. It is almost as if the boundary between Texas and Louisiana doesn't exist." See "Testimony of Dr. Daniel Jacobson at Hearing before Indian Claims Commission," in *(Creek) Indians Alabama-Coushatta: Ethnological Report and Statement of Testimony*, 213.

68. According to a 1934 memorandum, there were three hundred Alabama and Coushatta people living on the reservation, which was comprised of about one thousand acres purchased for them by the state of Texas and three thousand acres purchased by the federal government. The reservation is about twenty miles from the town of Livingston in Polk County. A. C. Monahan, "Memorandum to the Commissioner, regarding Alabama Indians, Alabama Reservation, near Livingston, Texas," January 30, 1934, folder 7, box 48, ser. 4C, Jennings.

69. Ernest Sickey, interview with author, April 29, 2015. The movement between tribes was captured in a report by C. F. Hauke, chief clerk for the U.S. Department of the Interior, to Cato Sells, commissioner of Indian Affairs, saying, "I was informed that, some years ago, two or three Choctaw Indians from Oklahoma visited this band [Alabama-Coushatta] and conversed with them, and also that a few Indians from this band had been in Oklahoma, always going to the neighborhood of the Choctaw Tribe." July 2, 1917, folder 7, box 48, ser. 4C, Jennings.

70. Sickey and Gregory interviews, November 19, 2015. Mobilian was a pidgin language that Emanuel Drechsel describes as "a linguistic compromise that evolved out of situations involving contact between speakers of several mutually unintelligible, often unrelated languages." See Drechsel, "Speaking 'Indian' in Louisiana,'" 6. For the results of Drechsel's work with Langley, see Drechsel, "Mobilian Jargon."

71. Jean-Luc Pierite, interview with author, February 8, 2016.

72. Klopotek, *Recognition Odysseys*, 48.

73. Linda Langley explained that this form of shared decision-making was reflected in the approach used by Red Shoes in the eighteenth century, during one of the tribe's moves. "Red Shoes saved the Coushatta people. I have this vision [that]

roughly half the tribe followed him and half did not. It was always an open discussion. You are free to stay or free to go." Linda Langley, interview with author, April 3, 2016.

74. Leland Thompson, quoted in Mueller et al., *Nations Within*, 68.

75. Ernest Sickey, interview with author, July 1, 2015. What Sickey described indicates the continuation of a form of government practiced by the Creeks and Coushattas in previous centuries in which great importance was placed upon town government (or a regionally defined portion of the population), with a head man, or *mikkó* (*micco*), representing the wishes of the people and presiding over a council of representatives. This was not a hereditary position, but an elected one generally bestowed upon a well-respected man with great orator abilities. See Bartram, *Travels* (reprint, 1792; Philadelphia: printed by James and Johnson, 1791), 389–90. For additional detail about the Muskogee form of government, see Deloria and Lytle, *American Indians, American Justice*, 84–87.

76. Bertney Langley remembered that his uncle Bel Abbey was the representative for his side of the family when community meetings were called. Interview with author, April 4, 2016. Also, the practice of shared governance was often interpreted as a *lack* of government by outside observers. After spending just one day at the Bayou Blue settlement, e.g., U.S. Indian Service supervisor Frank E. Brandon concluded in his 1920 report: "They have no tribal government although they have a head man. He attends to business for them in a general way but they have no elected counsel." Brandon didn't recognize what was unfamiliar to him, which prevented him from fully appreciating the endurance of Coushatta decision-making practices and the tribe's leadership structure. See Brandon to U.S. commissioner of Indian Affairs, January 12, 1920.

77. Sickey interview, July 28, 2015; Johnson and Leeds, *Patteran*, 143.

78. Stickball—also known as ball play—is among one of the oldest known team sports in North America. Although it originated among southeastern tribes, it was historically—and still is—practiced by tribes across the United States and Canada. Similar to lacrosse, it involves utilizing sticks shaped like large wooden spoons (that later evolved to include nets) in order to catch and throw balls into the opposing team's goal. Traditional stickball games were major events that could last for days. They were often used to settle intertribal or intra-village disputes and generally had spiritual significance. Hunter reported that "both areas [of the Bayou Blue Coushatta community] had stickball grounds and competed actively against one another in the games. This itself would seem to suggest that the idea of the old Creek intra-town divisions (moieties) persisted at least in terms of this sport. None of the present informants were able to give the exact locations of the old stickball fields, though the sport was conducted at the present location of the

church until the mid-1940s." See Hunter, "Settlement Pattern," 83. See also Adair, *History of the American Indians*, 430.

79. Bel Abbey was quoted by Hunter, "Settlement Pattern," 85. Hunter makes a convincing argument that the Coushattas exhibited cultural continuity in the manner in which they settled the Bayou Blue area. See "Settlement Pattern," 88. This argument was later supported by Kniffen, Gregory, and Stokes, who claimed that "the Koasati have maintained traditional values while modifying the architectural forms," *Historic Indian Tribes*, 117.

80. According to Sickey, there isn't a special Coushatta version of gumbo. See interviews September 16 and November 16, 2015.

81. Barbara Langley, interview with author, April 4, 2016.

82. Crystal Williams interview, April 5, 2016.

83. The Coushatta educational approach resonates with patterns in Indigenous education classified by Lomawaima and McCarty. See their book, *To Remain an Indian*, 28–42.

84. Langley et al., "Louisa Williams Robinson," 156.

85. Unidentified speaker, quoted in Giovo et al., *Jefferson Davis Parish*, 19.

86. Lelia Battise, interview with author, April 5, 2016.

87. Doris Robinson Celestine Battise and Jamison "Jimmy" Poncho, "How We Survived," 275–79.

88. Jonathan Cernek, interview with author, April 5, 2016.

89. Paula Abbey Manuel, interview with author, November 16, 2015.

90. Bertney Langley in Giovo et al., *Jefferson Davis Parish*, 16–17.

91. Sickey, interview with author, April 29, 2015.

92. Bertney Langley interview, April 4, 2016.

93. Sickey interviews, April 29 and May 13, 2015.

94. The Battise family's name often appears in the records under the spelling *Baptiste*. The census records list Ellisor "Baptiste" as being born in about 1882 in Texas before residing in Allen Parish by 1920. His occupation is listed as "salesman" in the sawmill industry. Burissa "Baptiste" is recorded as being born in about 1890 in Louisiana. U.S. Federal Census, 1920, Police Jury Ward 2, Allen Parish LA, Ancestry.com. Rev. Paul Leeds recorded the couple's baptism dates as Burissa (June 1907) and Ellisor (September 1909). See Leeds, *St. Peter's Congregational Church*.

95. Sickey interview, May 13, 2015.

96. "Services Commemorating Fifty Years in Ministry Are Dedicated to Rev. Paul Leeds of Kinder," *Lake Charles American Press*, November 12, 1943, 27.

97. Leeds gave multiple estimates of how many Coushattas lived at the Bayou Blue settlement upon his arrival, which varies between 150 and 300 people. Also, Leeds was not the first missionary to expose the Coushattas to Christianity. While still

living at Indian Village, a missionary named Sam Reed attempted to work with the tribe. See Jacobson, "Koasati Cultural Change," 87.

98. Aline Thompson, "Aid Forthcoming to Area's 'Orphan Indians,'" *Lake Charles American Press*, June 14, 1959, 22; Dorothy Seals, "He Taught Them of 'Minco-Chitto,'" *Lake Charles American Press*, February 19, 1956, n.p., scrapbook 4 (MR4-48), MRC.

99. According to the 1910 census, Paul Williams was a farmer born in about 1863 at Indian Village. He was married to Harriet Williams. U.S. Federal Census, 1910, Police Jury Ward 1, Calcasieu LA, Ancestry.com; Dorothy Seals, "Allen Indian Tribe Found Home—and God," *Alexandria Town Talk*, December 13, 1957, 9.

100. Leeds, *St. Peter's Congregational Church*; Thompson, "Aid Forthcoming," 22; and Seals, "He Taught Them." The original St. Peter's Congregational Church was torn down in the summer of 1934. A new church was constructed and opened that following September with materials purchased through gifts from the Scofield Memorial Church in Dallas. Jacobson, "Origin of the Koasati Community," 117.

101. Leeds explained why St. Luke's Congregational Church was built: "For the convenience of many Indians living on the West side of Bayou Blue, and because of dissatisfaction in the first church, St. Peter's, on the East side of the Bayou, a Sunday School was organized by Billie Henderson, at the Lastie Williams School, on July 13, 1913. Rev. D. A. D. Hayes assisted the Indians in organizing." Leeds, *St. Luke's Congregational Church*. Although this particular church closed, the community remained active and developed a new church in the western community.

102. Johnson and Leeds, *Patteran*, 26.

103. "Mrs. W. S. Kingrey of Kinder Hostess to D.A.R. Meeting," *Lake Charles American Press*, March 16, 1939, 21; and Dorothy G. Seals, "Forgotten Indians Long for Their Own Land," *Lake Charles American Press*, January 28, 1951, 11. Given the Coushattas' location on "the northern fringe of the Catholic Acadian region in Louisiana," it has been characterized as "ironic" that the Roman Catholic Church didn't have a documented impact on them. See Johnson, *Coushatta People*, 76–77, 81.

104. "Koasati Missionary Addresses WMS," *Lake Charles American Press*, February 5, 1956, 12; Johnson and Leeds, *Patteran*, 18.

105. "Biography of Pioneer Minister Published," *Lake Charles American Press*, July 5, 1965, 13.

106. Coushatta Tribe, "Struggle," 9; Langley et al., "Louisa Williams Robinson," 162–63. Donald Hunter argues: "The Koasati settlement on Bayou Blue is dispersed and the central area near the church, the *isha choba* ('big house'), approximates the old ceremonial center within a creek town. The church is no longer circular in shape and made of waddle daub, but the door still opens to the south." See "Settlement Pattern," 87; Sickey interview, October 5, 2016.

107. Sickey interview, May 13, 2015; Jacobson, "Origin of the Koasati Community," 107. Quotation from Edna Langley in press release for "Special Exhibition of Indian Crafts to Open at the Cabildo," issued by the U.S. Department of the Interior, Indian Arts and Crafts Board, November 23, 1973, 2, CTA.

108. Curtis Sylestine, quoted in Giovo et al., *Jefferson Davis Parish*, 21–22.

109. Paredes stated that southern tribes utilized schools and churches as mechanisms to ensure the continuation of Indian identity. Between the 1870s and the 1940s, he argued, these institutions "tended to become important anchors of local identity and have served as training grounds for Indians in the leadership styles and administrative patterns of the larger society." See "Paradoxes of Modernism," 353.

110. Untitled obituary, *Lake Charles American Press*, February 10, 1934, 6; Johnson and Leeds, *Patteran*, 144.

111. Langley et al., "Louisa Williams Robinson," 164; Leeds, *St. Peter's Congregational Church*; Sickey interview, October 5, 2016.

112. D. Seals, "He Taught Them."

113. Cernek interview, April 5, 2016. Cernek is the son of Gloria Battise Cernek, the youngest daughter of Solomon and Adeline Abbey Battise, and Rev. John Cernek, a missionary who came to Louisiana from Wisconsin. The other children of Solomon and Adeline Abbey Battise include Leonard, Willis Ralph, Reed, Janice, Ardeena, Glenna, and Faye.

114. Bertney Langley interview, April 4, 2016.

115. Darlene Langley Dunnehoo, interview with author, November 6, 2015; Sickey interviews, May 13 and September 16, 2015, and September 20, 2016.

116. Johnson, *Coushatta People*, 81–82.

117. For a discussion on the development of Indian churches (including St. Peter's) as institutions for survival in the eastern United States, see Bartl, "Importance of the 'Indian Church,'" 37–53.

2. REFUSING TO BE OVERLOOKED

EPIGRAPH: Letter, Jeff Abbey and Kinney Williams to John Collier, July 23, 1938, 720-Choctaw, box 475, Central Classified Files, 1907–39, record group 75, Records of the Bureau of Indian Affairs, National Archives Building in Washington DC (hereafter cited as NA-DC).

1. "Hon. Robert Campbell Culpepper," http://www.culpepperconnections.com/ss /p4182.htm.

2. The incident occurred on December 24, 1911, and received some newspaper coverage that misidentified the victims as Choctaws. See "Kinder, Choctaw Indian Instantly Killed by Freight Train," *New Orleans Times-Democrat*, December 26, 1911, 6. For the lawsuit that followed, see letter, Frank E. Powell (Powell & Perkins, Lawyers) to the Honorable Patrick E. Moore, April 3, 1913; petition, Jackson

Langley to the Honorable Judge of the Fifteenth Judicial District Court, Calcasieu Parish LA, prepared by Cline, Cline & Bell, n.d., both from the Allen Parish Clerk of Court, Oberlin LA.

3. Deposition, Jackson Langley and Alfred John, September 2, 1919; letter, R. C. Culpepper to Cato Sells, September 2, 1919, CTA.

4. Letter, Cato Sells to James B. Aswell, February 14, 1920, folder 7, box 48, ser. 4C, Jennings.

5. Literal translation of *Ihoochakittap Aati Imintohnoto*: "Working for the people long ago."

6. Letter, J. A. Williams to the commissioner of Indian Affairs, January 21, 1911, MC201, box 16, folder 1, Coushattas, 1911–73, Seeley G. Mudd Manuscript Library, Princeton University, Princeton NJ (hereafter cited as Byler).

7. Letter, Arsène Pujo to the commissioner of Indian Affairs, February 10 and May 28, 1911, Byler.

8. Letter, Robert G. Valentine to Rep. Pujo, March 1, 1911; C. F. Hauke to Rep. Pujo, June 21, 1911, Byler.

9. See Brightman, "Chitimacha," 642–52; Kniffen, Gregory, and Stokes, *Historic Indian*, 74–75; Usner, "'They Don't Like Indians around Here,'" 89–124.

10. "We don't know the Chittimache [*sic*]," wrote Jackson Langley in a letter to Jeff Dutch (acting chief clerk), May 29, 1917, exhibit L-17, box 4C335, Yarborough.

11. See U.S. Congress, Senate, *Journal of the Proceedings at the Treaty of Dancing Rabbit Creek*, S. Doc. 512, 21st Cong., 1st sess. (1830); and U.S. Congress, House Committee on Indian Affairs, "Land Claims &c. Under 14th Article Choctaw Treaty," May 11, 1836, H. Rep. 663, 24th Cong., 1st sess. (1836), microfiche 295.

12. U.S. House of Representatives, Committee on Indian Affairs, *Claims of Choctaw Indians of Mississippi*, 75th Cong., 3rd sess. (1938), Report No. 2233, 2. See also Adams, *Who Belongs*, 96–97.

13. For more detail on the Mississippi Choctaws' efforts to hold the federal government accountable for treaty obligations and how the tribe maneuvered Mississippi politics and religious organizations to secure alliances, see Osburn, *Choctaw Resurgence* and "Mississippi Choctaws and Racial Politics." Also, Kidwell's book *Choctaws and Missionaries in Mississippi, 1818–1918* provides some insightful coverage on the "Second Removal" of the Mississippi Choctaws and some of the events leading up to their recognition in 1918 (chaps. 9–10). Finally, Adams, *Who Belongs*, does a thorough job discussing the Mississippi Choctaws' case as it relates to citizenship and identity and how the tribe was able to maneuver its way through legal and racial barriers (chap. 3, 96–131).

14. Osburn, *Choctaw Resurgence*, 42 and 45; Adams, *Who Belongs*, 108.

15. Reverend Leeds wrote about a lawyer (likely the same one) in his journal: "An enterprising lawyer made an appointment to meet the tribe at Kinder to

get them to furnish money for him to go to Washington to secure the passage of legislation to give them financial aid. Seeing a large number of them in town, I asked the cause. I dropped in at their meeting and asked questions. The lawyer reluctantly told me his plan; then I told them that I had called on the Indian Agent in Washington a few months earlier and had discussed the matter with him, only to be informed that there was no way to grant these Indians help, because they were free citizens with the same status as any other Americans, and no such exception could be made. The lawyer, like the Arab, silently folded his tent and stole away." See Leeds and Johnson, *Patteran*, 147–48.

16. Adams, *Who Belongs*, 118–19; "A Find for Allen Ph. Indians," *Lake Charles American Press*, August 8, 1913, n.p., CTA. The actual value of Choctaw citizenship, if the case were to be won, according to P. J. Hurley in a 1915 report, was estimated at between $5,000 and $8,000. See "Report of P. J. Hurley to the Honorable Cato Sells for 1915," 4, folder 7, box 12, Patrick Jay Hurley Papers, Choctaw Manuscript Collections, University of Oklahoma Libraries, Western History Collections, Norman. Following Powell's visit to Louisiana, his efforts became part of a federal investigation the same year (1913); see letter, Brandon to U.S. commissioner of Indian Affairs, January 12, 1920; and Roy Nash, "The Indians of Louisiana in 1931," 11, folder 7, box 48, ser. 4C, Jennings.

17. "Find for Allen Ph. Indians."

18. Letters, Mark Robinson to U.S. commissioner of Indian Affairs, March 3, 1913; and acting commissioner (name illegible) to Mark Robinson, April 3, 1913. A local sawmill owner, Richard Powell, also wrote to the OIA on behalf of the tribe to directly validate Robinson's claims, see letter, Powell to commissioner of Indian Affairs, March 3, 1913. All letters from Byler.

19. Over the course of a year Jackson Langley sent the following letters to the Bureau of Indian Affairs: Langley to the commissioner of Indian Affairs, February 16, 1917; Langley to Jeff Dutch (acting chief clerk in the Bureau Office), May 29 and September 12, 1917; and Langley to Todd Hanke (chief clerk in the Bureau Office) January 20, 1918. All letters from exhibit L-17, box 4C335, Yarborough.

20. In the summer of 1917 C. F. Hauke conducted a site visit on the Alabama-Coushatta Reservation, offering recommendations to the commissioner for the purchase of land and equipment for the tribe (to be reimbursable) as well as federal investment in a school, hospital, and farm equipment (non-reimbursable). See Hauke to Sells, July 2, 1917, folder 7, box 48, ser. 4C, Jennings.

21. "The Mississippi Choctaw Claim," January 21, 1914, Library of Congress, HathiTrust Digital Library, https://catalog.hathitrust.org/Record/009606211/Cite.

22. William Webb Venable, notice in *Neshoba County Democrat*, March 15, 1917, n.p.; "Will Help Indians," *Jackson Daily News*, March 12, 1917, 5.

23. "The Choctaws," *Neshoba County Democrat*, March 22, 1917, 3; Osburn, *Choctaw Resurgence*, 54.

24. Kidwell, *Choctaws and Missionaries*, 196.

25. Langley's letter incited an immediate response from Lazaro, who revealed that he had not been properly informed about the meetings either. As a result, he wrote to OIA commissioner Cato Sells asking that his office "furnish me with the information desired." Cato was receptive, thanking Lazaro for alerting him to another neglected Indian community that he planned to investigate. See letters, Lazaro to Sells, January 14, 1918, and Sells to Lazaro, January 15, 1918, Choctaw 050, box 12, Central Classified Files, 1907–39, record group 75, NA-DC.

26. Letter, Langley to Lazaro, January 7, 1918, Choctaw 050, box 12, Central Classified Files, 1907–39, record group 75, NA-DC.

27. Johnson and Leeds, *Patteran*, 35; "10 Persons Reported Dead as Result of Tornado on Louisiana Coast Yesterday," *Monroe News-Star*, August 7, 1918, 1; "Storm Victims," *Alexandria Town Talk*, August 9, 1918, 1.

28. In 1918 there were over eight hundred newspaper articles in Louisiana alone regarding the Spanish influenza epidemic and how to avoid contracting the illness. Many parishes even closed schools and churches temporarily due to the epidemic. See "Influenza Brings General Closing by Health Board," *St. Landry Clarion*, October 12, 1918, 1. For the Mississippi Choctaws, one report stated that between 20 and 50 percent were killed by the influenza outbreak. Brescia, *Choctaw Tribal Government*, 21. Also see Kidwell, *Choctaws and Missionaries*, 196; and Osburn, *Choctaw Resurgence*, 58.

29. Brandon to U.S. commissioner of Indian Affairs, January 12, 1920, 11.

30. Langley appears in the following census records: 1880 (Hickory Flat, Calcasieu Parish LA), roll 449, film 1254449, p. 463A; 1910 (Police Jury Ward 1, Calcasieu LA), roll T624_510, p. 23B; 1920 (Police Jury Ward 2, Allen LA), roll T625_603, p. 29A; 1930 (Police Jury Ward 2, Allen LA), roll 782, p. 19A; and 1940 (Allen Parish LA), roll T627_1379, p. 19B All census data retrieved from Ancestry.com.

31. In 1929 Langley worked with ethnographer John R. Swanton to record the Koasati language. The results were published in Swanton, "Indian Language Studies in Louisiana," 195–200. According to Geoffrey D. Kimball, Langley's mother, Selin Williams Langley, served as the primary consultant to Swanton and Mary Haas. See *Koasati Traditional Narratives*, 4.

32. Langley interview, April 4, 2016.

33. Records demonstrate the large family Jackson Langley had by 1938. Married three times—to Sinnie Polyte Langley (date unknown), Alice Pocoto Langley (1919), and Maggie John Langley (1924)—he had three daughters and three sons. See 1938 family records entitled "Koasati Tribe—1938," 2, CTA; Robin Langley, interview with author, April 4, 2016.

34. Letters, Mark Robinson to commissioner of Indian Affairs, January 19 and February 23, 1920, Byler. Also, for a response to a letter written by Robinson a few years later, see E. B. Meritt (assistant commissioner of Indian Affairs) to Robinson, June 27, 1922, folder 7, box 48, ser. 4C, Jennings.

35. U.S. Senate, Committee on Indian Affairs, 71st Cong., 3rd sess., Survey of Conditions of the Indians in the United States: Hearings on S. Res. 79, 308, and 263, pt. 16, March 26, 28, and 31, 1930, and November 6, 8, and December 10, 1930 (Washington DC), 7932–41. Nash's 1931 report lists the "heads of family" as "Mark Robinson, Jacob Robinson, Mrs. Gossett Robinson, Louisa Robinson, Jeff Abbey, M. D. Abbey, Lindsay Abbey, Alfred John, Adam John, Ben John, Isaac John, Scott John, Edmond John, Foster Poncho, John Poncho, David Poncho, Anna Poncho, Asa Poncho, Gardner Langley, Jackson Langley, Joe Austin, Kinney Williams, Houston Williams, Joe Williams (no family living), Dock Williams, Davis Sickey, Charles Sickey (no family living), Ellison Batties, and Lonnie Abbott." Nash, "Indians of Louisiana in 1931," 1–2. Mention of this hearing was also made in a 1934 letter from R. E. Powell to the secretary of the interior, September 27, 1934, Byler.

36. Prucha, *Great Father*, 273.

37. Literal translation of *Tatka Mikkok Akohchokchanaakato*: "The White Chief went against us." Because of the lack of services, by the mid-1920s several Louisiana Coushattas moved back to Texas to work for the Carter Lumber Company. According to Nash, the Alabama-Coushatta Reservation residents voted unanimously against allowing those families to move onto the reservation and receive services. It is important to point out that the precise terms of what they voted on weren't explicit in the report, so it is difficult to accurately assess the circumstances. See Roy Nash, "The Indians of Texas" (March 1931), folder 12, box 22, ser. 4C, Jennings.

38. The "Brandon Report" was the result of an assessment on the status of four of Louisiana's Indian settlements and compiled in a document issued January 12, 1920. In it Brandon estimated that there were approximately 150 Coushatta living in a similar state of poverty as neighboring whites. He recommended the government purchase land for them at a later time—something that never happened. See Brandon to the U.S. commissioner of Indian Affairs, January 12, 1920.

39. Nash, "Indians of Louisiana in 1931," 6.

40. A 1940 study by Lyda Averill Taylor assessed the "useful" nature of remedies used by different southern tribal communities for a variety of ailments. Her conclusions were based on vague assessments; however, she determined that 50 percent of the Coushattas' remedies used by traditional healers are useful and 57 percent of those used by Choctaw healers are useful. See Taylor, *Plants Used as Curatives*, 70.

41. Leeds, *St. Peter's Congregational Church* and *St. Luke's Congregational Church*.

42. Nash, "Indians of Texas."

43. In a letter to Mark Robinson, E. B. Meritt claimed, "It does not appear that there have ever been any treaties negotiated [with] that particular band or tribe of Indians and the United States upon which a claim could be based for governmental assistance." June 27, 1922.

44. Memo, commissioner of Indian Affairs, April 22, 1936, Byler.

45. Brandon to commissioner of Indian Affairs, January 12, 1920. For more on the confounding manner in which race operated in Indian lives, see Greenbaum, "What's in a Label."

46. Letter, Brandon to commissioner of Indian Affairs, January 12, 1920.

47. Letter, E. B. Meritt (Indian commissioner) to Jackson Langley, April 26, 1923, folder 7, box 48, ser. 4C, Jennings.

48. Nash report (1931), 7.

49. Letter, Ray Lyman Wilbur to T. H. Harris, March 3, 1932, Choctaw 806, box 482, Central Classified Files, 1907–39, record group 75, NA-DC.

50. Long's Share Our Wealth movement was many years in the making. It proposed the redistributing of the nation's wealth through a series of actions, including a capital levy tax on the wealthy. See Snyder, "Huey Long and the Presidential Election of 1936."

51. Jacobson, "Koasati Cultural Change," 147; Johnson, *Coushatta People*, 72. A reference to Simmons learning to speak Koasati can be found in the Reeves report (1937).

52. Battise, "How We Survived Long Ago," 278.

53. Letter, Thos. J. Griffin (Allen Parish School Board superintendent) to L. W. Page (superintendent of the Choctaw Agency), September 26, 1938, CTA.

54. According to Brandon (1920), the two schools had a combined enrollment of approximately forty students. Details were also provided in "St. Patrick's Celebration at Recreation Center," *Lake Charles American Press*, March 16, 1939, 21.

55. John Collier is a controversial figure. He began his career working with immigrant populations in New York as a social worker during the Progressive Era. In 1920 he traveled to Taos Pueblo in New Mexico, where he dedicated himself to Indian affairs and critiqued the policies and practices of the OIA. Once his tenure with the OIA began, in 1933, he emphasized tribal communal land ownership, cultural preservation, and Indian controlled tribal governments. Some scholars credit him for "saving" tribes from the destruction of previous assimilationist policies. Others identify Collier as offering a new brand of assimilationist practices as tribal communities were organized into controlled governments with federal oversight. See Prucha, *Great Father*, 917–18; and Philip, *Indian Self-Rule*, 30–109.

56. Sec. 5 of the Alabama-Coushatta Constitution allows for the extension of tribal membership to any Louisiana Coushatta person who marries a member of the

Texas-based community. See U.S. Department of Interior Office of Indian Affairs, *Constitution and By-Laws of the Alabama and Coushatta Tribes of Texas, Approved*, August 19, 1938, art. 2, sec. 5; located in the appendix of Rothe, *Kalita's People*.

57. Quotation relayed by Ernest Sickey, interview with author, July 1, 2015.

58. Ryan report (1934), 1.

59. See Ryhner and Eder, *History of Indian Education*, 102–3.

60. Letter, W. Carson Ryan to Monahan, October 10, 1934, Choctaw 806, box 482, Central Classified Files, 1907–39, record group 75, NA-DC; Routh Trowbridge Wilby, "The Weave Goes On," *Dixie*, November 7, 1976, n.p.

61. Fickinger, "Memorandum to Mr. Monahan," October 3, 1935, Choctaw 806, box 482, Central Classified Files, 1907–39, record group 75, NA-DC; Narrative Section, Annual Statistical Report, 1935, sec. 4 ("Education"), Choctaw 919, box 484, Central Classified Files, 1907–39, record group 75, NA-DC; "V. L. Roy among 84 Louisiana Teachers Retired with Pensions," *Alexandria Town Talk*, July 17, 1937, 7; "Indian School near Oakdale Gets U.S. Aid: Tribe Pleased by Assistance, Which Permits 1935 Operation," *Shreveport Times*, October 10, 1935, 3; letter, Simmons to Superintendent Hector, January 6 and February 22, 1936, CTA.

62. Letter, Hector to the commissioner of Indian Affairs, June 10, 1937, Choctaw 806, box 482, Central Classified Files, 1907–39, record group 75, NA-DC; letter, Paul L. Fickinger to A. C. Hector, August 6, 1937, CTA.

63. Letter, Kinney Williams to A. C. Hector, June 23, 1937, Choctaw 806, box 482, Central Classified Files, 1907–39, record group 75, NA-DC.

64. The argument of permanence was issued in relation to the Jena Band of Choctaws who were discussed in the same letter as living a drifter lifestyle. The accompanying recommendation was to compel them to move to the Mississippi Choctaw community, which would "eliminate one school in Louisiana." See letter, Edna Groves to W. W. Beatty, January 17, 1938. This December 1937 trip was also reported by A. C. Hector to Paul L. Fickinger, December 15, 1937, Choctaw 806, box 482, Central Classified Files, 1907–39, record group 75, NA-DC.

65. Klopotek, *Recognition Odysseys*, 51.

66. Letter, Thos. J. Griffin (Allen Parish School Board) to A. C. Hector, October 19, 1937, CTA; letter, M. S. Robertson (WPA Education Program director) to A. C. Hector, December 17, 1937, Byler.

67. Letter, Griffin to Hector, November 4 and November 8, 1937, CTA.

68. Initial letter was sent by Hector to the U.S. commissioner of Indian Affairs, January 20, 1938. The response came from the U.S. commissioner of Indian affairs to Hector, February 25, 1938, CTA.

69. Letter, Abbey and Williams to Collier, July 23, 1938.

70. Letter, Fickinger to Abbey, August 15, 1938, Choctaw 720, box 475, Central Classified Files, 1907–39, record group 75, NA-DC.

71. Letter, Caroline Dorman to Commissioner of Indian Affairs, December 16, 1929, folder 7, box 28, ser. 4C, Jennings. Brandon reported that by 1920 the Coushatta landholdings had been "reduced to an average of seven acres per capita but not distributed [*sic*] on that basis." See Brandon report, 12.

72. Nash (1931) reported the Coushatta landholdings based on details provided by Mark Robinson, who offered information on the acreage held by each family: "Jeff Abbey—260, Mark Robinson—91, Mrs. Dock Williams—80, John Poncho—70, Mrs. Lonnie Abbott—51, Mrs. Gossett Robinson—51, Jacob Robinson—51, Mrs. Alfred John—40, M.L. Abbey—40, Ellison Battise—40, Houston Williams—10, and Jackson Langley—?" (2–3). It is important to point out that since the amount of property owned by Jackson Langley wasn't reported, the total number of acres held by the Coushattas was higher than the reported 784 acres. In fact, in a testimony before the U.S. Senate Committee in 1930, Reverend Leeds listed "their land holdings as 935 acres divided among 15 owners—8 married men, 5 married women, 1 widow, and 1 minor" U.S. Senate, Committee on Indian Affairs, 71st Cong., 3rd sess., Survey of Conditions, 3.

73. Letter, Vernon W. Scott (Associate Farm Management) to E. C. McInnis (Farm Security Administration), December 16, 1941, folder 20, box 7, ser. 3A, Jennings.

74. Letter, Mark Robinson to Roy Nash and printed in the "Nash Report" (1931), 3. See also Cushing, *Investigation of Alleged Loss*; Brandon to commissioner of Indian Affairs, January 12, 1920.

75. Letter, J. Phillips to commissioner of Indian Affairs, July 22, 1912, Byler.

76. Sickey interview, July 28, 2015. J. A. Bel left a sizable estate to his children, Marie, Katherine, and Ernest, upon his death in 1918. Bel's heirs organized the estate into three separate companies: Bel Oil, Bel Estate, and Quatre Parish Company. The history behind the three companies is detailed in an unpublished professional report, "Bel Oil Corporation," for the fulfillment of a master of business administration degree by one of the Bel heirs, Della Bel Blake.

77. This was reported by Jacobson (1954) based on information supplied to him in a letter by C. L. Marcantel, mayor of Elton.

78. Letter, L. W. Page to "Mr. Commissioner," August 23, 1938, Choctaw 806, box 482, Central Classified Files, 1907–39, record group 75, NA-DC.

79. Langley et al., "Louisa Williams Robinson," 166.

80. Davis, *Louisiana*, 353. The environmental degradation that the oil industry caused in south Louisiana was the subject of multiple lawsuits and subsequent regulations that are discussed by Theriot in "Oilfield Battleground."

81. Frazell, "North Elton Field, Allen Parish, Louisiana," 22.

82. Letter, L. W. Page to "Mr. Commissioner," August 23, 1938. There was a short period in which OIA officials looked into placing the new school on the Sissy Robinson Alabama homestead that had previously been taken into federal trust.

Alabama's heirs, Emily Alabama and Jane Battise, held title to the land by the time these discussions were under way, but for unknown reasons, that property was also deemed unsuitable for the school. Letter, G. A. Collins to Harvey K. Meyer, September 28, 1939, Byler.

83. Letters, Beatty to Hector, April 5, 1938, and Beatty to Page, September 2, 1938, Choctaw 806, box 482, Central Classified Files, 1907–39, record group 75, NA-DC.

84. Letters, Page to "Mr. Commissioner," August 23, 1938, and Harvey K. Meyer to commissioner of Indian affairs, December 26, 1939, folder 20, box 7, ser. 3A, Jennings; letter, Meyer to the commissioner of Indian affairs, February 26, 1940, Byler.

85. Letter, Meyer to "Sir," December 21, 1939, folder 20, box 7, ser. 3A, Jennings.

86. Johnson and Leeds, *Patteran*, 147.

87. Letter, Hector to Beatty, April 13, 1938, Choctaw 806, box 482, Central Classified Files, 1907–39, record group 75, NA-DC. Hector's efforts were furthered by Harvey K. Meyer the following year. See Meyer to J. A. Bel, December 21, 1939, folder 20, box 7, ser. 3A, Jennings.

88. Letters, Meyer to the commissioner of Indian affairs, March 12 and April 8, 1940, Byler.

89. Letter, Beatty to Meyer, June 11, 1940, CTA.

90. Letter, Juo M. Foote to T. J. Griffin, September 9, 1940, and memo to Mr. Foote, September 9, 1940, CTA.

91. Cushing, *Investigation of Alleged Loss*.

92. New Deal programs also provided opportunities for the Coushattas of Texas to work, particularly following the drought of 1934. See "A Benefit to Indians on the Alabama and Coushatta Reservation," *Indians at Work*, vol. 2, April 15, 1935, 33. Later the CCC also provided jobs in land management, revegetation, insect control, and waterway improvement. See Clenson Sylestine, "CCC at the Alabama-Coushatta Reservation, Livingston, Texas," *Indians at Work* 5, October 15, 1937, 18. Both found at https://catalog.hathitrust.org/Record/000058924.

93. Ernest Sickey, interview with author, August 12, 2015.

94. Literal translation of *Naksaamoosip Komawiichito*: "They helped us a little." Letter, Jeff Abbey to Harvey Meyer, December 8, 1939, CTA. Linda Langley shared how Douglas John produced the first Koasati dictionary in 1930. Langley, personal communication, July 16, 2018.

95. Clem F. Fain Jr. "White Chief's Tepee," *East Texas*, April 1928, 28–29; Nash report (1931), "Indians of Texas"; Hook, *Alabama-Coushatta Indians*, 41.

96. Klopotek, *Recognition Odysseys*, 53.

97. Dorothy Seals, "'Forgotten' La. Indians Seeking Government Aid," *Shreveport Times*, May 4, 1952, 2.

98. Letters, Abbey to Beatty, May 16, 1940, and Douglas John to the commissioner of Indian affairs, June 28, 1941, Byler.

99. "Allen Parish Church Is Tribute to Man Who Converted Keasati [*sic*] Indian Tribe," *Alexandria Town Talk*, February 3, 1951, 3; Dorothy Seals, "'Forgotten' La. Indians," 2; Dorothy Seals, "Forgotten Tribe Wary of Federal Offers of Loans," *Lake Charles American Press*, March 2, 1952, n.p.; Dorothy Seals, "Allen Indian Tribe Found Home—and God," *Alexandria Town Talk*, December 13, 1957, 9.

100. Letter, Beatty to Meyers, June 11, 1940, CTA.

101. Lomawaima and McCarty, *To Remain an Indian*, 49.

102. Letter, State Highway Department to Joe Jennings, September 25, 1940, folder 5, box 27, ser. 3B, Jennings; *Arizona Highways* (June 1940), author's private collection.

103. Letters, Joe Jennings to A. H. McMullen, April 7, 1942; E. C. McInnis (FSA state director) to Phil D. McDonald (RR supervisor); Gladys L. Martin (Farm Security Administration parish supervisors), March 3, 1942; and Joe Jennings to A. H. McMullen, January 30, 1943. All from folder 20, box 7, ser. 3A, Jennings.

104. Letters, McDonald to McInnis, March 6, 1942, and McMullen to "sir," March 11, 1942, folder 20, box 7, ser. 3A, Jennings; memorandum to Mr. McCaskill from Joe Jennings, July 15, 1942, Byler.

105. Letters, Jennings to McMullen, November 1 and December 1, 1941; Vernon W. Scott (farm management specialist) to E. C. McInnis, December 16, 1941; A. H. McMullen to "Sir," December 30, 1941; Joe Jennings, memorandum on the "Rehabilitation of the Coushatta Indians near Elton, Louisiana," December 30, 1941. All sources from folder 20, box 7, ser. 3A, Jennings.

106. Letters, Kenneth E. McCoy to L. W. Page, September 9, 1938, and Page to McCoy, September 9, 1938, CTA. Letter, J. C. McCaskill to George S. Mitchell (Farm Security Administration), December 3, 1941, folder 20, box 7, ser. 3A, Jennings.

107. Elizabeth Lansden wrote to the Choctaw Agency inquiring about how to keep her position as teacher of the Coushatta school once it became fully under the control of the Indian bureau. The response she received stated that she would have to take the civil service exam before being considered. In reality, however, taking the exam would have done little to secure her position. The Choctaw Agency was intent on hiring an agriculture teacher. See letters, Lansden to Meyer, May 14, 1939, and superintendent to Mrs. Lansden, May 19, 1939, CTA.

108. In 1939 and 1940 Lansden wrote several letters to Harvey Meyer, thanking him for sending toys and other supplies to the Coushatta school. The letters also offer insight into the school curriculum. See letters from April 19, 1939, and February 12 and May 30, 1940, CTA.

109. Letters, McMullen to Abbey, June 19, 1942 and McMullen to McCoy, June 23, 1942, CTA; letter, Jennings to P. W. Danielson, April 23, 1942, folder 20, box 7, ser. 3A, Jennings.

110. Letter, Abbey and Mr. and Mrs. McCoy to Jennings, August 25, 1942, folder 20, box 7, ser. 3A, Jennings.

111. Samuel H. Thomson (supervisor of Indian education) report to the commissioner of Indian affairs of the "Choctaw Indian Jurisdiction," February 20, 1946, 6, folder 5, box 30, ser. 3B, Jennings.

112. Sickey interview, April 6, 2015.

113. Thomson report, "Choctaw Indian Jurisdiction," February 6, 1946, vol. 7; "Coushatta Indians to Go to Elton, Kinder Schools," *Lake Charles American Press*, August 25, 1949, 37.

114. Sickey interviews, November 16, 2015, and October 5, 2016.

115. "Doctor Is Fined $2,500 for Illegal Sale of Narcotics," *Alexandria Weekly Town Talk*, July 26, 1947, 6.

116. Memorandum, A. C. Monahan to the commissioner, January 30, 1934, folder 7, box 8, ser. 4C, Jennings.

117. Sickey, "We Will Forever Remain Coushatta," 47.

118. Sickey interview, October 5, 2016.

119. See "Jones Compares Administration Promises with Performances," *Alexandria Weekly Town Talk*, December 30, 1939, 4; Robert D. Leighninger Jr., "Big Charity: The History of Charity Hospital," *Know Louisiana: The Digital Encyclopedia of Louisiana*, http://www.knowlouisiana.org/the-history-of-charity-hospital.

120. Leeds, *St. Peter's Congregational Church* and *St. Luke's Congregational Church*.

121. Jacobson, "Koasati Cultural Change," 157.

122. Ernest Sickey, Coushatta Tribe of Louisiana, Heritage Department Film (2012), CTA; Sickey interview, April 29, 2015.

123. Quotation attributed to Key, *Southern Politics*, 156.

124. Huey Long, quoted in Sanson, "'What He Did and What He Promised to Do,'" 214–15.

125. Ernest Sickey, Coushatta Tribe of Louisiana, Heritage Department Film (2012), CTA.

126. Barbara Langley interview, April 4, 2016. According to Nash (1931), Jeff Abbey owned 260 acres, nearly three times the amount of land owned by the next largest homestead, owned by Mark Robinson, who had 91 acres (2–3).

127. Ernest Sickey, interviews by author, April 29 and September 30, 2015.

128. Bernard, *Cajuns*, 15–16.

129. "Sheriff Told to Report All Japs in This Parish," *Opelousas Daily World*, December 8, 1941, 10.

130. "Oakdale Negro Indicted Again," *Alexandria Town Talk*, May 9, 1944, 7. The details of the case can also be found in Fairclough, *Race and Democracy*, 79.

131. Johnson, *Coushatta People*, 86.

132. "Lawsuit Seeks Return of Land to Indians," *Lake Charles American Press*, May 17, 1950, 24; "U.S. Is Seeking to Regain Land Sold by Indians," *Beaumont Enterprise*, May 17, 1950, n.p.

133. "Government Loses Indian Land Case," *Lake Charles American Press*, September 13, 1950, 41; *U.S. v. Della Bel Krause et al.*

134. "Elton Indians Mourn Death of Chief," unknown paper and date, CTA.

135. Senator Allen J. Ellender (Terrebonne Parish) remained in office from January 1937 until his death in July 1972.

136. Day, "Progressives and Conservatives," 60 and 63.

137. Sickey interview, April 6, 2015; Sickey, "We Will Forever Remain Coushatta," 45.

138. Sickey, Coushatta Tribe of Louisiana, Heritage Department Film (2012).

3. ABANDONED, NOT TERMINATED

EPIGRAPH: Bertney Langley, personal communication, July 12, 2018.

1. "Elton Indians Mourn Death of Chief," unknown paper (February 1951), CTA. Others who died between 1935 and 1953 and held positions within the Indian Church at various times included Alex Johnpierre (d. 1936, age 35), Alfred John (d. 1941, age 69), Lucy Robinson John (d. 1942, age 52), McKinley Williams (d. 1943, age 18), Charley Sickey (d. 1943, age 72), Doc Williams (d. 1944, age 63), Annie Alabama Poncho (d. 1946, age 52), and Jacob Robinson (d. 1948, age 60). Leeds, *St. Peter's Congregational Church*.

2. Literal translation of *Mikko Hahpon Hohachaalihchin, Immaayasin Kommaayatikkoto̜ Stathiiyato̜*: "They elected a new chief, and he spoke on our behalf more."

3. "Coushatti Tribe Names New Chief," *Lake Charles Southwest Citizen*, March 12, 1951, n.p., MRC; "Elect Chief for Koasati Indian Tribe," *Lake Charles American Press*, March 13, 1951, 3.

4. "Coushatti Tribe Names New Chief."

5. Ernest Sickey, interview with author, December 15, 2015.

6. Johnson, *Coushatta People*, 54; "Enterprise Club: Indian Mission School Visited," *Lake Charles American Press*, October 19, 1970, 8. Jacobson claimed that following his election, Martin Abbey moved to Texas and Bel Abbey served "as acting chief in his absence," "Koasati Cultural Change," 146. See also letter, Daniel Jacobson to William Byler (AAIA), March 20, 1973, folder 3, box 245, AAIA. There is a reference to Abbey's work-related reason for moving back and forth between Louisiana and Texas in Elvin Rees, "Candidates for Anti-Poverty," *Opelousas Daily World*, September 13, 1964, 17.

7. "'Year's Holidays' Theme of Elton Carnival Parade," *Lake Charles American Press*, March 11, 1962, 19; "Coushatti Indians Pay First Visit of Year to City Folks," *Lake Charles Southwest Citizen*, March 22, 1957, n.p., MRC; "70,000 People to View Jubilee at Jennings," *Lake Charles American Press*, September 20, 1951, 21.

8. "Elect Chief for Koasati Indian Tribe."

9. Dorothy G. Seals, "Forgotten Indians Long for Their Own Land," *Lake Charles American Press*, January 28, 1951, 11.

10. Dorothy G. Seals, "Lost La. Indians Seek Reservation," *Shreveport Times*, December 2, 1951, 67.

11. "Koasati Indians to Sell Wares Here," *Lake Charles American Press*, March 18, 1951, 16; "Indian Chief Will Be Presented with Headdress Here," *Lake Charles American Press*, March 21, 1951, 1; unspecified title, *Lake Charles American Press*, March 23, 1951, 31.

12. Larry Bell, "Coushatti Indians Pay First Visit of Year to City Folks," *Lake Charles Southwest Citizen*, March 22, 1951, n.p., MRC; "Koasati Indians Slate Exhibition at Rice Festival," *Lake Charles American Press*, October 13, 1951, 5.

13. "Two Tourist Couples Are Feted at Elton," *Lake Charles American Press*, May 7, 1959, 35; "Tourists Are Entertained at Elton," *Lake Charles American Press*, May 8, 1958, 33.

14. Barbara Langley interview, April 4, 2016.

15. Deloria, *Playing Indian*, 109; "Koasati Indians to Visit Pack 3," *Lake Charles American Press*, March 20, 1957, 40.

16. Langley interview, April 4, 2016; "Indians to Hold Sale in Elton," *Lake Charles American Press*, June 18, 1951, 33.

17. "Three Graduate from Cubs, Three Get Wolf Badges," *Lake Charles American Press*, September 1, 1951, 5.

18. Ernest Sickey, interview with author, October 28, 2016. Also see "Cub Scouts to Hold Program to Help Indians," *Lake Charles American Press*, December 8, 1954, 31. It is important to point out that Girl Scout troops also began to visit and provide donations to the Coushattas by the mid-1960s. See "Girl Scouts Bring Gifts for Indians," *Opelousas Daily World*, December 23, 1966, 15.

19. For more on Koasati house types from the 1700s to the mid-1950s, see Jacobson, "Koasati Cultural Change," 147.

20. According to Jacobson, "The first Koasati homes to procure electricity were those of Solomon Battisse [*sic*] and Joe Langley in the northeastern sector of the community in 1948." "Koasati Cultural Change," 136.

21. The initial letter cannot be located, but the response to Dugas's letter indicates its contents. See Robert M. Cullum (Choctaw Agency) to Tim Dugan [*sic*], April 9, 1952, CTA.

22. Letter, Ruby B. Ellis (chairwoman of Indian Affairs, Carroll Women's Club) to Russell Long, May 25, 1951, Byler; "Vinton Literary Club Plans Year's Projects," *Lake Charles American Press*, August 5, 1951, 16; Milton Turner, "Koasati Indians Will Get Library Books," *Lake Charles American Press*, September 19, 1951, n.p.,

CTA; "Indian Girl Gets Award," *Lake Charles American Press*, August 30, 1952, n.p., MRC.

23. "CAR to Send Representatives to State Conference," *Lake Charles American Press*, March 4, 1955, 30; "DAR Children to Make Pilgrimage," *Lake Charles American Press*, October 14, 1956, 17.

24. "Indian Basket Show and Sale Set near Elton," *Lake Charles American Press*, April 4, 1950, 18; "Koasati Indians Plan Sale Here," *Lake Charles American Press*, May 23, 1951, 41; "Indians to Hold Sale in Elton," *Lake Charles American Press*, June 18, 1951, 33.

25. "Allen Parish Church Is Tribute to Man Who Converted Keasati [*sic*] Indian Tribe," *Alexandria Town Talk*, February 3, 1951, 3.

26. "Allen Parish," *Lake Charles American Press*, October 8, 1954, 2.

27. Fixico, *Termination and Relocation*, 183–84.

28. See Commission on Organization of the Executive Branch of the Government, Indian Affairs: A Report to Congress (1949). Hoover Commission Report found at https://catalog.hathitrust.org/Record/008375278.

29. Letter, George W. Malone to Jeffery E. Fuller (Indian Civil Rights Committee), September 26, 1951, folder 3, box 1130, American Civil Liberties Union (ACLU) Records, Seeley G. Mudd Manuscript Library, Princeton University, Princeton NJ (hereafter cited as ACLU).

30. Cornell, *Return of the Native*, 121–23.

31. Fixico, *Termination and Relocation*, 94.

32. For a more robust discussion of the termination policy, see Pevar, *Rights of Indians and Tribes*, 11–12; Getches, Wilkinson, and Williams, *Cases and Materials*, 204–24; Fixico, *Termination and Relocation*.

33. Getches, Wilkinson, and Williams, *Cases and Materials*, 206–7.

34. Letter, Cullum to Dugan [*sic*], April 9, 1952.

35. The congressional schedule included bills to terminate the following tribes: Indians of Utah (Paiute and Shoshone) (S. 2670, H.R. 7390); Indians of Texas (S. 2744, H.R. 6382, H.R. 6547); Indians of Western Oregon (S. 2746, H.R. 7317); Sac and Fox and Iowa of Kansas and Nebraska and the Kickapoo and Potawatomi of Kansas (S. 2743, H.R. 7318); Klamaths of Oregon (S. 2745, H.R. 7320); Flatheads of Montana (S. 2750, H.R. 7319); Seminoles of Florida (S. 2747, H.R. 7321); Turtle Mountain Chippewas of North Dakota (S. 2748, H.R. 7316); Indians of California (S. 2749, H.R. 7322); and Menominees of Wisconsin (S. 2813, H.R. 7135). See Fixico, *Termination and Relocation*, 226.

36. Peroff, *Menominee Drums*, 4–5; Fixico, *Termination and Relocation*, 95–96.

37. Fixico, *Termination and Relocation*, 101.

38. For more details on how the Florida Seminoles confronted the termination bill that targeted them, see Kersey, "Termination and Turmoil," 23–50.

39. See Osburn, *Choctaw Resurgence*, 159–69.

40. Philp, *Termination Revisited*, 73 and 163.

41. Precht, "Coushatta Homesteading," 132.

42. Letters, Williard W. Beatty to Mr. Jennings, February 7, 1940, and Paul L. Fickinger to Harvey K. Meyer, February 17, 1940, folder 20, box 7, ser. 3A, Jennings.

43. Letter, Joe Jennings to A. H. McMullen, February 21, 1942, folder 20, box 7, ser. 3A, Jennings; "Coushatta Indians to Go to Elton, Kinder Schools," *Lake Charles American Press*, August 25, 1949, n.p.

44. Sickey interview, December 15, 2015.

45. Letter, Paul Vance to Martha John, September 22, 1953, exhibit MA-9 1953, box 4C335, Yarborough.

46. Members of the community who were recorded as being at the meeting on October 2, 1953, were Ed Williams, Newton Williams, Solomon Battise, Joe A. Langley, Abel John, Bel Abbey, Edward Sylestine, Ira B. John, Fred Langley, Joe Williams, Douglas John, Nora Abbey, Dalla Sylestine, Imagene Sylestine, Maggie Langley, Adeline Battise, Lizzie Robinson, and Mimmie Obe. Documented on stationery from the Bentley Hotel in Alexandria LA. Copied from the Yarborough Collection, CTA.

47. "Resolution," folder 3, box 245, AAIA.

48. Letter, Paul Vance to Aline Thompson, June 19, 1958, CTA.

49. Sickey, "We Will Forever Remain Coushatta," 46.

50. Letter, Newton Williams to Paul Vance, October 9, 1953, folder 3, box 245, AAIA.

51. Portions of the report appear in the Coushatta petition to the Department of Interior. The original report is referenced in S. Bobo Dean to Marvin Franklin (Department of the Interior), April 30, 1973, folder 3, box 245, AAIA.

52. "Red Shoes' People: Coushatta Victory," *Association on American Indian Affairs Newsletter* (July 1973): 6, folder 3, box 245, AAIA.

53. Sickey, "We Will Forever Remain Coushatta," 46.

54. Getches, Wilkinson, and Williams, *Cases and Materials*, 209.

55. Letter, Phillip Martin to Fred A. Seaton, September 27, 1960, folder 11, box 249, AAIA.

56. "Principle of Consent" attached to letter, I. George Nace (National Council of the Churches of Christ) to Jeffery Fuller (ACLU), February 23, 1954, folder 3, box 1130, ACLU.

57. Holland et al., "Geology of Beauregard and Allen Parishes," 15.

58. Rod Bertrand, interview with author, November 17, 2015. It wasn't until around 2000, after the tribe petitioned the parish, that the road was raised to ease flood damage.

59. Jacobson, "Koasati Cultural Change," 19; "Flood Waters Recede in Area Communities," *Lake Charles American Press*, May 21, 1953, n.p., CTA; "Koasate Indians Are

Evacuated off Bayou Blue," *Lake Charles American Press*, May 22, 1953, n.p., MRC; "Nearly 100 Families Homeless: Area Imperiled by South Winds," *Lake Charles American Press*, February 9, 1955, 1. Reportedly, no homes were destroyed, and no lives were lost.

60. After being taken out of federal trust, land patents were issued to Emily Alabama (no. 1139433) and Jane Battise (no. 1139439) on June 11, 1953, accession nos. 1139438–39, Serial Patent, LA, U.S. Department of the Interior Bureau of Land Management, General Land Records.

61. "Resolution."

62. Sickey, "We Will Forever Remain Coushatta," 46.

63. Philp, *Termination Revisited*, 73 and 163.

64. Brightman, "Chitimacha," 651.

65. To further extend the reach of the termination policy, Congress also passed Public Law 83-280 to accelerate the reduction its financial responsibilities to Indian populations in six states—Alaska, California, Minnesota, Nebraska, Oregon, and Wisconsin. A relocation program was also launched nationwide by 1956 to offer job training and housing in urban areas to Indian people living on reservations as a way of disbanding tribal communities. Approximately 100,000 Indian people from across the country relocated as a result of this program. Louisiana Coushattas were not among them. Pevar, *Rights of Indians and Tribes*, 12; Getches, Wilkinson, and, Williams, *Cases and Materials*, 209; Fixico, *Termination and Relocation*, 183.

66. The Coushattas and Chitimachas were included in an earlier document requesting suggestions for tribes to be proposed for termination. It was recommended that the "entire State of Louisiana including Chitimacha, Coushatta and miscellaneous bands" be included. Partial letter in response to memorandum of August 10, 1954, entitled "Proposed Legislative Program, 84th Congress, 1st Session," September 9, 1954, folder 12, box 40, ser. 3C, Jennings.

67. Reprinted in Fixico, *Termination and Relocation*, 207–9. Original source: memorandum no. 55, Work Paper on Termination, box 69, William A. Brophy Papers, Harry S. Truman Presidential Library, Independence MO.

68. The tribal membership of the Alabama-Coushatta Tribe at the time of termination was 450, with tribal landholdings of 3,200 acres, the Catawbas' population was 631, with tribal landholdings at 3,388 acres. Taylor, *States and Their Indian Citizens*, 180.

69. Fixico, *Termination and Relocation*, 208. Jonathan B. Hook provides details about the meeting between federal officials and the Alabamas and Coushattas of Texas regarding the proposed termination resolution and their concerns about the implications. *Alabama-Coushatta Indians*, 79–77.

70. In both cases the tribes regained a federally acknowledged status years later: the Alabama-Coushattas in 1987 and the Catawbas in 1993.

71. "Texas Indian Commission" summary accompanying letter to Earl Barbry (Tunica-Biloxi Tribe of Louisiana) from Raymond D. Apodaca (Texas Indian Commission), February 7, 1985, accession no. P95-72, 19202-1-P, Louisiana State Archives, Indian Affairs, Governor's Commission, Baton Rouge (hereafter cited as LSA).

72. Sickey interview, October 28, 2016. According to the Heyer report of 1959, the twelve to fifteen families of Coushattas living on or near the Texas reservation received the same services as the Alabamas under state Indian superintendent Howard Jones from 1954 to 1957. Once the new superintendent, Walter Broemer, took on the position, the Coushattas were cut off from these services. See Claude H. Heyer, "Report: The Coushatta" (July 1959): 3–4, folder 2, box 245, AAIA; 83rd Cong., 2nd sess., Senate, Report No. 1321, "Termination of Federal Supervision over the Property of the Alabama and Coushatta Indians of Texas," May 11, 1954; 83rd Cong., 2nd sess., House of Representatives, Report No. 2491, "Providing for the Termination of Federal Supervision over the Property of the Alabama and Coushatta Tribes of Indians of Texas, and the Individual Members Thereof," July 26, 1954.

73. Robert F. Kennedy, "Testimony before the Senate Subcommittee on Indian Affairs Pertaining to Senate Concurrent Resolution 11 Which Recommends a 'New National Indian Policy,'" March 5, 1968, folder 4, box 15, James Gaither Collection. Lyndon Baines Johnson Presidential Library, Austin TX.

74. Heyer report (1959), 1.

75. Sickey interview, October 28, 2016.

76. A count was taken based on the burial information for St. Peter's and St. Luke's cemeteries. Linda Langley communicated that she thought there were many more than twenty deaths during this period based on the number of graves in both cemeteries with missing markers. Personal communication, July 12, 2018.

77. Heyer report (1959), 1.

78. Sickey interview, April 6, 2015.

79. Battise interview, April 5, 2016.

80. Langley interview, April 4, 2016.

81. Loretta Williams, interview with author, April 4, 2016.

82. Marian Patterson, quoted in Giovo, Turner, and Langley, *Jefferson Davis Parish*, 6 and 38.

83. Sickey interview, April 29, 2015.

84. Betty LaFleur, "At Elton Mission: Shepherd of the Indians," *Opelousas Daily World*, April 23, 1967, 25; Ernest Sickey interview, October 28, 2016.

85. Alexander Lesser (executive director, AAIA), letter to the editor, *Medford Mail Tribune*, September 5, 1954, 5.

86. Cobb, *Native Activism*, 14.

87. Heyer report (1959), 1.

88. Letter, La Verne Madigan to Donald Johnson, August 25, 1959, folder 2, box 245, AAIA.

89. Letter, La Verne Madigan to Dr. Galen R. Weaver (Race Relations, Congregational Christian Churches), August 28, 1959, folder 2, box 245, AAIA.

90. "NAACP Urges Group to Probe Police Brutality," *Monroe Morning World*, March 28, 1964, 20; "Repeal of Unpledged Electors Plan Sought," *Opelousas Daily World*, May 21, 1964, 1.

91. There are multiple references throughout the 1960s of Wanda Johnson's efforts to educate the public about the Coushattas through speeches and tours. Some examples include, "'Is the Believer under the Law'? Set by Mainord," *Longview Daily News*, April 12, 1962, 18; "Special Meeting Is Called by Entre Nous Club," *Shreveport Times*, January 29, 1963, 14; "Jeff Davis HD Achievement Day Held at Fruge Home, Elton," *Lake Charles American Press*, November 21, 1964, 5; "Blue Birds Visit Indian Mission," *Opelousas Daily World*, March 30, 1965, 12; "Busy Meeting Is Held by DAR," *Lake Charles American Press*, January 12, 1966, 19; "P-T Group to Hear Talk on Indians," *Lake Charles American Press*, February 14, 1966, 6; Ellen Molloy, "Missionary to Sing, Talk at Meeting," *Shreveport Times*, November 11, 1969, 13.

92. Norman Richardson, "They Follow Mink-O-Chitto: The Koasatis—Louisiana's 'Lost Tribe,'" *Shreveport Times*, May 31, 1959, 73.

93. Betty LaFleur, "At Elton Mission: Shepherd of the Indians," *Opelousas Daily World*, April 23, 1967, 25.

94. Johnson, *Coushatta People*, 81. Reference to Battise signing for the land on behalf of the tribe also appears in a letter from David Garrison Jr. to William Byler, May 15, 1973, folder 3, box 245, AAIA.

95. Land Donation Deed to St. Peter's Congregational Church of Bayou Blue, State of Louisiana, March 28, 1960, folder 3, box 245, AAIA. Donors include John A. Bel, Della Bel Krause, Floy Moss Bel, Albert Bel Fay, Ernest Bel Fay, Marie G. Garrison, Katherine G. Sommers, and James W. Gardner. Witnesses include: Solomon Battise and Donald Johnson. By 1963 the Bel Oil Corporation also donated some swings for the school's playground. "Koasati Indian Tribe Members Stage Demonstration of Weaving Craft," *Opelousas Daily World*, June 18, 1963, 8.

96. Aline Thompson, "Aid Forthcoming to Area's Orphan Tribe," *Lake Charles American Press*, June 14, 1959, 22.

97. LaFleur, "At Elton Mission."

98. Letters, Donald K. Johnson to the AAIA, August 19, 1959, and Madigan to Johnson, August 28, 1959, folder 2, box 245, AAIA.

99. The Johnsons also reached out to local women's groups for book donations in the towns of Welsh, Raymond, and Elton. These groups even hosted Christmas parties for the children of the school. See "Elton WSCS Hears Mrs. Harold Hine,"

Opelousas Daily World, March 12, 1967, 12; "Indian Students Give Elton WSCS Program," *Lake Charles American Press*, September 18, 1967, 6; "Homemakers Initiated into Elton Club," *Opelousas Daily World*, November 30, 1970, 7; LaFleur, "At Elton Mission."

100. Sickey interview, April 6, 2015.

101. Davis and Daisy Sickey later had another son named Patrick, who was stillborn. Sadly, they also lost three daughters (Mary Ann, Lovinia, and another listed in the records as "Babe") as infants. Their only children to live to adulthood were Ernest and Bernetta. Sickey interview, September 20, 2016.

102. Earl Kemp Long served as Louisiana's governor in 1939–40, 1948–52, and 1956–60. For more on his life and career, see Peoples, "Earl Kemp Long."

103. Ernest S. Clements, "Clements Votes 'No' on Big Loan: 14th District Senator Opposes Borrowing for Charity Hospital," *Alexandria Weekly Town Talk*, June 19, 1937, 8.

104. For more on Senator Clements and his involvement with Earl Long's political faction, see Dodd, *Peapatch Politics*.

105. The Long administration and its successors relied on a system of patronage to secure political alliances and votes, which was often taken too far and in many cases undermined the democratic process. See Badger, "'When I Took the Oath of Office, I Took No Vow of Poverty,'" 235–36. It is a common Coushatta practice to name children in honor of an ancestor or other person of note. See Johnson, *Coushatta People*, 61; and Johnson and Leeds, *Patteran*, 18.

106. Sickey interview, April 6, 2015.

107. Sickey interviews, July 28 and September 2, 16, 2015, and October 28, 2016. The land continues to be private property, although it is located near the fifteen-acre circle that later became the Coushattas' first reservation put into federal trust. According to Jacobson, subsistence farming was part of the Coushatta's cultural history and one that they didn't practice when located at the old Indian Village site on the Calcasieu. It "was re-instituted in the Bayou Blue community." See Jacobson, "Origin of the Koasati Community," 117.

108. Langley interview, April 4, 2016.

109. Sickey interview, October 28, 2016.

110. Elvin Reed, "Letters, Yes; Anonymous, No," *Opelousas Daily World*, February 23, 1964, 23.

111. Sickey interviews, April 6 and November 17, 2015.

112. Bonner Miller Cutting, interview with author, November 18, 2015.

113. In addition to the judicial appointments Miller held over the course of his career, he also was president of the Louisiana District Judges Association and served on the Louisiana Judicial Council. He worked on multiple projects aimed at law revision conducted by the Louisiana Law Institute and oversaw several committees to

address problems of judicial administration appointments by the Supreme Court. See "Judge Miller Stepping Down," *Alexandria Town Talk*, September 24, 1976, 15; Jack Hildebrand, "District Court Opening Ceremonies Here Today," *Opelousas Daily World*, September 1, 1971, 1.

114. Sickey interviews, April 6 and November 18, 2015.

115. Cutting interview, November 18, 2015. Baker was also the U.S. secretary of the Treasury under President Ronald Reagan and the U.S. secretary of state under President George H. W. Bush.

116. Ernest Sickey, interview with author, November 18, 2015.

117. The implications of such provisions resulted in the disenfranchisement of 95 percent of eligible African Americans and 50 percent of whites. The loss of voting rights also impacted the ability of African Americans to receive fair trials since jury pools were drawn from voter registration rolls. In the early decades of the twentieth century, up to half of Louisiana's African American population responded to the state's institutional racism by moving elsewhere. See Allured and Martin, *Louisiana Legacies*, 178–79.

118. While approximately 40,000 white men took advantage of the "grandfather clause," 111 black men also were able to benefit from the provision. See Ayers, *Promise of the New South*, 298–99; and Woodward, *Strange Career of Jim Crow*, 84–85.

119. The Snyder Act of 1924 conferred American Indians full U.S. citizenship, although many had already been determined citizens as a result of serving in the military, accepting allotments, marrying whites, or paying taxes. Even with the citizenship bill, however, many Indians were still prevented from participating in elections because the Constitution left it up to the states to administer voting. For more on the impact of the Voting Rights Act in Indian communities, see McCool, Olson, and Robinson, *Native Vote*; and Blu, *Lumbee Problem*, 74.

120. Letter, R. E. Powell to the Office of Indian Affairs, March 3, 1913, Byler.

121. Solomon Battise, quoted in Giovo, Turner, and Langley, *Jefferson Davis Parish*, 13.

122. Ernest Sickey, interview with author, June 1, 2017.

123. "Allen Registrar Gives Itinerary," *Alexandria Town Talk*, August 8, 1959, 4.

124. Woodward, *Strange Career of Jim Crow*, 154–56.

125. Day, "Progressives and Conservatives," 66–68. For more on Russell Long's position on racial issues in general and segregation in particular, see Mann, *Legacy to Power*, 94–96.

126. Letter, Lawrence Speiser to Roger N. Baldwin, May 16, 1968, folder 13, box 1133, ACLU; press release, "Ervin Introduces Substitute Civil Rights Measure," November 1, 1967, folder 12, box 1133, ACLU. Ervin's argument contributed to the passage of the Indian Civil Rights Act in 1968. See Nelson, "States' Rights and American Federalism," 174–75.

127. Brinkley, *Voices of Protest*, 15.

128. Ernest Sickey, interview with author, June 3, 2015.

129. Ernest Sickey and Dewith Carrier, group interview with author, November 17, 2015. Bertney Langely also recalled how his mother, Loris Abbott Langley, served a similar role among Coushatta women by discussing what political candidates they should vote for. Personal communication, July 17, 2018.

130. Sickey interviews, April 6 and 29, 2015.

131. Sickey interviews, April 6 and 29, 2015, and September 20, 2016.

132. Sickey interview, November 17, 2015.

133. Blake, "Bel Oil Corporation," 1 and 8–9.

134. Sickey interviews, November 17 and 19, 2015.

135. Sickey interviews, November 17 and April 29, 2015.

136. "Airman Completes First Basic Phase," unknown newspaper and date, Sickey Family Papers.

137. Sickey interview, November 17, 2015.

138. Sickey interview, April 29, 2015.

4. POOR BUT NOT HOPELESS

EPIGRAPH: Sickey interview, November 16, 2015.

1. Elvin Reed, "The Case for the Coushattas," *Opelousas Daily World*, November 29, 1964, 17.

2. "Business and Finance: Role of Defense Spending," *Alexandria Town Talk*, June 15, 1964, 29.

3. In 1963 there were six large sawmills, five wood-preserving plants, one veneer mill, and one wood pulp mill in southwestern Louisiana. Timber products from Louisiana forests totaled 381 million cubic feet, mostly deriving from the saw-log harvest of soft woods like pine, cypress and red cedar. See Paul A. Murphy, "Louisiana Forests: Status and Outlook," *Bulletin* (New Orleans, Department of Agriculture, Forest Services, Southern Forest Experiment Station, 1975), 50–53, https://www.srs.fs.usda.gov/pubs/9174.

4. Johnson, *Coushatta People*, 91.

5. Battise interview, April 5, 2016.

6. "Along Blue Bayou in Allen Parish: Coushatta Tribal Home Is Not a Reservation," *Town Talk*, October 22, 1967, 2.

7. Williams interview, April 5, 2016.

8. Pratt Doucet, interview with author, November 18, 2015.

9. "The Koasatis—Louisiana's 'Lost Tribe,'" *Shreveport Times*, May 31, 1959, 73.

10. Dunnehoo interview, November 16, 2015.

11. "The Indian Craft Shop," http://www.indiancraftshop.com/ARCHIVES/DarlineRobinson.htm.

12. Eli Langley, interview with author, February 10, 2016.

13. Jacobson notes that Alfred John, Kinney Williams, Ed Wilson, Nicy Poncho, and Loris Langley all drove the school wagon at different times; see "Koasati Cultural Change," 156; Loris Abbott Langley, interview with Linda Langley, August 22, 2006, referenced in Langley, Oubre, and Precht, "Louisa Williams Robinson," 167.

14. Elvin Reed, "Tribe Facing Dispersal: One Ray of Hope Left for Coushattas," *Baton Rouge Sunday Advocate*, June 20, 1965, 3E.

15. Bertney Langley, interview with author, November 16, 2015.

16. Sickey interview, November 17, 2015.

17. Bertney Langley, quoted in "Folk Stories: Kinder Man Preserving Coushatta Indian Tales He Heard as a Child," *Alexandria Town Talk*, January 16, 1994, 33.

18. Langley interview, April 4, 2016.

19. There are two Coushatta graveyards within the community. According to Donald G. Hunter, "The oldest of these is situated approximately one-half mile to the east of the old church . . . With construction of the new St. Peter's, the new cemetery was the preferred place of burial . . . [The old cemetery] is still utilized by families who think that their deceased relatives would rather be buried there." "Settlement Pattern," 83–84.

20. Sickey interview, November 16, 2015.

21. Literal translation of *Bassi-tilka̱, Ittihaplitilkato̱*: "Fighting against being poor."

22. Elvin Reed, "Candidates for Anti-Poverty," *Opelousas Daily World*, September 13, 1964, 17.

23. Johnson reinforced his position on March 6, 1968, in a special message to Congress entitled "The Forgotten American," in which he called for an end to termination and promoted Indian policy based on "self-determination." See Fixico, *Termination and Relocation*, 199–200.

24. Deloria, "Era of Indian Self-Determination," 196.

25. Legal scholar Stephen Cornell argues that the combination of Native soldiers returning from combat in World War II and anxieties over Cold War Indian policies paved the way for Indian people to conceive of themselves as a unifying force, speaking the language of sovereignty, economic justice, and cultural preservation. See *Return of the Native*. This movement towards unification increased involvement with pan-Indian organizations, such as the National Congress of the American Indian (NCAI), which held its first convention in 1944. According to Laurence Hauptman and Jack Campisi, however, the NCAI was deemed too conservative by many tribal leaders (particularly in the East), who opted for an alternative route. See "Eastern Indian Communities Strive for Recognition," in Hurtado and Iverson, *Major Problems*, 461–71. In 1961 anthropologist Sol Tax coordinated the American Indian Chicago Conference, hosting over 450 Native

delegates, including representatives from several southern tribes. The conference culminated with the drafting of a document, entitled the *Declaration of Indian Purpose*, which was delivered to President John F. Kennedy and emphasized Indian self-determination and later served as a reference for the Johnson administration's War on Poverty programs. See Lurie, "Voices of the American Indian," 478–500; and Miller, *Forgotten Tribes*, 188.

26. Cobb, *Native Activism*, 80–81.

27. Elvin Reed, "Candidates for Anti-Poverty," *Opelousas Daily World*, September 13, 1964, 17.

28. In *Coushatta People* Johnson also indicated that the Coushattas were in contact with Congressman Theo Asthon Thompson of Evangeline Parish, 91.

29. Elvin Reed, "Compares with Hitler: Tate Holds Free Electors a Minority Move in LA," *Opelousas Daily World*, October 13, 1963, 28.

30. "Mamou Ready for 2-Day Veterans Day Fête," *Opelousas Daily World*, November 9, 1962, 30.

31. "Notes from Mamou," *Opelousas Daily World*, December 1, 1950, 17; Elvin Reed, "Tribe Facing Dispersal: One Ray of Hope Left for Coushattas," *Baton Rouge Sunday Advocate*, June 20, 1965, 3E; "Elect Tate to Congress," *Opelousas Daily World*, August 29, 1965, 24. For more on Shriver's role in Johnson's antipoverty programs and his position on Indian affairs, see Cobb, *Native Activism*, 89, 120–21, 122–23, 134–35.

32. Reed, "Candidates for Anti-Poverty."

33. Cobb, "Philosophy of an Indian War," 71–103; "'Us Indians Understand the Basics,'" 41–66; and *Native Activism in Cold War America*, 126–27.

34. "Allen Poverty Agency Meets," *Alexandria Town Talk*, September 3, 1965, 2; "Allen Action Board Names Two Officers," *Lake Charles American Press*, September 3, 1965, 25; "Allen Head Start Gets Money," *Lake Charles American Press*, June 21, 1966, 23; "Allen Measures Poverty Payroll," *Alexandria Town Talk*, May 11, 1966, 37; "Allen Poverty Unit to Get Jury's Aid," *Alexandria Town Talk*, July 15, 1966, 2; "Two Head Start Programs Okayed," *Alexandria Town Talk*, March 31, 1967, 13.

35. One of the largest criticisms of the antipoverty programs in Louisiana is that they were often run by individuals who were not considered part of the intended service population and who directed the programs to benefit middle-class white residents above everyone else. See Jong, *Different* Day, 201–3. Clyde Warrior had a similar complaint about antipoverty programs failing to effectively serve tribal communities on a national scale due to bureaucratic self-interest that continuously trumped Indian interests. See McKenzie-Jones, "'We Are among the Poor,'" 250.

36. Sickey interview, November 17, 2015.

37. Carrier interview, November 17, 2015.

38. Sickey interview, November 17, 2015. The Allen Action Agency, Inc., did eventually inquire about Indian health services for the Coushatta in 1970, which prompted an investigation into their status. See the next chapter.

39. Elvin Reed, "Tribe Facing Dispersal One Ray of Hope Left for Coushattas," *Baton Rouge Sunday Advocate*, June 20, 1965, n.p.; obituary, *Alexandria Town Talk*, October 31, 1991, 18.

40. In 1960, e.g., Janice Battise represented the Coushattas as a guest speaker at a Children of the American Revolution (CAR) meeting. No title, *Lake Charles American Press*, January 21, 1960, 31. In 1966 Ray Poncho was a guest speaker for the Fort Atkinson Society Children of the American Revolution. "CAR Hear Koasati Indian," *Lake Charles American Press*, November 18, 1966, 8. A few years later, in 1969, Ray Poncho, along with his wife and children, were invited back to speak to the same group. "Indians Are Guests of Local CAR Chapter," *Lake Charles American Press*, November 26, 1969, 12. In 1970 a newspaper reported that Fred and Lois Langley conducted a three-day workshop among approximately five hundred teachers in the area to discuss Coushatta history and culture. "Teachers Get First Hand Information from Indians," *Opelousas Daily World*, August 27, 1970, 12.

41. Because of his work with the Coushattas, Timothy J. Dugas was the recipient of the first Brotherhood Award of the Lake Charles Chapter of the National Conference of Christians and Jews in 1971. Ernest and Ena Mae Sickey attended his honoring on behalf of the tribe. See "Dugas Receives Local Unit's First Brotherhood Award," *Lake Charles American Press*, March 2, 1971, 8.

42. Deloria, *Playing Indian*, 135.

43. "Second Annual Indian Dance Program Slates," *Opelousas Daily World*, November 24, 1968, n.p. The referenced dance was a joint effort between members of the Louisiana and Texas Indian Hobbyist Associations.

44. "Pack 3 to Host Indian Picnic Day," *Lake Charles American Press*, May 9, 1961, 6; Barbara Langley interview, April 4, 2016.

45. "Carnival for Indians Set for November 19," *Lake Charles American Press*, November 11, 1966, 17; "Indians Will Visit LC Stores," *Lake Charles American Press*, November 12, 1966, 7; "Koasati Thanksgiving," *American Press*, November 16, 1966, 16; "Coe to Appear at Landry Fete," *Lake Charles American Press*, November 16, 1966, 39; and "Indian Festival," *Lake Charles American Press*, November 26, 1966, 4; Woodward, *Strange Career of Jim Crow*, 99.

46. Katherine M. O. Osburn also discussed how Mississippi Choctaw Princess contests placed Indian women in public relations positions, as contest winners represented both the tribe and city of Philadelphia at civic events. See *Choctaw Resurgence in Mississippi*, 173. Within the Coushatta community, princess contests are now organized and conducted by the tribe with its own guidelines, rules, and judges.

47. "Vanishing Indians to Appear at Rice Festival," *Opelousas Daily World*, October 15, 1950, 33; "5,000 View Allen Parish Fair Parade," *Shreveport Times*, October 10, 1953, 7; and "Allen Fair Opens Today in Oberlin," *Alexandria Town Talk*, October 5, 1960, 4.

48. "Koasati Indian Tribe Members Stage Demonstration of Weaving Craft," *Opelousas Daily World*, June 18, 1963, 8; Gene Benham, "Koasatis to Visit Monday: Indian Group to Demonstrate Basket Making Method Here," *Shreveport Times*, June 9, 1963, 10.

49. "In LC Today: Rodeo Street Dance Slated," *Lake Charles American Press*, February 19, 1964, 1.

50. "Art Exhibit Scheduled at Gardens," *Lake Charles American Press*, May 22, 1964, 9. By 1966 the festival also began inviting weavers from the Alabama-Coushatta community in Texas to participate. "Hodges Garden Arts Festival to Open Today," *Lake Charles American Press*, June 4, 1966, 17.

51. "At Allen Fair: Officials Hail Stock Exhibits," *Lake Charles American Press*, October 8, 1964, 33; de Caro and Jordan, *Louisiana Traditional Crafts*, 20–21.

52. "Surfacing of Jeff Davis Road Finished," *Lake Charles American Press*, July 27, 1966, 40.

53. Sickey interviews, September 28 and November 17, 2015.

54. For a discussion on the movement of some tribes to incorporate as nonprofit organizations in order to qualify for funding during the Johnson administration, see Paredes, "Paradoxes of Modernism," 353; and Deloria, "Era of Indian Self-Determination," 198. There is also a good discussion of the Menominee Tribe of Wisconsin's move to organize as a nonprofit in 1962, the year after its termination went into effect, in Ulrich, *American Indian Nations from Termination to Restoration*, 145–46.

55. Deloria, "Era of Indian Self-Determination," 198.

56. This name was used interchangeably with "The Coushatta Indians of Allen Parish, Inc." in personal narratives about this period.

57. Ernest Sickey, interview with author, June 24, 2015.

58. Ella Mitchell, "Coushatta Indian Lauds Non-Profit Tribal Charter," *Lake Charles American Press*, June 21, 1972, 12; "Elton Indians to Start Handcraft Trading Post," *Opelousas Daily World*, July 24, 1966, 1.

59. Sickey interview, April 29, 2015; Winston De Ville, "Louisiana . . . En Passant," *Alexandria Town Talk*, March 29, 1967, 25; "Indians to Take to Mall Thursday," *Lake Charles American Press*, May 19, 1971, 43.

60. "Elton Indian Tribe to Open Trading Post," *Lake Charles American Press*, January 28, 1967, 6; "Elton Indians to Open Trading Post," *Opelousas Daily World*, January 31, 1967, 12; "Indian Trading Post Opens," *Alexandria Town Talk*, January 31, 1967, 7. By the following year, the trading post increased its hours of operation to

include Saturdays. "Elton Indians Open Trading Post All Day Saturday," *Opelousas Daily World*, March 17, 1967, 5. By 1969 the shop was open every day accept for Sundays. "Louisiana's Only Indian Trading Post," *Opelousas Daily World*, July 31, 1969, 16.

61. "Elton Indians Open Trading Post All Day Saturday," 5.

62. Deloria, *Playing Indian*, 137. By 1975 the Trading Post also began carrying quilts made by tribal members. Ernest Sickey to William Byler, n.d., 1975, folder 4, box 245, AAIA. "Elton Indian Tribe to Open Trading Post," *Lake Charles American Press*, January 28, 1967, 6. For more on Indians in popular culture see Berkhofer, *White Man's Indian*, 71–111.

63. Ronnie Petree, interview with author, November 17, 2015; "Tepee Going Up to Welcome Visitors," *Opelousas Daily World*, June 28, 1967, 20; "Newest Attraction," *Opelousas Daily World*, July 18, 1967, 9.

64. See Mechling, "Florida Seminoles," 149–66; Finger, *Cherokee Americans*, 98–117; Beard-Moose, *Public Indians, Private Cherokees*, 212–35.

65. Sickey interview, April 6, 2015.

66. This is an estimate based on a search of the databases from the *Opelousas Daily World*, the *Shreveport Times*, the *Alexandria Town Talk*, and the *Lake Charles American Press*.

67. "Indian Plan Open House at Trading Post," *Opelousas Daily World*, January 25, 1968, 7; "Indian Craft Shown at Smithsonian," *Opelousas Daily World*, December 3, 1968, 7.

68. Edna Redlich, "Beadwork Rejuvenated: Indian Art Gets New Life," *Opelousas Daily World*, June 9, 1968, 21; Mrs. Oris Redlich, "Indian Artifacts Gain Recognition," *Opelousas Daily World*, February 1, 1970, 17.

69. The Voting Rights Act was signed into law by President Lyndon B. Johnson and underwent several amendments. It was designed to enforce the Fourteenth and Fifteenth Amendments. Louisiana senator Russell B. Long (who later became a big supporter of the Coushattas) created some controversy when he indicated that he would not oppose federal intervention if individual parishes continued to institute restrictions on black voters. As a result, members of White Citizens' Councils swarmed the governor's mansion in Baton Rouge and circulated petitions that attempted to remove Long from office. See Mann, *Legacy to Power*, 236–38.

70. The ruling covered schools in both Lafayette and Jefferson Davis Parishes. See "School Integration in Two Parishes Is Asked in Suits," *Shreveport Times*, March 6, 1965, 2.

71. Inger, "New Orleans School Crisis of 1960," 82–97. For accounts on race relations and integration in Elton and the surrounding area in the 1960s, see Giovo, Turner, and Langley, *Jefferson Davis Parish*, 46–48 and 160–74.

72. Sickey interview, June 3, 2015.

73. "Kindergarten Tots Go on Field Trip," *Opelousas Daily World*, April 21, 1967, 15; "Scouts, Cubs Make Totem Poles, Meet Real Indians," *Opelousas Daily World*, May 21, 1967, 27; "Kindergarten Enthused at Trading Post," *Daily World*, May 16, 1968, 6; "Eunice Cub Scouts Visit Indian Post," *Opelousas Daily World*, November 29, 1968, 18; "Elton Receives Homestead Roll," *Opelousas Daily World*, February 7, 1969, 11; "Nursery Tots Visit Indian Trading Post," *Opelousas Daily World*, May 1, 1969, 6; "Nursery School Students Visit Indian Village," *Opelousas Daily World*, May 5, 1970, 6; "Indian Hills Nursery Tots Visit Indians," *Opelousas Daily World*, April 1, 1971, 6; "Elton Group Tours School," *Opelousas Daily World*, March 5, 1972, 18.

74. Untitled, *Lake Charles American Press*, May 24, 1969, 32.

75. Sickey interview, November 16, 2015; Paredes, "The Emergence of Contemporary Eastern Creek Indian Identity," 68–80; and "Federal Recognition and the Poarch Creek Indians," 120–39; Vickery, *Rise of the Poarch Band of Creek Indians*.

76. Eloise M. Fruge, "Trading Post," *Lake Charles American Press*, February 18, 1967, 4.

77. Precht, "Coushatta Basketry and Identity Politics," 152.

78. Mary Alice Fontenot, "En Passant: Again the Indians," *Opelousas Daily World*, September 26, 1969, 16.

79. Ernest Sickey, interview with author, August 26, 2015; "Enterprise Club: Indian Mission School Visited," *Lake Charles American Press*, October 19, 1970, 8; "Dowling Circle Members Report on 'Gift Shop,'" *Opelousas Daily World*, February 3, 1970, 6.

80. Hasa Ortego, "Educational Field Trip: Lawtell Children 'Visit the Indians,'" *Opelousas Daily World*, May 15, 1966, 23.

81. Sickey interview, April 6, 2015.

82. Ernest Sickey, interview with author, July 8, 2015; Ernest Sickey, Heritage Department Film, 2012, CTA.

83. Sickey interviews, May 13 and July 1, 2015; Battise interview, April 5, 2016.

84. Langley interview, April 4, 2016.

85. Ernest Sickey, interview with author, November 17 and 30, 2015.

86. "Claiborne, Concordia, Allen Youth Corps Plans Okayed," *Shreveport Times*, December 15, 1965, 33; "Pretty Indian Maid Manages Trading Post," *Opelousas Daily World*, September 21, 1967, 12; "Indian Trading Post Manager Assumes Duties," *Lake Charles American Press*, September 21, 1967, 24.

87. "Indians Seeking Artifacts for Post," *Opelousas Daily World*, March 26, 1968, 11.

88. Mary Doran, "Coushatta Indians: River Cane Basket Weaving Taught," *Lake Charles American Press*, July 28, 1973, 19.

89. Sickey interview, May 13, 2015.

90. Edna Redlich, "Beadwork Rejuvenated: Indian Art Gets New Life," *Opelousas Daily World*, June 9, 1968, 21.

91. Sickey interviews, July 28 and November 16, 2015.

92. Langley interview, April 4, 2016.

93. Dunnehoo interview, November 16, 2015.

94. Ernest and Ena Mae Sickey's sons are Durwin (1969–2010), Kevin (b. 1970), Brock (b. 1971), Lyndon (b. 1974), David (b. 1978), and Clark (b. 1981).

95. Sickey interviews, July 28 and November 18, 2015.

96. David Sickey, interview with author, November 17, 2015.

97. Ernest Sickey interview, July 1, 2015; David Sickey interview, November 17, 2015.

98. Sickey interview, November 17, 2015.

99. Linda Langley interview, April 4, 2016.

5. AN UNUSUAL ROAD TO RECOGNITION

1. Sickey interview, April 6, 2015.

2. Literal translation of *Nashahpa Komponaak, Stintoliinolaho*: "Something new they were learning how to work with." President Richard Nixon, "Message to Congress on Indian Affairs," July 8, 1970, reprinted in Josephy, Nagel, and Johnson, *American Indians' Fight for Freedom*, 101–18, quotation on 104.

3. In December 1970 Congress passed Public Law 91-550, returning Blue Lake and forty-eight thousand acres of land in New Mexico to the Taos Pueblo. In 1971 the Alaska Native Claims Settlement Act recognized the land rights of Alaskan Natives. The same year, contested land was returned to tribes in Arizona and Oregon.

4. Hailed as "the first meeting of its kind" and reported on a few years later, Ernest Sickey joined Thomas Dion of the Houmas, Matilde Johnson of the Choctaws from Lacombe, and Joseph A. Pierite of the Tunica-Biloxi Tribe from Marksville. Irving Ward-Steinman, "Southeast Indians—Now and Then," *Alexandria Town Talk*, February 11, 1973, 42.

5. Sickey interview, July 8, 2015.

6. Letter, R. E. Weatherford to Emery A. Johnson (director, Indian Health Service), August 14, 1970, CTA.

7. Sickey interview, November 16, 2015.

8. Memorandum, Mose E. Parris (Office of Environmental Health) on the "Eligibility Status—Coushatta Indian Tribe," September 3, 1970; letter, Emery A. Johnson, MD (Indian Health Services [IHS]) to R. E. Weatherford, October 8, 1970, CTA.

9. Letter, Ernest Stevens to Emery A. Johnson, MD (IHS), January 5, 1971, Byler.

10. Letter, James A. Clark Jr. (Office of Environmental Health) to "Director, Indian Health Service," November 25, 1970, CTA.

11. Letter, James Hawkins (BIA) to Alfred Ryder (district attorney of Louisiana), April 30, 1971, folder 3, box 245, AAIA.

12. See Purser, "Administration of Indian Affairs in Louisiana, 1803–1820," 401–10.

13. Sickey interview, November 16, 2015; "J. Daniel Rivette Opens Law Office," *Opelousas Daily World*, March 29, 1970, 7; Ella Mitchell, "Elton Tribe Has Unlimited Growth in Tourism Industry," *Opelousas Daily World*, June 9, 1972, 5.

14. Draft legislation by J. Daniel Rivette, "Tribal Government of the Coushatta Indians of Louisiana," April 27, 1971, LSA.

15. Sickey interviews, June 3 and November 18, 2015.

16. "Rev. Cormier Receives Humanitarian of Year Award at Eunice Lions Banquet," *Opelousas Daily World*, February 25, 1975, 14; Malcolm Lewis, "ERA Zealots Answered," *Alexandria Town Talk*, October 4, 1973, 6. Although she was heavily involved in supporting the Louisiana Democratic Party, Miller also worked to challenge the status quo on many fronts. For more on the grassroots work of women in Louisiana, see Allured, *Remapping Second-Wave Feminism*. Quotation from letter, Ruth Loyd Miller to John Cade, December 16, 1980, LSA.

17. Sickey interviews, June 3 and November 16 and 18, 2015.

18. Letter, Russell Long to Dillon Meyer (BIA), July 27, 1951, Byler.

19. Both Senators Ellender and Long ensured that the Allen Action Agency, Inc., received federal funding for its antipoverty programs and legal aid services. See "Allen Poverty Unit to Get Jury's Aid," *Alexandria Town Talk*, July 15, 1966, 2; "$13,802 Is Approved for Allen Project," *Lake Charles American Press*, February 19, 1966, 13.

20. Sickey interview, November 16, 2015.

21. Letter, Miller to the Louisiana Political Educational Council, December 1, 1972, LSA. The Louisiana State Mineral Board was created in 1936 and given authority to administer Louisiana's proprietary interests in oil, gas, and mineral resources. In the mid-1970s the board was reorganized and given new administrative capabilities. Tom Wright, "Louisiana's Oil and Gas Leasing Process," Fox 8 Local First, http://www.fox8live.com/story/18125669/louisianas-oil-and-gas-leasing-process.

22. Letter, Miller to Edwards, April 11, 1972, LSA.

23. The company went from a return on assets of 18 percent in 1950 to 32 percent in 1976 and a return on equity of 27 percent in 1950 to 44 percent in 1976. Blake, "Bel Oil Corporation," 25 and 47.

24. "State Unit Created for Indian Affairs," *Lake Charles American Press*, June 8, 1972, 18.

25. Sickey interview, November 16, 2015.

26. Sickey interviews, June 3 and November 18, 2015.

27. "A Red Man's Plea," *Winn Parish Enterprise*, November 14, 1973, n.p.

28. Bee, "Riding the Paper Tiger," 154.

29. Sickey's view of tribal sovereignty fell in line with what David E. Wilkins described as "the intangible and dynamic cultural force inherent in a given Indigenous community, empowering that body toward the sustaining and enhancement of political, economic, and cultural integrity. It undergirds the way tribal governments relate to their own citizens, to non-Indian residents, to local governments, to the state government, to the federal government, to the corporate world, and to the global community." See *American Indian Politics*, 48.

30. Sickey interviews, November 17 and 19, 2015.

31. Sickey interviews, April 6 and June 24, 2015.

32. Sickey, "Reflection on a Lifetime of Leadership," 174–75.

33. Sickey interview, November 18, 2015.

34. Sickey interviews, November 16 and December 15, 2015.

35. Ernest Sickey, presentation at Arizona State University, February 8, 2018.

36. Heather Williams, interview with author, April 3, 2016.

37. Sickey interview, April 29, 2015.

38. Bonner Miller Cutting, David Sickey, Ernest Sickey, and I met on November 18, 2015, when Cutting learned, for the first time, the extent of her parents' involvement in helping to advocate for the Coushatta people.

39. Fairclough, *Race and Democracy*, 476.

40. Bill Crider, "Just One Big Party: A Sweet Night for Edwards," *Alexandria Town Talk*, February 2, 1972, 36.

41. Sickey interview, November 16, 2015; "Edwards about Decided on Constitution Group," *Shreveport Times*, November 30, 1972, 2.

42. Reference to their March conversation is made in a follow-up letter. See Miller to Edwards, April 11, 1972.

43. Letter, Edwin Edwards to Rogers C. B. Morton (Department of Interior), September 19, 1972, folder 3, box 245, AAIA.

44. Louisiana Senate Concurrent Resolution, No. 38, Regular Session, 1972, folder 3, box 245, AAIA. The resolution was sponsored by Senators Robert Jones of Lake Charles and Dr. John Tassin of Ville Platte, along with Representatives James Martin of Welsh and James D. Cain of Dry Creek. "House Votes Recognition of Indian Tribe," *Lake Charles American Press*, May 26, 1972, 3; James Stephenson and Robert G. Jones were also credited with authoring the resolution in "State Recognizes Coushatta Indians as Bonafide Tribe," *Lake Charles American Press*, May 17, 1972, 43; letters, C. W. Roberts (Louisiana Senate) to President Richard Nixon, May 29, 1972, and Bradley Patterson Jr. (on behalf of President Nixon) to C. W. Roberts, June 7, 1972, folder 3, box 245, AAIA.

45. For a more detailed examination on the development and functioning of the Louisiana Office of Indian Affairs, see Bates, *Other Movement*, 56–67, 69–70, 72, 78–79; and Klopotek, *Recognition Odysseys*, 65–68, 202–3. At different

points in its history, the LOIA is also referenced as the Louisiana Governor's Commission on Indian Affairs and the Louisiana State Commission on Indian Affairs.

46. State of Louisiana, Governor Edwards, Executive Order No. 3, May 30, 1972, folder 3, box 245, AAIA. The document that laid out the formal function of the commission and its executive director was signed by Garrison on June 19, 1973, LSA.

47. North Carolina (1971), Louisiana (1972), Florida (1974), Alabama (1978), South Carolina (1979), Virginia (1982), Tennessee (1983), and Georgia (1995).

48. Wilkins and Lomawaima, *Uneven Ground*, 177–79. For a critique on state tribal recognition, see Sturm, "States of Sovereignty," 228–42. For detailed case studies examining the impact and implications of federal recognition, see Schulze, "Rediscovery of the Tiguas," 15–16; Miller, *Forgotten Tribes*; and Klopotek, *Recognition Odysseys*.

49. Letter, Miller to Edwards, April 26, 1972, LSA.

50. Letter, Miller to Edwards, April 11, 1972, LSA.

51. Suggested letter drafted by Miller on behalf of Governor Edwards to Garrison, April 11, 1972, LSA. Additional appointments to the commission were made in June, which included William T. Dion, J. D. Langley, Archie Vilcan, Fred B. Kniffen, and Mike Duhon. See Garrison to Governor Edwards, June 6, 1972, LSA. Reference to the office space and telephones provided by the OEO was made by Governor Edwards in an official statement, December 11, 1972, LSA. Garrison's appointment first appeared in "Racing Panel Appointees Are Listed," *Shreveport Times*, June 6, 1972, 4. Edwards's communication to Garrison appeared in a letter on May 29, 1972, LSA.

52. "A Break for the Coushattas," *Opelousas Daily World*, July 1, 1973, 4.

53. Gulf South Research Institute, *American Indians of Louisiana: An Assessment of Needs* (Baton Rouge: Gulf South Research, 1973), LSA.

54. Governor Edwin Edwards, "Statement," December 11, 1972, LSA.

55. Letter, Garrison to Senator Ellender, July 11, 1972, CTA; letter, Garrison to Edwards, June 6, 1972, LSA.

56. Letter, Garrison to Edwards, March 15, 1973, LSA.

57. Letter, Ruth Loyd Miller to the Louisiana Political Educational Council, December 1, 1972, LSA.

58. Garrison, quoted in Carolyn Moffett, "Indian Affairs: Aid to Strengthen Culture Roots," *Lake Charles American Press*, n.d., 1972, 48, CTA.

59. In 1972 only the Chitimacha qualified for funding under the provisions of the IRA. As Governor Edwards proclaimed in a December 11, 1972, statement: "The other four main tribes which are recognizable entities are the Houmas, the Tunicas, the Coushattas and the Choctaws. Since most members of these various tribes

do not live together under tribal conditions a statewide intertribal council is the only way for them to qualify for . . . monies from such diverse sources as the Office of Housing and Urban Development of Labor, Office of Economic Opportunity, the Bureau of Indian Affairs and others," LSA.

60. The extent of coverage in Louisiana was assessed using the online newspaper archive at www.newspapers.com.

61. George Avery, "Louisiana 'Indian Angels' Aided Invasion of Alcatraz," *Alexandria Town Talk*, November 14, 1971, 21.

62. The meeting was referenced in "Louisiana's Indians Set Pow-Wow," *Opelousas Daily World*, May 17, 1972, 12.

63. "Coushattas Denounce BIA Office Seizure," *Lake Charles American Press*, December 13, 1972, 59. Multiple other tribal leaders also issued formal statements against AIM's activities. A compilation of such statements can be found in Mohawk Nation, *Trail of Broken Treaties*, 22–23.

64. "Indian Leader Works within System," letter to the editor, *Shreveport Times*, April 1, 1973, 21.

65. Klopotek, *Recognition Odysseys,* 65. Also for a discussion on the methods and objectives of the Indians Angels as compared to the LOIA, 302 (EN21).

66. Letter, Garrison to Edwards, June 6, 1972, LSA.

67. Resolution of the Coushatta Tribal Council, September 18, 1972, folder 3, box 245, AAIA.

68. Letter, David L. Garrison Jr. to Bertram E. Hirsch (AAIA), September 14, 1972; "Area Indians Try to Regain Service," *Lake Charles American Press*, December 23, 1972, 21. While Garrison was involved in advocating for Coushatta federal reinstatement since the beginning, Governor Edwards made his first effort toward this goal in a September 19, 1972 letter to Rogers C. B. Morton (Department of Interior), folder 3, box 245, AAIA.

69. The gathering was also part of a celebration of the renewal of the tribe's nonprofit charter to continue operating the Trading Post. Letter, Garrison to Edwards, June 6, 1972, LSA; Ella Mitchell, "Coushatta Indian Lauds Non-Profit Tribal Charter," *Shreveport Times*, June 21, 1972, 12.

70. For Buffalo Tiger's description of the Miccosukees' meeting with Castro, see Tiger and Kersey, *Buffalo Tiger*, 88–92.

71. Sickey interviews November 16 and 19, 2015. There is also a mention of Sickey visiting Buffalo Tiger in a letter from Byler to Sickey, July 25, 1973, folder 3, box 245, AAIA. "Miccosukee Indians Set Up Embassy to U.S.," *Florida Today*, October 28, 1984, 10B.

72. Bruce Broussard, "Cenla Indians Battle BIA," *Alexandria Town Talk*, June 23, 1973, 6; letters, Sickey to Byler, August 1, 1972, and Garrison to Byler, September 21, 1972, folder 3, box 245, AAIA; Sickey interview, November 16, 2015.

73. Letter, Sickey to Byler, January 17, 1973, folder 3, box 245, AAIA. The research efforts of the AAIA involved contacting Daniel Jacobson, the scholar who wrote his dissertation on the Coushattas in 1954 entitled "Koasati Culture Changes." See letter, Daniel Jacobson to AAIA, March 12, 1973. Evidence of Byler's personal research activities involving the Coushatta's migration from Alabama can be found in his correspondence. See letters, Byler to Dean, March 27, 1973, Byler to Sickey, April 13, 1973, and Byler to the University of Georgia Library, July 5, 1973, folder 3, box 245, AAIA.

74. "Fund Bill Extension Is Sought," *Shreveport Times*, October 11, 1974, 5; letters, David Garrison to Bertram E. Hirsch (AAIA), September 14, 1972, and Hirsh to Garrison, September 19, 1972; and Memorandum No. 72-18, AAIA, "Revenue Sharing," November 13, 1972, folder 3, box 245, AAIA. Reference to the Chitimachas' involvement in revenue sharing was made in Dean to Sickey, May 30, 1973, folder 3, box 245, AAIA.

75. Wunder, "Walter Echo-Hawk," 303; "Services for Coushattas Are Discussed," *Lake Charles American Press*, October 18, 1972, 23.

76. Britten, *National Council on Indian Opportunity*, 171–75.

77. Letters, Garrison to Ellender, July 11, 1972, and Carlisle B. Morrison (assistant to Senator Ellender) to L. M. Burgess (Chitimacha Tribe) and Ernest Sickey, July 20, 1972; Coushatta Tribe of Louisiana, "Resolution," June 11, 1972, CTA.

78. Letter, John O. Crow to C. W. Roberts (secretary, Louisiana state senate), August 15, 1972, Byler.

79. Letter, William Byler to Marie Rose Remmel, September 6, 1973, folder 3, box 245, AAIA.

80. Ernest Sickey, Report of Consultant to the Commission of Indian Affairs for the State of Louisiana, September 12–November 20, 1972, LSA.

81. Letter, Garrison to Edwards, March 15, 1973, LSA.

82. Sickey interview, November 16, 2015.

83. Letter, Sickey to Byler, January 17, 1973, folder 3, box 245, AAIA. Despite a shared support of the Coushattas' case by Governor Edwards and Senator Long, there were tensions between the two men. Evidence of this came out when in 1973 the governor refused to declare Huey Long's birthday (August 30) an official state holiday. This day had been reserved in honor of Long since his assassination in 1936. "No Birthday Note for Long," *Opelousas Daily World*, August 28, 1973, 2. Sickey interviews, July 1 and 8 and November 16, 17, and 18, 2015.

84. Sickey interview, July 1, 2015.

85. Paula Abbey Manuel interview, November 16, 2016.

86. Sickey, "Reflection on a Lifetime of Leadership," 173; Sickey interview, July 28, 2015.

87. AAIA, "Coushatta Land Acquisition Program," (1973), 1; Jojola, "Notes on Identity, Time, Space, and Place," 89.

88. Sickey interview, June 3, 2015.

89. Doucet interview, November 18, 2015.

90. David Sickey interview, November 18, 2015.

91. Langley interview, April 4, 2016.

92. Battise interview, April 5, 2016.

93. Sickey interview, July 28, 2015; letters, Dean to Sickey, January 16, 1973, with accompanying draft "Constitution and Bylaws of the Coushatta Indian Tribe of Louisiana," and Byler to Sickey, July 2, 1973, folder 3, box 245, AAIA.

94. Sickey interview, July 1, 2015.

95. Letter, Dean to Sickey, April 12, 1973, folder 3, box 245, AAIA. For specific examples of constitutional development and amendments among tribal nations, see Kalt, "Role of Constitutions in Native Nation Building," 78–114.

96. Letters, Dean to Sickey, February 15, 1973 and April 2, 1973, folder 3, box 245, AAIA; Johnson, *Coushatta People*, vi.

97. Letter, Dean to Sickey, January 2, 1974. The AAIA helped with the organization of the Coushatta Alliance, Inc., by drafting the "Articles of Incorporation." Letters, Dean to Sickey, January 16, 1973, and Garrison to Byler, March 16, 1973; Official Declaration Document from the Commissioner of Indian Affairs, March 12, 1973; LOIA Statement, March 13, 1973. All sources from folder 3, box 245, AAIA. Letter, Garrison to Marvin Franklin (Department of Interior), June 29, 1973, CTA; "Indian Alliance Elects Trustees at Tribe Event," *Baton Rouge Morning Advocate*, March 15, 1973, 4A; "Alliance Is Formed by Coushattas," *Lake Charles American Press*, March 16, 1973, 15.

98. "Coushatta Choose Corporate Chiefs," *Alexandria Town Talk*, March 17, 1973, 4.

99. LOIA statement (1973); "Five Trustees Named by Coushatta Alliance," *Beaumont Enterprise*, March 15, 1973, 3A.

100. Letter, Dean to Franklin, April 30, 1973, folder 3, box 245, AAIA.

101. "A Break for the Coushattas," *Opelousas Daily World*, July 1, 1973, 4.

102. Johnston's May 14 letter and the impending letter from McQuirter were both referenced in J. Bennett Johnston (U.S. Senate) to Marvin Franklin, June 8, 1973, folder 3, box 245, AAIA.

103. Letter, Sickey to Byler, July 9, 1973, folder 3, box 245, AAIA.

104. Letter, Franklin to Garrison, June 27, 1973, folder 3, box 245, AAIA.

105. "Coushatta Indians Seek Reservation after Gaining Governmental Recognition," *Opelousas Daily World*, July 6, 1973, 2.

106. "Red Shoes' People" (July 1973), n.p.

107. Coushatta Tribe, *Red Shoes' People*, n.p.

108. Letter, Daniel Jacobson to William Byler, July 12, 1973, folder 3, box 245, AAIA.

109. Letter, Ruth Miller to John Cade, December 16, 1980, LSA.

110. Sickey interview, September 30, 2015.

111. Letter, Franklin to Garrison, June 27, 1973, folder 3, box 245, AAIA; "Harry A. Rainbolt" obituary, December 24, 2014, https://www.fredericksburg.com /obituaries/harry-a-rainbolt/article_e8111a16-3015-5a79-a827-1f4c2f658ec7.html; Sickey interview, September 30, 2015.

112. Agenda for Coushatta Meeting, July 2, 1973, St. Peter's Church, CTA; letter, Sickey to Byler, July 3, 1973, folder 3, box 245, AAIA; Rainbolt, quoted in Darryl Drewett, "Full Recognition Goal: Coushattas' Road a Long One," *Lake Charles American Press*, July 3, 1973, 6; Sickey interview, September 30, 2015.

113. "Coushatta Indians Seek Reservation after Gaining Governmental Recognition," *Opelousas Daily World*, July 6, 1973, 2.

114. Les Gay, quoted in Byler to Sickey, July 10, 1973, folder 3, box 245, AAIA.

115. Peroff, *Menominee Drums*, 8.

116. AAIA, "Coushatta Land Acquisition Program," 1973, and "Coushatta File," September 27, 1972, folder 3, box 245, AAIA; Sickey interview, July 28, 2015.

117. This proved to be a wise approach because matters did indeed take longer to resolve following the Coushattas' federal reinstatement, as efforts to acquire land to place into federal trust were stalled. By November 1973 the taxes on the ten acres came due, which the AAIA paid. Letter, Daniel M. Singer (attorney) to Kermit Manuel (Great Southern Mortgage and Loan Corp.), January 3, 1973; Cash Warranty Deed issued to William Byler, trustee, File No. 227,065, Allen Parish, January 22, 1973; letter, Manuel to Singer, February 5, 1973, folder 3, box 245, AAIA. The original cash warranty deed mistakenly recorded a thirty-acre tract of land instead of ten acres and took weeks to clear up. See letters, Byler to Lazarus, April 3, 1973; Daniel M. Singer to William Byler, April 6, 1973; Byler to Dean, November 27, 1973; and Manuel to Dean, November 29, 1973, folder 3, box 245, AAIA.

118. Letter, Byler to Sickey, March 7, 1973, folder 3, box 245, AAIA.

119. Letter, Garrison to Byler, May 15, 1973, folder 3, box 245, AAIA. Ernest Sickey conducted research, identifying desirable landholdings and flagging the ones available for immediate purchase. See letter, Garrison to Byler, July 30, 1973; "Coushatta Land Acquisition Program," 1973, folder 3, box 245, AAIA; Sickey interview, November 19, 2015.

120. The additional five acres were attributed to the Abbey family by Ernest Sickey, interview with author, April 27, 2017, folder 3, box 245, AAIA. According to a letter from S. Bobo Dean to Leonard K. Knapp, January 15, 1974, the purchase price for the additional five acres was $750.

121. It is interesting to note that although Byler was alerted to the BIA's change of requirement on the expected acreage from twenty-five to ten acres in order to

qualify the Coushattas for services, he continued to purport to various people he corresponded with that they needed twenty-five acres. This was perhaps an attempt to generate donations toward more land since that was the ultimate goal. For the letter indicating the shift in BIA requirements, see Byler to Sickey, July 5, 1973. For an example of Byler's continuing claim that the Coushattas needed twenty-five acres, see Byler to John A. Williams, September 28, 1973, folder 3, box 245, AAIA.

122. Letter, Dean to Rainbolt, September 27, 1974, folder 4, box 245, AAIA; Sickey interview, November 17, 2015. The transfer of the land into federal trust was delayed for five reasons: (1) there were still mineral interests that needed clearing. See Dean to Knapp, January 7 and April 16, 1974; (2) there was confusion over the cancellation of the previous tax deed. See Dean to Manuel, January 7, 1974; (3) the description of the additional five acres was filed incorrectly in the original deed and tax notice. See Dean to Manuel, January 15, 1974, and Knapp to Dean, May 15, 1974; (4) there was a delay in the Interior Department Solicitor's office inspecting the proposed Coushatta Reservation. See Dean to Sickey, May 30, June 24, and August 1, 1974, and Dean to Hildegarde Forbes (AAIA secretary), September 16, 1974; and (5) all of the paperwork needed to be filed to transfer the property from the Bylers (Mrs. Byler also had to sign over the deed) to the tribe, including a donation deed. See Knapp to Byler, October 21, 1974, and Dean to Rainbolt, November 5, 1974. The AAIA submitted the official resolution to have the fifteen acres taken into federal trust on April 29, 1974. See Dean to Sickey, April 29, 1974, and Dean to Garrison, April 30, 1974. All documents from folder 4, box 245, AAIA; Sickey interview, November 16, 2015.

123. The proclamation that received the fifteen acres into federal trust for the Coushattas was signed by Commissioner Thompson on March 14, 1975. See Dean to Rainbolt, February 13, 1975, and Sickey to Byler, March 7, 1975, folder 4, box 245, AAIA. See also "Allen Land Is Recognized a Reservation," *Lake Charles American Press*, March 17, 1975, 2. The notice of the establishment of the reservation is dated May 27, 1975, as it appeared on the federal register of June 5, 1975.

124. The tribe experienced many hurdles between April 8, 1975, when the land was initially donated, and January 18, 1977, when it was officially declared part of the Coushatta reservation. In addition to the time it took to clear the title through multiple Bel Estate shareholders, as well as having to replace misplaced documents as a result of Garrison's move to Houston, the bureaucratic wheels of the federal government once again moved at a slow pace. Miscommunication and inaction stalled the process for months. Plus, the request of the estate's attorneys that the tribe had to agree not to conduct "operations in search of oil, gas or associated minerals, but that those reserved minerals will be extracted from the land by

virtue of operations conducted off the surface of the land herby donated" elicited further need for clarification by the Department of Interior before moving forward. Through all of this, the Coushattas continued to receive help from lawyer S. Bobo Dean of the AAIA, who sent letters and made several phone calls about the status of the land. See Richard E. Gerard to William Byler, June 30, 1976; "Act of Donation Inter Vivos," July 2, 1976; Knapp to Dean, November 6, 1975; Dean to Knapp, November 10, 1975; U.S Department of Interior, Regional Solicitor to Eastern Area director, BIA, May 13, 1976; Dean to Sickey, December 16, 1976; Dean to W. D. Wesley (John A. Bel Estate), December 7, 1976; Dean to Sickey, January 19, 1977. All sources from folder 5, box 245, AAIA.

125. Sickey interview, July 28, 2015. Reference to Garrison initiating these efforts during Rainbolt's visit to the Coushatta community is also found in some correspondence from Sickey to Dean, March 31, 1975, folder 4, box 245, AAIA.

126. Langley interview, April 4, 2016.

127. Letters, Sickey to Senator Johnston, November 5, 1976, and Senator Johnston to Sickey, November 29, 1976, folder 5, box 245, AAIA.

128. Letters, Ben Reitel (BIA) to Senator Johnston, January 4, 1977, and name illegible (acting deputy commissioner, BIA) to Johnston, February 24, 1977, folder 5, box 245, AAIA.

129. Letter, Robert C. Byrd to Senator Johnston, April 11, 1977, folder 5, box 245, AAIA.

130. "Coushatta Tribal Head Is Proud of His People," unknown source, January 6, 1980, n.p., LSA; Coushatta Tribe, Resolution No. 85-15, Road Maintenance, January 28, 1982, CTA.

131. Sickey interviews, November 18 and 19, 2015.

132. Knapp interview, November 18, 2015.

133. Williams interview, April 5, 2016.

134. Leonard Battise interview, April 5, 2016.

135. Sickey interview, July 1, 2015. At the time of this book's publication, the Coushatta tribal government continues to run without a constitution.

6. CONTROLLING THE CONVERSATION

EPIGRAPH: Ernest Sickey, "Chairman's Report," *Coushatta Smoke Signal*, February 28, 1977, 2, CTA.

1. "Naming State Balloon a Breeze," *Alexandria Town Talk*, July 29, 1983, 24.

2. Letter, Sickey to Byler, March 15, 1973, folder 3, box 245, AAIA.

3. Ernest Sickey, "Letter to the Editor," *Baton Rouge Enterprise*, March 16–22, 1977, 2.

4. KLFY (CBS affiliate) to Ernest Sickey, June 13, 1975, CTA.

5. For more on social justice discourse regarding Indigenous peoples, see Rowse, *Rethinking Social Justice*.

6. "Editorial: Coushatta Tribe Gets Break," *Lake Charles American Press*, June 24, 1973, n.p.; "A Break for the Coushattas," *Opelousas Daily World*, July 1, 1973, 4.

7. Leger interview, November 18, 2015.

8. Jacobson, "Koasati Cultural Change," 136–37.

9. Introduced by Harvison and Owens, "Bel Abbey: Koasati Stories," 80.

10. Langley interview, April 4, 2016.

11. Ed Cullen, "Tradition: Times Change," *Baton Rouge Sunday Advocate*, August 8, 1982, 1G; Harvison and Owens, "Bel Abbey: Koasati Stories," 81–82; Gregory interview, November 19, 2015.

12. "Folklife Center to Honor Artists," *Alexandria Town Talk*, June 15, 1983, 29; "Indian Arts, Crafts Show Features Three Tribes' Work," *Alexandria Town Talk*, December 3, 1983, 20; quotation from "Coushatta Indian Members Honored," *Lake Charles American Press*, June 13, 1982, 7.

13. Jacobson wrote that he "was [also] often an overnight guest in the home of the late Ency Abbott," who was Bel Abbey's mother. See "Ethnological Report and Statement of Testimony," preface.

14. Letter, Fred Kniffen to William Byler, November 9, 1973, folder 3, box 245, AAIA. For examples of these early works, see Harrington, "Among the Louisiana Indians"; Swanton, "Animal Stories," "Indian Language," *Indians of the Southeastern United States*, "Myths and Tales," "Religious Beliefs and Medical Practices of the Creek Indians," 473–672; Haas, "Men's and Women's Speech in Koasati," 142–49.

15. Jacobson, "Koasati Culture Change," 204.

16. Davis, *Louisiana*, 25.

17. Gregory interview, November 19, 2015.

18. The Coushatta Heritage Department has identified archeological, ethnographic, and linguistic work done by approximately twenty-five different researchers over the course of the past century. Among them were Lyda Averill Taylor and Daniel Jacobson, who are credited with carrying out extensive ethnographic studies in the Coushatta community between the 1930s and 1950s. See Taylor, *Plants Used as Curatives*; and Jacobson, "Koasati Cultural Change" and "Origin of the Koasati Community." Mary R. Haas was a linguist who worked with many Native languages in the Southeast, including Muskogean languages such as Koasati. In 1944 she published a sociolinguistic study based on some work she conducted with the Coushattas. See Haas, "Men's and Women's Speech in Koasati." Geoffrey D. Kimball also completed his dissertation on the Koasati language in 1985 and later published a version of it in 1990, entitled *Koasati Grammar*, and then the *Koasati Dictionary* (1994) and *Koasati Traditional Narratives* (2010). Recent works on Muskogean languages have resulted in a closer examination of Koasati. For some examples, see Martin, "Implications of Plural Reduplication, Infixation,

and Subtraction," 27–55; and Gordon, Martin, and Langley, "Some Phonetic Structures of Koasati," 83–118.

19. Sickey interview, October 5, 2016.

20. Stroud interview with Jay Precht, August 4, 2008, CTA.

21. Gregory interview, November 19, 2015.

22. Drechsel, "Speaking 'Indian' in Louisiana," 12.

23. Gregory interview, November 19, 2015.

24. Sickey interview, November 19, 2015.

25. Gregory interview, November 19, 2015; Sickey interviews, November 19 and July 8, 2015; Sickey, "We Will Forever Remain Coushatta," 48–49.

26. Sickey interviews, November 19, July 8, and June 3, 2015. For more on the increased role of tribes in writing their own histories, see Forbes, "Intellectual Self-Determination and Sovereignty."

27. Gregory interview, November 19, 2015.

28. Sickey interviews, July 8 and September 30, 2015; Gregory interview, November 19, 2015; "Anthropologists, Indian Meet," *Alexandria Town Talk*, February 21, 1974, 33; "Indians to Sell Wares," *Shreveport Times*, December 2, 1982, 26.

29. For examples of this evolving relationship among other southern tribal communities and researchers, see the collection of essays in Bonney and Paredes, *Anthropologists and Indians in the New South*. Also, Stephanie May De Montigny's work among the Louisiana Coushattas and Alabamas and Coushattas of Texas has demonstrated that "native consultants and collaborators to a great degree, and tribal members began to exercise greater control over research and representations." See "Chiefs, Churches, and 'Old Industries,'" 1–40 (quotation on p. 2).

30. O'Brien, "Interview with Theda Perdue and Michael D. Green," 13.

31. Letter, Jacobson to Byler, March 20, 1973, folder 3, box 245, AAIA.

32. Gregory interview, November 19, 2015.

33. Jacobson released *The First Americans* (1969) and devoted a whole chapter to the Coushattas. The following year, he published a young adult book called *Great Indian Tribes* (1970) and dedicated the book to the tribe. Jacobson wasn't the first to make an effort to give the Coushattas more visibility within mainstream educational materials, however. Fred Kniffen also wrote an educational reference book for schoolchildren called *The Indians of Louisiana* (1945). While the text mainly focused on Louisiana's early Indigenous history, it does emphasize modern Indian communities (83). Later Kniffen developed a more robust, academic version of his earlier book that emphasized archaeology, cultural history, and geography. This time he teamed up with Hiram F. Gregory and geographer George Stokes to produce *The Historic Indian Tribes of Louisiana from 1542 to the Present*, which was published in 1987.

34. U.S. Department of Interior, *Indians of the Gulf Coast States*.

35. Draft of the article found in Byler to Sickey, July 5, 1973. Also see letters, Sickey to Byler, July 30, 1973, and January 20, 1975, folders 3–4, box 245, AAIA.

36. Cheryl Crooks, "Started on Gamble, Indian Tribal Series Beats Odds and Wins Success," *Arizona Republic*, August 4, 1974, 141.

37. Letter, Henry F. Dobyns to Ernest Sickey, May 29, 1973, folder 3, box 245, AAIA.

38. Letter, William Byler to John Griffin, November 12, 1973, folder 3, box 245, AAIA.

39. Johnson, *Coushatta People*, 97.

40. The 1970s and 1980s saw an influx of southern Indians working with institutions or independent academics to tell both their historic and contemporary stories. Tribes in South Carolina, e.g., teamed up with the University of South Carolina for a publication. See Crediford, *Contemporary Native Americans in South Carolina*.

41. Coushatta Tribe, *Struggle Has Made Us Stronger*, n.p.

42. Literal translation of *Koasati Asaala Achoolihak Ommiifookon, Aatohyak Hokosobbaalito*: "Because of the Coushatta basket weavers, everyone started knowing us."

43. The creation of this Association was influenced by the Lafayette-based economic development group, The International Relations Association of Acadiana (TIRAA), which promoted Cajun heritage by uniting twenty-two parishes and advertising them as the "Heart of Acadiana." Although Allen and Jefferson Davis Parishes boasted large Cajun populations, they were excluded from TIRAA membership. Bernard, *Cajuns*, 80.

44. Ellis Byers, "Acadiana Trail: 'Trail' Prospects Aired at Assn. Meet," *Opelousas Daily World*, January 11, 1970, 22.

45. "Tourist Bureau Will Be Indian Day Site," *Lake Charles American Press*, November 10, 1971, 13.

46. Ella Mitchell, "Elton Tribe Has Unlimited Growth in Tourism Industry," *Opelousas Daily World*, June 9, 1972, 5.

47. "Big Thicket Park Movement Gains; Meeting at Beaumont," *Liberty Vindicator*, March 15, 1962, 9; "ARA Study Due," *Longview News-Journal*, April 30, 1964, 6. The evolving partnership between the Alabama-Coushatta community and the Texas Tourism Council saw steady news coverage. See Vern Sanford, "State Capital Highlights and Sidelights," *Wise County Messenger*, April 29, 1965, 2.

48. Walter W. Broemer, quoted in "Indians on Etex Reservation Whooping Up Tourism Drive," *Shreveport Times*, October 3, 1965, 19.

49. Norman Richardson, "Changes in Sight for Texas Indians," *Shreveport Times*, June 21, 1964, 58; Brown and Root, Inc., "Preliminary Planning Tourist Facilities—Alabama-Coushatta Indian Reservation—Polk County, Texas," 1967. John V. Dowdy Sr. Papers, Baylor Collections of Political Materials, Waco TX.

50. Play bill, East Texas Indian Reservation of the Alabama and Coushatta Tribes Presents "Beyond the Sundown," 1975, Fondren Library, Southern Methodist

University, Dallas; Verdis Dowdy, "Alabama Coushatta Reservation: White Man Welcome in Indian Country," *Alexandria Town Talk*, March 30, 1969, 20.

51. Sickey interview, September 16, 2015.

52. "Railroad to Give Depot," *Opelousas Daily World*, December 6, 1973, 2; "Rep. Breaux Speaker at Supper in Elton," *Opelousas Daily World*, December 30, 1973, 13; "Elton May Become 'The Indian Capital,'" *Jennings Daily News*, December 27, 1973, n.p. According to the *Lake Charles American Press*, the Senate passed a resolution declaring Elton the "Indian Capital of Louisiana" in 1974. "Senate Moves to Honor Coushattas," *Lake Charles American Press*, July 10, 1974, n.p., CTA.

53. "Donation for Indian Center Given," *Opelousas Daily World*, July 3, 1974, 12; "Bank Presents Donation for Indian Museum," *Lake Charles American Press*, July 8, 1974, n.p.; Bertney Langley, "Coushatta Indian Cultural Center," *Coushatta Smoke Signal*, March 25, 1977, 1; letters, Stephen M. Richmond to Judy McKee, July 23, 1974, and Stephen M. Richmond to Ernest Sickey, May 6, 1975; "Coushatta Tribal Bicentennial Proposal," June 16, 1975, 1–3. Archive sources all from the CTA.

54. In 1975 the tribe was awarded a $30,000 grant from the EDA, with an additional $42,000 awarded in 1978. Sandra Lantz, "Coushatta Indians: Basket Weaving Trade Changes," *Opelousas Daily World*, June 18, 1978, 17. They also received funding from the "America the Beautiful Fund" and the Imperial Calcasieu Regional Planning and Development Commission. "America the Beautiful Fund" brochure, ca. 1975, folder 4, box 245, AAIA; Ann Muchison, "Calcasieu Imperial Commission: Bicentennial Funds Distributed," *Lake Charles American Press*, February 17, 1976, 46; "Coushatta Indians Open Cultural Center in Elton," *Lake Charles American Press*, September 11, 1974, n.p., CTA.

55. Johnson, *Coushatta People*, 96.

56. Sandra Lantz, "Coushatta Indians: Basket Weaving Trade Changes," *Opelousas Daily World*, June 18, 1978, 17.

57. Letter, Jan Van der Poll to Ernest Sickey, October 22, 1976; Ernest Sickey, "Chairman's Report," and Bertney Langley, "Cultural Center," *Coushatta Smoke Signal*, February 28, 1977, 1–2, CTA.

58. "Basket Classes Planned," *Alexandria Town Talk*, May 15, 1981, 17; "Folklife Center to Honor Artists," *Alexandria Town Talk*, June 15, 1983, 29; deCaro and Jordan, *Louisiana Traditional Crafts*, 23.

59. Sickey interview, April 29, 2015.

60. It is uncertain exactly how many baskets Richmond purchased, but in 2000 nine baskets from the Bayou Blue community (including an owl effigy basket woven by Rosabel Sylestine and three basket trivets) were transferred to the National Museum of the American Indian in Washington DC. For an inventory and acquisition information of the baskets that were transferred from the Indian Arts and

Crafts Board to the National Museum of the American Indian, see http://www
.nmai.si.edu/searchcollections/results.aspx?catids=0&cultxt=Coushatta&src=
1–1&size=75&page=1.

61. Haynes, "Constructing Authenticity," 19; letters, Sickey to Richmond, September
    29 and October 20, 1976; Richmond to Sickey, October 28, 1976, CTA.

62. Letter, Sickey to Richmond, August 18, 1976, CTA.

63. "Coushatta Pine Needle Coiled Basketry," by Rosabel Sylestine, September
    9–December 30, 1973, container 34, file 186A-Marketing Materials, Cherokee
    Field Office Records, 1968–83, Records of the Indian Arts and Crafts Board,
    record group 435, National Archives at Atlanta (hereafter cited as NA-A).

64. Letter, Richmond to Sickey, March 28, 1973, CTA.

65. Letters, David L. Garrison Jr. to Mitchell Wilder, July 19, 1974, and Richmond to
    Garrison, July 3, 1973, CTA. U.S. Department of Interior Indian Arts and Crafts
    Board, exhibition on Coushatta Pine Needle Coiled Basketry, by Rosabel Sylestine,
    1973, LSA; "Elton Indian Basketry Exhibit in Jackson Square," *Opelousas Daily
    World*, July 13, 1973, 2; "Coushatta Indian Basket Exhibition to Open Sunday,"
    New Orleans States-Item, July 11, 1973, n.p.; "Coushatta Indian: Elton Artist Has
    N.O. Show," *Lake Charles American Press*, July 14, 1973, 22.

66. Letter, Stephen Richmond to Robert G. Hart, July 18, 1973, container 11, file F65-E,
    Cherokee Field Office Records, 1968–83, Records of the Indian Arts and Crafts
    Board, record group 435, NA-A.

67. Letter, Frieda Morford (Louisiana State Museum) to Stephen Richmond, August
    13, 1973, container 23, file 305, Cherokee Field Office Records, 1968–83, Records of
    the Indian Arts and Crafts Board, record group 435, NA-A. Based on an itemized
    invoice prepared by Richmond at the start of the exhibit, the total value of the
    pine needle baskets were approximately $650; however, the demand prompted
    Sylestine to offer more pieces, resulting in over $1,000 worth of sales, as reflected
    in a note produced after the exhibition ended. See Louisiana State Museum Receipt
    of Objects, Coushatta pine needle coiled basketry by Rosabel Sylestine for exhibit,
    July 15–August 31, 1973; and "Geoff" to Stephen Richmond, October 18, 1973,
    container 34, file 186A, Cherokee Field Office Records, 1968–83, Records of the
    Indian Arts and Crafts Board, record group 435, NA-A.

68. Letter, Morford to Richmond, August 20, 1973, container 23, file 305, Cherokee
    Field Office Records, 1968–83, Records of the Indian Arts and Crafts Board, record
    group 435, NA-A.

69. Press release, "Special Exhibition of Indian Crafts to Open at the Cabildo," Novem-
    ber 23, 1973, CTA.

70. Letter, Langley to Richmond, January 21, 1974, CTA.

71. U.S. Department of the Interior, Indian Arts and Crafts Board, "Crafts by the
    Langley Family," December 20, 1972–January 17, 1973, folder 3, box 245, AAIA;

"Coushatta Indian Crafts by Edna Langley," brochure for exhibition, December 9, 1973–January 31, 1974, LSA; "Contemporary Coushatta Fashions by the Langleys," brochure, May 1, 1978, container 2, file SE 1978, Cherokee Field Office Records, 1968–83, Records of the Indian Arts and Crafts Board, record group 435, NA-A; "Lorena Langley Sews Best of Both Worlds," *Houston Chronicle*, May 3, 1978, n.p.

72. Richmond prematurely sought help for Langley from an outside source with clothes construction; however, she made it clear that she wanted her exhibit to be Coushatta-made and created. Letter, Stephen M. Richmond to Ruth Fontenot, July 28, 1976, CTA.

73. Marian John's biographical sketch draft was included with a letter from Michael Scott (editor of the *Crafts Report*) to Marion John, September 15, 1976, CTA. John, quoted in "Coushatta Indian Pine Needle Basketry by Marian John," August 5–September 15, 1974, container 1, file SE 1974, Cherokee Field Office Records, 1968–83, Records of the Indian Arts and Crafts Board, record group 435, NA-A. See also "Baskets Full of Art: Coushatta Indian Basketweaver," *Houston Post*, August 4, 1974, 3.

74. Letters, Stephen Richmond to Dallas Johnson, May 6, 1974, and Stephen Richmond to Margaret Prince, June 5, 1974, container 1, file SE 1974, box 1, Cherokee Field Office Records, 1968–83, Records of the Indian Arts and Crafts Board, record group 435, NA-A.

75. Letter, Marian John to National Endowment for the Arts, May 11, 1976, CTA.

76. Letter, Sickey to Richmond, March 17, 1975; Marian John, quoted in "Coushatta Indian Pine Needle Basketry by Marian John," August 5–September 15, 1974; letter, Stephen M. Richmond to Elena Canavier, November 20, 1974; letter, Peg Bolton to Stephen M. Richmond, October 24, 1974, CTA. In 1975 John was one of the headlining attractions at the First United Methodist Church's Annual Art Festival. "Pine Needles Baskets," *Town Talk*, April 4, 1975, 18. Quotation from letter, William A. Reedy to Ernest Sickey, December 5, 1974, CTA.

77. Letter, Sickey to Richmond, September 18, 1973, CTA. Richmond specifically pointed out how Marian John's basket prices were "extremely low" when she first began her exhibitions, but following her Houston show "was able to derive greatly increased prices for her creations." Letter, Stephen M. Richmond to Elena Canavier, November 20, 1974, CTA.

78. Letter, Edwards to Sickey, November 3, 1976, CTA.

79. De Caro and Jordan, *Louisiana Traditional Crafts*.

80. Letters, Richmond to Fletcher, June 14, 1979; Richmond to Sickey, March 30, 1981, Ernest Sickey to Nancy Hanks (National Endowment for the Arts), July 1, 1977, container 6, file 15, Cherokee Field Office Records, 1968–83, Records of the Indian Arts and Crafts Board, record group 435, NA-A.

81. Letter, A. John Tassin Jr. to Ernest Sickey, August 25, 1973, CTA.

82. Mary Catherine Bounds, "Premiere of LODA Play 'A Magnificent Thrill,'" *Times*, June 20, 1976, 1; "Arts Workshop Set in B.R.," *Alexandria Town Talk*, June 16, 1977, 38.

83. "Indian Arts Show Open at Museum," *Lake Charles American Press*, October 13, 1973, 8.

84. Sickey interview, November 16, 2015; letters, Ruth Loyd Miller to John Cade, December 16, 1980, LSA.

85. Clover, "In Case of Emergency, Break Convention," 299–313.

86. Literal translation of *Komaatik Stibachasakato Im-iltolihnok*: "We built up our people by working."

87. Sickey interviews, June 24, September 30, and November 19, 2015; letter, Sickey to Dean, March 31, 1975, folder 4, box 245, AAIA.

88. Letter, Dean to Sickey, November 23, 1976, folder 5, box 245, AAIA. The grant amount has been reported as different amounts by different sources. The $100,000 reporting comes from the quarterly report for the Louisiana Division of Human Services, Office of Indian Affairs, March 1–May 31, 1975, 4, LSA. "New Officers Installed at Em-Mok-La Meeting," *Opelousas Daily World*, January 16, 1977, 19.

89. Rodney Williams as told to Crystal Williams, interview with author, April 5, 2016.

90. Johnson, *Coushatta People*, 89.

91. Sickey interview, August 26, 2015; Knapp interview, November 18, 2015.

92. Sickey interviews, November 17 and 19, 2015.

93. Quotation attributed to Kelly, but sentiment affirmed by Ray. Ray and Kelly Rush in interviews with author, both November 19, 2015.

94. Sickey interviews, November 16 and 17, 2015.

95. In 1975, in his capacity as president of the Coushatta Alliance, Inc., Sickey applied for and managed an ONAP grant. This action was instantly flagged as a conflict of interest, and he was asked to resign from one of his positions. Given the situation, the tribe was granted an extension to find someone else to oversee the grant. Letters, George Blue Spruce Jr. to Ernest Sickey, December 8, 1975, and S. Bobo Dean to George Clark, December 22, 1975, folder 4, box 245, AAIA.

96. Sickey interview, November 17, 2015; letter, Sickey to Byler, August 6, 1976, folder 5, box 245, AAIA.

97. The position was advertised in the newspapers. Ernest Sickey, "Chairman's Report," *Coushatta Smoke Signal*, March 25, 1977, 2, CTA; "Health Planner Wanted," *Alexandria Town Talk*, January 17, 1978, 26; Bertrand interview, November 17, 2015; Sickey interviews, July 28 and November 17, 2015; Coushatta Tribe, *Red Shoes' People*, n.p.

98. Sickey interviews, July 28 and September 2, 2015; Johnson, *Coushatta People*, 89; O'Brien, *American Indian Tribal Governments*, 270. The term *suburban character*

is attributed to Ted Jojola in his description of other reservation living spaces. See "Notes on Identity, Time, Space, and Place," 94.

99. Letter, Robert F. Jaggers to Helen Gindrat, May 20, 1982, LSA. This letter provides the history of this funding as context for the tribe applying for an additional $86,300 in 1982 to continue rehabilitating substandard homes. Coushatta Tribe Resolution No. 82-12, Housing Improvement Program, January 28, 1982, CTA.

100. Langley interview, April 4, 2016; and Sickey interview, July 28, 2015.

101. Williams interview, April 4, 2016.

102. Williams interview, April 3, 2016.

103. Battise interview, April 5, 2016.

104. Peter D. Mora (LOIA) to the Inter-Tribal Council of Louisiana Board of Directors, October 27, 1977, 2, ITC; Battise interview, April 5, 2016.

105. Petree interview, November 16, 2015; Ernest Sickey to Margaret Sloan (Office of Elderly Affairs), March 14, 1983, LSA.

106. "Experts Study Indians' Lifespans," *Baton Rouge Morning Advocate*, October 7, 1985, n.p.

107. Williams interview, April 5, 2016.

108. Sickey interviews, July 28 and November 16, 2015. Eventually the old health services building was demolished and replaced with a new facility dedicated as the Ernest Sickey Medical Center.

109. Langley interview, November 16, 2015.

110. Sickey interview, May 13, 2015; Langley interview, November 16, 2015.

111. Eleyna Langley, interview with author, February 18, 2016.

112. Bertney Langley, joint interview with Ernest Sickey for the "Koasati Documentation Project," http://koasati.blogs.wm.edu/interviews/ernest-sickey-bertney -langley-tribal-history/; Sickey interview, November 16, 2015; Langley interview, November 16, 2015.

113. Report summarized in "Education, Higher Income Go Hand-in-Hand," *Shreveport Times*, July 17, 1976, 29.

114. Spicker, Steiner, and Walden, *Survey of Rural Louisiana Indian Communities*; John LaPlante, "Unemployed, Says Study," *Alexandria Town Talk*, July 30, 1978, 49.

115. Battise interview, April 5, 2016. According to the Gulf Research Institute report, *American Indians of Louisiana*, the median income for Louisiana Indian families was $4,650.

116. See Taylor, *States and Their Indian Citizens*; Wilkins, "Tribal-State Affairs," 1–28; National Conference of State Legislatures, "Promoting Effective State-Tribal Relations," v. Quotation from Johnson, Kaufmann, Dossett, and Hicks, *Government to Government*, 1.

117. "Sickey Appointed," *Basile Weekly*, December 27, 1972, n.p.

118. Carolyn Moffett, "Indian Affairs: Aid to Strengthen Culture Roots," *Lake Charles American Press*, July 9, 1972, 48.

119. Jeanette Alcon Campos, interview with author, November 17, 2016.

120. The Governor's Commission on Indian Affairs was given a zero operating budget during the fiscal year 1974. Letter, David Garrison Jr. to Charles C. Mary, May 14, 1973, LSA.

121. Campos interview, November 17, 2016; letter, Garrison to Edwards, March 15, 1973, and LOIA Meeting Minutes, September 24, 1973, 3, LSA. In 1977 the LOIA was moved to the Louisiana Department of Urban and Community Affairs and became referenced as the Division of Indian Affairs.

122. See "Policy Regarding Services to Indians Under the Comprehensive Employment and Training Act, Title III, Section 302," n.d.; Inter-Tribal Council of Louisiana, Inc., Board of Directors Meeting Minutes, February 25, 1977, ITC. The sub-granting of the CETA funding to what became the ITC generated questions about whether it could be released to the newly chartered nonprofit organization. Full cooperation during an internal audit, paired with legal counsel and a special trip to Washington DC by Sickey and Campos to discuss the situation, resolved the issue, and the state was "de-obligated" from any further responsibility for the grant. This was not where the trouble ended, however, and amid accusations of funding misappropriation during the transfer of funds, an audit was initiated for the 1976–77 fiscal years—a process that dragged on until it was finally resolved in 1984. See Indian Manpower Services, Inc., Meeting Minutes, September 5, 1975, and August 14, 1976, ITC Meeting Minutes, June 22, 1983, and October 17, 1984, ITC.

123. The meeting minutes for the first several years (beginning in June 1975) reveal that the Coushattas were represented by not only Ernest Sickey but also Lovelin Poncho, Myrna Wilson, Leonard Battise, and Barbara Langley. Indian Manpower Services, Inc., Meeting Minutes, June, September, November, and December 1975, ITC. The Houma Alliance (domiciled in Dulac) was organized in 1975 and merged with the Houma Tribe (domiciled in Golden Meadow) by 1979 to create the United Houma Nation, with headquarters in Golden Meadow.

124. Inter-Tribal Council of Louisiana, Inc., Resolution 80-01, December 14, 1979, ITC; Campos interview, November 17, 2016; "Coushatta: Closely-Knit Elton Tribe," *Baton Rouge Morning Advocate*, June 2, 1978, n.p.

125. Indian Manpower Services, Inc., Meeting Minutes, November 1, 1975; Indian Manpower Services, Inc., Fiscal Year 1976 Report, ITC.

126. Coushatta Tribe of Louisiana, Employment Assistance Adult Vocational Training Report, January 1982, CTA.

127. Ernest Sickey, "Koasati Documentation Project," http://koasati.blogs.wm.edu/interviews/ernest-sickey-bertney-langley-tribal-history/.

128. Manuel interview, November 16, 2015.

129. Battise interview, April 5, 2016.

130. Williams interview, April 4, 2016. Part of Loretta's story was also relayed by her daughter Heather Williams April 3, 2016.

131. Jeanette Campos, quoted in "Indian Youth Hold Conference in BR," *Alexandria Town Talk*, June 6, 1984, 6C. Lora Ann Chaisson discussed her involvement with the program when Thompson was a participant, in interview with author, March 31, 2016; Kevin Billiot, interview with author, April 1, 2016.

132. Quarterly report for the LOIA, March 1–May 31, 1975, 4, LSA; Sickey interview, May 13, 2016; Kenneth Bruchhaus, interview with author, November 19, 2015; Linda Langley, personal communication, July 11, 2018.

133. Sickey interview, May 13, 2016.

134. Ron Grant, "State to Get Indian Education Funds," *Alexandria Town Talk*, February 21, 1974, 33.

135. Letter, Jeanette Campos to John R. Dupre (Louisiana State Department of Education), May 26, 1983; ITC Meeting Minutes, August 9, 1983, ITC.

136. "Jury to Aid Indian Tribe," *Beaumont Enterprises*, July 14, 1974, n.p.; Dillard Hardin, "Fun Time for YCC Campers," *Alexandria Town Talk*, July 29, 1976, 17; Sickey interview, July 28, 2015.

137. Bertney Langley interview, November 16, 2015; Sickey interviews, July 28, August 26, and September 2, 2015; Bertney Langley, "Koasati Documentation Project."

138. See, e.g., "Tourneys Set in Elton," *Lake Charles American Press*, August 23, 1979, 15.

139. "Coushatta: Closely-Knit Elton Tribe," *Baton Rouge Morning Advocate*, June 2, 1978, n.p.

140. Sickey interview, July 28, 2015; Coushatta Tribe, Resolution No. 82-15, Road Maintenance, January 28, 1982; Robert O. Benn (superintendent, Choctaw Agency), memo on Coushatta Contract and Grant Proposals for FY 1983, August 13, 1982; Coushatta Tribe, Resolution No. 82-18, Water Resources, January 26, 1982, CTA.

141. Gene Paul, interview with author, November 19, 2015; Sickey interviews, July 28 and November 19, 2015.

142. Bruchhaus interview, November 19, 2015.

143. Sickey interviews, July 28 and August 12, 2015.

144. "Chairman's Report," *Coushatta Smoke Signal* 1:3, February 28, 1977, 2, CTA.

145. Literal translation of *Konnaathiihilkaak Kolkafihliichito*: "The language of keeping our people strong."

146. For more on the development and symbolism of the Coushatta tribal seal, see Bates, "What's in a Seal?" and "Symbolism of the Coushatta Tribal Seal and Heritage Logo," Coushatta Tribe of Louisiana website, http://koasatiheritage.org /blog/2013/sep/03/symbolism-coushatta-tribal-seal-and-heritage-logo/. The

emblem's color scheme has also been attributed to the four seasons to emphasize the Coushattas' identity as a woodlands people whose traditions were rooted in agriculture. Sickey interview, August 26, 2015. The emblem was created by an artist who worked for the Bibb Company, a textile manufacturer that included Coushatta basket designs as part of their "First Americans Collection" for home fashions from 1973 to 1974. The designs appeared on bedspreads, draperies, blankets, and sheets and were featured in major department stores, such as Sears, Roebuck, and Company. As a follow-up, the Bibb Company commissioned the creation of tribal seals for tribes that offered designs to the collection. See Paul McClung, "Kiowas to Benefit from Sale of Items," *Lawton (OK) Constitution*, November 3, 1974, 20; letters, William Byler to James H. Byler (Bibb Company), October 25, 1973; Byler to Sickey, December 10, 1973; Stephen W. Tabasko (Bibb Company) to Ernest Sickey, April 15, 1977, folder 4, box 245, AAIA.

147. Carrier interview, November 17, 2015.

148. Sickey interview, June 3, 2015.

149. Sickey interviews, June 24, September 2, and November 17, 2015; Paul interview, November 19, 2015. Carolyn Moffett wrote that Coushattas were "traditionally known as 'good neighbors,'" in "Ancient Art of Basketry Coushatta Handicraft Favorite," *Lake Charles American Press*, August 16, 1972, 9; ITC Board of Directors Meeting Minutes, August 5, 1978, ITC; "Kinder Knights," *Alexandria Town Talk*, August 5, 1970, 11.

150. Sickey interview, June 24, 2015.

151. Michelle Krebs, "Choctaw and the Auto Industry: Chief Martin—the Indians' Lee Iacocca," *Automotive News*, December 26, 1985, 20. For more on the economic development of the Mississippi Choctaws, see Martin, *Chief*; Dement, *Mississippi Entrepreneurs*, 94–97; McKee and Murray, "Economic Progress," 122–36; Ferrara, *Choctaw Revolution*.

152. Sickey interview, November 19, 2015; Dunnehoo interview, November 16, 2015.

153. Sickey interview, November 19, 2015; letter, Sickey to Byler, August 12, 1976, folder 5, box 245, AAIA.

154. Donna Pierite, interview with author, February 8, 2016.

155. Anna Neal, interview with author, February 23, 2016.

156. Sickey interviews, April 6 and November 19, 2015.

157. "Inter-Tribal Council of Louisiana," 1979, LSA.

158. Larry Burgess, quoted from ITC Board of Directors Meeting Report, November 17, 1979, ITC.

159. In addition to the five tribes served by the ITC (the Coushattas, Chitimachas, Jena Band of Choctaws, United Houma Nation (state recognized) and Tunica Biloxis), at the publication of this book there are nine other organized, state-recognized tribes in Louisiana. These include the Addai Caddo Tribe, the Biloxi-Chitimacha

Confederation of Muskogee, the Choctaw-Apache Community of Ebarb, the Clifton Choctaw, the Four Winds Tribe Louisiana Cherokee Confederacy, the Grand Caillou / Dulac Band, the Isle de Jean Charles Band, the Louisiana Choctaw Tribe, and the Pointe-Au-Chien Indian Tribe. National Conference of State Legislators, "Federal and State Recognized Tribes," http://www.ncsl.org/research /state-tribal-institute/list-of-federal-and-state-recognized-tribes.aspx#State.

160. "La. Indian Women Form Task Force," *Alexandria Town Talk*, February 26, 1978, 37; ITC Board of Directors Meeting Minutes, June 11, 1977, ITC.

161. Helen Gindrat to Jodi Cohen, November 8, 1982, LSA.

162. William P. Kellogg was the last Republican governor from 1873 to 1877.

163. "Aide Says Money Lacking to Empower Indian Panel," *Baton Rouge Morning Advocate*, December 16, 1980, n.p.; Operations Committee Meeting Minutes, ITC, January 21, 1978, ITC; Daniel Lombardo, meeting transcription, Clifton LA, August 22, 1981; Nelson Clay, meeting transcript, DUCA Office, Baton Rouge, September 24, 1981; Executive Director's Report, Governor's Commission on Indian Affairs, December 7, 1983, LSA.

164. The earliest block grants were enacted by a Democratic Congress during the Johnson administration in the 1960s as a way of combining a few targeted programs and comprising less than 1 percent of all federal aid to state and local governments. The surge in use of block grants was associated with Republican administrations, first with Nixon's failed proposal of consolidating 129 different programs into six grants and then with Congress's creation of three large new block grants—the Community Development Block Grant, the Social Services Block Grant, and the Comprehensive Employer and Training Act Program—by the end of the Ford administration. While the block grants of the 1970s actually provided additional money along with the reformulation of the funding structure, the continued use of the block grant system under the Reagan administration reversed this trend. See Urban Institute, "Block Grants: Historical Overview and Lessons Learned," http://www.urban.org/url.cfm?ID=310991; Conlan, "Back in Vogue."

165. Governor's Commission on Indian Affairs Board of Commissioners Meeting Minutes, December 29, 1983, LSA.

166. Letter, Ernest Sickey to Helen Gindrat, September 1, 1981, LSA; ITC Meeting Minutes, February 18 and March 15, 1983, ITC.

167. Report, Tribal Chairman Meeting of All Tribes in Louisiana, April 11, 1981, LSA.

168. The Undersigned Sovereign American Indian Tribal Governments of Louisiana, "Building Bridges: Old Problems—Present Issues, Tribal Governments/Louisiana State Government," position paper, May 31, 1981, LSA.

169. LOIA, Proposal for Emergency Food and Shelter Program, July 13, 1983; letter, Jane R. Steele (Louisiana DUCA) to Helen Gindrat (LOIA), September 1, 1983, LSA; DUCA Report on the Coushatta Tribe, September 23, 1983, CTA.

170. Letter, Ernest Sickey to Senator John Saunders, September 2, 1982, CTA; Bertrand interview, November 17, 2015.

171. Letter, Ernest Sickey to Governor Dave Treen, July 8, 1982, CTA; Coushatta Tribe, Resolution No. 83-9, Economic Development, September 2, 1982; letter, Ernest Sickey to Clyde Jackson (LOIA), September 14, 1983; Darrell Williamson (Office of Public Works) to Kenneth A. Beoubay (special assistant to governor), October 5, 1982, LSA; Bob Odom (Louisiana Department of Agriculture) to Ernest Sickey, August 20, 1981, LSA; Coushatta Tribe, Resolution No. 82-14, Business Management, January 26, 1982, and Coushatta Tribe, Resolution No. 82-17, Agriculture, January 26, 1982, CTA. The agricultural development programs didn't begin until 1986, with the new aquaculture program beginning in 1989 in which tribal members started working their own rice fields and crawfish farms. Other economic development ventures that came to fruition in the late 1980s included a new retail development that was completed adjacent to the administration building (1987), which was expanded to include a gift shop and restaurant (1991). In 1992 the tribe purchased eighty additional acres of land for cattle production and began the process of building a gaming and resort complex on tribal land along U.S. 165 north of Kinder. Grand Casino Coushatta opened in 1995. See Coushatta Tribe, *Red Shoes' People*, n.p.

172. The opening of the Seminole bingo hall in 1979 was a watershed moment that tested the parameters of tribal sovereignty when the county sheriff threatened to shut the operation down. The tribe fought back and won an injunction from a federal judge who allowing the continuation of their operation. The Coushattas experienced a similar response when their bingo hall was raided by local law enforcement, resulting in a lawsuit that the tribe won, reaffirming the outcome of the Seminole case. *Langley v. Ryder*, 602 F. Supp. 335 (W.D. La. 1985); *Langley v. Ryder*, 778 F. Supp. 1092 (W.D. La. 1985); Bertney Langley interview, April 4, 2016; Precht, "Nine from the Pines"; "Problems Raised by Indians' Arrest," *Baton Rouge Morning Advocate*, November 26, 1984, 2B.

173. Clark Sickey, interview with author, November 17, 2015.

174. David Sickey interview, November 17, 2015.

175. Sickey, "A Reflection on a Lifetime of Leadership," 171.

EPILOGUE

1. Langley v. Ryder, 602 F. Supp. 335 (W.D. La. 1985); Langley v. Ryder, 778 F. Supp. 1092 (W.D. La. 1985).

BIBLIOGRAPHY

ARCHIVAL SOURCES

Allen Parish Clerk of Court, Oberlin, Louisiana.

American Civil Liberties Union Records. Seeley G. Mudd Manuscript Library, Princeton University, Princeton, New Jersey.

Association on American Indian Affairs (AAIA) Records. Seeley G. Mudd Manuscript Library, Princeton University, Princeton, New Jersey.

William A. Brophy Papers. Harry S. Truman Presidential Library, Independence, Missouri.

Bureau of Indian Affairs Records, U.S. Department of the Interior, Central Classified Files, 1907–39, Record Group 75. National Archives and Records Administration, Washington DC.

Bureau of Indian Affairs Records, U.S. Department of the Interior, Cherokee Field Office Records, 1968–83, Records of the Indian Arts and Crafts Board, Record Group 435. National Archives at Atlanta, Morrow, Georgia.

Bureau of Land Management, U.S. Department of the Interior, General Land Office Records Database. https://www.blm.gov/services/land-records.

William Byler Papers. MC201, Box 16, Folder 1 (Coushattas, 1911–73). Seeley G. Mudd Manuscript Library, Princeton University, Princeton, New Jersey.

Coushatta Tribal Archives. Coushatta Tribe of Louisiana Heritage Department. Elton, Louisiana.

John V. Dowdy Sr. Papers. Baylor Collections of Political Materials, Waco, Texas.

Fondren Library, Southern Methodist University, Dallas, Texas.

James Gaither Collection. Lyndon Baines Johnson Presidential Library, Austin, Texas.

Patrick Jay Hurley Papers. Choctaw Manuscript Collections, University of Oklahoma Libraries Western History Collections, Norman, Oklahoma.

Inter-Tribal Council of Louisiana Records, Houma, Louisiana.

Joe Jennings Bureau of Indian Affairs Records. Archives of Appalachia, East Tennessee State University, Johnson City.

Louisiana State Archives, Indian Affairs, Governor's Commission. Accession no. P95-72, 19202-1-P, Baton Rouge.

Maude Reid Collection. Scrapbook 4, Ser. 1 (on loan from the Calcasieu Parish Public Library). Archives and Special Collections Department, Frazar Memorial Library, McNeese State University, Lake Charles, Louisiana.

Sickey Family Papers, Iowa and Elton, Louisiana.

Ashbel Smith Papers. Dolph Biscoe Center for American History, University of Texas, Austin.

James Ludwell Davis Sylestine Papers. Archives and Information Services Division, Texas State Library and Archives Commission, Austin.

U.S. Federal Census Database. 1880 (Hickory Flat, Calcasieu Parish, Louisiana); 1910 (Police Jury Ward 1, Calcasieu, Louisiana); 1920 (Police Jury Ward 2, Allen Parish, Louisiana); 1920 (Justice Precinct 5, Polk, Texas); 1930 (Police Jury Ward 2, Allen Parish, Louisiana); 1940 (Allen Parish, Louisiana). Access source: Ancestry.com.

U.S. Grave Index, 1600s–current. Access source: Ancestry.com.

U.S. Indian Census Rolls. Parsons and Abbott Roll, 1832 Creek Census, Cussetaw Town; Choctaw Rolls from Union Agency, 1885. Access source: Ancestry.com.

U.S. National Archives and Records Administration, World War II Army Enlistment Records, Group 64. National Archives at College Park, College Park, Maryland.

U.S. Social Security Applications and Claims Index, 1936–2007. Access source: Ancestry.com.

United States, World War I Draft Registration Cards, 1917–18. Access source: Ancestry.com.

Richard Yarborough Collection (RYC), 1849–1986. Dolph Briscoe Center for American History, University of Texas, Austin.

PUBLISHED SOURCES

Adair, James. *History of the American Indians*. 1775. Reprint, Johnson City TN: Watauga Press, 1930.

Adams, Mikaëla M. *Who Belongs? Race, Resources, and Tribal Citizenship in the Native South*. New York: Oxford University Press, 2016.

Allured, Janet. *Remapping Second-Wave Feminism: The Long Women's Rights Movement in Louisiana, 1950–1997*. Athens: University of Georgia Press, 2016.

Allured, Janet, and Michael S. Martin, eds. *Louisiana Legacies: Readings in the History of the Pelican State*. Malden MA: Wiley-Blackwell, 2013.

Ayers, Edward L. *The Promise of the New South: Life after Reconstruction*. New York: Oxford University Press, 1992.

Badger, Anthony J. "'When I Took the Oath of Office, I Took No Vow of Poverty': Race, Corruption, and Democracy in Louisiana, 1928–2000." In *Louisiana Legacies: Readings in the History of the Pelican State*, edited by Janet Allured and Michael S. Martin, 235–36. Malden MA: Wiley-Blackwell, 2013.

Banner, Stuart. *How the Indians Lost Their Land: Law and Power on the Frontier*. Cambridge: Belknap Press of Harvard University Press, 2005.

Bartl, Renate F. "The Importance of the 'Indian Church' for Native American Survival in the Eastern United States." *Journal of the Swedish Americanist Society* 8:2 (2000): 37–53.

Bartram, William. *Travels, and Other Writings*. Vol. 84. New York: Library of America, 1996.

Bates, Denise E. *The Other Movement: Indian Rights and Civil Rights in the Deep South*. Tuscaloosa: University Press of Alabama, 2012.

——. "Reshaping Southern Identity and Politics: Indian Activism during the Civil Rights Era." *Native South* 9 (2016): 125–51.

——. "What's in a Seal? How a Fish Came to Represent the Coushatta Tribe of Louisiana." *Southern Cultures* (Fall 2017): 128–33.

Battise, Doris Robinson Celestine, and Jamison "Jimmy" Poncho. "How We Survived Long Ago." In *A Listening Wind: Native Literature from the Southeast*, edited by Marcia Haag, 275–80. Lincoln: University of Nebraska Press, 2016.

Beard-Moose, Christina Taylor. *Public Indians, Private Cherokees: Tourism and Tradition on Tribal Grounds*. Tuscaloosa: University of Alabama Press, 2009.

Bee, Robert L. "Riding the Paper Tiger." In *State and Reservation: New Perspectives on Federal Indian Policy*, edited by George Pierre Castile and Robert L. Bee, 139–64. Tucson: University of Arizona Press, 1992.

Berkhofer, Robert F., Jr. *The White Man's Indian: Images of the American Indian from Columbus to the Present*. New York: Vintage Books, 1978.

Bernard, Shane K. *The Cajuns: Americanization of a People*. Jackson: University Press of Mississippi, 2003.

Blake, Della Bel. "Bel Oil Corporation: A Five Generation Experience." Thesis, University of Texas, Austin, 1981.

Blu, Karen I. *The Lumbee Problem: The Making of an American Indian People*. Lincoln: University of Nebraska Press, 1980.

Bonney, Rachel A., and J. Anthony Paredes, eds. *Anthropologists and Indians in the New South*. Tuscaloosa: University of Alabama Press, 2001.

Bounds, John H. "The Alabama-Coushatta Indians of Texas." *Journal of Geography* 70 (March 1971): 175–82.

Brasseaux, Carl A. *Acadian to Cajun: Transformation of a People, 1803–1877*. Jackson: University Press of Mississippi, 1992.

Brescia, William, ed. *Choctaw Tribal Government: A New Era*. Philadelphia MS: Choctaw Heritage Press, 1982.

Brightman, Robert A. "Chitimacha." In *Handbook of North American Indians, Southeast*, edited by William C. Sturtevant and Raymond D. Fogelson, 14:642–52. Washington DC: Smithsonian Institution, 2004.

Brinkley, Alan. *Voices of Protest: Huey Long, Father Coughlin, and the Great Depression.* New York: Vintage Books, 1982.

Britten, Thomas A. *The National Council on Indian Opportunity: Quiet Champion of Self-Determination.* Albuquerque: University of New Mexico Press, 2014.

Bruyneel, Kevin. *The Third Space of Sovereignty: The Postcolonial Politics of U.S.-Indigenous Relations.* Minneapolis: University of Minnesota Press, 2007.

Cahill, Cathleen D. "Making and Marketing Baskets in California." In *The Women's National Indian Association: A History,* edited by Valerie Sherer Mathes, 126–49. Albuquerque: University of New Mexico Press, 2015.

Cajete, Gregory A. "Indigenous Education and the Development of Indigenous Community Leaders." *Leadership* 12:3 (2016, reprint): 364–76.

Calliou, Brian. "The Culture of Leadership: North American Indigenous Leadership in a Changing Economy." In *Indigenous Peoples and the Modern State,* edited by Duane Champagne, Karen Jo Torjesen, and Susan Steiner, 47–68. Walnut Creek CA: Altamira Press, 2005.

Chang, David A. *The Color of the Land: Race, Nation, and the Politics of Landownership in Oklahoma, 1832–1929.* Chapel Hill: University of North Carolina, 2010.

Clarkin, Thomas. *Federal Indian Policy in the Kennedy and Johnson Administrations, 1961–1969.* Albuquerque: University of New Mexico Press, 2014.

Clifton, James. *The Prairie People: Continuity and Change in Potawatomi Indian Culture, 1665–1965.* Lawrence: Regents Press of Kansas, 1977.

Clover, Darlene E. "In Case of Emergency, Break Convention: Popular Education, Cultural Leadership, and Public Museums." In *Grassroots Leadership and the Arts for Social Change,* edited by Susan J. Erenrich and Jon F. Wergin, 299–313. Bingley, UK: Emerald Publishing, 2017.

Cobb, Daniel M.

——. *Native Activism in Cold War America: The Struggle for Sovereignty.* Lawrence: University Press of Kansas, 2008.

——. "Philosophy of an Indian War: Indian Community Action in the Johnson Administration's War on Indian Poverty, 1964–1968." *American Indian Culture and Research Journal* 22:2 (1998): 71–103.

——, ed. *Say We Are Nations: Documents of Politics and Protest in Indigenous America since 1887.* Chapel Hill: University of North Carolina Press, 2015.

——. "'Us Indians Understand the Basics': Oklahoma Indians and the Politics of Community Action, 1964–1970." *Western Historical Quarterly* 33 (Spring 2002): 41–66.

Cobb Daniel M., and Loretta Fowler, eds. *Beyond Red Power: American Indian Politics and Activism since 1900.* Santa Fe NM: School for Advanced Research Global Indigenous Politics Book, 2007.

Coleman, Arica L. *That the Blood Stay Pure: African American, Native Americans, and the Predicament of Race and Identity in Virginia.* Bloomington: Indiana University Press, 2013.

Conlan, Timothy J. "Back in Vogue: The Politics of Block Grant Legislation." *Intergovernmental Perspective* 7:3 (Spring 1981): 8–15.

Cook, Samuel R. *Monacans and Miners: Native American and Coal Mining Communities in Appalachia.* Lincoln: University of Nebraska Press, 2000.

Cornell, Stephen. *The Return of the Native: American Indian Political Resurgence.* New York: Oxford University Press, 1988.

Cornell, Stephen, and Joseph P. Kalt. "Two Approaches to the Development of Nation Nations: One Works, the Other Doesn't." In *Rebuilding Native Nations: Strategies for Governance and Development,* edited by Miriam Jorgensen, 3–33. Tucson: University of Arizona Press, 2007.

Coushatta Tribe of Louisiana. *Red Shoes' People: 25 Years of Sovereignty.* Elton: Coushatta Tribe of Louisiana, 1999.

——. "The Struggle Has Made Us Stronger." Elton: Coushatta Tribe of Louisiana, 1977.

Crediford, Gene J. *Contemporary Native Americans in South Carolina: A Photo Documentation Covering the Years 1983–1985.* Columbia: Department of Media Arts, College of Applied Professional Sciences, University of South Carolina, 1985.

Davis, Edwin Adams. *Louisiana: A Narrative History.* 2nd ed. Baton Rouge: Claitor's Book Store, 1965.

Day, John Kyle. "Progressives and Conservatives? Louisiana's Bifactional Politics and Massive Resistance." In *Louisiana beyond Black and White: New Interpretations of Twentieth-Century Race and Race Relations,* edited by Michael S. Martin, 57–84. Lafayette: University of Louisiana at Lafayette Press, 2011.

Debo, Angie. *And Still the Waters Run: The Betrayal of the Five Civilized Tribes.* 1940. Reprint, Princeton NJ: Princeton University Press, 1991.

——. *The Road to Disappearance.* Norman: University of Oklahoma Press, 1941.

De Caro, F. A., and R. A. Jordan. *Louisiana Traditional Crafts.* Baton Rouge: Louisiana State University Press, 1980.

De Jong, Greta. *A Different Day: African American Struggles for Justice in Rural Louisiana, 1900–1970.* Chapel Hill: University of North Carolina Press, 2002.

Deloria, Philip J. *Playing Indian.* New Haven CT: Yale University Press, 1998.

Deloria, Philip S. "The Era of Indian Self-Determination: An Overview." In *Indian Self-Rule: First-Hand Accounts of Indian-White Relations from Roosevelt to Reagan,* edited by Kenneth R. Philip, 191–207. Logan: Utah State University Press, 1995.

Deloria, Vine, Jr., and Clifford M. Lytle. *American Indians, American Justice.* Austin: University of Texas Press, 1983.

Dement, Polly. *Mississippi Entrepreneurs.* Canada: Cat Island Books, 2014.

De Montigny, Stephanie May. "Chiefs, Churches, and 'Old Industries': Photographic Representations of Alabama-Coushatta and Coushatta Culture and Identity." *American Indian Culture and Research Journal* 32:4 (2008): 1–40.

Dodd, William J. *Peapatch Politics: The Earl Long Era in Louisiana Politics*. Baton Rouge: Claitor's Publishing, 1991.

Dominguez, Virginia R. *White by Definition: Social Classification in Creole Louisiana*. New Brunswick NJ: Rutgers University Press, 1986.

Drechsel, Emanuel. "Mobilian Jargon: Linguistic, Sociocultural, and Historical Aspects of an American Indian *Lingua Franca*." PhD diss., University of Wisconsin, Madison, 1979.

———. "Speaking 'Indian' in Louisiana: Linguists Trace the Remnants of a Native American Pidgin." *Natural History* 9 (1986): 4–13.

Ethridge, Robbie. *Creek Country: The Creek Indians and Their World*. Chapel Hill: University of North Carolina Press, 2003.

Evans, Laura E. *Power from Powerlessness: Tribal Governments, Institutional Niches, and American Federalism*. New York: Oxford University Press, 2011.

Evans, Michelle, and Amanda Sinclair. "Containing, Contesting, Creating Spaces: Leadership and Cultural Identity Work among Australian Indigenous Arts Leaders." *Leadership* 12:3 (2016): 270–92.

Fabre, Geneviève, and Robert O'Meally, eds. *History and Memory in African-American Culture*. New York: Oxford University Press, 1994.

Fairclough, Adam. *Race and Democracy: The Civil Rights Struggle in Louisiana, 1915–1972*. Athens: University of Georgia Press, 1995.

Ferrara, Peter J. *The Choctaw Revolution: Lessons for Federal Indian Policy*. Washington DC: Americans for Tax Reform Foundation, 1998.

Finger, John R. *Cherokee Americans: The Eastern Band of Cherokees in the Twentieth Century*. Lincoln: University of Nebraska Press, 1991.

Fixico, Donald. *Termination and Relocation: Federal Indian Policy, 1945–1960*. Albuquerque: University of New Mexico Press, 1986.

Flores, Dan L. "The John Maley Journal: Travels and Adventures in the American Southwest, 1810–1813." Master's thesis, Northwestern State University, 1972.

———. "The Red Branch of the Alabama-Coushatta Indians: An Ethnohistory." *Southern Studies* 16 (Spring 1977): 55–72.

Foner, Eric. *Reconstruction: America's Unfinished Revolution, 1863–1877*. New York: Harper & Row, 1988.

Forbes, Jack D. "Intellectual Self-Determination and Sovereignty: Implications for Native Studies and for Native Intellectuals." *Wicazo Sa Review* 13:1 (Spring 1998): 11–23.

Fox, Vivian. *The Winding Trail: The Alabama-Coushatta Indians of Texas*. Austin TX: Eakin Press, 1983.

Frank, Andrew K., and Kristofer Ray. Guest editors' intro. "Indians as Southerners; Southerners as Indians: Rethinking the History of a Region." *Native South* 10 (2017): vii–xiv.

Frazell, W. D. "North Elton Field, Allen Parish, Louisiana." *Typical Oil and Gas Fields of Southwest Louisiana* 2 (1970): 22.

Gelo, Daniel J., and Tammy J. Morales. "The Alabama-Coushatta Indians: An Annotated Bibliography." *East Texas Historical Journal* 33:2 (1995): 35–63.

Getches, David H., Charles F. Wilkinson, and Robert A. Williams Jr. *Cases and Materials on Federal Indian Law.* 4th ed. St. Paul MN: West Publishing Co., 1998.

Giovo, Jack, I. Bruce Turner, and Linda Parker Langley. *Jefferson Davis Parish: An Oral History.* Jennings: Jefferson Davis Arts Council, Louisiana Endowment for the Humanities, 2000.

Gipp, Gerald E., Linda Sue Warner, Janine Pease, and James Shanley, eds. *American Indian Stories of Success: New Visions of Leadership in Indian Country.* Santa Barbara CA: Praeger, 2015.

Gordon, Matthew, Jack B. Martin, and Linda Langley. "Some Phonetic Structures of Koasati." *International Journal of American Linguistics* 81:1 (January 2015): 83–118.

Greenbaum, Susan. "What's in a Label? Identity Problems of Southern Indian Tribes." *Journal of Ethnic Studies* 19:2 (July 1991): 107–26.

Gregory, Hiram F. "The Louisiana Tribes: Entering Hard Times." In *Indians of the Southeastern United States in the Late 20th Century*, edited by J. Anthony Paredes, 162–82. Tuscaloosa: University Press of Alabama, 1992.

Gulf Research Institute. *American Indians of Louisiana: An Assessment of Needs.* Baton Rouge: Gulf South Research, 1973.

Haas, Mary R. "Men's and Women's Speech in Koasati." *Language* 20 (1944): 142–49.

Haggard, Villasana J. "The Neutral Ground between Louisiana and Texas, 1806–1821." *Louisiana Historical Quarterly* 28 (October 1945): 1001–1128.

Hahn, Steven C. *The Invention of the Creek Nation, 1670–1763.* Lincoln: University of Nebraska Press, 2014.

Hall, Jacquelyn Dowd. "The Long Civil Rights Movement and the Political Uses of the Past." *Journal of American History* (March 2005): 1233–63.

Harrington, Mark Raymond. "Among the Louisiana Indians." *Southern Workman* 37:12 (1908): 656–61.

Hartman, George B. "The Calcasieu Pine District of Louisiana." *Ames Forester* 10:13 (1922): 53–68.

Harvison, C. Renée, and Maida Owens. "Bel Abbey: Koasati Stories: Elton, Jefferson Davis Parish." In *Swapping Stories: Folktales from Louisiana*, edited by Carl Lindahl, Maida Owens, and C. Renée Harvison, 80–104. Jackson: University of Press of Mississippi, 1997.

Hasselbacher, Stephanie. "Koasati and 'All the Olden Talk': Ideologies of Linguistic Conservatism and the Mediation of Linguistic Authority." *Native South* 8 (2015): 31–62.

Hauptman, Laurence M., and Jack Campisi. "Eastern Indian Communities Strive for Recognition." In *Major Problems in American Indian History*, edited by Albert L. Hurtado and Peter Iverson, 461–71. 2nd ed. Boston: Houghton Mifflin, 2000.

Haynes, Joshua S. "Constructing Authenticity: The Indian Arts and Crafts Board and the Eastern Band of Cherokees, 1935–1985." *Native South* 3 (2010): 1–38.

Hill, Sarah H. "Marketing Traditions: Cherokee Basketry and Tourism Economics." In *Selling the Indian: Commercializing and Approaching American Indian Cultures*, edited by Carter Jones Meyer and Diana Royer, 212–35. Tucson: University of Arizona Press, 2001.

——. *Weaving New Worlds: Southeastern Cherokee Women and Their Basketry*. Chapel Hill: University of North Carolina Press, 1997.

Holland, Wilbur C., et al. "Geology of Beauregard and Allen Parishes." *Geology Bulletin: Louisiana Geological Survey*, no. 27 (May 1952): 15.

Hook, Jonathan B. *The Alabama-Coushatta Indians*. College Station: Texas A&M University Press, 1997.

Hoxie, Frederick E. *A Final Promise: The Campaign to Assimilate the Indians, 1880–1920*. Lincoln: University of Nebraska Press, 1984.

Hudson, Charles. *The Southeastern Indians*. Knoxville: University of Tennessee Press, 1976.

Hunter, Donald G. "The Settlement Pattern and Toponymy of the Koasati Indians of Bayou Blue." *Florida Anthropologist* 26:2 (June 1973): 79–88.

Hutchinson, Elizabeth. *The Indian Craze: Primitivism, Modernism, and Transculturation in American Art, 1890–1915*. Durham NC: Duke University Press, 2009.

Inger, Morton. "The New Orleans School Crisis of 1960." In *Southern Businessmen and Desegregation*, edited by Elizabeth Jacoway and David R. Colburn, 82–97. Baton Rouge: Louisiana State University Press, 1982.

Jacobson, Daniel. "The Alabama-Coushatta Indians." In *(Creek) Indians Alabama-Coushatta: Ethnological Report and Statement of Testimony*, edited by David Agee Horr, n.p. New York: Garland Publishing, 1974.

——. "Ethnological Report and Statement of Testimony" (Docket No. 226). Indian Claims Commission, The Alabama-Coushatta Indians of Texas and Coushatta Indians of Louisiana, 1972.

——. *Great Indian Tribes*. N.p.: Hammond, 1970.

——. "Koasati Cultural Change." PhD diss., Louisiana State University, 1954.

——. "The Origin of the Koasati Community of Louisiana," *Ethnohistory* 7:2 (Spring 1960): 97–120.

Johnson, Bobby H. *The Coushatta People*. Phoenix: Indian Tribal Series, 1976.

Johnson, Kathryn S., and Paul Leeds. *Patteran: The Life and Works of Paul Leeds*. San Antonio: Naylor Co., 1964.

Johnson, Susan, Jeanne Kaufmann, John Dossett, and Sarah Hicks. *Government to Government: Understanding State and Tribal Governments*. Washington DC: National Conference of State Legislators, 2000.

Jojola, Ted. "Notes on Identity, Time, Space, and Place." In *American Indian Thought*, edited by Anne Waters, 87–96. Malden MA: Blackwell Publishing, 2004.

Jolivette, Andrew J. *Louisiana Creoles: Cultural Recovery and Mixed-Race Native American Identity*. Lanham MD: Lexington Books, 2007.

Josephy, Alvin M., Jr., Joane Nagel, and Troy Johnson, eds. *The American Indians' Fight for Freedom: Red Power*. 2nd ed. Lincoln: University of Nebraska Press, 1999.

Jurney, David. "Diaspora of the Alabama-Coushatta Indians across Southeastern North America." PhD diss., Southern Methodist University, 2001.

Kalt, Joseph P. "The Role of Constitutions in Native Nation Building: Laying a Firm Foundation." In *Rebuilding Native Nations: Strategies for Governance and Development*, edited by Miriam Jorgensen, 78–114. Tucson: University of Arizona Press, 2007.

Kein, Sybil, ed. *Creole: The History and Legacy of Louisiana's Free People of Color*. Baton Rouge: Louisiana State University Press, 2000.

Kenny, Carolyn, and Tina Ngaroimata Fraser, eds. *Living Indigenous Leadership: Native Narratives on Building Strong Communities*. Vancouver: University of British Columbia Press, 2012.

Kersey, Harry A., Jr. *An Assumption of Sovereignty: Social and Political Transformation among the Florida Seminoles, 1953–1979*. Lincoln: University of Nebraska Press, 1996.

Key, V. O., Jr. *Southern Politics in State and Nation*. 1949. Reprint, Knoxville: University of Tennessee Press, 1984.

Kidwell, Clara Sue. *Choctaws and Missionaries in Mississippi, 1818–1918*. Norman: University of Oklahoma Press, 1995.

Kievit, Joyce Ann, ed. "A Discussion of Scholarly Responsivities to Indigenous Communities." *American Indian Quarterly* 27:1–2 (Winter–Spring 2003): 3–45.

Kimball, Geoffrey D. *Koasati Dictionary*. Lincoln: University Press of Nebraska, 1994.

——— . *Koasati Grammar*. Lincoln: University Press of Nebraska, 1990.

——— . *Koasati Traditional Narratives*. Lincoln: University Press of Nebraska, 2010.

Klopotek, Brian. "Indian Education under Jim Crow." In *Indian Subjects: Hemispheric Perspectives on the History of Indigenous Education*, edited by Brenda J. Child and Brian Klopotek, 48–72. Santa Fe NM: School for Advanced Research Press, 2014.

——— . *Recognition Odysseys: Indigeneity, Race, and Federal Tribal Recognition Policy in Three Louisiana Indian Communities*. Durham NC: Duke University Press, 2011.

Kniffen, Fred B. *The Indians of Louisiana*. 1945. Reprint, Gretna LA: Pelican Publishing, 1998.

Kniffen, Fred B., Hiram F. Gregory, and George A. Stokes. *The Historic Indian Tribes of Louisiana: From 1542 to the Present*. Baton Rouge: Louisiana State University Press, 1987.

Langley, Linda. "Koasati (Coushatta) Literature." In *A Listening Wind: Native Literature from the Southeast*, edited by Marcia Haag, 263–68. Lincoln: University of Nebraska Press, 2016.

———. "The Tribal Identity of Alexander McGillivray: A Review of the Historical and Ethnographic Data." *Louisiana History* 46:2 (Spring 2005): 231–39.

Langley, Linda, Susan G. LeJeune, and Claude Oubre, eds. *Les Artistes: Crafters Tell Their Tales*. Folklife Series 2. Eunice: Louisiana State University, 1996.

Langley, Linda, Claude Oubre, and Jay Precht. "Louisa Williams Robinson, Her Daughters, and Her Granddaughters (1855–1932): Recognizing the Contributions of Three Generations of Coushatta Women in Louisiana." In *Louisiana Women: Their Lives and Times*, edited by Janet Allured and Judith F. Gentry, 155–74. Athens: University of Georgia Press, 2009.

Lanza, Michael L. *Agrarianism and Reconstruction Politics: The Southern Homestead Act*. Baton Rouge: Louisiana State University Press, 1990.

Leeds, Paul. *St. Luke's Congregational Church on West Side of Bayou Blue (1913–1921)*. Reprinted by the Allen Parish Genealogical and Historical Society, 2005.

———. *St. Peter's Congregational Church Records, Bayou Blue, Elton, Louisiana (1901–1958)*. Reprinted by the Allen Parish Genealogical and Historical Society, 2005.

Leeper, Clare D'Artois. *Louisiana Place Names: Popular, and Forgotten Stories of Towns, Cities, Plantations, Bayous, and Even Some Cemeteries*. Baton Rouge: Louisiana State University Press, 2012.

Levine, Victoria Lindsay. "Arzelie Langley and a Lost Pantribal Tradition." In *Ethnomusicology and Modern Music History*, edited by Stephen Blum, Philip V. Bohlman, and Daniel M. Neuman, 190–97. Urbana: University of Illinois Press, 1991.

Lomawaima, K. Tsianina, and Teresa L. McCarty. *To Remain an Indian: Lessons in Democracy from a Century of Native American Education*. New York: Teachers College Press, 2006.

Louisiana Health and Human Resources Administration. Division of Human Services. *The Elderly Indians of Louisiana and Their Needs*. Report. Baton Rouge: Office of Indian Affairs, December 1, 1975.

Lowery, Malinda Maynor. *Race, Identity, and the Making of a Nation*. Chapel Hill: University of North Carolina Press, 2010.

Lurie, Nancy Oestreich. "The Contemporary Indian Scene." In *North American Indians in Historical Perspective*, edited by Eleanor Burke Leacock and Nancy Oestreich Lurie, 418–80. New York: Random House, 1971.

———. "The Voices of the American Indian: Report on the American Indian Chicago Conference." *Current Anthropology* 2:5 (December 1961): 478–500.

Mann, Robert. *Legacy to Power: Senator Russell Long of Louisiana*. New York: Paragon House, 1992.

Martin, Howard N. *Myths and Folktales of the Alabama-Coushatta Indians of Texas*. Austin TX: Encino Press, 1977.

Martin, Jack. "Implications of Plural Reduplication, Infixation, and Subtraction for Muskogean Subgrouping." *Anthropological Linguistics* 36 (1994): 27–55.

Martin, Phillip. *Chief*. Brandon MS: Quail Ridge Press, 2009.

May, Stephanie A. "Alabama and Koasati." In *Handbook of North American Indians, Southeast*, edited by William C. Sturtevant and Raymond D. Fogelson, 14:407–14. Washington DC: Smithsonian Institution, 2004.

McCool, Daniel, Susan M. Olson, and Jennifer L. Robinson. *Native Vote: American Indians, the Voting Rights Act, and the Right to Vote*. New York: Cambridge University Press, 2007.

McCrocklin, Claude. "The Red River Coushatta Indian Villages of Northwest Louisiana, 1790–1835." *Louisiana Archaeology* 12 (1985): 129–78.

McDonnell, Janet A. *The Dispossession of the American Indian, 1887–1934*. Bloomington: Indiana University Press, 1991.

McKee, Jesse O., and Steve Murray. "Economic Progress and Development of the Choctaw since 1945." In *After Removal: The Choctaw in Mississippi*, edited by Samuel J. Wells and Roseanna Tubby, 122–36. Jackson: University Press of Mississippi, 1986.

McKenzie-Jones, Paul. "'We Are among the Poor, the Powerless, the Inexperienced and the Inarticulate': Clyde Warrior's Campaign for a 'Greater Indian America.'" *American Indian Quarterly* 34:2 (Spring 2010): 224–57.

Mechling, Jay. "Florida Seminoles and the Marketing of the Last Frontier." In *Dressing in Feathers: The Construction of the Indian in American Popular Culture*, edited by S. Elizabeth Bird, 149–66. Boulder CO: Westview Press, 1996.

Merrill, Ellen C. *Germans of Louisiana*. Gretna LA: Pelican Publishing, 2004.

Mihesuah, Devon. "Commonality of Difference: American Indian Women and History." *American Indian Quarterly* 20 (Winter 1996): 15–27.

———, ed. *Natives and Academics: Researching and Writing about American Indians*. Lincoln: University of Nebraska Press, 1998.

Miller, Bruce Granville. *Invisible Indigenes: The Politics of Nonrecognition*. Lincoln: University of Nebraska Press, 2003.

Miller, Mark Edwin. *Claiming Tribal Identity: The Five Tribes and the Politics of Federal Acknowledgment*. Norman: University of Oklahoma Press, 2013.

———. *Forgotten Tribes: Unrecognized Indians and the Federal Acknowledgement Process*. Lincoln: University of Nebraska Press, 2004.

Millet, Donald J. "The Lumber Industry of 'Imperial' Calcasieu, 1985–1900." *Louisiana History* 7:1 (Winter 1966): 51–69.

Mohawk Nation. *Trail of Broken Treaties: B.I.A., I'm Not Your Indian Anymore*. Roos-eveltown NY: Akwesasne Notes, 1973.

Mueller, Timothy, Sarah Sue Goldsmith, and Risa Mueller. *Nations Within: The Four Sovereign Tribes of Louisiana*. Baton Rouge: Louisiana State University Press, 2003.

Mullin, Molly H. *Culture in the Marketplace: Gender, Art, and Value in the American Southwest*. Durham NC: Duke University Press, 2001.

National Conference of State Legislatures (NCSL). "Promoting Effective State-Tribal Relations: A Dialogue." Proceedings of a national issues seminar hosted by NCSL. Denver CO: NCSL, 1989.

Nelson, Lynn. "States' Rights and American Federalism from the New Deal to the Present, 1940–1999." In *States' Rights and American Federalism: A Documentary History*, edited by Frederick D. Drake and Lynn R. Nelson, 174–75. Westport CT: Greenwood Press, 1999.

O'Brien, Greg. "An Interview with Theda Perdue and Michael D. Green." In *The Native South: New Histories and Enduring Legacies*, edited by Tim Alan Garrison and Greg O'Brien, 1–32. Lincoln: University of Nebraska Press, 2017.

O'Brien, Sharon. *American Indian Tribal Governments*. Norman: University of Oklahoma Press, 1989.

Osburn, Katherine M. B. *Choctaw Resurgence in Mississippi: Race, Class, and Nation Building in the Jim Crow South, 1830–1977*. Lincoln: University of Nebraska Press, 2014.

——. "Mississippi Choctaws and Racial Politics." *Southern Cultures* 14:4 (Winter 2008): 32–54.

Paredes, J. Anthony. "The Emergence of Contemporary Eastern Creek Indian Identity." In *Social and Cultural Identity: Problems of Persistence and Change*, edited by Thomas K. Fitzgerald, 68–80. Athens: Southern Anthropological Society Proceedings, no. 8, 1974.

——. "Federal Recognition and the Poarch Creek Indians." In *Indians of the Southeastern United States in the Late 20th Century*, edited by J. Anthony Paredes, 120–39. Tuscaloosa: University of Alabama Press, 1992.

——. "Paradoxes of Modernism and Indianness in the Southeast." *American Indian Quarterly* 19:3 (Summer 1995): 341–60.

Peoples, Morgan D. "Earl Kemp Long: The Man from Pea Patch Farm." *Louisiana History: The Journal of the Louisiana History* 17:4 (Fall 1976): 365–92.

Perdue, Theda. "Indians in Southern History." In *Indians in American History: An Introduction*, edited by Frederick Hoxie and Peter Iverson, 121–39. 2nd ed. Wheeling IL: Harlan Davidson, 1998.

——. "Native Americans, African Americans, and Jim Crow." In *indiVisible: African-Native American Lives in the Americas*, edited by Gabrielle Tayac, 21–33. Washington DC: Smithsonian Institution, Nation Museum of the American Indian, 2009.

Peroff, Nicholas C. *Menominee Drums: Tribal Termination and Restoration, 1954–1974.* Norman: University of Oklahoma Press, 1982.

Peters, Kurt, and Terry Straus, eds. *Visions and Voices: American Indian Activism and the Civil Rights Movement.* New York: Albatross Press, 2009.

Pevar, Stephen L. *The Rights of Indians and Tribes.* 4th ed. New York: Oxford University Press, 2012.

Philp, Kenneth R., ed. *Indian Self-Rule: First Hand Accounts of Indian-White Relations from Roosevelt to Reagan.* Logan: Utah State University Press, 1995.

——. *John Collier's Crusade for Indian Reform, 1920–1954.* Tucson: University of Arizona Press, 1977.

——. *Termination Revisited: American Indians on the Trail to Self-Determination, 1933–1953.* Lincoln: University of Nebraska Press, 1999.

Pope, Christie Farnham. "Southern Homesteads for Negroes." *Agricultural History* 44 (April 1970): 201–12.

Post, Lauren C. *Cajun Sketches: From the Prairies of Southwest Louisiana.* 1962. Reprint, Baton Rouge: Louisiana State University Press, 1990.

——. "The Rice Country of Southwestern Louisiana," *Geographical Review* 30 (1940): 574–90.

Precht, James (Jay) H. "Coushatta Basketry and Identity Politics: The Role of Pine-Needle Baskets in the Federal Rerecognition of the Coushatta Tribe of Louisiana." *Ethnohistory* 62 (2015): 145–67.

——. "Coushatta Homesteading in Southwest Louisiana and the Development of the Community at Bayou Blue." *Journal of Southern History* 84:1 (February 2018): 113–38.

——. "'The Lost Tribe Wanders No More': Indian Gaming and the Emergence of Coushatta Self-Determination." PhD diss., Arizona State University, 2007.

——. "The Nine from the Pines: High-Stakes Bingo and Federal Intervention in Coushatta Tribal Affairs in the 1980s." *Native South* 6 (2013): 142–69.

Prucha, Francis Paul. *The Great Father: The United States Government and the American Indians.* Abridged ed. 1984. Reprint, Lincoln: University of Nebraska Press, 1986.

Purser, Joyce. "The Administration of Indian Affairs in Louisiana, 1803–1820." *Louisiana History* 5:4 (Fall 1964): 401–10.

Raibmon, Paige. "Meaning of Mobility on the Northwest Coast." In *New Histories for Old: Changing Perspectives on Canada's Native Pasts*, edited by Theodore Binnema and Susan Neylan, 175–95. Vancouver: University of British Columbia Press, 2008.

Roth, George. "Federal Tribal Recognition in the South." In *Anthropologists and Indians in the New South*, edited by Rachel A. Bonney and J. Anthony Paredes, 49–70. Tuscaloosa: University of Alabama Press, 2001.

Rothe, Aline. *Kalita's People: A History of the Alabama-Coushatta Indians of Texas.* Waco TX: Texian Press, 1963.

Rowse, Tim. *Rethinking Social Justice: From "Peoples" to "Populations."* Canberra: Aboriginal Studies Press, 2012.

Roy, Ewell P., and Don Leary. "Economic Survey of American Indians in Louisiana." *American Indian Journal* 11 (1977): 11.

Rushing, Dorothy M. "The Promised Land of the Alabama-Coushatta." Master's thesis, East Texas State University, Commerce, 1974.

Ryhner, Jon, and Jeanne Eder. *A History of Indian Education.* Billings: Native American Studies, Montana State University–Billings, 1989.

Sanson, Jerry P. "'What He Did and What He Promised to Do . . .': Huey Long and the Horizons of Louisiana Politics." In *Louisiana Legacies: Reading in the History of the Pelican State,* edited by Janet Allured and Michael S. Martin, 212–19. Malden MA: Wiley-Blackwell, 2013.

Saunt, Claudio. "The Native South: An Account of Recent Historiography." *Native South* 1 (2008): 45–60.

Schulze, Jeffry M. "The Rediscovery of the Tiguas: Federal Recognition and Indianness in the Twentieth Century." *Southwestern Historical Quarterly* 105:1 (2001): 14–39.

Shoemaker, Nancy, ed. *Negotiators of Change: Historical Perspectives on Native American Women.* New York: Routledge, 1995.

Shreve, Bradley G. *Red Power Rising: The National Indian Youth Council and the Origins of Native Activism.* Norman: University of Oklahoma Press, 2011.

Shuck-Hall, Sheri M. "Alabama and Coushatta Diaspora and Coalescence in the Mississippian Shatter Zone." In *Mapping the Mississippian Shatter Zone: The Colonial Indian Slave Trade and Regional Instability in the American South,* edited by Robbie Ethridge and Sheri M. Shuck-Hall, 250–71. Lincoln: University of Nebraska Press, 2009.

——. *Journey to the West: The Alabama and Coushatta Indians.* Norman: University of Oklahoma Press, 2008.

Sibley, John. "Historical Sketches of the Several Indian Tribes in Louisiana, South of the Arkansas River, and between the Mississippi and River Grand." *American State Papers,* Class 2, United States Indian Affairs. New York: Hopkins & Seymour, 1806.

Sickey, Ernest. "A Reflection on a Lifetime of Leadership." In *We Will Always Be Here: Native Peoples on Living and Thriving in the South,* edited by Denise E. Bates, 171–76. Tallahassee: University Press of Florida, 2016.

——. "We Will Forever Remain Coushatta and We Will Always Be Here." In *We Will Always Be Here: Native Peoples on Living and Thriving in the South,* edited by Denise E. Bates, 45–50. Tallahassee: University Press of Florida, 2016.

Sider, Gerald. *Living Indian Histories: Lumbee and Tuscarora People in North Carolina.* Chapel Hill: University of North Carolina Press, 1993.

Smither, Harriet. "The Alabama Indians of Texas." *Southwestern Historical Quarterly* 36:2 (1932): 83–108.

Smith-Ferri, Sherrie. "The Development of the Commercial Market for Pomo Indian Baskets." *Expedition* 40:1 (1998): 15–22.

Snyder, Robert E. "Huey Long and the Presidential Election of 1936." *Louisiana History* 16:2 (Spring 1975): 117–43.

Spicker, Jean R., Halk R. Steiner, and Rupert Walden. *A Survey of Rural Louisiana Indian Communities.* Pamphlet. Baton Rouge: Inter-Tribal Council of Louisiana, 1977.

Stremlau, Rose. *Sustaining the Cherokee Family: Kinship and the Allotment of an Indigenous Nation.* Chapel Hill: University of North Carolina Press, 2011.

Sturm, Circe. "States of Sovereignty: Race Shifting, Recognition, and Rights in Cherokee County." In *Beyond Red Power: American Indian Politics and Activism since 1900,* edited by Daniel M. Cobb and Loretta Fowler, 228–42. Santa Fe NM: School for Advanced Research Press, 2007.

Swanton, John R. "Animal Stories from the Indians of the Muskhogean Stock." *Journal of American Folklore* 26 (1913): 119–218.

——. "Indian Language Studies in Louisiana." *Explorations and Field-Work of the Smithsonian Institution,* 195–200. Washington DC: U.S. Government Printing Office, 1930.

——. *The Indians of the Southeastern United States.* Bureau of American Ethnology, Bulletin 137. 1946. Reprint, Washington DC: Smithsonian Institution Press, 1979.

——. "Myths and Tales of the Southeastern Indians." Bureau of American Ethnology, Bulletin 88, 275. Washington DC: U.S. Government Printing Office, 1929.

——. "Religious Beliefs and Medical Practices of the Creek Indians." *Bureau of American Ethnology, Forty-Second Annual Report,* 473–672. Washington DC: U.S. Government Printing Office, 1928.

Taylor, Graham D. *The New Deal and American Indian Tribalism.* Lincoln: University of Nebraska Press, 1980.

Taylor, Lyda Averill. *Plants Used as Curatives by Certain Southeastern Tribes.* 1940. Reprint, New York: AMS Press, 1978.

Taylor, Melanie Benson. *Reconstructing the Native South: American Indian Literature and the Lost Cause.* Athens: University of Georgia Press, 2011.

Taylor, Theodore W. *The States and Their Indian Citizens.* Washington DC: United States Department of the Interior, 1972.

Theriot, Jason. "Oilfield Battleground: Louisiana's Legacy Lawsuits in Historical Perspective." *Louisiana History* 57:4 (Fall 2016): 403–62.

Tiger, Buffalo, and Harry A. Kersey, Jr. *Buffalo Tiger: A Life in the Everglades.* Lincoln: Bison Books, University of Nebraska Press, 2002.

Trammell, Camilla Davis. *Seven Pines: Its Occupants and Their Letters, 1825–1872.* Houston: Southern Methodist University Press, 1986.

Trepanier, Cecyle. "The Cajunization of French Louisiana: Forging a Regional Identity." *Geographical Journal* 157:2 (July 1991): 161–71.

Trump, Erik. "'The Idea of Help': White Women Reformers and the Commercialization of Native American Women's Arts." In *Selling the Indian: Commercializing and Approaching American Indian Cultures*, edited by Carter Jones Meyer and Diana Royer, 159–89. Tucson: University of Arizona Press, 2001.

Ulrich, Roberta. *American Indian Nations from Termination to Restoration, 1953–2006.* Lincoln: University of Nebraska Press, 2010.

Usner, Daniel H., Jr. *American Indians in the Lower Mississippi Valley: Social and Economic Histories.* Lincoln: University of Nebraska Press, 1998.

——. "From Bayou Teche to Fifth Avenue: Crafting a New Market for Chitimacha Indian Baskets." *Journal of Southern History* 79:2 (May 2013): 339–74.

——. *Indian Work: Language and Livelihood in Native American History.* Cambridge: Harvard University Press, 2009.

——. "'They Don't Like Indians around Here': Chitimacha Struggles and Strategies for Survival in the Jim Crow South." *Native South* 9 (2016): 89–124.

——. *Weaving Alliances with Other Women: Chitimacha Indian Work in the New South.* Athens: University of Georgia Press, 2015.

U.S. Congress. House Committee on Indian Affairs. "Land Claims &c. Under 14th Article Choctaw Treaty," May 11, 1836. H. Rep. 663, 24th Cong., 1st sess. (1836), microfiche 295.

——. House of Representatives, 83d Cong., 2d sess. Report No. 2491, "Providing for the Termination of Federal Supervision over the Property of the Alabama and Coushatta Tribes of Indians of Texas, and the Individual Members Thereof" (July 26, 1954).

——. Senate. Committee on Indian Affairs. 71st Cong., 3d sess. Survey of Conditions of the Indians in the United States: Hearings on S. Res. 79, 308, and 263, pt. 16: March 26, 28, and 31, November 6 and 8, and December 10, 1930 (1931), 7932–41.

——. Senate. Select Committee on Indian Affairs. 95th Cong., 2d sess., on S. 2375 (April 18, 1978).

——. Senate. 21st Cong., 1st sess. *Journal of the Proceedings at the Treaty of Dancing Rabbit Creek.* S. Doc. 512 (1830).

——. Senate. 83d Cong., 2d sess. Report No. 1321, "Termination of Federal Supervision over The Property of the Alabama and Coushatta Indians of Texas" (May 11, 1954).

U.S. Department of the Interior. Office of Indian Affairs. Constitution and By-Laws of the Alabama and Coushatta Tribes of Texas, Approved (August 19, 1938).

——. Bureau of Indian Affairs. *Indians of the Gulf Coast States.* Washington DC: U.S. Government Printing Office, 1968.

Vickery, Lou. *The Rise of the Poarch Band of Creek Indians.* Atmore AL: Upword Press, 2009.

Voyageur, Cora, Laura Brearley, and Brian Calliou, eds. *Restoring Indigenous Leadership: Wise Practices in Community Development.* Banff, Alberta: Banff Centre Press, 2014.

Wickman, Patricia Riles. *Warriors without War: Seminole Leadership in the Late Twentieth Century*. Tuscaloosa: University of Alabama Press, 2012.

Wilkins, David E. *American Indian Politics and the American Political System*. Lanham MD: Rowman & Littlefield, 2002.

——. "Tribal-State Affairs: American States as 'Disclaiming' Sovereigns," In *The Tribes and the States: Geographies of Intergovernmental Interaction*, edited by Brad A. Bays and Erin Hogan Fouberg, 1–28. Lanham MD: Rowman & Littlefield, 2002.

Wilkins, David E., and K. Tsianina Lomawaima. *Uneven Ground: American Indian Sovereignty and Federal Law*. Norman: University of Oklahoma Press, 2001.

Wilkins, Teresa J. *Patterns of Exchange: Navajo Weavers and Traders*. Norman: University of Oklahoma Press, 2008.

Winfrey, Dorman H., and Jack Bryant. *Indian Tribes of Texas*. Waco TX: Texian Press, 1971.

Winfrey, Robert Hill, Jr. "Civil Rights and the American Indian: Through the 1960s." PhD diss., University of Oklahoma, 1986.

Woodward, C. Vann. *The Strange Career of Jim Crow*. 2nd rev. ed. London: Oxford University Press, 1966.

Wunder, John R. "Walter Echo-Hawk: Pawnee." In *The New Warriors: Native American Leaders since 1900*, edited by David Edmunds, 299–321. Lincoln: University of Nebraska Press, 2001.

INDEX

baskets, 104, 110, 124, 161, 173, 174, *176*, 180; buying, 181; designs, 282n146; exhibits of, 69, 178–79, 182; making, 9, 10, 22, *117*, 209, 228n35; pine needle, 8, 18, 175, 176, 179, 276n67; public relations campaigns and, xiv; river cane, 176, 177; selling, 8, 98, 108; swamp cane, 8

Baton Rouge, xiii, 82, 92, 95, 134, 135, 148, 164, 172; meetings in, 127, 146

Baton Rouge City Municipal Building, 163

Battise, Adeline Abbey, *117*, 235n113, 249n46

Battise, Ardeena, 235n113

Battise, Burissa, 25, 233n94

Battise, Doris Robinson Celestine, 8

Battise, Ellisor, 25, 233n94, 239n35

Battise, Faye, 235n113

Battise, Glenna, 235n113

Battise, Jane, 76, 243n82, 250n60

Battise, Janice, 235n113, 258n40

Battise, Lelia, 22, 185–86, 191

Battise, Leonard, 79, 98, 115, 149, 151, 160, 186, 189, 235n113, 280n123

Battise, Reed, 235n113

Battise, Solomon, 18, 25–26, 29, 79, 82, 84, 98, 109, 111, *117*, 149, 151, 157, *175*, 196, 230n59, 235n113; baskets by, 135; election and, 66, 170; electricity and, 247n20; on politics/elections, 90; Sickey and, 115, 116

Battise, Willis Ralph, 235n113

Bayou Blue, xiii, xvii, xxii, 2, 6, 11, 16, 18, 20, 27, 31, 60, 68, 87, 95, 98, 131, 148, 166, 173; Alabamas in, 224n3; community in, 38; Coushattas in, 34–35, 38, 39, 40; farming at, 253n107; IHS and, 127; improvements for, 181; land ownership around, 156; natural

disaster in, 76; residential patterns at, 50; settlement at, xix, xxiii–xxiv, 5, 15, 25, 26, 59, 81, 89, 161, 173, 233n76, 233n79, 234n106; tourism in, 105–13

Bayou Dularge, 229n46

Bayou Grand Caillou, 229n46

Bayou Lafourche, 229n46

Bayou Point aux Chenes (or Chien), 229n46

Bayou Teche, 33

Bayou Terrebonne, 229n46

beadwork, 119, 173, 176

Beatty, Willard W., 51, 52

Beauregard Parish, 2, 86

Bee, Robert L., 133

Bel, Ernest, 242n72

Bel, Floy Moss, 252n95

Bel, John Albert, 5, 50, 131, 242n76, 252n95

Bel, Katherine, 242n76

Bel, Marie, 242n76

Bel Estate, 44, 49, 50, 61, 84, 109, 131, 157, 159, 242n76, 270n124

Bel Lumber Company, 5, 52

Bel Oil Corporation, 5, 87, 93, 121, 125, 131, 167, 242n76, 252n95, 263n23

Bernard, Shane K., 60

Bertrand, A. L., xvii

Bertrand, Odell, 5

Bertrand, Roderick "Rod," 184

BIA. *See* Bureau of Indian Affairs

Bibb Company, 282n146

Bicentennial Project, 172

Billiot, Kevin, 192

Biloxi-Chitimacha Confederation, 282–83n159

Biloxis, 19

Bismarck, Otto Von, 227n17

Blake, Della Bel, 242n76

block grants, 145, 185, 202, 203, 283n164

bloodlines, 14, 83, 152
Blume, Lucille, 181
Boy Scouts, 68, 69, 106, 107, 111, 165
Branch of Acknowledgment and Research (BAR), 139
Brandon, Frank E., 39, 41, 232n76, 240n54
Brandon Report, 41, 239n38, 242n71
Brearley, Laura, 223n46
Breaux, John, 130, 153, 174
Brinkley, Alan, 91
Broemer, Walter W., 173, 251n72
Broken Bow, 230n60
Brown v. Board of Education of Topeka (1954), 90
Bruchhaus, Kenneth, 192, 196
Bruyneel, Kevin, 222n37
Buffalo Tiger, 143, 200, 266n71
Bureau of Catholic and Indian Missions, 120
Bureau of Indian Affairs (BIA), 69, 70, 71, 72, 73, 75, 76, 79, 84, 85–86, 87–88, 90, 99, 100, 127–28, 138, 140, 141, 145, 146, 148, 152, 153, 154, 155, 156, 158, 159, 170, 195; acreage and, 269–70n121; Bicentennial Project of, 172; Coushattas and, 182; decentralization of, 102; funding, 183; Miccosukees and, 143; petition process, 160; presence of, 74; requirements of, 270n121; services, 78, 128, 143; termination and, 77
bureaucracy, xx, 72, 159, 182, 191
Burgess, Larry, 201
Bush, George H. W., 89, 254n115
Byler, Mary Lou, 270n122
Byler, William, 144, 145–46, 270n121; BIA and, 158; Garrison and, 151; Griffin and, 171; Sickey and, 153, 156, 157, 164, 170
Byrd, Robert C., 159

Cain, James D., 264n44
Cajete, Gregory A., 221n36
Cajun Power, 137
Cajun Prairie, 7
Cajuns, xvii, 5, 6, 60, 78, 80, 93, 137, 184, 195, 198, 226n17, 274n43
Calcasieu Parish, 6, 7, 86, 219n22; employment in, 223n47; settling in, 2
Calliou, Brian, 223n46
Camp Fire Girls, 111, 165
Campisi, Jack, 256n25
Campos, Jeanette Alcon, 190, 192, 280n122
Carrier, Dewith, 6, 91, 105, 198
Carter Lumber Company, 239n37
Casino Grand Coushatta, 284n171
casinos, 209, 284n171
Castro, Fidel, 144
Catawbas, 181, 250n68, 250n70; termination and, 77
Catholics, 11, 120, 226–27n17, 234n103
CC Bel Road, 52, 122, 158
CCC. *See* Civilian Conservation Corps
cemeteries, 169, 193, 251n76, 256n19
Cernek, Gloria Battise, 235n113
Cernek, Jonathan, 23, 29–30, 235n113
CETA. *See* Comprehensive Employment Training Act
"Chairman's Report" (Sickey), 163
Chaisson, Lora Ann, 281n131
Charity Hospital System, 57
charity hospitals, xxii, 57
Cherokees, 9, 32, 111, 181, 283n159; Eastern Band of, 143; termination of, 77
chiefs: electing, 66–70; term, 20
Chikapoo, 229–30n57
Children of the American Revolution (CAR), 258n40
Chitimachas, xviii, 9, 10, 18, 33, 34, 35, 73, 83, 140, 142, 145, 150, 190, 201,

Green Corn ceremonies, 19

Gregory, Hiram F., 18, 166, 167, 168, 169, 233n79, 273n33

Griffin, John, 170, 171

Griffin, Thomas J., 47

Groves, Edna, 47

Gulf South Research Institute, 140

Haas, Mary R., 166, 238n31, 272n18

Hahn, Steven C., 218n9

Hall, Jacquelin Dowd, 220n26

Hall of Master Folk Artists, 165

Harrington, Mark, xvii, 7, 17, 166, 227–28n30

Harris, T. H., 42

Hauke, C. F., 33, 231n69, 237n20

Hauptman, Laurence, 256n25

Havasupai Tribe, 170–71

Hayes, D. A. D., 234n101

Hays, Marie, 73, 74, 76

Head Start, 105, 149

health care, 74, 95, 101–2, 132, 154, 186, 187, 188, 189, 193; funding for, xviii; improving, 182; public, 57; records, 40, 78; resources for, xxiv

Health Department and Clinic, 209

health issues, 40, 172

Hector, A. C., 45, 46, 47, 51, 243n82

Henderson, Billie, 234n101

Henderson, Isaac M., 6–7

Herbert, Oday, 66

heritage, 80, 83, 106, 135, 138, 173

Heyer, Claude H., 81, 82

Heyer report, 251n72

Hill, Sarah H., 9

The Historic Indian Tribes of Louisiana from 1542 to Present (Kniffen, Gregory, and Stokes), 273n33

history: Coushatta, 40, 41, 69, 165, 223n50; cultural, xv, 83, 219n20, 253n107, 273n33; economic, 219n20;

migration, 170; political, xv; tribal, 210, 273n26

Homestead Act (1862), 2, 3, 4, 225n5, 225n10

homesteaders, xxii, 2, 4, 6, 15, 49, 225n5

homesteading, 2, 3, 225n5, 225n10

homesteads, xxiii–xxiv, 30, 33, 51, 61–62, 223n50, 226n11; Alabama, 224n3; Coushatta, 4, 5, 14–15, 19 (map), 42, 51, 157, 224n3

Hook, Jonathan B., 250n69

Hoover Commission on Indian Affairs, 70

Houma Alliance, 280n123

Houmas, 11, 140, 141, 203, 229n46, 262n4, 265n59, 280n123; population of, 220n28

House Concurrent Resolution 108, 70–71

housing, 132, 182, 184, 193; Indian, 82, 185, 247n19; programs, 185, 186; rehabilitation of, 279n99; tar paper-covered, 136; urban, 250n65

Houston, Sam, xv

HUD. *See* Department of Housing and Urban Development

human rights, 104, 164

Hunter, Bonner, 131

Hunter, Donald G., 232n78, 233n79, 234n106, 256n19

Hunter, Edwin Kidd, 131, 140

Hurley, P. J., 237n16

identity, 93, 110, 209, 236n13; Coushatta, xix, xxv, 10, 24, 282n146; cultural, 91, 142, 226n17; ethnic, 138; Indian, xxi, xxii, 35, 60, 107, 112, 217n4, 222n39, 235n109; language and, xxv; preserving, 104; public, 222n40; racial, 10, 41; religious, 91

IHS. *See* Indian Health Services

John, Edmond, 239n35
John, Ira B., 249n46
John, Isaac, 239n35
John, Lycia, 117
John, Marian, 179–80, 277n73, 277n76, 277n77
John, Martha, 74
John, Mrs. Alfred, 242n72
John, Scott, 239n35
Johnpierre, Alex, 29, 246n1
Johnson, Bobby H., 30, 171, 176
Johnson, Donald K., 81, 115, 144, 252n95, 252n99; Coushattas and, 83–84, 183; Madigan and, 82
Johnson, Lyndon B., 145, 257n25, 260n69, 283n164; message from, 256n23; poverty and, 102, 126
Johnson, Matilde, 262n4
Johnson, Wanda Kuntz, 80, 81, 85, 252n99; Coushattas and, 83–84, 252n91; Madigan and, 82
Johnston, J. Bennett, Jr., 130, 153, 154, 159
Jones, Howard, 251n72
Jones, Robert G., 264n44

Kalt, Joseph P., 221n31
Kellogg, William P., 283n162
Kennedy, John F., 97, 102, 257n25
Kennedy, Robert F., 78
Kickapoo, termination of, 248n35
Kidwell, Clara Sue, 36
Kimball, Geoffrey D., 272n18
Kinder, xvii, 7, 26, 32, 55, 80, 93, 236n15; founding of, 6
Kinder, Jim, 6
Kinder (LA) Courier News, 164
Kiwanis Clubs, 183
Klamaths, termination of, 248n35
Klopotek, Brian, xxiii, 11, 47, 142
Knapp, Leonard, Jr., 157, 160, 183

Kniffen, Fred B., 166, 233n79, 265n51, 273n33
Koasati Culture Change, 166
Koasati Dictionary (Kimball), 272n18
Koasati Grammar (Kimball), 272n18
Koasati language, xiii, 7, 25, 29, 38, 66, 69, 93, 118, 160, 163, 165, 167, 168, 188, 223n50, 223–24n51, 224n52, 272n18; Coushattas and, xiv, xxv, 217n1; losing, 80; protecting, 208; revitalization of, 209; speaking, 42, 79, 80, 101, 240n51; translations/feedback and, 210; worshipping in, 27
Koasati Traditional Narratives (Kimball), 272n18
Krause, Della Bel, 252n95
Kulturkampf, 227n17

LaFleur, Betty, 84
LaFleur, Mildred "Millie," 174, 175
Lake Charles, 6, 33, 50, 51, 68, 87, 106, 109, 113, 119, 121, 133, 157, 171, 191; Coushattas and, 78; Langley and, 107; meetings in, 146; tri-racial event in, 107
Lake Charles American Press, 5, 113, 260n66
Lake Charles Rodeo, 108
Lake Charles Tourist Bureau, 173
Land and Water Conservation Fund, 195
landowners, 3, 11, 61, 156; private, 73, 184–85; tribal, 31, 49
lands, xv, 34, 49, 250n68, 269n119; acquiring, xvii, 157; agricultural, 71; Coushatta, 20, 31, 48, 242n71, 242n72; foreclosures, 157–58; grazing, 51; patents, 250n60; private, 185; public, 2; reservation, 156, 157, 185, 209; surplus, 3; tribal, 126; trust, 71, 156, 160, 185, 204

Meritt, E. B., 240n43
Meyer, Harvey K., 51, 243n87, 244n208
Miccosukee Tribe, 143, 150, 154, 200;
recognition for, 144
migration, xxii; Choctaw, 230n61;
Coushatta, 217n7
mikkó (micco), 20, 232n75
Miller, Minos D., 131, 132, 137, 253n113;
Sickey and, 88, 89, 91–92, 129–30, 133,
134, 135
Miller, Ruth Means Loyd, 88, 89, 129–30,
131, 140, 141, 144, 152, 155; Edwards
and, 137, 138; gender inequality and,
130; lobbying by, 139; Sickey and, 133,
134, 135, 146
minerals, 84, 263n19, 270–71n124
Mississippi Choctaw Tribe, 76, 143, 181,
200, 222n41, 238n28, 241n64, 258n46;
constitution for, 150; life expectancy
of, 185; termination and, 72, 77
Missouri-Pacific Railroad Company, 5, 174
Monacan Tribe, 11
Morales, Tammy J., 219n20
mortality rates, 40, 57
Muscogee Confederacy, 218n9
Muskogee Area Office, 71
Muskogee Field Office, 73
Muskogees: Biloxi-Chitimacha Confederation of, 282–83n159; government
of, 233n75

NARF. *See* Native American Rights Fund
Nash, Roy, 39–40, 44, 242n72; on
Coushattas, 41–42, 239n35
National Association for the Advance-
ment of Colored People (NAACP), 82
National Conference of Christians and
Jews, 258n41
National Congress of American Indian
(NCAI), 256n25

National Council on Indian Opportunity
(NCIO), 145
National Endowment for the Arts,
179, 180
National Museum of the American
Indian, 227–28n30, 275–76n60
National Science Foundation, 224n51
National Youth Corps Program, 116
Native American Rights Fund (NARF),
xix, 145, 152
Neal, Anna, 200
networks: building, 63; information,
143; strategic, xxi; support, 183
Nevils, James, 219n22
New Deal, 42–52, 243n92
New Orleans, Texas and Mexico
Railroad Company, 32
New Orleans Times-Democrat, 7
New South, xxi; social/economic
development of, 9
Nixon, Jorge Antonio, xv
Nixon, Richard M., 126, 127, 139
nonprofit organizations, 109, 110, 151,
259n54, 266n69, 280n122
Nooksacks, 221n29
North Elton Gas Field, 93, 158

Oakdale Rotary Club, 183
Obe, Mimmie, 249n46
Oberlin, 6, 86, 88, 92, 93, 101, 116, 198
O'Brien, Sharon, 218n9
Office of Economic Opportunity (OEO),
102, 265n51
Office of Environmental Health, 128
Office of Indian Affairs (OIA), 3, 32, 33,
35, 39, 40, 44, 45, 46–47, 48, 49,
50, 54, 55, 69; allocations from, 56;
pressuring, 38; promises of, 53
oil, 49, 50, 93, 263n19, 270n124; leases,
157; lights, 84

CPSIA information can be obtained
at www.ICGtesting.com
Printed in the USA
LVHW090734181219
640689LV00008BA/95/P